Intellectual Property and Antitrust

NEW HORIZONS IN COMPETITION LAW AND ECONOMICS

Series Editors: Steven D. Anderman, *Department of Law, University of Essex, UK* and Rudolph J.R. Peritz, *New York Law School, USA*

This series has been created to provide research based analysis and discussion of the appropriate role for economic thinking in the formulation of competition law and policy. The books in the series will move beyond studies of the traditional role of economics – that of helping to define markets and assess market power – to explore the extent to which economic thinking can play a role in the formulation of legal norms, such as abuse of a dominant position, restriction of competition and substantial impediments to or lessening of competition. This in many ways is the *new horizon* of competition law policy.

US antitrust policy, influenced in its formative years by the Chicago School, has already experienced an expansion of the role of economic thinking in its competition rules. Now the EU is committed to a greater role for economic thinking in its Block Exemption Regulations and Modernisation package as well as possibly in its reform of Article 102. Yet these developments still raise the issue of the *extent* to which economics should be adopted in defining the public interest in competition policy and what role economists should play in legal argument. The series will provide a forum for research perspectives that are critical of an unduly-expanded role for economics as well as those that support its greater use.

Titles in the series include:

Antitrust and Regulation in the EU and US
Legal and Economic Perspectives
Edited by François Lévêque and Howard Shelanski

Competition Law, Innovation and Antitrust
An Analysis of Tying and Technological Integration
Hedvig Schmidt

Intellectual Property and the Limits of Antitrust
A Comparative Study of US and EU Approaches
Katarzyna Czapracka

Microsoft on Trial
Legal and Economic Analysis of a Transatlantic Antitrust Case
Edited by Luca Rubini

Intellectual Property and Antitrust
A Comparative Economic Analysis of US and EU Law
Mariateresa Maggiolino

Intellectual Property and Antitrust

A Comparative Economic Analysis of US and EU Law

Mariateresa Maggiolino

Assistant Professor of Commercial Law, Bocconi University, Milan, Italy

NEW HORIZONS IN COMPETITION LAW AND ECONOMICS

Edward Elgar

Cheltenham, UK • Northampton, MA, USA

Published by
Edward Elgar Publishing Limited
The Lypiatts
15 Lansdown Road
Cheltenham
Glos GL50 2JA
UK

Edward Elgar Publishing, Inc.
William Pratt House
9 Dewey Court
Northampton
Massachusetts 01060
USA

A catalogue record for this book
is available from the British Library

Library of Congress Control Number: 2010932040

FSC
www.fsc.org
MIX
Paper from
responsible sources
FSC® C018575

ISBN 978 1 84844 340 2

Typeset by Servis Filmsetting Ltd, Stockport, Cheshire
Printed and bound by MPG Books Group, UK

To my family

Contents

Foreword

Mariateresa Maggiolino's *Intellectual Property and Antitrust: A Comparative Economic Analysis of US and EU Law* is an excellent and long-needed one-volume comparative study of what we in the United States sometimes refer to as 'IP and Antitrust,' or the intersection of intellectual property law and competition policy. This book brings to bear Professor Maggiolino's considerable skills as a comparative competition law scholar on what is perhaps the single most important competition policy issue facing us today – namely, how to use IP policy and competition policy in tandem to further both economic competition and competition in innovation.

Professor Maggiolino's book covers a large range of IP practices by dominant firms where competition law can be invoked, including 'sham' litigation and product design, improper infringement actions, predation, and refusals to license. In some of these areas European and United States policies have always been similar or have largely converged. In others, particularly the law of unilateral refusal to license, they remain quite far apart. In each case Professor Maggiolino outlines the key features of both European and United States law, pointing out similarities and differences and defending her position. She does a particularly fine and thorough job of explaining the important differences between the United States and European cases brought against Microsoft Corp.

This book is well-researched, well-written, and completely up to date. Every serious competition law/antitrust and intellectual property scholar and practitioner should regard it as 'must' reading.

Herbert Hovenkamp

Acknowledgements

Many people have contributed to the completion of this three-year book with their academic and human prowess. It is impossible to thank everyone who has offered such much-valued support, but a few names should, however, be mentioned.

I owe gratitude to Herbert Hovenkamp whose inspiring guidance led to the birth of this book. I am deeply indebted to Steven Anderman, who constantly improved my reasoning and the overall text through his critical and provoking observations. I am beholden to Federico Ghezzi – my 'chief' – who was the first to show me that antitrust law represents a theoretical and practical challenge for lawyers, economists and policy makers. Special thanks go to Chiara Battistini, Elisa Brodi, Paola Magnani, Maria Lillà Montagnani, and Federico Morando for their precious comments, lively discussion and the reassurance they gave me when subjected, often involuntarily (!), to my long monologues on the topic of this book. I am very grateful to Nina Segre for giving her valuable time in reading and patiently reviewing the drafts. And, on a personal note, I thank my parents and friends for warmly supporting my efforts.

March 2010, Milano
Mariateresa Maggiolino

Introduction

THE COURSE OF THE ARGUMENT

This book examines *whether*, *when*, and *why* the antitrust authorities[1] of the United States of America and European Union have enforced Section 2 of the Sherman Act[2] and Article 102 of the TFEU[3] in order to *shape*

[1] In the United States, antitrust law is primarily enforced by federal judges. Actually, two public bodies are also entrusted with its application: the Antitrust Division of the Department of Justice and the Federal Trade Commission (FTC). The former influences competition law by making speeches, negotiating settlements, and issuing guidelines; the latter enjoys administrative adjudicatory powers. Yet, by and large, they both act as prosecutors rather than as decision-makers: in the end, what they can do is to bring antitrust actions before ordinary federal courts. In contrast, EU competition law is primarily applied by the European Commission, which is an administrative and political body, whose decisions can be challenged in the Court of First Instance (CFI) and in the European Court of Justice (ECJ). In fact, even national competition authorities and national judges can enforce EU competition law but, in order to guarantee a uniform and harmonized enforcing structure, their action is to some extent subject to that of the Commission. See, in this regard, Commission Notice on cooperation within the Network of Competition Authorities – OJ 2004, C101/43 – and Commission Notice on the cooperation between the Commission and the courts of the EU Member States in the application of Articles 101 and 102 TFEU – OJ 2004, C101/54. In sum, given the differences between the US and EU enforcing systems, the choice to use hereinafter the generic term 'antitrust (or competition) authorities' to address who is entrusted with the duty to apply competition law in the two jurisdictions could appear superficial and improper. Yet, it helps to simplify the written exposition, and the book will, however, distinguish between US and EU enforcing authorities when the outcomes of its analysis rest with the prerogatives and skills that they enjoy.

[2] US Code, Title 15, Chapter 1, available at http://www.law.cornell.edu/uscode/. Section 2 establishes that, 'Every person who shall monopolize, or attempt to monopolize, or combine or conspire with any other person or persons, to monopolize any part of the trade or commerce among the several States, or with foreign nations, shall be deemed guilty of a felony, and, on conviction thereof, shall be punished by fine not exceeding $100,000,000 if a corporation, or, if any other person, $1,000,000, or by imprisonment not exceeding 10 years, or by both said punishments, in the discretion of the court'.

[3] Because of the Treaty of Lisbon – OJ 2007, C306/1 – the European provision regarding the 'abuse of dominant position' changed from article 82 TEC to article 102 TFEU. 'TEC' is the acronym for the past Treaty on the European Community – OJ 2002, C325/33. 'TFEU' is the acronym for the actual Treaty on the Functioning of the European Union – OJ 2008, C115/1. Indeed, with the Treaty of Lisbon, the latter has substituted the former. Article 102 states that, 'Any abuse by one or more undertakings of a dominant position within the internal market or in a substantial part of it shall be prohibited as incompatible with the internal market in so far as it may affect trade between Member States. Such abuse may, in particular, consist of: (a) directly or indirectly imposing unfair purchase or selling prices or

the scope of dominant firms' IPRs, such as patents and copyrights.[4] This research question leads to two inquiries.

On the one hand, since one can expect that such enforcement actions assume the existence of an *ideal* yardstick to measure the proper scope of dominant firms' IPRs, Chapter 1 clarifies that, from a general perspective, that is to say, without a case-by-case analysis, even economic theory[5] cannot establish conclusively how broad the scope of dominant firms' patents and copyrights must be.

On the other hand, since Section 2 and Article 102 are the 'tangible tools' that courts and administrative bodies must employ to carry out such enforcement actions, Chapter 2 discusses how, over the years, US and EU antitrust authorities have interpreted the two provisions, establishing their aims and enforcing criteria.

The will to protect competition and innovation or, to put it in another way, the will to protect consumer welfare over the short and long run,[6] is one of the threads that links these two chapters.[7] Indeed, Chapter 1 explains that social planners would like to establish the scope of market dominance, patents, and copyrights in order to promote competition and innovation. Chapter 2 observes that, nowadays, antitrust authorities would like to employ Section 2 and Article 102 in order to prohibit dominant firms' practices that strengthen market power and harm competition and innovation. Together, the two chapters show that what should motivate US and EU enforcement actions that are aimed at shaping the scope of monopolists' IPRs is the protection of competition and innovation.

---

other unfair trading conditions; (b) limiting production, markets or technical development to the prejudice of consumers; (c) applying dissimilar conditions to equivalent transactions with other trading parties, thereby placing them at a competitive disadvantage; (d) making the conclusion of contracts subject to acceptance by the other parties of supplementary obligations which, by their nature or according to commercial usage, have no connection with the subject of such contracts.'.

[4] Hereinafter, the book uses the acronym 'IPRs' for intellectual property rights and the terms 'monopolists' and 'dominant firms' as synonyms.

[5] The choice to look at what the economic theory teaches as to the scope of dominant firms' IPRs is not accidental. As Chapter 1 shows, economics moulds competition law and contributes to justify the rationale of patents and copyrights.

[6] Indeed, Chapter 1 explains that there is a theoretical relationship between the everyday notions of competition and innovation, on the one hand, and the technical economic concepts of short- and long-run consumer welfare, on the other hand.

[7] There are other threads between Chapters 1 and 2. For instance, Chapter 1 shows that, away from perfect competition, it is up to policy makers to fix the objectives of competition law and the main features of its enforcing system; Chapter 2 discusses the many policy and enforcing objectives that, over time, Section 2 and Article 102 have pursued. Chapter 1 explains that economic theories cannot establish *directly* how long market monopolies should last in order to promote competition and innovation; Chapter 2 remarks that the legal standards that antitrust authorities elaborate to assess dominant firms' conduct and thus establish *indirectly* the proper duration of market monopolies follow from specific policy choices.

Chapters 3 to 6 test this conclusion from economic and legal standpoints. They describe certain economic models that explain that monopolists may harm consumer welfare by engaging specific behaviors that are expressly authorized by applicable IP systems, and they describe the cases in which US and EU antitrust authorities have enforced Section 2 or Article 102 against these IP-consistent behaviors.[8] More exactly, these chapters assess, in economic and legal terms, dominant firms:[9]

(i) developing and/or acquiring patentable inventions and copyrightable creative works (see Chapters 3 and 4);
(ii) refusing to license their own IPRs to third parties (see Chapter 5); and
(iii) bringing infringement lawsuits and other IP administrative actions against their actual and potential rivals (see Chapter 6).[10]

Therefore, Chapters 3 to 6 analyze *both* whether economics can establish, at least from a case-by-case perspective, how broad the scope of dominant firms' IPRs should be, *and* whether the US and EU legal standards that anti-

---

[8] In this light, therefore, the book's analysis has a backward look: it focuses on past US and EU case law.

[9] The book does not analyze whether and when IPRs as such grant monopoly power, though it must be recognized that it happens rarely since there is no 'one-to-one' relationship among IPRs, products, and relevant markets. See, e.g., Robert P. Merges, *Intellectual Property Rights and the New Institutional Economics*,53 VAND. L. REV. 1857 (2000); and Frank H. Easterbrook, *Intellectual Property is still Property*, 13 HARV. J. L. PUB. POL. 1 (1990). Indeed, at least in applying Section 2 and Article 102, antitrust authorities have never presumed market power to arise from patents and copyrights. See, on the US side, *United States v. E. I. du Pont de Nemours & Co.*, 351 U.S. 377 (1956); and *United States v. Loew's, Inc.*, 371 U.S. 38 (1962); and, on the EU side, Case 24/67, *Parke, Davis and Co. v Probel, Reese, Beintema-Interpharm and Centrafarm*, February 29 1968, [1968] ECR 55, and Case 78/70 *Deutsche Grammophon Gesselschaft mbH v Metro-SB-Großmärkte GmbH & Co. KG.*, June 8 1971, [1971] ECR 487.

[10] The behaviors that the book chooses to analyze are unlikely to cover all the monopolistic practices involving IPRs. Rather they have a peculiar heuristic value as to US and EU antitrust attitudes towards both dominant firms' conduct and the interface between competition and IP laws. On the one hand, the behaviors in question call for a clear definition of what antitrust authorities should prohibit via Section 2 and Article 102 because, although they may contribute to strengthen monopolists' market power, they do not always harm consumer welfare, even when they serve to realize predation, entry-deterrence, or leverage. On the other hand, these behaviors lie at the very heart of IP laws by consisting of the enforcement of some of the quintessential prerogatives that IPR holders (or would-be IPR holders) boast. Therefore, to analyze how these behaviors do violate antitrust laws means, first, setting up the case for a conflict between antitrust provisions and IP rules. Then it entails acknowledging that an antitrust intervention aimed at striking those practices curbs IPRs prerogatives and, hence, reduces the scope of IPRs as though antitrust authorities could act as second-tier regulators. Third, analyzing these behaviors allows discussing how the two jurisdictions' antitrust authorities have managed this legal conflict, trying to find out whether, when and why they applied different legal standards and make antitrust law prevail over IP laws or vice versa.

trust authorities have applied in their case law are responsive to what economic models suggest as to the protection of competition and innovation.

This compound inquiry – which also deals with the confrontation between the antitrust and the IP worlds – allows the reader to consider several other topics. They all deal with the differences that distinguish the US and EU jurisdictions, and can be easily summarized with one simple question: why do US and EU antitrust authorities follow different approaches in shaping the scope of patents and copyrights that dominant firms hold?

The Conclusion explores the policy issues that contribute to the answer to this question, and explains the convergences and divergences between the two jurisdictions. Notwithstanding the role that economics plays in fashioning antitrust (or competition) law and in justifying the rationale of patents and copyrights, the book shows that *non-economic principles* can explain whether, when, and why antitrust authorities apply Section 2 and Article 102, in order to shape some dominant firms' IPRs, such as patents and copyrights.

The scheme shown in Figure 0.1 reproduces what is stated above, by portraying diagrammatically the course of the book's argument.

SOME CAVEATS

According to the legal tradition of civil law countries, a study that intends to deal with the interface between antitrust and IP laws should start by discussing in full detail what scholars have elaborated about the terms of such a comparison, namely, what antitrust law,[11] IP laws, and their

[11] Definitions are never expected to be conclusive or exhaustive. Rather, they can work as effective analytical tools aimed at simplifying inquiries, like the definitions regarding the terms that the book will use hereinafter. For instance, the book employs the stricter meaning of the EU expression 'competition law' as a synonym of the US term 'antitrust law', in order to address the rules dealing with anticompetitive agreements and monopolistic conduct, i.e. Sections 1 and 2 of the Sherman Act and Articles 101 and 102 of the TFEU. Actually, the above expressions can also address both the rules concerning merger control, and, in the sole European Union, the provisions that aims to regulate Member States' involvement in business practices. See Section 7 of the Clayton Act (US code, Chapter 1, Title 15, Sections 12 et seq.), Council regulation (EC) No.139/2004, OJ 2004, L24/1, and Article 106 of TFEU. Second, the book makes a distinction between 'antitrust (or competition) law' and 'antitrust (or competition) policy', viewing the former as a branch of the latter. The former addresses the prohibitions concerning specific firms' behaviors. The latter refers to a larger array of rules that: (i) encompasses not only proscriptions but also prescriptions; (ii) addresses not only firms but also governments; and (iii) aims to determine not only the impact that a single firm's practice has on market's outcome and development, but the general level of competition within the borders of one jurisdiction. For instance, the so-called 'competition (or antitrust) policy' also includes the enforcement of antidumping regulation, the scrutiny of public restrictions on entry into

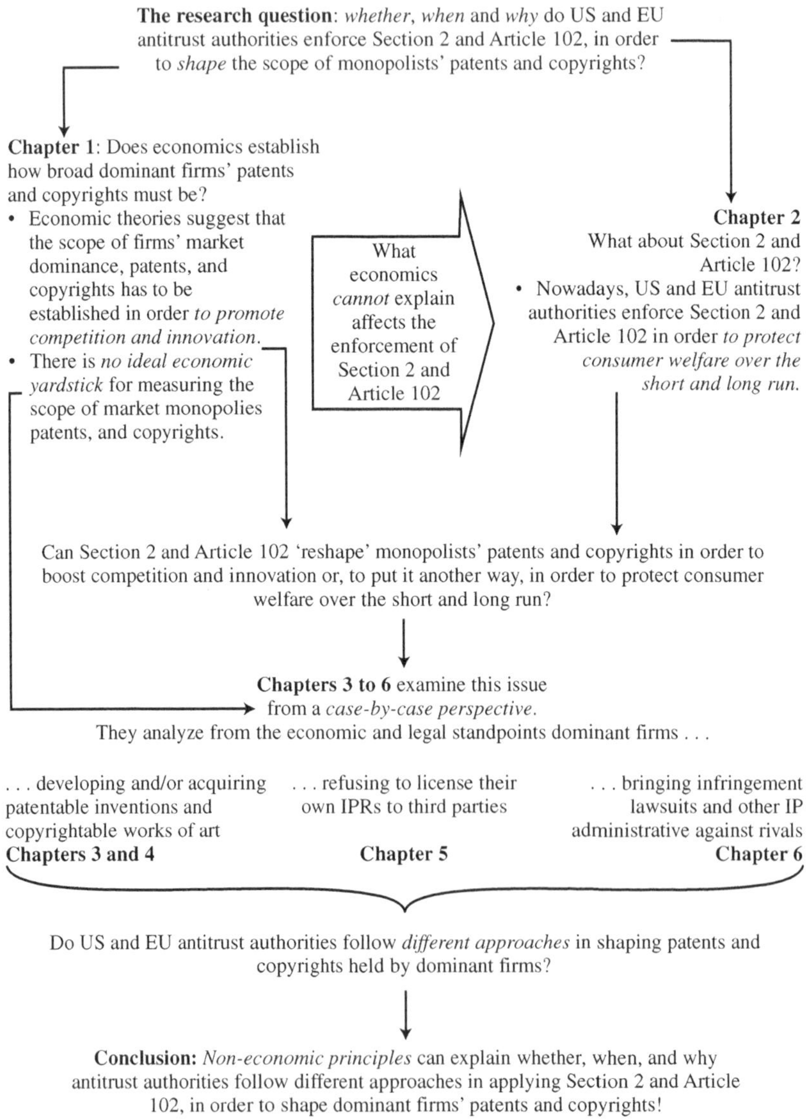

Figure 0.1 The course of the arguments

interface are. It should continue by elaborating the general principles that govern such an interface, first indentifying whether and when antitrust and IP laws enter into conflict, and then analyzing whether these conflicts should be solved by making antirust law prevail over IP laws, or vice versa. Finally, it should conclude by stating whether courts and administrative authorities have acted in accordance with these theoretical guidelines.

Yet, such an analysis would not fit well with a comparative examination of the antitrust rules affecting monopolists' behaviors because, both in the United States and in the European Union, competition law stems more from economics, case law, and industrial policies, rather than from articulated pieces of legislation and universal legal principles. Therefore, the book adopts a different approach: by following a more analytical and inductive analysis, it teases out the policy issues that antitrust authorities face in dealing with monopolists' practices involving IPRs.

Without lingering over transatlantic doctrinal debates it is, however, useful to give some definitions as to what antitrust law, IPRs, and their interface are, or, at the very least, are taken to be in this context.

As to antitrust law, it is assumed that this is a set of prohibitions concerning firms' specific behaviors, so that it can be analogized to a surgical intervention adept at excising specific illnesses, rather than to a steady cure aimed at treating a chronic disease.[12] Hence, competition law should not be considered a tool for forging market structures, the initial distribution of market opportunities, or the early allocation of incentives to compete and innovate. Rather, antitrust law is a means for prosecuting those firms' behaviors that worsen existing markets' performance, [13] that is to say, those behaviors

---

a market, the choice to subsidize a specific industry (or a specific firm, as in the case of the European doctrine of state aid), and even suggestions for adjustments in the design of intellectual property systems. See, e.g., Richard Gilbert & Oliver Williamson, 'Antitrust Policy', *in The New Palgrave Dictionary of Economics and the Law* 82 (Peter Newman ed. 1988); Andrew I. Gavil, William E. Kovacic, & Jonathan B. Baker, *Antitrust Law in Perspective: Cases, Concepts and Problems in Competition Policy* 4 (2008); and Herbert J. Hovenkamp, 'Innovation and the Domain of Competition Policy' 1, University of Iowa Legal Studies Research Paper, Number 08–07, March, 2008 (stating that, "Competition policy' refers to the full range of public rules and sanctions designed to ensure that markets are as competitive as they can realistically be, consistent with these other policies. In the United States the term 'competition policy' certainly includes the antitrust laws as a central component, but competition policy is in fact much broader.'). Third, the term 'policy' when referred to antitrust enforcement can also address the several issues that lie behind prosecuting choices. In other words, it is common to say that whether a specific competition action is worthwhile is a matter of 'policy', meaning a matter that regards the efficient use of the scarce resources available to those who enforce competition law. As the following chapters show, such a question becomes pressing when it turns to the study of the antitrust intervention against dominant firms.

[12] For this analogy see Frederic M. Scherer, David Ross, *Industrial Market Structure and Economic Performance* 12 (1990).

[13] As Chapter 2 explains, no antitrust concepts exist in nature: antitrust aims as well

that, given preliminary firms' endowments, prevent markets' outcomes that should follow from the natural interaction between demand and supply.

As to IPRs, two clarifications are due.[14] First, in the following discussion IPRs are primarily meant to be *ius excludendi alios*, without discussing whether this is enough to consider them as property rights.[15] For the purpose of the arguments developed in this book, indeed, it is enough to consider that IPRs grant to their owners the right to *exclude* anybody else from using and reproducing them and, hence, the power to decide who to *include* in their enjoyment.[16] Secondly, because of the role that economics plays in shaping antitrust law, IPRs are here analyzed from the eco-

---

as antitrust rules derive from specific policy choices. Therefore, what has been described here as the 'natural interaction between demand and supply' is what society expects to achieve through the operation of market forces. See, e.g., Andrew I. Gavil, William E. Kovacic, Jonathan B. Baker, *Antitrust Law in Perspective: Cases, Concepts and Problems in Competition Policy* 16 (2008); Carl Kaysen, Donald F. Turner, *Antitrust Policy; An Economic And Legal Analysis* 14 (1959).

[14] For a general discussion of what IPRs are, see, e.g., David I. Bainbridge, *Intellectual Property* (2007); Adam D. Moore, *Intellectual Property & Information Control. Philosophic Foundations and Contemporary Issues* (2001); William R. Cornish & David Llewelyn, *Intellectual Property: Patents, Copyrights, Trademarks and Allied Rights* (1999); Lawrence C. Becker, 'Deserving to Own Intellectual Property', 68 *Chicago-Kent Law Review* 609 (1993); Michael Lehmann, 'The Theory of Property Rights and the Protection of Intellectual and Industrial Property', 16 *International Review of Industrial Property and Copyright Law* 525 (1985).

[15] In other words, the book does not discuss what the right of property is, for instance whether it should be viewed as either 'a bundle of rights', or 'the right to exclude others from the use of its subject matter'; or 'the unrestricted right of using, enjoying and disposing of its subject matter'. For the first theory see, e.g., Wesley Newcomb Hohfeld, 'Fundamental Legal Conceptions as Applied in Judicial Reasoning', 26 *Yale L.J.* 710 (1917); and id., 'Some Fundamental Legal Conceptions as Applied in Judicial Reasoning', 23 *Yale L.J.* 16 (1913) (arguing that property is a set of rights, duties, privileges, powers, liabilities, disabilities, and immunities that courts interpret in disputes). For the second theory see, e.g., Thomas W. Merrill, 'Property and the Right to Exclude', 77 *Neb. L. Rev.* 730 (1998) (arguing that, 'The right to exclude others is more than just 'one of the most essential constituents of property – it is the sine qua non'); and Richard A. Epstein, *Takings, Private Property and the Power of Eminent Domain* 65 (1985) (arguing that, 'The idea of property embraces the absolute right to exclude.') The third definition comes directly from the Roman tradition, where property was conceived as *jus utendi et abutendi re sua quatenus iuris ratio patitur*. A different issue is speaking about the 'propertization' of IPRs. With this expression, indeed, scholars want just to address the fact that recently IP laws have been subject to subsequent reforms, which have not only created new IPRs, included new items in the subject matter of traditional IPRs, but have also enlarged the duration and the scope of traditional IPRs. Therefore, nowadays the prerogatives of IPR holders seem to be 'unlimited' as much as the rights of the holders of traditional property rights. Yet, though they are said to be 'absolute', even traditional property rights suffer some limitations, as well as several IP doctrines work as 'antibodies' against the on-going enlargement of IPRs. See Gustavo Ghidini, *Intellectual Property and Competition Law* (2006), and Michael A. Carrier, 'Cabining Intellectual Property through a Property Paradigm', *54 Duke L.J.* 1, 4–7 (2004).

[16] See Ghidini, *supra* note 15. To be sure, IPRs can be conceptualized according to different theories. For instance, see Ilkka Rahnasto, *Intellectual Property Rights, External Effects and Antitrust Law* 49 (2002).

nomic perspective, that is to say, by deeming them as tools for promoting efficiency, technological and cultural innovation. Yet, it is worth to recall that over the years, political and legal scholars have put forward several non-economic theoretical justifications for explaining the rationale of IPRs[17] – explanations that, perhaps apart from the theory of natural rights,[18] can soundly be applied to both US and EU IPRs. For instance,

---

17 See, e.g., Lionel Bentley & Brad Sherman, *Intellectual Property Law* 39 (2009); Edwin C. Hettinger, 'Justifying Intellectual Property', 18 *Philosophy and Public Affairs* 31, 37 (1989).

18 Natural law views property rights as arising out of the logic of nature and, as such, independent from any specific kind of civil society. See generally David Hume, *A Treatise of Human Nature* (1740); and John Locke, *Second Treatise of Government* (1690). According to the natural rights theory, therefore, patents and copyrights flow from the fundamental, inalienable, and undeniable rights that humans have by virtue of what they are, such as the (moral) right to 'have one's own identity connected to one's own creations and inventions'. Ideas must belong to their creators because they are the manifestation of their creators' personalities. See, e.g., Wendy J. Gordon, 'A Property Right in Self-Expression: Equality and Individualism in the Natural Law of Intellectual Property', 102 *Yale L. J.* 1533 (1993); Tom G. Palmer, 'Are Patents and Copyrights Morally Justified?', 13 *Harvard Journal of Law and Public Policy* 817 (1990); Alfred C. Yen, 'Restoring the Natural Law: Copyright as Labor and Possession', 91 *Ohio St. L. J.* 517 (1990). Further, consider that Art. 27(2) of the Universal Declaration of Human Rights states that 'everyone has the right to the protection of the moral and material interests resulting from any scientific, literary or artistic production of which he is the author'. True, as mentioned in the text, it is often said that on the European continent IP is perceived as having its roots in natural law, while in Anglo-American jurisdictions IP laws have utilitarian foundations. Indeed, the concept of moral rights was specifically rejected by the drafters of the US Constitution, as Thomas Jefferson wrote, 'inventions then cannot, in nature, be a subject of property. Society may give an exclusive right to the profits arising from them, as an encouragement to men to pursue ideas which may produce utilities, but this may or may not be done according to the will and convenience of society, without claim or complaint from anybody' – Walton H. Hamilton, *Patents and Free Enterprise. Investigation of Concentration of Economic Power* 21 (1941). Nevertheless, this argument cannot be pushed too far: intimations of both natural rights-based and utility-based claims can be found in most countries. See Jane C. Ginsburg, 'A Tale of Two Copyrights: Literary Property in Revolutionary France and America', 64 *Tul. L. Rev.* 991 (1990); and Justin Hughes, 'The Philosophy of Intellectual Property', 77 *Geo. L. J.* 287, 288 (1988) (arguing that, 'rights in our society cannot depend for their justification solely upon statutory or constitutional provisions'). Further see e.g. Roberta R. Kwall, 'Copyright and the Moral Right: Is an American Marriage Possible?', 38 *Vand. L. Rev.* 1, 5–16 (1985) (suggesting the US should converge towards the European law which recognizes moral and personal rights rather than mere pecuniary interests); Michael Katz, 'The Doctrine of Moral Rights and American Copyright Law – A Proposal', 24 *S. Cal. L. Rev.* 375, 391–409 (1951) (proposing that the US should incorporate the European concept of moral rights into copyright law); and Martin A. Roeder, 'The Doctrine of Moral Rights: A Study in the Law of Artists, Authors and Creators', 53 *Harv. L. Rev.* 554, 558–65 (1940). Broadly speaking, the natural right approach to IPRs is named 'axiomatic'. It differs from the consequentialist theory according to which the existence of IPRs is to be decided on the consequences that they produce on the whole society. Nevertheless, see Peter Lewin, 'Creativity or Coercion: Alternative Perspectives on Rights to Intellectual Property', 71 *Journal of Business Ethics* 441 (2007) (claiming that, upon examination, this distinction is misleading and that ultimately all legal-ethical-moral justification schemes have to be based on a consideration of consequences).

one should not forget that, according to the Lockean theory of labor and property rights,[19] IPRs derive from the universal right to 'own oneself' and the consequential universal right to 'own the fruits of one's own labor', such as intellectual goods.[20] Indeed, when one mingles one's efforts with 'the raw stuff of the world', any resulting product ought to be one's own.[21] Likewise, it is by endorsing the so-called contractarian theory that patents can be described as what governments grant to inventors in exchange for the knowledge that they disclose via the patenting process.[22] Similarly, from a political standpoint, copyrights have been conceptualized as 'state measures' designed to fortify democracy by promoting the public debate and feeding expressive diversity and pluralism.[23]

Finally, as to the interface between antitrust and IP laws, it can be portrayed in a very simple way, by stating that each firm's practice involving IPRs can be found legal or illegal pursuant to IP provisions, and legal or illegal pursuant to competition rules, so that the four-scenario scheme shown in Table 0.1 is conceivable:

Table 0.1 The Antitrust-IP Interface

	IP Law	
Competition Law	**I** Illegal *Legal*	**III** Legal *Legal*
	II Illegal *Illegal*	**IV** Legal *Illegal*

[19] For a discussion of two possible interpretations of the Lockean conception of labor – i.e. the avoidance theory and the value-added view – see Hughes, *supra* note 18, at 302–310.

[20] See, e.g., Hughes, *supra* note 18, at 301–302 (arguing that, 'Locke . . . begins his justification of property with the premise that initially only our bodies are our property. [. . .] Our handiwork becomes our property because our hands – and the energy, consciousness, and control that fuel their labor – are our property. [. . .] [Therefore, the Author concluded that] Locke linked property to the product of the individual person's labor.').

[21] See, e.g., Frank I. Michelman, 'Property, Utility, and Fairness: Comments on the Ethical Foundations of "Just Compensation" Law', 80 *Harv. L. Rev.* 1165, 1204 (1967).

[22] This is the main intuition underpinning the so-called 'consideration doctrine', which – as said in the text – can be led inside the frame of a more general theory, the so-called 'contractarian theory'. According to this theory IPRs exist because they fit into the 'social contract' upon which the whole society has been built up.

[23] See, e.g., Neil Weinstock Netanel, 'Copyright and a Democratic Civil Society', 106 *Yale L.J.* 283, 291 (1996).

Now, as a matter of logic, it should be noted that a 'legal conflict' happens only when, once the range of action of IP and antitrust rules are understood and fixed,[24] a dominant firm's practice is legal according to the former (IP) and illegal according to the latter (antitrust), or vice versa. In other words, whereas no issue arises when a dominant firm either complies with or violates both IP and antitrust laws, certain issues of coordination and setting priorities arise when the two bodies of law qualify particular conduct in a conflicting way.

From an antitrust standpoint, which is the one focused upon in this book, the case of conduct that infringes IP provisions but does not violate competition law does not lead to difficulties of enforcement. Indeed, it is hard to conceive of a case in which the EU antitrust authorities (whether communitarian or national), though devoid of interest, would take the initiative to act in lieu of IP national judges when, in addition, they would have no power to act under IP national laws against firms that do not comply with them.[25] Likewise, it is hard to conceive of a case in which US judges, though they can act to interpret IP law and use it against the illegal behavior, would nonetheless prefer to act against it in the name of an unfounded antitrust claim. In effect, Chapters 3 to 6 show that, perhaps because of the costs that the antitrust enforcement entails, antitrust authorities have not tended to enlarge their jurisdictions to cover behaviors that are antitrust-compliant but not IP consistent. Such behaviors would be handled within the IP realm.

Instead, from the antitrust standpoint, it becomes crucial to understand how to manage the conflict between IP laws and competition provisions when the latter prohibits behavior that the former permits.

The research question beneath the book, indeed, falls within the boundaries of this last 'square' of the Antitrust–IP interface.

---

24 To be sure, it can be difficult to draw the limits of IPRs' and competition rules' range of action: for instance, as seen in Chapter 2, it is complex to establish limits of dominant firms' liability. Equally, though this book does not face such a topic, it is questionable whether, for instance, some practices represent an IP misuse or fall under those doctrines that establish the exceptions to IP rules. Therefore, not every case is easy to place in one of the four finals cells of the above diagram.

25 Indeed, as Chapter 1 explains, European antitrust authorities have no jurisdiction upon IP issue, because IPRs are mainly a matter of national laws.

1. Antitrust law, IPRs and economics: the leeway for policy choices

A GENERAL YARDSTICK FOR THE SCOPE OF DOMINANT FIRMS' IPRS

US and EU antitrust rules are poorly defined prohibitions,[1] which barely address certain firms' practices.[2] Economics is in an excellent position to imbue these rules with meaning[3] because its primary aim is to explain firms' behaviors.[4]

---

1 For such a well-established fact see, e.g., 1 Phillip E. Areeda & Herbert Hovenkamp, *Antitrust Law: An Analysis of Antitrust Principles and Their Application* ¶103.d (2007); David J. Gerber, *Law and Competition in Twentieth-Century Europe* 345 (1988), and OECD, 'Competition on the Merits' 21 (2005), available at http://www.oecd.org/dataoecd/7/13/35911017.pdf (addressing directly Section 2 of the Sherman Act and Article 82 of the EC Treaty). However, see Timothy J. Brennan, 'Saving Section 2: Reframing US Monopolization Law', in *The Political Economy of Antitrust* 417 (Vivek Ghosal & John Stennek eds. 2007) (arguing that Section 2 remains a vital part of US economic policy because of its brevity and its ability to be morphed by case law according to changing circumstances and advances in knowledge). Likewise, Article 102, poor language grants a great flexibility to EU antitrust institutions. For instance, without such leeway what the EU Commission did with the 2009 Communication about dominant firms' exclusionary behaviors – that is to say, the *Guidance on the Commission's Enforcement Priorities in Applying Article 82 of the EC Treaty to Abusive Exclusionary Conduct by Dominant Undertakings*, OJ 2009, C45/7 – would have not been possible. Indeed, though not expressly, the 2009 Communication half restates the existing law and half changes the meaning to be associated with the most famous slogans of the past EU antitrust practice. See in this regard Chapter 2.

2 As antitrust law is immediately directed at checking firms' conduct, the markets where antitrust law is expected to intervene the most are those where firms are really free to choose how to behave and, in that case, whether to harm competition. This is the reason why several textbooks associate antitrust law with free market economies – that is, with economic regimes where the allocation of resources does not rest with government planning – as well as the reason why the enforcement of antitrust law in regulated markets, such as telecommunications and securities, gives rise to several concerns, among others, about the possibility that firms receive orders from 'two different chiefs': antitrust authorities and regulators. See, e.g., Alison Jones & Brenda Sufrin, *EC Competition Law* (2008); Richard Whish, *Competition Law* (2008); and 2A Phillip E. Areeda & Herbert Hovenkamp, *Antitrust Law: An Analysis of Antitrust Principles and Their Application* (2002).

3 See, e.g., Timothy J. Muris, 'Economics and Antitrust', 5 *Geo. Mason L. Rev.* 303 (1997); Michael S. Jacobs, 'An Essay on the Normative Foundations of Antitrust Economics', 74 *North Carolina L. Rev.* 219 (1996); Richard A. Posner, *Antitrust Law* (1976) (first advocating expressly this role for economics); Paolo Buccirossi, 'Introduction', in *Handbook of Antitrust Economics* I, IX and XI–XII (Paolo Buccirossi ed. 2008) (arguing that whatever the language

Therefore, this chapter looks at economics – which is also universal by nature and, hence, well suited to comparative inquiries[5] – in order to find a general yardstick to measure the scope of dominant firms' IPRs.[6] It highlights that economic concepts and principles,[7] which today play a

---

used to prohibit anticompetitive behaviors, their identification must hinge on some economic models, because 'economics lies at the heart of competition, or antitrust, law. While in the early days the application of antitrust rules was almost entirely left to the wit of people with only a legal background, it is now widely accepted that the proper interpretation of these rules requires an understanding of how markets work and of how firms can alter their functioning. This knowledge is the realm of economic science.' '[T]he economic science is the only body of knowledge that provides the rational foundation for the proper interpretation of any substantive antitrust rule'); Jonathan B. Baker, 'Recent Developments in Economics That Challenge Chicago School Views', 58 *Antitrust L. J.* 645, 646 (1989) (stating firmly that 'economics has become the essence of antitrust'); Herbert Hovenkamp, 'Antitrust Policy After Chicago', 84 *Mich. L. Rev.* 213, 220 (1985) (observing that 'one must go all the way back to the first thirty years of antitrust enforcement to find a policy that can reasonably be characterized as having little or no economic content'); and James May, 'Antitrust in the Formative Era: Political and Economic Theory in Constitutional and Antitrust Analysis, 1880–1918', 50 *Ohio St. L. J.* 257, 283–8 (1989) (sustaining that even in the earliest days of the antitrust history, policymakers employed economic models to inform the state of the law).

4 See Ginevra Bruzzone, Marco Boccaccio, 'Identifying Infringements of Competition Rules: The Role of Economic and Legal Thinking 3', paper presented to the VIII Conference 'Antitrust Between EC Law and National Law', Treviso, 22–23 May 2008, available at http://www.emagazine.assonime.it/upload/Identifying%20infringements%20def.pdf (arguing 'since antitrust rules directly concern an economic process, i.e. the operation of the market, the definition of substantive enforcement criteria inevitably requires an economic view'). Other social sciences may explain how firms behave. Nevertheless, nowadays economics does it in the most systematic and complete way possible. Therefore, as long as it searches for a reliable and comprehensive interpretative yardstick for understanding firms' behaviors, antitrust law cannot set aside economics.

5 See, e.g., Buccirossi, *supra* note 3, XI-XII (arguing that economics may well represent a point of convergence between the US and EU jurisdictions in as much as it does not rest with the institutional, cultural, and political differences that distinguish them); Hanns Ullrich, 'The Interaction between Competition Law and Intellectual Property Law: An Overview', in *European Competition Law Annual 2005: The Interaction between Competition Law and Intellectual Property Law* 4 (Claus-Dieter Ehlermann & Isabela Atanasiu eds. 2006) (stating that, 'the economics-based approach contributes enormously to bringing US and EU competition policy on a path of practical convergence, and possibly even of theoretical dependence'); and Mario Monti, 'Convergence in EU—US Antitrust Policy Regarding Mergers and Acquisitions. An EU Perspective', speech at UCLA Law First Annual Institute on US and EU Antitrust Aspects of Mergers and Acquisitions, Los Angeles, February 28, 2004, available at http://www.europa.eu.intlcommfcompetition/speeches/ (claiming that nowadays US and EU competition laws are largely consistent not only because they pursue the same ultimate aim, that is ensuring consumer welfare, as Chapter 2 explains, but also because they rely on the same micro-economic analytical tools).

6 In other words, since this book discusses the application of competition law to dominant firms' behaviors involving IPRs, it makes sense to use economics as an analytical bridge between antitrust and IP laws. Indeed, to read IP laws with the economic lenses could help the reader acquire a better understanding of the consequences that a likely antitrust action (or inaction) against IPRs may produce on IPRs.

7 In fact, in order to give readers a proper 'toolbox', this first chapter overviews some of the main economic ideas, to which the following chapters refer.

significant role in shaping antitrust and IP rules[8],[9] leave nonetheless policy makers with no conclusive arguments to establish the optimal scope of *both* market monopolies *and* IPRs. Thus, the chapter concludes that, when antitrust law confronts dominant firms' IPRs, *a fortiori* it cannot rely on a general economic measure of their duration and broadness.

ANTITRUST LAW, MARKET MONOPOLIES, AND MAINSTREAM ECONOMICS: SOME REASONS FOR LOOKING AT FIRMS WITH MONOPOLY POWER WITH SUSPICION

Mainstream economic theories – whether they stem from subsequent elaborations of classical principles,[10] arise solely within the frame of

---

[8] The chapter omits to consider whether specific rules concerning business practices or IPRs are efficient. Using economics for imbuing legal words with meaning is different from using economics for understanding either the rationale of a legal system or the effects that a specific legal rule has on some economic variables, such as efficiency. In the former case, economics bridges legal rules with the empirical phenomena that these rules address. In the latter case, economics works for testing what good comes with the relevant legal regime taken as a whole, or divided into its parts.

[9] While describing some economic concepts that shape competition and IP laws, the chapter addresses various historical developments of economic thinking. Nevertheless, the following sections are not intended to trace a comprehensive and exhaustive history of these developments. In this regard see, e.g., Ernesto Screpanti & Stefano Zamagni, *An Outline of the History of Economic Thought* (2005). Neither are the following sections intended to piece together the way in which US and EU antitrust authorities and IP enforcers morph their policies according to the developments of economic thinking. For various overviews about the relationship between economics and antitrust case law see, e.g., Herbert Hovenkamp, 'The Harvard and Chicago Schools and the Dominant Firm', in *How the Chicago School Overshot the Mark* 109 (Robert Pitofsky ed. 2008); William Kovacic, 'The Intellectual DNA of Modern U.S. Competition Law for Dominant Firm Conduct: The Chicago/Harvard Double Helix', 2007 *Colum. Bus. L. Rev.* 1 (2007); Daniel L. Rubinfeld, 'Antitrust Policy', in 1 *International Encyclopedia of the Social and Behavioral Sciences* 553 (Neil J. Smelser and Paul B. Baltes eds. 2001); Patrick Van Cayseele & Roger Van den Bergh, 'Antitrust Law', in *Encyclopedia of law and economics* 467 (Boudewijn Bouckaert & Gerrit De Geest eds. 1999); William H. Page, 'Areeda, Chicago, and Antitrust Injury: Economic Efficiency and Legal Process', 41 *Antitrust Bull.* 909 (1996); and Herbert Hovenkamp, 'The Antitrust Movement and the Rise of Industrial Organization', 68 *Tex. L. Rev.* 105, 107–108 (1989).

[10] The term 'classical school' is usually used to address the first economic school of the modern age, which elaborated on economic growth, the theory of value, and the idea that free markets can regulate themselves. Adam Smith, David Ricardo, Thomas Malthus and John Stuart Mill are among the most relevant economists associated with this school. Some economists, who came afterwards, worked on its outcomes. For instance, in *The Wealth of Nations* (1776) Adam Smith maintained that each economic agent, by promoting his own gain, is led by an 'invisible hand' to promote public interest. In the 1950s, several neoclassical economists provided a more sophisticated, mathematically based version of this insight. Namely, they elaborated the 'two fundamental theorems of welfare economics' that gave a full analytical

neoclassical economics,[11] or come from industrial organization doctrines[12] – explain that competitive markets deliver better outcomes than monopolistic ones. In particular, the neoclassical perfect competition model[13] shows that competition is the state of world that guarantees the

---

justification of the laissez faire principle. See, in this regard, Screpanti & Zamagni, *supra* note 9, at 396–400.

11 For brevity's sake, it can be stated that five simple ideas lie at the heart of neoclassical economics (also named orthodox or mainstream economics) and combine to create the so-called neoclassical theoretical system; namely: (i) the scarcity assumption, according to which resources are available only in limited quantities; (ii) the *Homo Oeconomicus* paradigm, which prescribes that (a) economic agents are self-interested individuals (and not political bodies or social classes) with Olympian rationality, exogenous preferences, complete information, and homogeneous motivations; and (b) the human good consists in nothing other than economic welfare; (iii) the utilitarian approach, according to which any human behavior is exclusively reducible to a rational calculation aimed at the maximization of welfare; (iv) the subjective theory of value, which states that something has a value as long as an economic agent considers it valuable; and (v) the substitution principle, according to which economic agents pursue their goals deciding the optimal choice among alternative possibilities. See, in this regard, Screpanti & Zamagni, *supra* note 9, at 165–7. Economic neoclassicism arose in the 1870s and 1880s, but it established itself in the 1920s, after about 30 years of struggle against the old-school classicists.

12 Industrial organization doctrines, such as the Harvard, the Chicago and the post-Chicago schools (see footnotes 30 ff. and the accompanying text), share neoclassical economics' founding principles. Simply, they study markets that move away from the specific hypotheses underpinning the perfect competition model (see footnote 20 and the accompanying text). They look at markets where economic agents do not always act independently of one another but may instead collude; where resources may be immobile and products may be differentiated; where information is incomplete; and where there are economies of scale, externalities, and barriers to entry. In other words, industrial organization models pivot around the concept of market power, inquiring whether and how particular firms' behaviors and specific market features allow maintaining, strengthening, and prolonging such power. For a brief history of the industrial organization thinking, see, Richard Schmalensee, 'The New Industrial Organization and the Economic Analysis of Modern Markets', in *Advances in Economic Theory* 253 (Werner Hildebrand ed. 1982).

13 Thinking economic theories as a gradual refinement of the single conception of 'competition as a state of affairs' would be a mistake. Classical economists and the earlier neoclassical writers, indeed, saw competition as a rivalry, a dynamic process. See, in this regard, Frank M. Machovec, *Perfect Competition and the Transformation of Economics* 236 (1995); Paul J. McNulty, 'Economic Theory and the Meaning of Competition', 82 *Quarterly Journal of Economics* 639 (1968); and Paul J. McNulty, 'A Note on the History of Perfect Competition', 75 *J. Pol. Econ.* 395 (1967). It was not until the 1920s that, thanks to Frank Knight, *Risk, Uncertainty and Profit* (1921), the conception of perfect competition, born with Antoine A. Cournot, *Researches into the Mathematical Principles of the Theory of Wealth* (1838) and Francis Y. Edgeworth *Mathematical Psychics* (1881), was finally received into the corpus of mainstream economics. See George J. Stigler, 'Perfect Competition. Historically Contemplated', 65 *Journal of Political Economy* 1 (1957). Yet, the real consecration of the (ideal) of perfect competition happened with Joan Robinson, *The Economics of Imperfect Competition* (1933) and Edward Chamberlin, *The Theory of Monopolistic Competition* (1933). See, in this regard, Israel Kirzner, *Competition and the Market Process: Some Doctrinal Milestones*, in *The process of competition* 11, 12 (Jackie Krafft ed. 2000); Mark Blaug, 'Competition as an End-State and Competition as a Process', in *Trade, Technology and Economics* 241–2 (B. Curtis Eaton and Richard G. Harris eds.

achievement of allocative efficiency[14] and productive efficiency,[15] together with maximum consumer welfare,[16] maximum producer welfare,[17] and maximum total welfare.[18] Therefore, the more a market moves away from perfect competition by approaching a monopoly regime, that is to say, the

---

1997); and Scott Moss, 'The History of the Theory of the Firm from Marshall to Robinson and Chamberlin: The Source of Positivism in Economics', 51 *Economica* 307 (1984). Subsequently, the concept of perfect competition has been seriously criticized since the 1940s from, at least, three standpoints, that is by: (i) questioning the effective occurrence of its hypothesis (see footnotes 20 ff. and the accompanying text); (ii) observing that the model is not very suitable for explaining economic growth (see footnotes 37 ff. and the accompanying text); and (iii) opposing to it a different conception of competition, i.e., the idea of competition as a rivalry that was dear to classical economists (see footnotes 53 ff. and the accompanying text).

[14] Allocative efficiency (also named Pareto Efficiency) is reached when the existing stock of (final and intermediate) goods is assigned via the system of market prices to those purchasers who value them most in terms of willingness to pay or willingness to forego other consumption possibilities. When allocative efficiency is achieved, market prices are equal to the marginal costs of producing and supplying those goods; no more mutually advantageous bargains or contracts can be made as none of the players, sellers or buyers, could be made better off without someone being made worse off. For this definition and the other economic definitions presented in this chapter, see Roger J. Van den Bergh & Peter D. Camesasca, *European Competition Law and Economics: A Comparative Perspective* (2006); W. Kip Viscusi, John M. Vernon & Joseph E. Harrington, Jr, *Economics of Regulation and Antitrust* (2005); Massimo Motta, *Competition Policy* (2004); and Mike Walker & Simon Bishop, *The Economics EC Competition Law: Concepts, Application and Measurement* (2002).

[15] Productive efficiency (also named operating efficiency) is achieved when a particular firm is able either to produce the maximum output possible for any given level of inputs cost, or to employ the cheapest combination of inputs possible for any given level of output. When operating efficiency is achieved, firms produce at the minimum average cost permitted by the existing input prices and technology. Indeed, whereas input prices determine which combination of inputs is the one that entails the lowest production costs for any given level of output, technology conditions determine what alternative combinations of inputs can produce a given amount of output. During the 1970s, in its fight against the Harvard school, the Chicago School stressed greatly the importance of productive efficiency to show that economies of scale derive from a more efficient use of existing resources by larger firms as compared with smaller ones, rather than from markets' structural features. See on this topic, footnote 31 and the accompanying text. In accord, Josef Drexl, 'Is There a "More Economic Approach" to Intellectual Property and Competition Law?', in *Research Handbook on Intellectual Property and Competition Law* 39 (Josef Drexl ed. 2008).

[16] The welfare (or surplus) of an individual consumer results from the difference between the consumer's willingness to pay for a specific good – that is her valuation of the good – and the price she really has to pay for it. Thus, consumer welfare is nothing more than the sum of the individual surplus of all the consumers. For a discussion of what consumer welfare is see Liza Lovdahl Gormsen, *A Principled Approach to Abuse Of Dominance In European Competition Law* 20 (2010).

[17] The welfare of an individual producer results from the difference between the price at which she sells the good and the costs she has to sustain in order to produce it. Thus, producer welfare is (again) nothing more than the sum of all the profits that producers make in an industry.

[18] Total welfare results from the sum of consumer surplus and producer surplus. It is the standard concept that economics uses to measure how well a market performs.

higher market power that a firm holds,[19] the higher are the social costs that the monopolized market produces. Namely, as the following scheme shows, if a monopolist can profitably impose over-competitive prices and sub-optimal output both a dead weight loss – which is a net harm to allocative efficiency – and a wealth transfer from consumers to producers – which equals a net reduction of consumer welfare – occur.

Further, mainstream economics proves that competitive markets deliver better outcomes than monopolistic ones even by relaxing some of the unrealistic hypothesis beneath the perfect competition model.[20] For instance, by abandoning the idea that firms are black boxes that adapt passively to market features and rivals' behaviors,[21] it explains that a monopolist can: (i) reduce productive efficiency because it suffers a kind of slack, and is slow in searching for either cost-saving or quality-improving goods and

---

[19] If market power is the power to charge over-competitive prices in a profitable way, monopoly power is a significant and persistent amount of market power. See in this regard, William M. Landes, Richard A. Posner, 'Market Power in Antitrust Cases', 94 *Harv. L. Rev.* 937, 939 (1981) (observing that, 'the fact of market power must be distinguished from the amount of market power [. . . so that . . .] when the deviation of price from marginal cost is trivial, or simply reflects certain fixed costs, there is no occasion for antitrust concern, even though the firm has market power'). In other words, monopoly power is generally understood to be: 'The ability (1) to price substantially above the competitive level *and* (2) to persist in doing so for a significant period without erosion by new entry or expansion.' – See Areeda, Hovenkamp, *supra* note 2, at ¶ 501.

[20] Stated briefly, the conditions that must hold for having perfect competition are that: (a) consumers and producers do maximize their welfare; (b) sellers and buyers act independently of one another; (c) all the capital and human input can move freely among markets, also because there are no barriers to entry or exit; (d) there are no externalities; (e) sellers and buyers are so numerous that no one has the power to condition market price via her production or consumption decisions – i.e., all the economic agents are price takers; (f) all the economic agents have perfect knowledge about all the relevant market variables.

[21] For neoclassical economics firms are simple 'technological black boxes' that produce output by combining the existing inputs and work as neurons of the Smith's invisible hand. They are mere algorithms: their performances are just a matter of optimal use of the given factors. Instead, for industrial organization doctrines, firms interact with rivals, consumers, and markets in order to affect them. Their behaviors, indeed, become 'strategies', that is to say, cooperative and non-cooperative practices, which condition industrial structure and competitors' practices. Indeed, as explained in Dennis W. Carlton & Jeffrey M. Perloff, *Modern Industrial Organization* 350–1 (2005), 'a strategic behavior is a set of actions a firm takes to influence [. . .] all factors that influence the market outcome (prices, quantities, profits, welfare), including the beliefs of customers and of rivals, the number of actual and potential rivals, the production technology of each firm, and the costs or speed with which a rival can enter the market. By manipulating [all these factors], a firm may be able to increase its profits'. Given that as noticed by McNulty, *supra* note 13, at 645, 'in a free enterprise economy [. . .] there are two primary institutions through which resources are organized, transformed, and channeled for ultimate consumption as goods or services: the private business firm and the market', it can be acknowledged that with industrial organization doctrines the focus of the economic and antitrust analyses shifted in part from the market (and, thus, from the issues connected to exchange, determination of economic value, prices) to the firm (and, hence, to the matters related to production, determination of physical form, and quality).

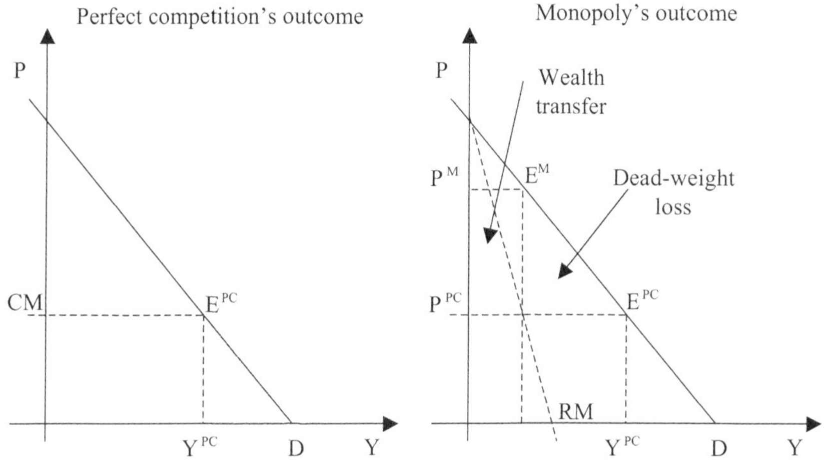

Figure 1.1 Graphs to show perfect competition and perfect monopoly regimes

production techniques;[22] and (ii) waste part of the mentioned welfare transfer in order to prolong its market power, by endorsing strategic behaviors – also called 'rent seeking activities'[23] – such as brand proliferation, wasteful research and development expenses, predatory innovations, and sham litigation.[24]

---

[22] See, e.g., Motta, *supra* note 14, at 47–50 (2004) (discussing in detail the economic models that can support or contest such a conclusion); and Harvey Leibenstein, 'Allocative Efficiency vs. "X-Efficiency"', 56 *Am. Econ. Rev.* 392 (1966) (addressing managers' slack as 'X-inefficiency', meaning the sum of inefficiencies that stem not from imperfections in the structure of the market but rather from the fact that 'for a variety of reasons people and organizations normally work neither as hard nor as effectively as they could').

[23] See, e.g., Frederic M. Scherer & David Ross, *Industrial market structure and economic performance* 28–9 (3d ed. 1990); Frederic M. Scherer, 'Antitrust, Efficiency, and Progress', 62 *N.Y.U. L. Rev.* 998, 999–1000 (1987); Richard Posner, 'The Social Costs of Monopoly and Regulation', 83 *J. Pol. Econ.* 807 (1975); Anne O. Krueger, 'The Political Economy of the Rent-Seeking Society', 64 *Am. Econ. Rev.* 291 (1974); and Gordon Tullock, 'The Welfare Costs of Tariffs, Monopolies and Theft', 5 *W. Econ. J.* 224 (1967).

[24] In particular, this book will face a wide range of strategies that incumbents can employ in dealing with market rivalry, seeking to protect or extend their monopoly power against their actual and potential rivals' encroachments. See, for a general picture on the subject, Janusz A. Ordover & Garth Saloner, 'Predation, Monopolization, and Antitrust', in *1 Handbook of Industrial Organization* 537, 538 and 541 (Richard Schmalensee & Robert D. Willing eds. 1989) (arguing that 'the hallmark of these strategies is that, invariably, they reduce the expected level of profits that incumbent's rivals – present and future – can hope to earn.' Further, these authors clarified that a firm can engage in 'potentially anticompetitive conduct on three fronts. First, they can engage in practices designed to deter potential entrants. [. . .] Second, they can engage in practices that disadvantage actual rivals, without

In brief, *with such an analysis of competitive and monopolistic markets as the backdrop*, antitrust authorities have reasons to look with suspicion at firms that aim at possessing – or already possess and aim at strengthening – market power. They can argue that market monopolies are hurtful for competition, because firms with market power may: (i) 'harm total and consumer welfare', by increasing market price and lowering market output; and (ii) 'deprive consumers of choice', by degrading the quality and variety of their own products that, in the end, are the majority of the products available on the market.

Instead, notwithstanding the above analysis of competitive and monopolized markets, antitrust authorities have no reasons to oblige markets and firms to comply with the requirements beneath the perfect competition model – in other words, they cannot use their enforcing powers to achieve efficiency and maximize welfare.[25] This action would in fact reproduce that of a regulator, while antitrust authorities are aware that they are not supposed to remedy the many imperfections – such as scale economies,[26] externalities,[27] and barriers to entry[28] – that may characterize real markets.

---

necessarily causing their exit [. . .]. Third, they can engage in actions that actually cause the exit of an existing rival or rivals. These types of action can have a substantial deterrence effect on potential rivals and, in fact, may only be rational if they have this demonstration effect.'). The business practices involving IPRs analyzed in this book, which are all non-price business practices, are well-suited for fulfilling each of these three aims.

[25] This is why it would be wrong to affirm that antitrust authorities aim at *maximizing* consumer welfare as such. As Chapter 2 explains, stating that consumer welfare is one (or the sole) of the antitrust goals means that antitrust authorities aim to prevent firms' behaviors that harm consumer welfare, trying not to prohibit those practices that enhance it. See, in this regard, Bruzzone, Boccaccio, *supra* note 4, at 12.

[26] The term 'economies of scale' addresses the case of a firm that reduces its average cost as it increases the output is produces. Often, they occur when a large initial outlay is required, but incremental production is relatively cheap, as happens with the production of software. The existence of economies of scale runs against the idea, proper to perfect competition and to the so-called 'structuralist approach' of the first Harvard School (see footnote 30), that the greater the number of firms in the market, the more the market is competitive. In other words, the existence of economies of scale spurs a trade-off between allocative efficiency and productive efficiency: more firms push prices down to marginal costs, but increase average costs. Therefore, in a market with economies of scale antitrust authorities would make a mistake if, by pointing to realize the market structure of perfect competition regimes, they undertook a policy aimed at increasing the plurality of small competitors by protecting them from being forced to exit, or by aiding them to enter. Indeed, as Scherer & Ross, *supra* note 23, at 1006 noticed, with the exception of *United States v. Aluminum Co. of Am.*, 91 F.Supp. 333 (1950), since the end of World War II it is hard to find US monopolization cases that have actually deconcentrated industries with important scale economies. Further, see Bruzzone, Boccaccio, supra note 4, at 8.

[27] Each economic activity may cast costs and benefits not only upon the agent who endorses that activity but also upon someone else, even upon the whole society. A conduct is said to produce negative externalities when it entails costs that the individual does not have to pay – this typically happens with pollution. Instead, a conduct is said to produce positive externalities when it produces benefits that individuals other than those who sustain its costs

Rather, over times antitrust authorities have learned to 'face' and 'manage' these market imperfections with analytical tools and frameworks[29]other than the perfect competition model, such as the *structuralist approach* of the first Harvard school;[30] the *price theory* of the Chicago

---

can reap – this typically happens with intellectual goods (see footnote 109 ff. and the accompanying text). The existence of externalities unbalances the calculus that economic agents undertake to understand the extent to which they endorse a specific activity. Therefore, when externalities exist, whereas negative externalities entail that more resources will be devoted to the regarded activity, positive externalities imply that less resources will be devoted to it, and the market fails. Yet, it is up to legal provisions, such as tax systems and IP regimes, and not to antitrust authorities, to internalize these externalities.

[28] The concept of barrier to entry has been deeply discussed, since Joe S. Bain, *Barriers to New Competition* 3 (1956) (arguing that the 'conditions of entry' to an industry should be 'evaluated roughly by the advantages of established sellers in an industry over potential entrants, these advantages being reflected in the extent to which established sellers can persistently raise their prices above a competitive level without attracting new firms to enter the industry'). More exactly, Bain thought that three factors could prevent entry; namely, economies of scale (at 53–6), absolute cost advantages (at 114–20), and product differentiation (144–7). Only in Joe S. Bain, *Industrial organization* 239 (1959) does Bain give a general definition of barriers to entry, stating that they are 'some source of disadvantage to potential entrants as compared with established firms'. Afterwards, Stigler proposed another definition of entry barriers, in George J. Stigler, *The Organization of Industry* 67 (1968) (describing barriers to entry in terms of differential costs for potential entrants. Indeed, Stigler stated: 'A barrier to entry may be defined as a cost of producing (at some or every rate of output) which must be borne by a firm which seeks to enter an industry but is not borne by firms already in the industry'). Therefore, according to Stigler, product differentiation is a barrier to entry only if the costs of differentiation (design, advertising, etc.) are higher for a new firm than an existing firm. The following literature moved back and forth between Bain and Stigler. In the wake of Bain, see, e.g., Scherer & Ross, *supra* note 23, at 360; Jean Tirole, *The Theory of Industrial Organization* 305 (1988); Richard J. Gilbert, 'Mobility Barriers and the Value of Incumbency', in *1 Handbook of Industrial Organization* 475, 480-508 (Richard Schmalensee & Robert D. Willig eds. 1989). In contrast, in the wake of Stigler, see Carlton, Perloff, *supra* note 21, at 79; William J. Baumol, John C. Panzar & Robert D. Willig, *Contestable Markets and the Theory of Industry Structure* 282 (1982); Franklin M. Fisher, John J. McGowan & Joen E. Greenwood, *Folded, Spindled, and Mutilated: Economic Analysis and U.S. v. IBM* 165 (1983); and in particular Harold Demsetz, 'Barriers to Entry', 72 *Am. Econ. Rev.* 47 (1982).

[29] True, the 'schools' mentioned in the text have also developed policy suggestions. See, in this regard, footnotes 75 ff. and the accompanying text.

[30] Indeed, put aside its focus on empirical inquiries, the first Harvard school, which arose and became established during the first two decades after World War II, is famous for the so-called Structure-Conduct-Performance (SCP) paradigm, according to which the market structure determines firms' conduct that, in turn, determines market performance. In other words, the Harvard school directly linked a non-concentrated market structure to desirable firms' performances in terms of market price, market quantity, product quality, variety, and innovation. Therefore, it predicted monopoly-like behaviors and welfare losses by heavily weighting the number of buyers and sellers and the entry conditions. See, e.g., Carl Kaysen & Donald F. Turner, *Antitrust Policy: An Economic and Legal Analysis* (1959); and Edward S. Mason, 'The Current State of the Monopoly Problem in the United States', 62 *Harv. L. Rev.* 1265, 1282–5 (1949). For a general discussion of the structural approach see, e.g., James W. Meehan, Jr & Robert J. Larner, 'The Structural School, Its Critics, and Its Progeny: An Assessment 182', in *Economics and Antitrust Policy* (Robert J. Larner & James W. Meehan, Jr, eds. 1989).

school,[31] often combined with[32] the *transaction costs insights* of the so-called New Institutional Economics;[33] and the *strategic interaction approach* of the post-Chicago scholars.[34] Thanks to the compounded

---

[31] Indeed, the Chicago School, based on neoclassical microeconomic theory, encouraged the following ideas, namely that: markets are robust enough to discipline anticompetitive behavior; firms do maximize their profits; monopolies, when they occur, tend to be self-correcting; natural barriers to entry are more imagined than real; and since economies of scale are based on productive efficiency, they are far more pervasive then the structuralist approach believed. In particular, the Chicago School used price theory – see, George J. Stigler, *The Theory of Price* (1946) – to show that the search for efficiencies justifies many types of vertical conduct, such as vertical agreements, vertical unilateral practices like tie-ins and refusals to deal, and vertical mergers. See, e.g., Richard A. Posner, 'The Chicago School of Antitrust Analysis', 127 *U. Pa. L. Rev.* 925 (1979).

[32] See Michelle M. Burtis, 'Modern Industrial Organization: A Comment', 12 *Geo. Mason L. Rev.* 39, 44 (2003) (noticing that whereas 'the Chicago School criticized the antitrust policies hostile to vertical practices on the basis of their impact on allocative efficiency', 'the New Institutional Economics offered a much more detailed and developed framework for explaining the efficiencies that can guide these [practices]').

[33] New Institutional Economics examined how transaction costs – i.e., the costs that a firm sustains by trading with other parties – affect the outcomes of the neoclassical models, thanks to Ronald Coase, *The Nature of the Firm* (1937) and Oliver Williamson, *Transaction Costs Economics: The Governance of Contractual Relations* (1979). The analysis of the New Institutional Economics, which depicted firms as the nexus of contracts, made it possible to identify the efficiency reasons for which firms use various contracts and, in particular, vertical agreements and vertical mergers. See, e.g., Peter Klein, 'New Institutional Economics', in *Encyclopedia of Law and Economics* 456 (Boudewijn Bouckaert & Gerrit De Geest eds. 2000); Glenn R. Carroll & David J. Teece (eds.), *Markets and Hierarchies. The Transaction Cost Economics Perspective* (1999); and Paul L. Joskow, 'The Role of Transaction Cost Economics in Antitrust and Public Utility Regulatory Policies', 7 *J. L. Econ. & Organ.* 53 (1991).

[34] While endorsing many Chicagoan basic microeconomic hypotheses, post-Chicago scholars questioned various Chicagoan central theses about the welfare impact of some behaviors. See, e.g., Steven C. Salop, 'Strategy, Predation, and Antitrust Analysis: An Introduction', in *Strategy, Predation, and Antitrust Analysis* 1, 2 (Steven C. Salop ed. 1981) (arguing that antitrust inquiries should focus not only on entry barriers, like the Harvard school suggested, but also on behaviors' welfare implications, because, differently from what the Chicago School believed, the existence of efficiencies cannot be deemed as a sufficient justification of business behaviors). Further, see Baker, *supra* note 3, 646 and Oliver Williamson, 'Delimiting Antitrust', 76 *Geo. L. J.* 271, 273–4 (1987) (characterizing the post-Chicago School's work not as an alternative to Chicago thinking but as a refinement of it, an effort to provide decision makers with a more accurate picture of the marketplace and more sensitive tools for detecting inefficient behavior). For instance, the post-Chicago School explained the likely anticompetitive nature of some vertical restraints such as exclusive dealings, tie-ins, and refusals to deal, by enlightening via game theory how these strategies can be used as non-price entry deterrence devices. Yet, game theory – see, e.g., John Von Neumann & Oskar Morgenstern, *Theory of Games and Economic Behavior* (1944) –has not consensus among lawyers, judges and jurors because it relies on very sophisticated mathematics, non-testable hypotheses, and because it leads to conclusions that are very sensitive to the way problems are defined and to the assumptions that follow. In other words, taken alone, game theory cannot offer good arguments to sustain a claim. See, e.g., Sam Peltzman, 'The Handbook of Industrial Organization: A Review Article', 99 *J. Pol. Econ.* 201 (1996); Herbert Hovenkamp, 'Post-Chicago Antitrust: A Review and Critique', 2001 *Colum. Bus. L. Rev.* 257 (2001); Bruce H. Kobayashi, 'Game Theory and Antitrust: A Post-Mortem', 5 *Geo. Mason L. Rev.* 411

results of these modern doctrines,[35] current antitrust authorities know that certain behaviors can increase consumer and total welfare as well as improve consumer choice, even if practised by dominant firms.[36] In other words, as the economic thinking developed, antitrust authorities began to enjoy an understanding of dominant firms' conduct and monopolistic markets, which is less simplistic than that which the perfect competition model supplies.

Yet, even the whole elaboration of these industrial organization doctrines have a flaw, which is not trivial in connection to the treatment of market monopolies and in relation to those business behaviors that, by involving IPRs, produce short- and long-run effects on competition and innovation. These industrial organization doctrines cannot fully explain how markets equilibria change,[37] and how market monopolies

---

(1997); and William E. Kovacic, 'The Influence of Economics on Antitrust Law', 30 *Econ. Inquir.* 294 (1992), Burtis, *supra* note 32, at 44–5; and Dennis W. Carlton, 'The Relevance for Antitrust Policy of Theoretical and Empirical Advances in Industrial Organization', 12 *Geo. Mason L. Rev.* 47, 58–60 (2003).

[35] Indeed, nowadays the technical legacy of the mentioned industrial organization doctrines can be synthesized – in spite of some simplifications – in few guidelines. It cannot disregard the role, as the Harvard school first illustrated, that market structure, market power, and barriers to entry play in affecting firms' practices. It also has to acknowledge the Chicago School teaching that, thanks to a rigorous economic analysis, several horizontal and vertical practices do not affect allocative efficiency. Else, the present antitrust analysis has to consider the lesson of the New Institutional Economics about the efficiency reasons for which firms use contractual techniques, especially vertical ones. And, finally, it cannot forget the post-Chicago insights that in a few specific scenarios the horizontal and vertical practices that the Chicago School deemed harmless may, on the contrary, serve as strategic tools to strengthen and prolong market power. See, in this regard, Jacobs, *supra* note 3, at 222–5 and Giorgio Monti, *EC Competition Law* 35 (2007).

[36] See James Kavanagh, Neil Marshall, Gunnar Niels, 'Reform of Article 82 EC – Can the law and economics be reconciled?', in *Article 82 EC: Reflections On Its Recent Evolution* 1, 3 (Ariel Ezrachi ed., 2009).

[37] Some industrial organization models approach the idea of change by employing game theory. They look at the mechanisms of entry and exit and at the interaction between scale economies and irreversible investments. For instance, the model of contestable markets describes an easy entry-exit mechanism by connecting it to business investments that can be easily liquidated. See William J. Baumol, John C. Panzar and Richard D. Willig, *Contestable Markets and the Theory of Industry Structure* (1982) and the rich literature that grew out of it, such as Joseph Stiglitz, 'Technological Change, Sunk Costs, and Competition', *Brookings Papers on Econ. Activity* 883 (1987); Steven C. Salop, 'Measuring Ease of Entry', 31 *Antitrust Bull.* 551 (1986); and Joseph Farrell, 'How Effective is Potential Competition', 9 *Econ. Letters* 67 (1986). However, even these models lost the focus on innovation and industry evolution. See, Franco Malerba, 'Innovation and the Evolution of Industries' in *Innovation, Industrial Dynamics and Structural Transformation. Schumpeterian Legacies* 7, 8 (Uwe Cantner & Franco Malerba eds. 2006); Rudolph J. R. Peritz, 'Competition Policy and Its Implications for Intellectual Property Rights in the United States', in *The Interface between Intellectual Property Rights and Competition Policy* 125, 175–7 (Steven D. Anderman ed. 2007); and Salop, *supra* note 34, at 1.

affect the pace of innovation,[38] although it is further acknowledged[39] that increases in dynamic efficiency – that is to say, in the rate of innovation – accelerate economic growth far more than does the elimination of static inefficiencies.[40] In fact, these models remain focused on short-run price

---

[38] Broadly speaking, the term 'innovation' is used to address the act of developing and spreading new ideas, processes, and products. According to Schumpeter, innovations may also be distinguished as five different types; new products, new methods of production, new sources of supply, the exploitation of new markets, and new ways to organize business. However, in economics, most of the focus has been on the first two, where a product innovation is a new or improved good or service, while a process innovation is a new or improved process that lowers the cost of producing a good or service. See, e.g., Jacob Schmookler, *Invention and Economic Growth* 166 (1966); and Charles Edquist, Leif Hommen & Maureen McKelvey, *Innovation and Employment, Process versus Product Innovation* (2001). Another kind of classification is possible by distinguishing between 'sustaining innovations' and 'disruptive innovations'. The former offer consumers more of the same basic set of product features, enabling consumers to do what they already do in a more efficient way, such as new computers with more computing speed and new cars that drive faster. Often, this kind of innovation builds on existing skills and, hence, is said to be 'competence-enhancing'. Disruptive innovations, instead, offer consumers quite a different set of product characteristics and, hence, enable them to do different things, or familiar things quite differently. Their effect is thus to displace existing technologies and also to reduce the value of firms' existing skills and expertise, as disruptive innovations require firms to develop new skills and expertise. They are thus sometimes named 'competence destroying' innovations. See, in this regard, Clayton M. Christensen, *The Innovator's Dilemma* (1997). This distinction is rooted in Schumpeter's distinction between 'incremental innovations' and 'radical innovations', respectively. See, in particular, Bengt-Åke Lundvall, *National Systems of Innovation: Towards a Theory of Innovation and Interactive Learning* (1992). For a more detailed picture, see Jan Fagerberg, 'Innovation: A Guide to the Literature', in *The Oxford Handbook of Innovation* 1 (2005).

[39] See, e.g., David Audretsch, William L. Baumol & Andrew Burke, 'Competition Policy in Dynamic Markets', 19 *International Journal of Industrial Organization* 613 (2001); Richard J. Gilbert & Willard K. Tom, 'Is Innovation King at the Antitrust Agencies? The Intellectual Property Guidelines Five Years Later', 69 *Antitrust L. J.* 43 (2001); Richard J. Gilbert & Steven C. Sunshine, 'Incorporating Dynamic Efficiency Concerns in Merger Analysis: The Use of Innovation Markets', 63 *Antitrust L. J.* 569 (1995); Thomas M. Jorde & David J. Teece, 'Rule of Reason Analysis of Horizontal Arrangements: Agreements Designed to Advance Innovation and Commercialized Technology', 61 *Antitrust L. J.* 579 (1993); and William L. Baumol & Janusz A. Ordover, 'Antitrust: Source of Dynamic and Static Inefficiencies?', in *Antitrust, Innovation, and Competitiveness* 82 (Thomas M. Jorde & David J. Teece eds. 1992).

[40] See, e.g., Thomas M. Jorde & David J. Teece, 'Introduction', in *Antitrust, Innovation, and Competitiveness* 3, 4 (Thomas M. Jorde & David J. Teece eds. 1992) (arguing that 'competition driven by innovation generally stimulates rivalry and promotes economic welfare far more effectively than does competition that focuses on price reductions. Yet innovation-driven competition is not what U.S. antitrust laws emphasize. [. . .] Unfortunately – and importantly – in static analysis there is almost no reference to innovation and its importance to competition and economic welfare.'). To be sure, the concept of equilibrium – proper of mainstream economics – does not necessarily represent an antinomy to the concept of change. See Fritz Machlup, 'Commenting on Clark's Competition: Static Models and Dynamic Aspects', 45 *Am. Econ. Rev.* 480, 481 (whereas Clark spoke 'of a gap between theories of equilibrium and theories of growth and development [. . .] equilibrium is a tool of thinking needed to explain change, no matter whether it is change in market prices or in business investment or in employment or in the rate of growth. Equilibrium is a valuable concept

and output effects: they share, by and large, the same static perspective that underpins the perfect competition model,[41] without discussing the relationship between today's and tomorrow's competition.

To be sure, the perfect competition model, when applied to analyze long-run change,[42] states that competitive markets and small firms enjoy the proper set of incentives to innovate.[43] For instance, it teaches that whereas competitive pressure sharpens management's incentives to avoid sloth and slack,[44] managers in monopolies may resist innovations that would threaten the existing organizational structure. Moreover, it could be maintained that a dominant firm may have less to gain from innovation than its rivals because, unlike them, it already has most of the business that there is to get.[45] Further, whereas the price competition that occurs in competitive markets may arguably induce firms to search for competitive advantages to escape it,[46] the monopoly's quiet life could induce dominant

---

both in models which disregard time-lags static theory and in models which present sequences in time-dynamic theory. Since a theory of growth will ordinarily use the equilibrium concept, there can be no contrast between theories of equilibrium and of growth. What Clark meant, I suppose, was the contrast between 'static theories of price and output' and 'theories of growth and development'').

41 See Joseph E. Stiglitz, *Whither Socialism?* 140 (1997) (arguing that, 'The standard Arrow-Debreu model (the competitive paradigm) not only does not include (endogenous) changes in technology but its framework is fundamentally inconsistent with incorporating technological change. What is more, it is not just that competition is imperfect – that firms are not price takers – but that the form and nature of competition – competition to develop new and different products – is simply not well captured by the standard Arrow-Debreu model.').

42 See, in this regard, George Stigler, 'Competition', in *The New Palgrave. A Dictionary of Economics* 51, 55 (John Eatwell, Murray Milgate & Peter Newman eds. 1987) (arguing that a partial adaptation to change of the competitive model was made by stressing the possibility that welfare is maximized over time, by trading off consumption and production gains across different time periods). With this new conceptualization of competition, change appears as a breaking point between two different static situations: the ante-change scenario, and the post-change scenario. However, this 'comparative statics' still ignores the process of change from one to the other situations.

43 See Herbert Hovenkamp, *The Antitrust Enterprise: Principle and Execution* 13 (2005); and Whish, *supra* note 2, at 5.

44 This insight can be traced back to Adam Smith, *An Inquiry into the Nature and Causes of the Wealth of Nations* 163–4 (R. H. Campbell, A. S. Skinner, & W. B. Todd eds. 1976).

45 See Kenneth J. Arrow, 'Economic Welfare and the Allocation of Resources for Innovation', in *The Rate and Direction of Inventive Activity* 609–25 (National Bureau of Economic Research ed.) (1962). In this seminal work, indeed, Arrow explained that once a successful monopolistic innovation displaces the existing old technology, it does not bring new profits to the monopolist but it replaces the old ones with new ones. To put it another way, dominant firms have a strong incentive to slow the pace of technological change so as to increase the profits that they can extract from existing products – an effect that Tirole named the 'replacement effect' – see Tirole, *supra* note 28, at 395.

46 Such an incentive to invest in R&D in order to gain a competitive advantage, via product differentiation and innovation, that allows escaping price competition, has been named in several different ways, such as the 'escaping competition incentive' – see Philippe Aghion et al., 'Competition and Innovation: An Inverted-U Relationship', 120 *Quarterly*

firms to economize on R&D and creative activities by imitating rather than innovating.

Nevertheless, these arguments regarding the incentives to innovate that small firms enjoy in competitive markets are not conclusive. Antitrust authorities cannot rely solely on them in order to have a further reason for looking with suspicion at market monopolies. Indeed, several other insights[47] explain that monopolies and large firms spur innovation more than competitive markets with several small firms.[48] For instance, for dominant firms innovative activity may be either less expensive or more profitable than it is for small firms.[49] The former, indeed, can attract specialized equipment and personnel and are more likely to enjoy scale economies in producing, promoting, and distributing the results of R&D than are the latter. In addition, being diversified, dominant firms are likely to realize a larger internal payoff from R&D. Further, given the extra profits and a better access to the imperfect market for capital, they may have deep pockets and, hence, can afford risky projects. Moreover, as fighting for a competitive advantage that consists in a better product or in a less expensive producing process is costly, no firm engages in such a battle without the right to appropriate the incomes and benefits that come from that competitive advantage. Therefore, no firm would fight in order to smite its rivals via innovation if markets could not move from perfect competition to monopoly regimes.

Therefore, focusing theoretical analysis – as well as empirical studies – on what market structure[50] and on what business size[51] are more conducive

---

J. Econ. 701, 714 (2005) – and the 'stimulus factor' – see Scherer & Ross, *supra* note 23, at 637.

47 For recent antitrust scholars' analysis of the market features and other factors that affect innovation, see Jonathan B. Baker, 'Beyond Schumpeter vs. Arrow: How Antitrust Fosters Innovation', 74 *Antitrust L. J.* 575 (2008); Richard J. Gilbert, 'Looking for Mr. Schumpeter: Where Are We in the Competition—Innovation Debate?', in *Innovation Policy and the Economy* 159 (Adam B. Jaffe, Josh Lerner & Scott Stern eds. 2006).

48 See, e.g., Dennis W. Carlton, 'A General Analysis of Exclusionary Conduct and Refusal to Deal – Why Aspen and Kodak Are Misguided', 68 *Antitrust L. J.* 659, 674 (2001) (arguing that the constant pursuit of monopoly power is the central driving thrust of new economy industries); John E. Lopatka, '*United States v. IBM*: A Monument to Arrogance', 68 *Antitrust L. J.* 145, 156 (2000) (stating that, 'periods of 'monopoly' profits drive innovation, and it is the innovative process, more so than lower prices, that best serves consumers'); and David J. Teece & Mary Coleman, 'The Meaning of Monopoly: Antitrust Analysis in High-Technology Industries', 18 *Antitrust Bull.* 801, 824 (1998) (observing that 'it is the quest for profits that encourages innovation in the first place').

49 See, e.g., Robert Pitofsky, 'Antitrust and Intellectual Property: Unresolved Issues at the Heart of the New Economy', 16 *Berkeley Tech. L. J.* 535 (2001); Frederic M. Scherer, 'Schumpeter and Plausible Capitalism', 30 *Journal of Economic Literature* 1416 (1992); and Scherer & Ross, *supra* note 23, at 652.

50 Virtually all of the evidence suggests that market structure is not obviously the most important driver of innovation. See, e.g., Jorde Gual, 'Time to Rethink Merger Policy', 3

to innovation[52] does not help antitrust authorities to deal with change and economic growth. Thus, it does not serve to understand whether they can find in the protection of innovation a further reason to look with suspicion at market monopolies.[53]

Competition Policy International 29 (2007), available at http://ssrn.com/abstract=987093; George Symeonides, 'Innovation, Firm Size and Market Structure: Schumpeterian Hypotheses and Some New Themes' § 44, Economics Department Working Papers No. 161, London School of Economics (1996) (emphasizing the inconclusiveness of the R&D-market concentration relationship); and Wesley M. Cohen & Richard C. Levin, 'Empirical Studies of Innovation and Market Structure', in 2 *Handbook of Industrial Organization* 1059 (Richard Schmalensee & Robert D. Willig eds. 1989) (observing that the empirical 'results leave little support for the view that industrial concentration is an independent, significant, and important determinant of innovative behavior and performance.'). See further, Patrick Van Cayseele, 'Market Structure and Innovation: A Survey', 146 *De Economist* 391 (1998); Paul A. Geroski, 'Innovation, Technological Opportunity, and Market Structure', 42 *Oxford Econ. Papers* 586 (1990); William L. Baldwin & John T. Scott, *Market Structure and Technological Change* 63–113 (1987); and Bruzzone, Boccaccio, supra note 4, at 8 (arguing that the structuralist approach that deems competition as a market structure is ill-suited to explain innovation).

[51] Empirical studies on innovation and firm size are somewhat more definitive than the ones mentioned in the previous footnote, finding that smaller firms (beyond a minimum threshold) are as research-intensive as larger firms and are more productive. However, the contribution of small firms to innovation is known to vary greatly by industry. See, in this regard, Daniel L. Rubinfeld & John Haven, 'Innovation and Antitrust Enforcement', in *Antitrust, Innovation, and Competitiveness* 75 (Thomas M. Jorde & David J. Teece eds. 1992). There is also a substantial body of evidence that leading incumbents prefer a different path of innovation than challengers. See Nancy S. Dorfman, *Innovation and Market Structure: Lessons from the Computer and Semiconductor Industries* (1987) (observing that whereas leading companies generally use technology as a means of reinforcing their position for the already mentioned substitution effect, small firms and major firms working outside their main area of specialization are more conducive to the introduction of path-breaking technological breakthroughs).

[52] A related issue, given a developed innovation, is to understand who is in the best position to extract profits from it via its use and commercialization. Indeed several studies suggest that the innovation's profitability might strongly depend on the expectations and the history of the firm. Therefore, it can be that a firm is not in the best position to understand the real market value of an innovation, hence choosing not to patent and market it when its development and commercialization would have been optimal for the whole society. See, e.g., Neus Palomeras, 'Sleeping Patents: Any Reason to Wake Up?', Working Paper no. 506 (2003), available at www.ebcenter.org. Indeed, the author inquired whether neglected innovative projects are actually low value inventions or whether they in fact hide a potential value that could be exploited in other hands or in another industry. This is a problem of bound rationality and, at most, of excessive transaction costs. For a peculiar solution to this problem, see Carl A. Kukkonen, 'The Use of Patent Licensing Center as an Intermediary for Facilitating the Licensing of Commercially Viable, Unused Patents', 3 *Va. J. L. & TECH.* 10–11 (1998) (discussing a kind of 'patents collective society' as a vehicle to promote the marketing of unused patents); and Kurt M. Saunders & Linda Levine, 'Better, Faster, Cheaper–Later: What Happens When Technologies Are Suppressed', 11 *Mich. Telecomm. & Tech. L. Rev.* 1, 9 (2002) (proposing, among the other things, 'that all patentees file, as a matter of public record, an annual statement that simply indicates whether their patents are being used and, if not, the reasons that the patents are not being used or licensed to others for use').

[53] Recently, it has been argued from both a theoretical and empirical standpoint that some intermediate levels of competition might be optimal for dynamic efficiency, as if there was

Perhaps, also, this kind of analysis has an intrinsic flaw: it tries to explain change, innovation, and economic growth by placing them into a static scenario, despite the fact that change, innovation, and economic growth are all dynamic phenomena.[54] New economic models are thus necessary. The debate about the nature of competition may disclose some 'out of the box' insights about change and innovation.[55]

ANTITRUST LAW, MARKET MONOPOLIES, AND HETERODOX ECONOMICS: ARE OTHER REASONS FOR LOOKING AT FIRMS WITH MONOPOLY POWER WITH SUSPICION?

Over time,[56] scholars developed numerous theories that represent competition as a process that places change and innovation at its heart.[57] For

---

an inverted–U relationship between competition and innovation. See Frederick M. Scherer, 'Market Structure and the Employment of Scientists and Engineers', 57 *Am. Econ. Rev.* 524 (1967) (assuming that the relationship between market structure and innovation follows an inverted-U pattern: innovation is observed to be low at high levels of competition, reach its peak at intermediate levels of oligopoly (where the four leading firms control roughly half the market), and then fall off as market structure approaches monopoly. Several studies replicated and confirmed Scherer's results. For the empirical side of this theory, see Aghion et al., *supra* note 46; and Richard C. Levin et al., 'R&D Appropriability, Opportunity and Market Structure: New Evidence on Some Schumpeterian Hypotheses', 75 *Am. Econ. Rev.* 20 (1985).

[54] Indeed, see Richard R. Nelson, *The Sources of Economic Growth* 87 (1996) (arguing that much economic research urged by the Schumpeterian hypothesis is based on 'a misreading of Schumpeter or, at least, a failure to think through what was basic in Schumpeter's arguments'. The simple-minded search for correlations between market structure and innovation neglects the dynamism and disequilibrium that was the essential element of Schumpeter's vision of capitalism). The development of mainstream economic research does not have much in common with the original spirit of Schumpeter's work. See also Malerba, *supra* note 37, at 8.

[55] To be sure, the debate about what competition is differs from the debate about the drivers of competition and innovation. Nevertheless, a stream of theories portrays competition as a process (i.e., a process of learning and coordination, a process of discovery, a process of trial and error, or else a process of selection) that places innovation at its heart. Further, the 'time dimension' links the idea of competition as a process and that of innovation. Indeed, innovation itself can be seen as a process – a process that entails the development of a new technology, the transformation of the productive structures, a change in cost conditions, the modification of consumer preferences, a change even in the level and quality of the available information. See, in this regard, Mario Amendola, Jean-Luc Gaffard & Patrick Musso, 'Innovative Choice and Competition Process', in *The Process of Competition* 65, 66 (Jackie Krafft ed. 2000). Further, as to the concepts of competition that US and EU authorities seemed to have endorsed, see Robert H. Bork, *The Antitrust Paradox* 58–61 (1993); and Eugene Buttigieg, *Competition law: Safeguarding the Consumer Interest. A comparative Analysis of US Antitrust Law and EC Competition law* 3–7 (2009).

[56] See Alfred Marshall, *Principles of Economics XV* (1920) (stating that: 'the main concern of economics is [. . .] with human beings who are impelled, for good and evil, to change and progress. Fragmentary statical hypotheses are used as temporary auxiliaries to dynamical – or rather biological – concepts: but the central idea of economics [. . .] must

instance, the Schumpeterian school described competition as a fight for innovations through which the economy is constantly shaped to superior kinds of equilibrium.[58] Similarly, the evolutionary school assumed that competition is an open-ended process of innovation and experimentation where firms, being unable to calculate single best practices,[59] used 'routines' (that is to say, sets of 'learned behaviors') to guide their responses to unforeseen market conditions.[60] Alternatively, the Austrian school thought

---

be that of living force and movement.'). On the concepts of competition, see also John Vickers, 'The Concepts of Competition', 47 *Oxford Economic Papers* 1 (1995); Israel Kirzner, *Competition and Entrepreneurship* (1973) (arguing that the idea of competition as a state of affairs is that of economists, whereas that of competition as a process is that of businessman. Therefore, perhaps it was for sociological reasons that 'the businessman's perception of active competition was dismissed as a crude expression of the way in which imperfect reality falls short of the sophisticated analytical ideal which the PC model expresses.').

[57] See Jerry Ellig & Daniel Lin, 'Introduction', in *Dynamic Competition and Public Policy. Technology, Innovation, and Antitrust issues* 1, 4 and 7 (Jerry Ellig ed. 2001), arguing that the greatest similarity shared by all of these theories – i.e., Schumpeterian, Evolutionary, Austrian, and Path-dependence – is their focus on innovation as a key component of the competitive process. Further, see Kirzner, *supra* note 13, at 14 (stating that, until Hayek's *The Meaning of Competition* 'no one in the profession had seen or at least made explicit the crucial difference between competition as a state of affairs and competition as a driving, dynamic process').

[58] See, e.g., Joseph Schumpeter, *Capitalism, Socialism, and Democracy* 105 (1942) (arguing that 'the introduction of new methods and new commodities is hardly conceivable with perfect – and perfectly promptly – competition'). In other words, according to Schumpeter, innovation is what makes the economy jump from one state of equilibrium to another, superior one. The point is that Schumpeter studied the transition step observing that whereas innovations allow the innovating firm to gain a competitive advantage and earn extra profits over its rivals, imitation is what the other firms use to reduce the gap to the point where the economy will be driven to another, but superior, state of equilibrium, where no firm will earn extra profits. As developing innovations is costly, the most innovative firms should have a large stream of resources for R&D. The incentive to innovate is greatest where there is little threat of imitation, so the most innovative firms should have few competitors. Therefore, as seen before, Schumpeter suggested that large firms are more innovative than small firms, monopolistic industries are more innovative than competitive ones, and firms will be more innovative when they anticipate that they will be allowed to exploit the advantages created by their innovations.

[59] According to the evolutionary school, indeed, firms do not enjoy Olympic rationality but 'bounded rationality', that is to say, they can take their decisions only by using a limited amount of information and time and by suffering from their cognitive limitations. Therefore, these firms are not able to detect the behaviors that maximize their profits.

[60] See, e.g., Nicolai J. Foss, 'Theories of the Firm: Contractual and Competence Perspectives', 9 *Journal of Evolutionary Economics* 127 (1993); Giovanni Dosi et al., *Technical Change and Economic Theory* (1988); Richard N. Langlois, *Economics as a Process: Essays in the New Institutional Economics* (1986); and Richard R. Nelson & Sidney G. Winter, *An Evolutionary Theory of Economic Change* (1982). For these economists, firms learn how to do things by doing, by using, by searching, by interacting, and by monitoring new developments. Therefore, developing new routines by putting together old ones, by copying some from rivals, and by developing brand new ways of doing things, is the way of surviving the selection that happens in the market. During their lives firms search for better routines by experimenting with new ways of doing things, such as new production techniques, new organizational

of competition as a dynamic process for new products, new techniques, new management methods, corporate culture, and organizational processes, so that uncovering previously hidden knowledge is the only way of coping with uncertainty over time.[61]

From these streams of economic thinking antitrust authorities can gain guidance about competition, market monopolies and innovation. For instance, they could conclude that what may appear inefficient today, such as monopolies and barriers to entry, may actually turn out to be a necessary passage toward achieving efficiency tomorrow. Likewise, they could realize that market power, barriers to entry, and over-competitive prices are not a sign of inefficiency but evidence that the dominant firm has made a substantial contribution to economic growth, by developing new products, processes, and organization models that satisfy consumers better. On the contrary, they could acknowledge that firms unable to develop new products, production techniques, or models of organization should not be 'saved' and that, if a kind of intervention has to be sustained, it should elaborate on ways to encourage discovery and innovation. In sum, thanks to the described conceptions of competition as a dynamic process, antitrust authorities could acknowledge that market monopolies have to be tolerated because they work as 'appropriability tools':[62] by rewarding with extra profits and other advantages firms that have smitten their rivals via superior performances, market monopolies give to those firms and to their rivals the incentives to develop new competitive advantages.

Yet, unfortunately, these suggestions not only clash with what was said above about the perfect competition model, but also contrast with another

---

cultures, and new products. Only when the market selects the better innovation, rewarding it with extra profits, will the firm succeed in surviving. The firm can also imitate the routines that were cultivated by rivals, if they proved to be the most preferred. Further, see Richard R. Nelson, 'Understanding Economic Growth as the Central Task of Economic Analysis', in *Perspectives on Innovation* 27, 30 (Franco Malerba & Stefano Brusoni eds. 2007), 'What Winter and I did, of course, was to marry an evolutionary theory of technological change with a behavioral theory of the firm, augmented to include innovation as a central firm activity, and placed in a context of Schumpeterian competition'.

61 See, e.g., Dina Kallay, *The Law and Economics of Antitrust and Intellectual Property. An Austrian Approach* (2004); L. M. Lachmann, *The Market as an Economic Process* (1986); Israel M. Kirzner, *Methods, Process and Austrian Economics* (1982); Ludwig von Mises, *Human Action: A Treatise on Economics* (1949); Friederich A. Hayek, *Individualism and Economic Order* (1948); and Friederich A. Hayek, 'Economics and Knowledge', 4 *Economics* 33 (1937).

62 Broadly speaking, the term 'appropriability' when referred to goods, addresses one's ability to earn their net value. See, e.g., Richard C. Levin et al., *supra* note 53 (showing via a survey that patents were generally rated the least effective of the mechanisms of appropriation. Indeed natural secrecy, lead time and recognition lags, learning curves, first-mover advantages accruing to the innovator, and sale or service efforts, were regarded as substantially more effective than patents, especially in protecting product inventions).

theory: the so-called path-dependence doctrine, which antitrust scholars have recently looked at because it focuses mainly on new economy markets.[63] This last theory, indeed, proposes that antitrust authorities should intervene in young markets, helping deconcentration before lock-in occurs, to prevent any firm from gaining too much market power and, hence, allow consumers to reach superior alternatives that they do not otherwise enjoy. Indeed, the path-dependence doctrine introduces the idea – questioned from an empirical standpoint[64] – that in particular scenarios, such as those of the so-called new economy, competition might not select the most efficient firm.[65] More exactly, this theory maintains that those who succeed in being dominant firms might just have benefited from small events unrelated to the superiority of their product or processes,[66] but connected to some market features, such as increasing network effects,[67] and tipping

---

63 See John T. Soma & Kevin B. Davis, 'Network Effects in Technology Markets: Applying the Lessons of Intel and Microsoft to Future Clashes between Antitrust and Intellectual Property', 8 J. *Intell. Prop. L.* 1, 3–4 (2000) (arguing 'that the need for compatibility between different machines and programs and network effects causes a company that has already achieved a 30–40 per cent market share to rise, virtually automatically, to a market share equal to 80–90 per cent. Therefore, antitrust remedies need to be applied earlier, while the negative economic effects of monopolies can be most efficiently dealt with by the appropriate enforcement authorities.'); Michael L. Katz & Carl Shapiro, 'Antitrust in Software Markets', in *Competition, Innovation and the Microsoft Monopoly: Antitrust in the Digital Marketplace* 65, 70, 78 (Jeffrey A. Eisenach & Thomas M. Lenard eds., 1999); id., 'Systems Competition and Network Effects', 5 *Journal of Economic Perspectives* 93 (1994); id., 'Network Externalities, Competition, and Compatibility', 75 *Am. Econ. Rev.* 93 (1986); id., 'Technology Adoption in the Presence of Network Externalities', 94 *J. Pol. Econ.* 822 (1986); and Stanley M. Besen & Joseph Farrell, 'Choosing How to Compete: Strategies and Tactics in Standardization', *J. Econ. Persp.* 117 (1994). However, see Jonathan M. Jacobs, 'Do We Need a 'New Economy' Exception for Antitrust?', 16 *Antitrust* 89 (2001) (arguing that 'new economy exceptions are almost as old as the Sherman Act', and that, indeed, the attributes mostly associated with today's new economy industry are not really new).

64 Stan J. Liebowitz and Stephen E. Margolis argued in a series of articles that the evidence indicates that this has not actually occurred; see, e.g., 'Are Network Externalities a New Source of Market Failure?', in 17 *Research in Law and Economics* 1 (Richard O. Zerbe, Jr & William Kovacic eds. 1995); 'Path Dependence, Lock-In and History', 11 *J. L. Econ.. & Org.* 205 (1995); 'Network Externality: An Uncommon Tragedy', 8 *J. Econ. Persp.* 133 (1994); 'The Fable of the Keys', 33 *J. L. & Econ.* 1 (1990).

65 In other words, according to this theory a product could lose out to an objectively inferior alternative if it enjoys peculiar market advantages. See W. Brian Arthur, 'Competing Technologies, Increasing Returns, and Lock-In by Historical Events', 99 *Econ. J.* 116 (1989); Paul A. David, 'Clio and the Economics of QWERTY', 75 *Am. Econ. Rev.* 332 (1985); and Joseph Farrell & Garth Saloner, 'Standardization, Compatibility, and Innovation', 16 *Rand J. Econ.* 70 (1985).

66 Market participants do not have enough information to identify dominant products or standards, *ex ante*. There is enough uncertainty about production technologies that firms can learn as they use the technology more. Therefore, individuals cannot dispose of one product or technology in the course of adopting another.

67 There are two kinds of network effects; direct and indirect network effects. See, beyond Katz & Shapiro, *supra* note 63, John E. Lopatka & William H. Page, 'Antitrust on Internet

effects,[68] that are hence completely unrelated to the particular firm's merits.[69] Therefore this theory, trusting governments more than markets in picking up winning technologies,[70] suggests to antitrust authorities the

---

Time: Microsoft and the Law of Economics and Exclusion', 7 *Sup. Ct. Econ. Rev.* 157, 160 (1999); and Mark A. Lemley & David McGowan, 'Legal Implications of Network Economic Effects', 86 *Cal. L. Rev.* 479, 481 (1998). Direct network effects occur when the benefit to one person from using a product increases as more people use the product; in other words, when average consumer benefit rises as output increases. For instance, direct network effects spring off with telephones and computers as each telephone and computer acquires a larger value as more people are able to communicate one with the other, in this case exchanging compatible files. Because of direct network effects, without some offsetting advantage a potential entrant has no prospect of success, so that an incumbent may employ some strategies just in order to reach a number of consumers to enjoy direct network effects. For a similar discussion in the specific context of PC software, see David S. Evans & Richard L. Schmalensee, 'Be Nice to Your Rivals: How the Government Is Selling an Antitrust Case Without Consumer Harm in *United States v. Microsoft*', in *Did Microsoft Harm Consumers? Two Opposing Views* 45, 65–6 (David S. Evans et al., 2000), available at http://www.aei.brookings/publications/books/consumers.pdf. Instead, the term 'indirect network effects' serves to address the consequences that the existence of a network has on the production of complements. See, generally, Neil Gandal, 'A Selective Survey of the Literature on Indirect Network Externalities: A Discussion of Liebowitz and Margolis', in 17 *Research in Law and Economics* 1 (Richard O. Zerbe, Jr & William Kovacic eds. 1995). For empirical evidence of an indirect network effect in the software industry, see Neil Gandal, Michael Kende & Rafael Rob, 'The Dynamics of Technological Adoption in Hardware/Software Systems: The Case of Compact Disc Players', 31 *Rand J. Econ.* 43 (2000); and Neil Gandal, 'Competing Compatibility Standards and Network Externalities in the PC Software Market', 77 *Rev. Econ. & Stat.* 599 (1995). With indirect network effects, the potential entrant's disadvantage relates to the availability of complements of various sorts. To the extent that the complements are incompatible in some way, an entrant might have to establish its own complementary network.

[68] Tipping effects occur when one network has taken such a large portion of the market that competing networks no longer have enough members to be viable. Even though an individual consumer may prefer a competing network's technology, the benefits (due to network effects) from joining a dominant network may swamp these considerations. Thus, marketing techniques, or anti-competitive practices that gain large market share for a network, may 'tip' the market in favor of that network. See, in this regard, Max Schanzenbach, 'Network Effects and Antitrust Law: Predation, Affirmative Defenses, and the Case of *U.S. v. Microsoft*', 2002 *Stan. Tech. L. Rev.* 4, 6 (2002); and Lemley & McGowan, *supra* note 67, at 495–500. An often cited example of market tipping is the VCR industry, in which the Beta technology essentially vanished. See, e.g., W. Brian Arthur, 'Positive Feedback in the Economy', 262 *Scientific Am.* 92 (1990).

[69] See Gregory J. Werden, 'Network Effects and Conditions of Entry, Lessons from the Microsoft Case', 69 *Antitrust L. J.* 87 (2001); and Joel Klein & Preeta Bansal, 'International Antitrust Enforcement in the Computer Industry', 41 *Vill. L. Rev.* 173 (1996).

[70] See, e.g., Stan Liebowitz & Stephen E. Margolis, 'Network Effects and the Microsoft Case', in *Dynamic Competition and Public Policy*, at 190–1 (Jerry Ellig ed. 2001) (arguing that network markets, such as software products and operating systems, are highly competitive even though some firms have large market shares); Ronald A. Cass & Keith N. Hylton, 'Preserving Competition: Economic Analysis, Legal Standards and Microsoft', 8 *Geo. Mason L. Rev.* 1, 36–7 (1999) (noting while entry barriers may be higher in network markets, payoffs to successful entry are higher as well); Robert A. Levy, 'Microsoft and the Browser Wars', 31 *Conn. L. Rev.* 1321, 1352–8 (1999) (disputing the significance of network effects in the Microsoft case).

need to carry on such a duty rather than to leave markets to operate freely and tolerate market monopolies.

In sum, there is currently no consensus on a microeconomic theory [71] that explains change, economic growth, and – in the end – whether market monopolies should be tolerated and how long they should last in order not to harm competition and innovation,[72] that is to say, in order to give firms, whether dominant or not, enough incentives to search, and to keep searching, for competitive advantages.

---

[71] Since the 1950s economists have employed different macroeconomic frameworks for analysing the relationship between innovation and economic growth. Indeed, it was only with Robert M. Solow, 'A Contribution to the Theory of Economic Growth', 70 *Quarterly J. Econ.* 65 (1956) that the economic thinking went back to focus on economic growth via technological innovation. However, this pioneering writing treated technological change as an exogenous phenomenon, like population growth. It used technological change to justify the growth that the model could not explain in terms of increased quantities of labor and capital, to some extent as if innovation was a kind of 'explanatory factor of last resort'. See, for this expression, Bart Verspagen, 'Innovation and Economic Growth Theory: A Schumpeterian Legacy and Agenda', in *Perspectives on Innovation* 42, 43 (Franco Malerba & Stefano Brusoni eds. 2007). In particular, Moses Abramovitz, 'Resource and Output Trends in the US since 1870', in 46 *Am. Econ. Rev.* 5 (1956) and Robert M. Solow, 'Technical Change and the Aggregate Production Function', 39 *Rev. of Economics and Statistics* 312 (1957) showed in the first empirical studies about factors that cause economic growth that 87.5 per cent of growth could be justified by looking at increased efficiency, that is to say, by looking at a set of factors able to affect productivity, such as a better division of labor, better managers, more IT devices, better governments, and innovation, which is difficult to detect, define, and measure. He named this percentage 'the measure of our ignorance'. Afterwards, several other empirical studies (belonging to the stream of literature named 'accounting growth') tried to explain the residual part, looking at the importance of R&D expenses; at the education system and the quality of labor; and at the role of information technologies. For this new generation of empirical studies, the amount of our ignorance equals the 55 per cent. Meanwhile, on the theoretical side, two new approaches emerged: the 'evolutionary' and 'new growth' theory (also named the endogenous growth theory). In this regard, see Bart Verspagen, 'Innovation and Economic Growth', in *The Oxford Handbook of Innovation* 487 (2005); and Malerba, *supra* note 37, at 8–10. These two approaches differ on the precise mechanisms through which innovation affects growth. Whereas the evolutionary *weltanschaung* is one of historical circumstances – complex causal mechanisms that change over time, so that innovation follows unforeseeable and unsettled patterns – the new growth theory, which belongs to the neoclassical tradition, considers growth as an ordered, steady-state phenomenon. *A latere*, another stream of literature – the so-called post-Kaysian literature – starts off assuming that knowledge is not a public good but a private good, specific to each agent that develops it and does not spill over easily to other agents. That said, a more detailed discussion of all these theories goes beyond the aims of the book, as they do not provide insights about market characteristics and competition mechanisms – insights that are instead crucial for the antitrust analysis. This accords with Marcus Glader, *Innovation Markets and Competition Analysis* 25 (2006).

[72] See, David M. Hart, 'Antitrust and Technological Innovation in US: Ideas, Institutions, Decisions, and Impacts, 1890–2000', 30 *Research Policy* 923, 924 (2001).

THE LEEWAY FOR POLICY CHOICES IN THE ANTITRUST WORLD: WHAT INTEREST TO PROTECT, WHAT ENFORCING SYSTEM TO ADOPT, WHAT ECONOMIC THEORY TO APPLY, AND WHAT SCOPE FOR MARKET MONOPOLIES

What has been said up to now helps to illustrate the current boundaries of economic theory when it comes to antitrust law. First, in real markets it is not the same to pursue efficiency or welfare, allocative efficiency or productive efficiency, consumer or total welfare.[73] Further, in the stochastic contexts of imperfect markets not only may business practices' short- and long-run effects diverge, but also actual and likely market performances may be different. Therefore, before enforcing any antitrust provision, courts and agencies have to choose what interest to protect and whether to typify business behaviors according to the kind of efficiency and welfare effects that they do produce, will produce, and are likely to produce. These are policy choices that explain whether and when business conduct should be prohibited. In other words, economic theories do not suggest what is illegal:[74] as Chapter 2 shows, the answer to this question rests with the objectives that antitrust authorities want to pursue – whether competition and innovation, for instance – and with the features that they want their enforcing systems to have.

Second, economic models are not always easy to administer because antitrust authorities do not always have the information necessary to decide whether the facts that they ascertain can fit the applied model. Thus, since uncertainty and the risk of making mistakes weigh down the enforcement of these models, antitrust authorities have to decide the level of complexity that they want to embrace in making their analysis, and how much they want to intervene in the market. In this regard, the above industrial organization doctrines have supplied antitrust authorities with several policy suggestions other than the mentioned analytical tools and frameworks[75]. The Chicago school has always suggested employing very

---

[73] See, e.g., Joseph F. Brodley, 'The Economic Goals of Antitrust: Efficiency Consumer Welfare and Technological Progress', 62 *N.Y.U. L. Rev.* 1020, 1026–8 and 1033–4 (1987); Scherer, *supra* note 23, at 1002; McNulty, *supra* note 13, at 652.

[74] David J. Gerber, 'The Future of Article 82: Dissecting the Conflict' 12–13, paper presented at the 12th Annual Competition Law and Policy Workshop, Robert Schuman Centre EUI, Florence (2007), available at http://www.eui.eu/RSCAS/Research/Competition/2007(papers).shtml (observing that the 'fact-interpretive' role of economics is a *plus* whatever the objectives that antitrust law wants to pursue: as it can provide more and better tools for assessing the consequences of firms' conduct, so improving competition authorities' performances).

[75] See, *supra* note 29.

simple and clear-cut economic intuitions, and has always been very skeptical about antitrust intervention, arguing that it could be more harmful than non-action.[76] On the other hand, the second Harvard school and the post-Chicago school have believed in the effectiveness of antitrust action. Over the years while the second Harvard school has expressed more caution about the administrability of legal rules,[77] the post-Chicago school has seemed more confident in the capacity of legal institutions to implement even sophisticated economic models.[78] Nevertheless, it rests that antitrust authorities have to choose from these different policy suggestions the enforcing approach that they want to follow, as Chapter 2 shows.

Third, since sometimes economics deals with a specific phenomenon by offering divergent explanations of it – explanations that, in addition, are equally plausible and empirically verifiable[79] – antitrust authorities' determinations about that phenomenon are based on non-economic

---

[76] See, indeed, Frank H. Easterbrook, 'Ignorance and Antitrust'119, in *Antitrust, Innovation, and Competitiveness* (Thomas M. Jorde & David J. Teece eds. 1992); id., 'Workable Antitrust Policy', 84 *Mich. L. Rev.* 1696 (1986) (suggesting the reduction of antitrust enforcement to 'little other than plain vanilla cartels and mergers to monopoly', that is, proposing to disregard illegal monopolizations, and vertical practices); and id., 'The Limits of Antitrust', 63 *Texas L. Rev.* 1, 2 (1984).

[77] Indeed, whereas 'the first Harvard school' sustained the need for a strong antitrust intervention and the faith in the effectiveness of it, in the late 1970s a kind of 'second Harvard school' arose. It was much less ambitious about the goals of antitrust, and significantly more skeptical about the benefits of aggressive judicial intervention, also questioning authorities' skillfulness to address dominant firms' conduct. See Hovenkamp, *supra* note 9, at 109 (speaking about a 'chastised Harvard school' that emerged in the late 1970s in the writings of Philip E. Areeda and Donald T. Turner, the authors of the present most prominent US treatise).

[78] See, e.g., Uwe Cantner & Franco Malerba (eds.) *Innovation, industrial dynamics and structural transformation: Schumpeterian legacies* (2007) (arguing that post-Chicagoan theoretical findings and prescriptions are difficult to translate into workable and enforceable standards that in actual market settings would, without fail, promote conduct that enhances social welfare and would discourage conduct that harms welfare. In particular, the authors noticed that the source of the problem is the strategic setting itself. In the context of strategic interactions, it is difficult to distinguish between those actions which are intended to harm actual and potential rivals that stifle competition, and thereby reduce economic welfare, and those actions which harm present and discourage future entry but which, nevertheless, promote economic welfare). To be sure, more post-Chicago scholars ended up suggesting the 'hands off' approach, after having recognized the complexity of their economic analysis. Nevertheless, it seems that they do succeed in persuading antitrust authorities on both sides of the Atlantic Ocean to take seriously claims of anticompetitive harm from horizontal and vertical exclusion, as the following chapters show, mainly discussing the Microsoft saga.

[79] See, e.g., David Evans & Richard Schmalensee, 'Some Economic Aspects of Antitrust Analysis in Dynamically Competitive Industries', in 2 *Innovation Policy and the Economy* (Jaffee et al. eds. 2002); J. David Balto & Robert Pitofsky, 'Challenges of the New Economy: Issues at the Intersection of Antitrust and the New Economy', 68 *Antitrust* 913 (2001); and Michael L. Katz & Howard A. Shelanski, '"Schumpeterian" Competition and Antitrust Policy in High-Tech Markets' 2, available at http://ssrn.com.

principles.[80] For instance, whether to explain a dominant firm's behavior with a static or dynamic model is a policy determination.[81] Likewise, whether to judge business behaviors that prolong market monopolies as improper is a policy choice,[82] because current economic theories, whether static or dynamic, suggest antitrust law to allow temporary monopolies,[83]

---

[80] See Richard M. Brunell, 'Appropriability in Antitrust: How Much is Enough?', 69 *Antitrust L. J.* 1, 6 (2001); R. Hewitt Pate, 'The Common Law Approach and Improving Standards for Analyzing Single Firm Conduct', in *International Law Policy: Fordham Corporate Law* 2003 195 (Barry E. Hawk ed. 2004); and Jacobs, *supra* note 3, 224–6 and 259–64 (1995) (arguing in particular that these policy choices should be express and not covered by fake-economic technicalities).

[81] Oliver Budzinsky, 'Modern Industrial Economics and Competition Policy: Open Problems and Possible Limits' 8 (2009), available at www.ssrn.com. However, consider that, once dynamic theories are well developed, Occam's razor suggests that dynamic theories are better only where they are needed. Where a case can be solved with the simpler, less realistic, static theories, these last remain preferable. On the other hand, the search for simplicity cannot lead to misleading analysis. In this regard, see Timothy J. Brennan, 'Should Innovation Rationalize Supra-Competitive Prices? A Skeptical Speculation' 15–17, prepared for the Pros and Cons of High Prices Seminar, Swedish Competition Authority/ Konkurrensverket Stockholm, Sweden, November 9, 2007 (speaking about Microsoft and arguing that 'reduction of a difficult dynamic case to an easy static case had at least three consequences. First is the foregone opportunity to clarify how monopolization or abuse of dominance law should work in dynamic or 'new-economy' industries characterized by Schumpeterian competition. Second, avoiding the hard work of a dynamic case undercuts the basis for consequential relief. [. . .] Third is that allegations involving control over distribution of other forms of software, e.g., media players, are held (by some commentators) to an inappropriate dynamic standard, when they should be brought only as straightforward static exclusion cases.').

[82] Indeed it could be argued that no legal issue should arise if monopolies' duration rests with the combination of the following factors: on the one hand, the quality of the competitive advantages that monopolists have developed and keep on developing; and, on the other hand, their potential and actual rivals' capacity to fill in the competitive gap. In fact, Section 2 and Article 102 would like to prohibit those monopolistic behaviors that strengthen dominance with tools other than competitive advantages. Further, see Schumpeter, *supra* note 58, at 88 (arguing that dominant firms' restrictive practices are devices aimed to protect competitive advantages like patents). Indeed, IP laws are pieces of legislation that try to protect specific kinds of competitive advantages, such as inventions and some functional copyrightable materials.

[83] See, Schumpeter, *supra* note 58, at 93 (portraying that in a scenario with few small firms whoever innovates acquires a temporary monopoly, that is to say, a monopoly that will last until other firms will be able to reproduce the innovation); Sydney G. Winter, 'The Logic of Appropriability: From Schumpeter to Arrow to Teece', 35 *Research Policy* 1110, 1111 (2006) (arguing that the role of a market that is perfectly prompt to reproduce perfect competition is 'to exclude lead-time as a mechanism of appropriability for the innovator'). Therefore – as the following Chapter 2 explains – it should not come as a surprise that EU and US competition laws do not strike monopolies as such: the prospect of really enjoying some market power by appropriating the benefits that flow from it is a strong incentive for firms to invest and innovate. Further, see Lawrence A. Sullivan & Ann I. Jones, 'Monopoly Conduct, Especially Leveraging Power from One Product or Market to Another', in *Antitrust, Innovation, and Competitiveness* 166–7 (Thomas M. Jorde & David J. Teece eds. 1992) (stating that 'when the law considers what a monopolist may do, it may not evaluate social consequences solely on the assumption that the monopoly already exists. In that *ex post* posture, the more efficient

but do not establish how long these monopolies should last, in order to, on the one hand, effectively reward firms that achieve competitive advantages and, on the other hand, give their rivals the proper incentives to fill that competitive gap, maybe by innovating.[84]

ECONOMICS AND IPRS: THE LIMITS OF THIS INTERPRETATIVE TOOL

Whereas competition provisions are so poorly defined that they grant a great deal of leeway to any external source of interpretation and, in particular, to economics, IP legal systems encompass numerous detailed and specific rules that deal with IPRs scope and, hence, do not leave much open to interpretation.[85] For instance, whereas in the US and EU jurisdictions

---

solution would be to insist on prices related to cost. But the law must take account also of the *ex ante* constraint – the social goal of encouraging firms to be dynamic and efficient by tolerating monopolies when attained by such conduct. In the context of innovation, this [*ex ante*] constraint acknowledges (following in large measure the policy rationales for patent and other intellectual property protection) that in order to provide a firm with the stimuli needed to ensure *the maximum degree of innovative activities*, there must be a defined zone of permissible conduct and an opportunity to exploit, with supracompetitive prices and profits, the spoils of a firm's innovative efforts.').

[84] See Jonathan B. Baker, 'Promoting Innovation Competition through the Aspen/Kodak Rule', 7 *Geo. Mason L. Rev.* 495, 512 (1999) (arguing that 'as a matter of economic theory, it is impossible to say for certain whether enforcement of the antitrust prohibition against monopolization, which might restrict the conduct of a dominant firm, will on balance enhance or reduce aggregate industry innovation in general'). As footnote 156 and the accompanying text will show, this time-consistency issue, meaning the difficulty of striking a balance between *ex ante* and *ex post* incentives to compete fiercely by innovating, that lies behind the duration of monopolies, also underpins the definition of the scope of IPRs.

[85] To be sure, IP systems do not consist only of statutes. For instance, they also include standards for granting IPRs and determine the resources that IP authorities can spend to review IPRs' applications. When it comes to the antitrust-IP interface these rules are also important. For instance, a very superficial and quick patents-granting process may generate an excessive number of weak and ill-based patents that, in the end, retard innovation by increasing the risk that a good would-be patent will be infringing the already existing ones. See, in this regard, James Bessen, 'Patent Thickets: Strategic Patenting of Complex Technologies' (2003), available at www.ssrn.com (presenting a model discussing the results of having low or high standards requirements for the issuing of a patent); and Robert M. Hunt, 'Patent Reform: A Mixed Blessing for the U.S. Economy?' (1999), available at http://ideas.repec.org/a/fip/fedpbr/y1999inovp15-29.html (observing that relaxing of the non-obviousness requirement in the US patent system reduces expected return from R&D in high-tech industries and therefore has a negative impact on R&D spending and innovation). With such a scenario as the backdrop, antitrust authorities could be inclined to use competition law as a rough tool for remedying improvidently granted patents. See, in this regard, William E. Kovacic, 'Competition Policy and Intellectual Property: Redefining the Role of Competition Agencies', in *Antitrust and IPRs. EU and US Perspectives* 1, 3 (François Leveque & Howard Shelanski eds. 2005). For a similar argument, see John Temple Lang, 'Anticompetitive Abuses Involving Intellectual Property Rights', in *European Competition Law Annual 2003: What is*

there is only a single antitrust rule regarding dominant firms, at present there are 376 and 155 federal patent and copyright provisions,[86] and the patent and copyright laws of the 27 EU Member States[87] contain hundreds of provisions.[88] Therefore, it should not come as a surprise that often IP rules state holders' prerogatives so clearly that many theoretical economic elaborations are directed toward largely settled issues. For instance, one of the hottest IP debates of the last few decades has concerned optimal patent duration, though patent law plainly establishes patent duration.[89]

---

an Abuse of Dominant Position 589 (Claus Dieter Ehlermann, Isabela Atanasiu eds. 2003). For a deeper discussion of this last topic see Chapter 5.

86 See Patent Act 35 U.S.C.A. §§ 1 also 376 (1790) and Copyright Act, 17 U.S.C.A. §§ 101–1332 (1790).

87 Article 345 of TFUE, indeed, states that the Treaty 'shall in no way prejudice the rules in Member States governing the system of property ownership'. Further, the ECJ stated clearly that, 'the determination of the conditions and procedures under which the protection of [European IPRs] is granted is a matter for the national rules of each Member State. It is for the national legislature to determine which products may benefit from protection, even where they form part of a unit which is already protected as such.' – Case 238/87, *Volvo AB v Erik Veng (UK) Ltd*, October 5, 1988, [1988] ECR 6211, § 7. Therefore, in the European Union, IPRs are mainly a matter of national law, creating a *hiatus* between the community level of antitrust law and the national level of IPRs that does not exist in the USA, where IP and antitrust laws are all a matter of federal law. As Chapter 5 shows, such a different distribution of consideration between IPRs and antitrust law – in other words, the existence in the sole EU jurisdiction of a 'vertical relationship' between competition law and IPRs – produces substantial and jurisdictional consequences that affect the interface between antitrust and IPRs.

88 To be sure, the European Union has always been interested in harmonizing national IP law and creating community IPRs. Therefore, though the European Union has not been able to create community patents and copyrights yet, beyond the community trademark regulation several harmonizing measures have been enacted. See, e.g., Council Directive 87/57 of 16 December 1986 on the legal protection of topographies of semiconductor products, OJ 1987 L24/36; Council Directive 91/250 of 14 May 1991 on the legal protection of computer programs, OJ 1991 L122/42, repealed in part OJ 1993 L290/9; Council Regulation 1768/92 of 18 June 1992 concerning the creation of a supplementary protection certificate for medicinal products, OJ 1992 L182/1; Council Regulation 2081/92 of 14 July 1992 on the protection of geographical indications and designations of origin for agricultural products and foodstuffs, OJ 1992 L208/1; Council Directive 92/100 of 19 November 1992 on rental right and lending right and on certain rights related to copyright in the field of intellectual property, OJ 1992 L346/61, repealed in part, OJ 1993 L290/9; Council Directive 93/83 of 27 September 1993 on the coordination of certain rules concerning copyright and rights related to copyright applicable to satellite broadcasting and cable retransmission, OJ 1993 L248/15; Council Directive 93/98 of 29 October 1993 harmonizing the term of protection of copyright and certain related rights, OJ 1993 L290/9; Council and Parliament Directive 96/9 of 11 March 1996 on the legal protection of databases, OJ 1996 L77/20; Council and Parliament Regulation 1610/96 of 23 July 1996 concerning the creation of a supplementary protection certificate for plant protection products, OJ 1996 L198/30; Council and Parliament Directive 98/44 of 6 July 1998 on the legal protection of biotechnological inventions, OJ 1998 L213/13; Council and Parliament Directive 98/71 of 13 October 1998 on the legal protection of designs, OJ 1998 L289/28; Council and Parliament Directive 2001/29 of 22 May 2001 on the harmonization of certain aspects of copyright and related rights in the Information-Society, OJ 2001 L167/10.

89 See, for a concurring opinion, Robert P. Merges & Richard R. Nelson, 'On the Complex Economics of Patent Scope', 90 *Colum. L. Rev.* 839, 840 (1990) (arguing that

Similarly, suppose that an economic model shows that, under given conditions, a dominant firm refusing to license its IPRs is strengthening its market position and harming consumer welfare.[90] Whereas US courts and EU antitrust institutions can interpret Section 2 and Article 102 in order to prohibit that conduct and, therefore, comply with what the economic model states, IP enforcers cannot.[91] As Chapter 5 explains, in order to satisfy the economic model IP enforcers should evade the statutes that expressly grant IPRs holders the exclusive right to use the intellectual good and, therefore, contest and overcome what the IP legislator has already mandated.[92]

In addition, the IP analysis cannot be confined to simple economic issues:[93] IP laws deal as well with innovations – for instance, medical drugs

---

scholarly attention to patent duration has been closeted inside universities and, at most, triggered a legislative process regarding patent terms on pharmaceuticals to compensate for regulatory lag).

[90] See Chapter 2 explaining that nowadays this is the twofold requirement for a dominant firm's conduct to be held unlawful in both the US and EU jurisdictions.

[91] See in this regard William E. Kovacic & Carl Shapiro, 'Antitrust Policy: A Century of Economic and Legal Thinking', 14 *J. Econ. Persp.* 43 (2000) (stating in relation to the Sherman Act that 'by these open-ended commands, Congress gave federal judges extraordinary power' and 'by enlisting the courts to elaborate the Sherman Act's broad commands, Congress also gave economists a singular opportunity to shape competition policy'). See, further, Bruzzone, Boccaccio, *supra* note 4, at 1 (arguing, in connection to both the US and the EU antitrust rules, 'this legal framework gives competition authorities and judges, who apply the law to specific sets of facts, a crucial role in defining the scope of substantive competition rules').

[92] As Chapter 5 shows, the different hierarchical *status* between the ones that could make the law comply with what economic models state – IP legislators vis à vis antitrust courts – introduces, especially in the United States, a second 'vertical relationship' between competition law and IPRs which cannot but affect their interface via the so-called 'separation of power argument'. In the European Union, another 'vertical relationship', meaning that between national IPRs and the EU competition law, almost nullifies the 'separation of power argument' (see footnote 87 and accompanying text).

[93] See, e.g., Jessica Silbey, 'The Mythical Beginnings of Intellectual Property', 15 *Geo. Mason L. Rev.* 319, (2008) (explaining how intellectual property protection can be rooted in narrative theory); Madhavi Sunder, 'IP3', 59 *Stan L. Rev.* 257 (2006) (questioning the economics foundations of IP law); Pam Samuelson, 'Copyright and Freedom of Expression in Historical Perspective', 10 *J. Intell. Prop. L.* 319, 319–27 (2003); Neil Weinstock Netanel, 'Copyright and a Democratic Civil Society', 106 *Yale L. J.* 283, 288 (1996) (arguing that 'neoclassicism cannot serve as the basis for copyright doctrine because copyright's primary goal is not allocative efficiency, but the support of a democratic culture'); Mark Rose, *Authors and Owners: The Invention of Copyright* 48 (1993) (remarking on the importance of honor and reputation in authorship); Jane C. Ginsburg, 'Creation and Commercial Value: Copyright Protection of Works of Information', 90 *Colum. L. Rev.* 1865, 1873 (1990) (describing early copyright law as a device for the promotion of learning); Steven Cherensky, 'Agreements, Property, and Personhood', 81 *Cal. L. Rev.* 595, 646, 646–53 (1993) (suggesting that an inventor's work is a 'product of original thought,' and therefore inventors have a 'personality stake in their inventions'); Edward J. Damich, 'The Right of Personality: A Common Law Basis for the Protection of Moral Rights', 23 *Ga. L. Rev.* 1, 4 (1988) (stressing that even though US courts have provided for some protection of personality rights through copyright,

and works of art – which find a private or public raison d'être independent of any economic consideration. In fact, several European IP statutes do not depend directly on an explicit economic rationale,[94] though it must be noted that the 'economic soul' of US federal IPRs is quite marked, because of the utilitarian vision[95] underpinning Article I, Section 8 of the US Constitution, which provides a constitutional basis for the patent and copyright statutes.[96]

---

privacy, defamation, unfair competition, and contract laws, such protection lacks the substantial and coherent basis it has under French law); and Margaret Jane Radin, 'Property and Personhood', 34 *Stan. L. Rev.* 957, 968 (1982) (observing that, because 'property may have an important relationship to certain character traits that partly constitute a person', the expectation of continuing control over such property should be protected).

[94] See, e.g., Olav Kolstad, 'Competition Law and Intellectual Property Rights – Outline of an Economics-based Approach', in *Research Handbook on Intellectual Property and Competition Law* 3, 6 (Joseph Drexl ed. 2008).

[95] The act of granting a property right over an innovation in exchange for the production of the same innovation can be interpreted as endorsing either a 'retrospective approach', or a 'forward looking approach'. In the former case, patents and copyrights reward inventors and creators for their already developed innovative and creative process; in the latter case, it is the promise of receiving a reward via those IPRs that gives inventors and creators the incentives to produce their future innovations. These two visions are both said to be consequentialist and utilitarian because they link the acts of innovating to the consequences that they produce and interpret these outcomes in terms of utility, value, costs, and benefits. For a more detailed discussion of them and, in particular, of the forward looking approach, see footnote 114 and the accompanying text.

[96] More precisely, in 1790 the Congress enacted the Patent and Copyright Acts pursuant to Article I, Section 8, of the US Constitution, which grants to the Congress the power 'to promote the progress of science and useful arts, by securing for limited times to authors and inventors the exclusive right to their respective writing and discoveries'. See, e.g., Herbert Hovenkamp, Mark D. Janis & Mark A. Lemley, 1 *IP and Antitrust. An Analysis of Antitrust Principles applied to Intellectual Property Law* § 1.1 (2009), and *Mazer v. Stein*, 347 U.S. 201, 219 (1954) (where the Supreme Court stated that 'the economic philosophy behind the clause empowering Congress to grant patents and copyrights is the conviction that encouragement of individual effort by personal gain is the best way to advance public welfare [. . .] sacrificial days devoted to such creative activities deserve rewards commensurate with the services rendered'). In connection with this seminal opinion, and as evidence that these categorizations about the philosophical foundations of IPRs cannot be interpreted too strictly, see Justin Hughes, 'The Philosophy of Intellectual Property', 77 *Geo. L. J.* 287, 303 (1988) (arguing that there is a strong connection between such an instrumental/utilitarian vision of IPRs and the Lockean theory about the relationship between property rights and labor. Hughes argues that while the Lockean theory has a 'normative flavor' as it pivots around the moral imperative of rewarding with property the unpleasantness of labor, the instrumental/utilitarian argument is directly concerned with the consequences that property rights create: it proposes that the unpleasantness of labor is to be rewarded with property because people must be motivated to perform labor. Hughes adds, 'in principle, the two propositions can coexist but neither requires acceptance of the other. In practice, however, the two not only coexist, but the instrumental argument often seems to be treated as a 'proof' of the normative argument. The instrumental claim has a utilitarian foundation: we want to promote labor because labor promotes the public good. Once we recognize that property is needed to motivate work for the public good, we may transform the reward into a right just as we often convert systematically granted benefits into rights *deserved* by the recipients. [. . .] As *Mazer* demonstrates, it is

In summary, the choice to use economics as an ideal *koiné* for the antitrust-IP dialog finds some external limits in what IP legislations state in full details and – at least, sometimes – in the wake of explicitly non-economic needs and wants.

Nevertheless, from the 1960s onwards, the literature on the economics of IPRs, and patents in particular,[97] has grown significantly.[98] Not only does the rise of IP protection coincide with industrialization and economic progress,[99] and its recent legislative expansion[100] responds to extraordinary technological developments that advanced economies are experiencing, especially in industries that are innovative and information-knowledge-intensive.[101] Further, whether rightly or not, the public institutions of the United States and European Union have often relied on IP protection in

strikingly easy to move from an instrumental discussion of consequences to an assumption of just rewards.'. For the jurisprudence about the Constitutional clause, see also *Zacchini v. Scripps-Howard Broadcasting Co.*, 433 U.S. 562, 576 (1976); *Goldstein v. California*, 412 U.S. 546, 555 (1973); *United States v. Paramount Pictures*, 334 U.S. 131, 158 (1948); *Grant v. Raymond*, 31 U.S. (6 Pet.) 218, 241–2 (1832).

97 For a review of the economics of the patent system, see Roberto Mazzoleni & Richard R. Nelson, 'The Benefits and Costs of Strong Patent Protection: A Contribution to the Current Debate', 27 *Research Policy* 273 (1998).

98 This literature has discussed several topics: from the opportunity of introducing an IP protection to the magnitude that IPRs' scope should have in relation to the business interests of IP producers as opposed to the interests of the public and other producers. See Stanley M. Besen & Leo J. Raskind, 'An Introduction to the Law and Economics of Intellectual Property', 5 *J. Econ. Persp.* 3, 27 (1991) (encouraging economists to research intellectual property issues, which could play a key role in affecting America's future competitiveness); Stanley M. Besen, 'Intellectual Property', in *The New Palgrave Dictionary of Economics and the Law* 348 (1998) (arguing that a different branch of studies regards how final consumers' copies can affect IPRs' holders' interests). Further, see Ove Gran Strand, 'Innovation and Intellectual Property Rights' 266, 279, in *The Oxford Handbook of Innovation* (2005).

99 IP protection dates back to the fifteenth century, when the Venetian State granted exclusive rights to inventors and printers. In the sixteenth century, England, the Netherlands, France and Germany all had patent systems. The English Statute of Monopolies of 1624 and the Statute of Queen Anne of 1710 were the first written laws that, respectively, granted a monopoly for an invention for a limited period of time, and gave authors exclusive powers to reprint a book for 14 years after it was first published.

100 See, e.g., Jane C. Ginsburg, 'Legal Protection of Technological Measures Protecting Works of Authorship: International Obligations and the US Experience' (2005), available at http://lsr.nellco.org/columbia/pllt/papers/0593; Severine Dusollier, 'Technology as an Imperative for Regulating Copyright: From the Public Exploitation to the Private Use of the Work', 27 *European Intellectual Property Review* 201(2005); and id., 'Exceptions and Technological Measures in the European Copyright Directive of 2001 – An Empty Promise', 34 *IIC* 62 (2003).

101 See, e.g., Ian C. Forrester, 'Regulating Intellectual Property Via Competition? Or Regulating Competition Via Intellectual Property? Competition and Intellectual Property: Ten years on, the debate still flourishes' 2 (2005), available at http://www.eui.eu/RSCAS/Research/Competition/2005/200510-CompForrester.pdf (arguing that the growing importance of 'knowledge-based' industries and the shift of traditional manufacturing industries to low cost countries have strengthened the demand for intellectual property protection in the developed countries).

order to drive economic growth. IPRs affect firms' behaviors and markets' actual and future functioning by governing the spread of information and knowledge and by establishing the limits of ownership of resources, such as inventions and creations, which can be likely competitive advantages. In other words, IP systems distribute the incentives and the opportunities to innovate and compete. It is not coincidental, therefore, that today IPRs result more from business lobbies' pressures[102] than from the most developed explanatory theories.[103] Moreover, the costs of today's R&D investments and today's mass production and distribution, as well as the high amounts of money in the form of IP licensing fees,[104] require major business companies to be involved, although no-profit innovative and creative activities do exist – more and more using the internet – at the moment this is just a minor market niche.

To conclude, today IPRs can largely be deemed to be economic tools,[105] whose rationale and scope can be interpreted employing the instrumental/

---

[102] Christina Bohannan, 'Reclaiming Copyright', 23 *Cardozo Arts & Ent. L. J.* 567, 568 (2006); in accord, Joseph P. Liu, 'Copyright and Time: A Proposal', 101 *Mich. L. Rev.* 409, 448 (2002); William F. Patry, 'Copyright and the Legislative Process: A Personal Perspective', 14 *Cardozo Arts & Ent. L. J.* 139, 141 (1996); and Stewart E. Sterk, 'Rhetoric and Reality in Copyright Law', 94 *Mich. L. Rev.* 1197, 1246 (1996) ('It is hardly shocking to discover that interest-group power has shaped copyright legislation. [. . .] What is surprising is the paucity of criticism – from Congress, public interest groups, and the academic community – that has accompanied each new expansion of copyright protections.').

[103] For the UK experience, see Paul Torremans, *Intellectual Property Law* 16 (2008). For the US experience, instead, see Hovenkamp, *supra* note 43, at 249–53; William M. Landes & Richard A. Posner, *The Economic Structure of Intellectual Property Law* 407–15 (2003); Robert P. Merges, 'One hundred Years of Solicitude: Intellectual Property Law', 1900–2000, 88 *Cal. L. Rev.* 2187 (2000); and Merges & Nelson, *supra* note 89, at 1876–77 (premising the New Institutional Economics approach to IP regimes on the idea that 'IPRs, like all property rights, are granted by governments. Changes in property rights, like all legislation, are lobbied over, negotiated, and otherwise subject to the political process.'). For example, consider Frederic M. Scherer, *Patents, Economics, Policy and Measurement* 20–21 (2005) (arguing that, 'every attempt to alter the U.S. law in this direction has been beaten down as a result of determined opposition from industrial groups and the patent bar' although 'the substantial amount of evidence now available suggests that compulsory patent licensing, judiciously confined to cases in which patent-based monopoly power has been abused [. . .] would have little or no adverse impact on the rate of technological progress.').

[104] *KSR Intern. Co. v. Teleflex, Inc.*, 127 S.Ct. 1727, 1842 (2007) (where Justice Kennedy noticed that today 'an industry has developed in which firms use patents not as a basis for producing and selling goods but, instead, primarily for obtaining licensing fees').

[105] See William Fisher, 'Theories of Intellectual Property', in *New Essays in the Legal and Political Theory of Property* 168, 169 (Stephen R. Munzer ed. 2001) (deeming the utilitarian theory as the 'most popular' theory of intellectual property); William R. Johnson, 'The Economics of Copying', 93 *J. Pol. Econ.* 158, 172 (1985) (concluding that restrictions on copying may enhance social surplus under certain circumstances); and Ejian Mackaay, 'Economic and Philosophical Aspects of Intellectual Property Rights', in *The Socio-Economic Role of Intellectual Property Rights* 1 (Mark Van Hoecke ed. 1991).

utilitarian approach[106] and the cost-benefit analysis dear to mainstream economics.[107]

ECONOMICS AND IPRS: THE MAINSTREAM APPROACH

The economic thinking regarding patents and copyrights can be depicted as a 'skein' of intuitions and insights.[108] One way to disentangle it is to consider that for mainstream economics intellectual goods are different from tangible goods because, like public goods, they are not rivalrous and not excludable.[109]

---

[106] Endorsing the consequentialist approach does not necessarily mean looking at the consequences that IPRs produce in terms of benefits and costs. It can also signify considering non-economic consequences, such as personal satisfaction, and the quest for respect and esteem. See, e.g., William M. Landes & Richard A. Posner, 'An Economic Analysis of Copyright Law', 18 *J. Legal Studies* 325, 331 (1989) (observing that 'many authors derive substantial benefits from publication that are over and beyond any royalties. This is true not only in terms of prestige and other non-pecuniary income, but also pecuniary income in such forms as a higher salary for a professor who publishes than for one who does not.'); and Lloyd Weinreb, 'Copyright For Functional Expression', 111 *Harv. L. Rev.* 1149, 1226 and 1233 (1998).

[107] Within the so-called utilitarian stream of the consequentialist approach that focuses on the consequences of conduct, using economics means (i) identifying all the likely beneficial consequences that a system of property rights can entail; (ii) choosing the best among those consequences; and (iii) identifying the tools to reach this best consequence. This cost-benefit analysis together with the idea that any agent (without distinction among human beings, firms, and institutions) acts in order to fulfill its objectives in the best way possible, represent the heart of mainstream economics, that is to say, of economics as 'the science which studies human behavior as a relationship between ends and scarce means which have alternative uses'. See, in this regard, Lionel Robbins, *The Great Depression* 16 (1934); Paul A. Samuelson, *Foundations of Economic Analysis* (1947) (arguing that there is a simple principle at the heart of all economic problems: a mathematical function to maximize under constraints); and Gary Becker, *The Economic Approach to Human Behavior* 5 (1976) (observing that 'the combined assumptions of maximizing behaviors, market equilibrium, and stable preferences, used relentlessly and unflinchingly, form the heart of the economics approach as I see it').

[108] In the past, there has been far more emphasis on the economic analysis of patents because they were seen as a much more important tool for economic growth than the other IPRs. Nowadays, however, the economic justification developed regarding patent law can also be applied to copyright law because, over the years, the entertainment and service industries that serve as intermediaries between the authors and the public, have grown faster than manufacturing; copyright has increasingly been used to protect such a commercial exploitation of these works of art; and new, more technologically orientated, and really profitable types of works, such as software, have been protected by copyright and not by patents. See, e.g., Christian Handke, Paul Stepan, & Ruth Towse, 'Development of the Economics of Copyright', in *Research Handbook on Intellectual Property and Competition Law* 373 (Josef Drexl ed. 2008); Richard Watt, *Copyright and Economic Theory: Friends or Foes?* (2000).

[109] See Richard R. Nelson, 'The Simple Economics of Basic Scientific Research', 67 *J. Pol. Econ.* 297 (1959); and Arrow, *supra* note 45, at 614–16. In other words, because of firms'

They are not rivalrous, because one's consumption of intellectual goods does not deplete them of their value. Intellectual goods do not risk being used up.[110] Therefore, economic agents cannot price these goods and bargain them.

They are not excludable because those who produce[111] them cannot appropriate all the advantages that they entail: very often their competitors are likely to discover and/or disclose the intellectual good, especially after the creator has commercialized it. In particular, the greater the gap between the costs sustained for producing the goods and the benefits that their producers cannot appropriate: (i) the less likely it is that producers will be able to recoup their production fixed costs through higher revenues; (ii) the more likely it is that a significant post-creation rivalry will occur lowering the producers' expected profits and, hence, their *ex ante* incentives to produce; and (iii) the more likely it is that each producer will strategically wait with its producing activities so as to be the one who takes a free ride on the producing efforts of others.[112]

Therefore, the twofold idea beneath patent and copyright regimes is that such property rights are allocative and appropriability tools, without which the market would fail and innovation would be impaired.

They are allocative tools because, as the Coase theorem shows,[113] the mere existence of property rights allows their holders to give them a price and, hence, to bargain their ownership until the achievement of a Pareto

inability to appropriate sufficient returns of their R&D investments; private investment in R&D is less than what is optimal for the whole society.

[110] The tragedy of the commons argument states that absent private property, the economic agents that use a good do not internalize the costs that such a use entails and the good is thus depleted by overuse. Yet, intellectual goods are non-rivalrous in consumption. In facts, as Judge Easterbrook recently wrote in *Wallace v. IBM*, 467 F.3d 1104, at 1107 (7th Circ. 2006), 'intellectual property can be used without being used up'. Intellectual goods can be easily replicated infinite times without causing depletion or any direct injury to their original owners. In other words, intellectual goods are not scarce: for them the tragedy of the commons argument does not hold. See, e.g., Paul Rommer, 'When Should We Use Intellectual Property Rights', 92 *Am. Econ. Rev.* 213–16 (1992).

[111] Instead, the activities of commercializing and distributing intellectual goods do not suffer risks of free-riding. See, e.g., F. Scott Kieff, 'Facilitating Scientific Research: Intellectual Property Rights and the Norms of Science – A Response to Rai and Eisenberg', 95 *Nw. U. L. Rev.* 691 (2001). Further, see Mark A. Lemley, 'Ex ante versus ex post Justifications for Intellectual Property', 71 *U. Chi. L. Rev.* 129, 135–8 and 149 (2004) (arguing that whereas the creation of intellectual goods entails a public good issue, their distribution does not. Therefore, justifying the existence of IPRs by arguing that they serve to encourage distribution is a mistake. To assure an efficient distribution, competitive and free market is enough.).

[112] See Janusz A. Ordover, 'Economic Foundations and Considerations in Protecting Industrial and Intellectual Property', 53 *Antitrust L. J.* 503, 505–6 (1985).

[113] See Ronald H. Coase, 'The Problem of Social Cost', 3 *Journal of Law and Economics* 1 (1960).

superior equilibrium, that is to say, until their owner is whoever values them the most highly.

IPRs are appropriability tools[114] because they allow economic agents to capture the social value of intellectual goods,[115] in order to be *ex ante* properly incentivized to produce them,[116] and to keep on investing in innovative and creative activities.[117]

In particular, this appropriability function rests with: (i) the right to exclude others from using, reproducing, and selling the IPR and, hence, from the twofold right to pursue a special pricing strategy for the IPR – often a non-linear pricing strategy[118] – and to license it; and (ii) the right

---

114 See, Winter, *supra* note 83; and Jonathan M. Barnett, 'Private Protection of Patentable Goods', 25 *Cardozo L. Rev.* 1251 (2004).

115 For the argument that property rights limit the creation of uncompensated externalities, see Harold Demsetz, 'Toward a Theory of Property Rights', 57 *Am. Econ. Rev.* 347 (1967). However, even traditional property rights can be viewed as serving two main utilitarian purposes: providing incentives for development and preventing the depletion of finite resources. See Richard A. Posner, *Economic Analysis of Law* (2003); C. C. von Weizsacker, *Barriers to Entry. A Theoretical Treatment* 5-7 (1980); and Bruce A. Ackerman, *Economic Foundations of Property Law* (1975). Intellectual property rights instead do not have to deal with the scarcity issue. See footnote 110 and the accompanying text.

116 See Frank H. Easterbrook, 'Foreword: The Court and the Economic System in The Supreme Court 1983 Term', 98 *Harv. L. Rev.* 4, 21–9 (1984) (naming the Supreme Court's utilitarian and instrumental approach to IPRs as the '*ex ante* perspective on intellectual property').

117 What said in the text is true as long as patent and copyright regimes work actually as property regimes. Indeed, see Herbert Hovenkamp, 'Innovation and the Domain of Competition Policy' 18 (2008), available at https://ssrn.com; and James Bessen & Michael J. Meurer, *Patent Failure: How Judges, Bureaucrats, and Lawyers Put Innovators at Risk* (2008) (arguing 'while the patent system is said to create 'property' rights, the boundaries of intellectual property are often very poorly delineated, giving non-holders inadequate timely information about when they might be committing a trespass; this serves as a major deterrent to invention', and then adding that several patents, particularly those regarding software and business methods, have been granted despite vague and abstract claims that, hence, can be construed very broadly).

118 Intellectual property is often very costly to create, but it has very low marginal costs for reproduction. Indeed, the costs of creation, being invariant to output, are fixed costs once incurred. In contrast, the costs that vary with output, which is to say the costs incurred in actually providing the intellectual property to consumers, often are very low, at least relative to the fixed costs. In the case of software distributed over the internet (including digitized musical recordings), variable cost, and hence marginal cost, is close to zero. When fixed costs are a high percentage of total costs, a price equal to marginal cost is unlikely to cover total costs unless marginal cost is sharply rising. Therefore, a price above marginal costs is necessary. Marginal-cost pricing would maximize access to existing intellectual property and deter or expel inefficient entrants, but it would reduce, indeed often eliminate, the incentive to create the property in the first place. On the other hand, the same reasoning explains why imitating the subject matter of IPRs entails a zero marginal cost. See, in particular, Arrow, *supra* note 45, at 609 (1962); Hanns Ullrich, 'The Importance of Industrial Property Law and Other Legal Measures in the Promotion of Technological Innovation', 28 *Industrial Property* 102–103 (1989).

to control complementary[119] and follow-on inventions as well as derivative creative works,[120] thus enabling innovators and creators to appropriate the benefits that flow from future innovative and creative spillovers, as well as prior positions in related markets.[121]

However, patents and copyrights do entail costs as well to society, owners, and users. First, these IP systems involve protection costs, that is to say, the costs connected to the choice of using IP protection instead

---

[119] David J. Teece, 'Profiting from Technological Innovation: Implications for Integration, Collaboration, Licensing and Public Policy', in 15 *Research Policy* 285 (1986) (arguing further that the successful exploitation and commercialization of an innovation requires it to be utilized in conjunction with other complementary capabilities and assets and suggesting, hence, that public policy should grant to developers of IPRs ownership over complementary assets but leaving a large part of the profits to imitators and other competitors). This issue resembles that underpinning the profitability of corporate spinoffs. Whereas society as a whole has an interest in the creation of corporate spinoffs (they rationalize the offer and better satisfy the demand), the mother firm cannot want them because they represent competitors and, hence, subtract profits or, at least, transfer to them only a part of their profits.

[120] In particular, see Edmund W. Kitch, 'The Nature and Function of the Patent System', 20 *J. L. & Econ.* 265, 271–275 (1977) (observing that privatizing inventions encourages their owners to improve them. In particular, Kitch argued that granting a patent early in the development process allows the inventor to invest in development without fear that another firm will steal his or her work, thus encouraging the inventor to improve the innovation and to coordinate activities with other firms. Kitch states that this 'prospect function' of patents necessarily implies broad patents in favor of pioneers); and see footnote 128 ff. and the accompanying text. Instead, looking at copyright see, e.g., Orrin G. Hatch & Thomas R. Lee, '"To Promote the Progress of Science": The Copyright Clause and Congress's Power to Extend Copyrights', 16 *Harv. J. L. & Tech.* 1, 20–21 (2002) (commenting on the Sonny Bono Copyright Term extension Act by stating that the 20-year extension of copyright protection provides the production and dissemination of copies that require intermediaries' investments that otherwise would not occur); and Orrin G. Hatch, 'Toward a Principled Approach to Copyright Legislation at the Turn of the Millennium', 59 *U. Pitt. L. Rev.* 719, 736–7 (1998) (arguing that this term extension creates as well incentives to preserve existing works).

[121] A different – and non-economic – issue requires understanding whether the benefits that IPR holders gain because of these appropriability rules are 'just' or produce a windfall that the whole society is not willing to accept. In this regard, it has been argued that if an activity involving an IPR produces profits, then that activity belongs within the scope of the IPR. This is the so-called 'if value, then right' theory. Yet see Felix Cohen, 'Transcendental Nonsense and the Functional Approach', 35 *Colum. L. Rev.* 809, 815 (1935) (arguing that 'the vicious circle inherent in this reasoning is plain. It purports to base legal protection upon economic value, when, as a matter of actual fact, the economic value of a sales device depends upon the extent to which it will be legally protected.'); and Wendy J. Gordon, 'Introduction', 108 *Yale L. J.* 1611, 1615–16 (1999). Further see Schumpeter, *supra* note 58, 73–4 (arguing 'spectacular prizes much greater than would have been necessary to call forth the particular effort are thrown to a small minority of winners, thus propelling much more efficaciously than a more equal and more 'just' distribution would, the activity of that large majority of businessmen who receive in return very modest compensation or nothing or less than nothing, and yet do their utmost because they have the big prizes before their eyes and overrate their chances of doing equally well.'). Nevertheless, empirical studies show that the majority of innovative efforts confer only modest rewards, while the median project yields less than the capitalized cost of invested funds. See Frederic M. Scherer & Dietmar Harhoff, 'Technology Policy for a World of Skew-distributed Outcomes', 29 *Res. Policy* 559 (2000).

of other means to boost innovative and creative activity. In other words, these costs question directly whether intellectual property protection is the best among the available tools able to solve the above mentioned appropriability issue.[122]

Second, the mere existence of IP laws may impose transaction costs, connected to the difficulties of identifying intellectual properties and, hence, of transferring them.[123]

Third, as public officials have to be relied upon to implement IP policies in the public interest, IP regimes create public choice problems.[124]

Fourth, IP laws produce rent-seeking costs, that is to say the social costs due to an excessive (and, thus, suboptimal) level of investments in

---

[122] See, e.g., Scherer & Ross, *supra* note 23, at 624 (noticing that 'although devised to solve an important incentive problem, the patent system is a crude and imperfect instrument. Because of diverse real-world complications, the patent protection given an innovator may be too little, too much, or of the wrong kind.'). Indeed, a huge quantity (and quality) of intellectual goods had been produced before governments enacted patent and copyright statutes. Moreover, there are other means than sale to protect intangible goods. The most famous example is a public subsidy that relieves authors and creators of the need for revenue, as happened during the times of the Roman statesman and patron, Maecenas. Yet, such an option involves several problems: first, it requires tax subsidy schemes; second, calculating in advance the optimal reward or how much compensation any artist should receive to induce him to produce something is hard to establish; third, such a system would be politicized. However, see Michael Abramowicz, 'Perfecting Patent Prizes', 56 *Vand. L. Rev.* 115 (2003) (analyzing a reward system as a substitute for an intellectual property system); Steven Shavell & Tanguy van Ypersele, 'Rewards versus Intellectual Property Rights', 44 *J. L. & Econ.* 525, 537–40 (2001) (arguing, among other things, that IPRs do not possess a fundamental social advantage over reward systems); Steve P. Candrillo, 'An Economic Analysis of Intellectual Property Rights: Justifications and Problems of Exclusive Rights, Incentives to Generate Information, and the Alternative of a Government-run Reward System', 9 *Fordham Intell. Prop. Media & Ent. L. J.* 301 (1998); Pamela Samuelson et al., 'A Manifesto Concerning the Legal Protection of Computer Programs', 94 *Colum. L. Rev.* 2308 (1994); Stephen Breyer, 'The Uneasy Case for Copyright: A Study of Copyright in Books, Photocopies, and Computer Programs', 84 *Harv. L. Rev.* 281 (1970); R. Hurt & R. Schuchman, 'The Economic Rationale for Copyright', 56 *Am. Econ. Rev.* 421 (1966); Arnold Plant, 'The Economic Theory concerning Patents for Inventions', 1 *Economica* 67 (1934); and Paul David, 'Intellectual Property Institutions and the Panda's Thumb: Patents, Copyrights, and Trade Secrets in Economic Theory and History', in *Global Dimensions of Intellectual Property Rights in Science & Technology* 19, 54–7 (Mitchel B. Wallerstein, Mary Ellen Mogee, & Roberta Schoen eds. 1993).

[123] Better, whereas all property rights may be flawed and, hence, bring some element of uncertainty, the ambiguity of patents has been deemed 'especially striking and endemic'. See, in this regard, Mark A. Lemley & Carl Shapiro, 'Probabilistic Patents', 19 *Journal of Economic Perspectives* 75 (2005) (arguing that patents are probabilistic rights mainly because, being based on a brief, inconclusive *ex parte* process, they are not strong titles in courts. Therefore, inventors obtaining patents from the PTO face grave uncertainty over their ability to exclude others from using their invention). As Alan Devlin, 'The Stochastic Relationship between Patents and Antitrust', 5 *Journal of Competition Law and Economics* 75, 77 (2009) noticed – it is neither feasible nor cost-effective for an inventor to predict either the validity or likely pecuniary worth of its future patent rights determinatively.

[124] Richard A. Posner, 'Intellectual Property: The Law and Economics Approach', 19 *Journal of Economic Perspectives* 57, 58 (2005).

intellectual goods to the prospects of the pricing level that they make available – a waste of resources that is typically referred to via the case of the so-called 'patent race'.[125]

Finally, IP laws entail denied-access costs:[126] by allowing firms to deny access to the intellectual good and/or to charge overcompetitive prices, IPRs on the one hand, exclude some buyers from consuming intellectual goods[127] and, on the other hand, reduce the ability of other inventors and creators to copy them in order to exercise their own creativity and skill.

In this last regard, consider that historically IPRs resulted from balancing two opposing interests: the interest to incentivize and protect first generations of inventors and creators through granting them exclusive rights, and the interest to spur further generations of innovators and creators by enlarging the public domain.[128] Especially in industries characterized by cumulative knowledge and/or overlapping cross-markets knowledge,[129]

---

[125] See, e.g., Robert P. Merges, 'Rent Control in the Patent District: Observations on the Grady-Alexander thesis', 78 *Vand. L. Rev.* 359, 381 (1992); Matthew Erramouspe, 'Comment, Staking Patent Claims on the Human Blueprint: Rewards and Rent-dissipating Races', 43 *UCLA L. Rev.* 961, 962 (1996) (arguing that patent races can waste resources not only directly, but also because follow-on prospectors bid resources away from higher valued uses); Mark F. Grady & Jay I. Alexander, 'Patent Law and Rent Dissipation', 78 *Vand. L. Rev.* 305 (1992); Jennifer F. Reinganum, 'The Timing of Innovation: Research, Development, and Diffusion', in 1 *Handbook of Industrial Organization* 849 (Richard Schmalensee & Robert D. Willig, eds. 1989) (discussing the costs of patent races); and Donald G. McFetridge & Douglas A. Smith, Patents, 'Prospects, and Economic Surplus: A Comment', 23 *J. L. & Econ.* 197, 198 (1980).

[126] See Ordover, *supra* note 112, at 505.

[127] Stating that IPRs allow overcompetitive prices to be charged does not mean concluding that IPRs allow firms to charge monopoly prices. This outcome is likely only when the market for the intellectual good and the relevant market overlap, that is to say, it happens when the market power that IPRs do concede becomes significant, by morphing into monopoly power, often because the proprietary innovation turned out to be straightforward.

[128] See Michael A. Carrier, 'Cabining Intellectual Property through a Property Paradigm', 54 *Duke L. J.* 1, 4 (2004); and Robert P. Merges & Glenn H. Reynolds, 'The Proper Scope of the Copyright and Patent Power', 37 *Harv. J. on Legis.* 45, 52–3 (2000) (arguing in connection to the Constitutional Clause upon which the US Patent and Copyright premise upon that, 'the constitutional footing for intellectual property protection was constructed with inherent limitations, as well as with a grant of power. The specific language ('to promote progress,' and 'for limited times'), the history, and the context of the Clause dictate that the congressional power to create property rights does not extend to nonproductive rent-seeking. Congress exceeds its authority to grant property rights when those rights do not promote progress, or are not sufficiently limited in time [. . . T]he courts must exercise their authority to enforce constitutional limits on the Copyright and Patent power. To ignore this duty is to risk the kinds of abuse that threatened the economic progress of seventeenth-century Britain, and to turn our backs on the historical transformation of ad hoc grants of rent-seeking privileges into rule-based systems for recognizing intellectual property rights.').

[129] For a description of the different types of innovative regimes see, e.g., Jorde & Teece, *supra* note 40, at 4–5 (distinguishing between the regime of incremental innovation, which occurs when new products are introduced in rapid succession, each one as an improvement on the previous product so that the new drives out the old; and the regime of radical innovation,

it is likely that patents and copyrights on first innovations can decrease R&D incentives and block future innovations.[130] Indeed, if one conceives of innovative output as a natural outcome of complex processes, then strengthening pioneer patents and copyrights and, hence, protecting initial innovators from the competitive effects of subsequent innovations, or giving initial innovators the option to monopolize subsequent innovations, can have a surprisingly depressing effect over subsequent' R&D investments.[131]

---

where each innovation represents a clearly displacing factor for the old products); and Kitch, *supra* note 120, *passim* (observing that some kinds of inventions can arise from coordination among different researchers working in related fields of technology). Then empirical studies show that whereas in the pharmaceutical, chemical, plastics and medical instruments sectors and sometimes in all or parts of special machinery industries, the innovative process is not cumulative, in industry where there is little 'networking,' or need for inter-product compatibility, such as high-tech industry, mainly computer software and related technology, the innovative process is cumulative. See, e.g., Levin, *supra* note 53. In particular, most cumulative technologies are in the nature of system products, that is, products that permit or require the simultaneous functioning of a number of complementary components.

[130] Traditionally, scholars have assumed that stronger patent rights increase R&D investments, because – as said in the text – the extent of patent rights has direct implications for the expected return on innovations. See, e.g., Vincenzo Denicolò, 'Patent Races and Optimal Patent Breadth and Length', 44 *Journal of Industrial Economics* 249 (1996); Richard Gilbert & Carl Shapiro, 'Optimal Patent Length and Breadth', 21 *Rand Journal of Economics* 106 (1990); and Paul Klemperer, 'How Broad Should the Scope of Patent Protection Be?', 21 *Rand Journal of Economics* 113 (1990); Frederic M. Scherer, 'Nordhaus's Theory of Optimal Patent Life: A Geometric Reinterpretation', 62 *Am. Econ. Rev.* 422 (1972); and William D. Nordhaus, *Invention, Growth, and Economic Welfare* (1969). Likewise, theoretical literature on the reverse causality is almost unanimous in assuming a positive correlation between the numbers of patents and the amount of R&D investments. See, e.g., Mariko Sakakibara & Lee Branstetter, 'Do Stronger Patents Induce More Innovation? Evidence from the 1988 Japanese Patent Law Reforms', 32 *Rand Journal of Economics* 77 (2001). However, these results were derived considering only isolated inventions, that is to say, by disregarding the fact that in some industries innovation is cumulative.

[131] With cumulative, sequential, or complementary technological progress patents can, in the long run, deter innovation and give rise to such hold-up phenomena as the so-called patent thickets and the tragedy of the anti-commons. See, in particular, Robert M. Hunt, 'When Do More Patents Reduce R&D?' (2006), available at http://ideas.repec.org/e/phu40.html; Nancy Gallini, 'The Economics of Patents: Lessons from Recent U.S. Patent Reform', 16 *Journal of Economic Perspectives* 131 (2002); Wendy J. Gordon, 'Authors, Publishers, and Public Goods: Trading Gold for Dross', 36 *Loyola L. Rev.* 159, 164–5 (2002); Rosemarie Ham Ziedonis & Bronwyn H. Hall, 'The Effects of Strengthening Patent Rights on Firms Engaged in Cumulative Innovation: Insights from the Semiconductor Industry', 32 *Rand Journal of Economics* 101 (2001); Adam B. Jaffe, 'The U.S. Patent System in Transition: Policy Innovation and the Innovation Process', 29 *Research Policy 531* (2000); and James Bessen & Eric Maskin, 'Sequential Innovation, Patents, and Imitation' (2000), available at www.ssrn.com; Carl Shapiro, 'Navigating the Patent Thicket: Cross Licenses, Patent Pools, and Standard-Setting', in 1 *Research on Innovation Policy & the Economy* 1 (Adam B. Jaffe, Josh Lerner, & Scott Stern eds.) (2000); Michael Heller & Rebecca Eisenberg, 'Can Patents Deter Innovation?' 'The Anticommons in Biomedical Research', 280 *Science* 698 (1998); Mark A. Lemley, 'The Economics of Improvement in Intellectual Property Law', 75 *Tex. L. Rev.* 989 (1997) (discussing the follow-on innovation problem and analyzing patent and copyright law's

However, in order not to favor IPRs holders too much, US and EU IP legislators intentionally conceived some constraints, consisting in some IP doctrines[132] such as patent and copyright misuse,[133] exhaustion,[134] experimental use,[135] compulsory licenses,[136] copyright and trademark fair use,[137] reverse engineering,[138] and interoperability obligations.[139]

---

responses to it); Jerry R. Green & Suzanne Scotchmer, 'On the Division of Profit in Sequential Innovation', 26 *Rand J. Econ.* 20 (1995); Suzanne Scotchmer, 'Standing on the Shoulders of Giants: Cumulative Research and the Patent Law', 5 J. *Econ. Persp.* 29 (1991); and Suzanne Scotchmer & Jerry Green, 'Novelty and Disclosure in Patent Law', 21 *Rand J. Econ.* 131 (1990).

132 See Herbert Hovenkamp, *supra* note 11, at 1–2 (stating that 'well established rules within Intellectual Property policy, such as the doctrines of patent and copyright 'misuse,' or the first sale doctrine serve to protect competition by applying the policies of those statutes as a kind of substitute for the antitrust laws').

133 Patent misuse doctrine, which has arisen as a defense in patent infringement cases in order to prevent patentees obtaining relief, has always been construed in order to deem illegal patentees' practices that improperly extend patents' scope. Nowadays, not only common law but also section 271(d) of the Patent Act defines the most important aspects of the misuse defense stating that, 'No patent owner otherwise entitled to relief for infringement or contributory infringement of a patent shall be denied relief or deemed guilty of misuse or illegal extension of the patent right by reason of his having done one or more of the following: (1) derived revenue from acts which if performed by another without his consent would constitute contributory infringement of the patent; (2) licensed or authorized another to perform acts which if performed without his consent would constitute contributory infringement of the patent; (3) sought to enforce his patent rights against infringement or contributory infringement; (4) refused to license or use any rights to the patent; or (5) conditioned the license of any rights to the patent or the sale of the patented product on the acquisition of a license to rights in another patent or purchase of a separate product, unless, in view of the circumstances, the patent owner has market power in the relevant market for the patent or patented product on which the license or sale is conditioned.'. Analogously, copyright misuse, which is a judicially created doctrine, establishes that a copyright holder is not allowed to extend their exclusive right beyond the limits of the statutory grant. See Thomas F. Cotter, 'Misuse', 44 *Hous. L. Rev.* 901 (2007); id., 'The Procompetitive Interest in Intellectual Property Law', 48 *Wm. & Mary L. Rev.* 483 (2006).

134 The doctrine of exhaustion denies IPRs holders the right to control subsequent sales of trademarked, patented, or copyrighted goods after they have been marketed with the consent of the right owner.

135 US patent law has always encompassed a common law 'experimental use' defense to patent infringement and, further, featured a statutory safe harbor provided for by section 271(e)1, which states, 'It shall not be an act of infringement to make, use, offer to sell, or sell within the United States or import into the United States a patented invention (other than a new animal drug or veterinary biological product (as those terms are used in the Federal Food, Drug, and Cosmetic Act and the Act of March 4, 1913) which is primarily manufactured using recombinant DNA, recombinant RNA, hybridoma technology, or other processes involving site specific genetic manipulation techniques) solely for uses reasonably related to the development and submission of information under a Federal law which regulates the manufacture, use, or sale of drugs or veterinary biological products'.

136 The Copyright Act contains a few compulsory licensing provisions, such as Sections 111 and 119.

137 This doctrine, which was born as a judicial-made doctrine and was then codified in Section 107 of the 1976 Copyright Act, establishes that in certain situations unauthorized copying is however permissible. In trademarks, fair use covers descriptive uses of marks,

In summary, both the simple existence of IP regimes, and the definition of patent and copyright scope resulting from the combination of IP provisions and IP doctrines requires striking a balance between opposing interests in a scenario where mainstream economics, by portraying the costs and benefits that each specific situations presents, cannot suggest 'right' solutions.

Besides, heterodox economic theories supply some insights as to the appropriability function of IPRs and the alleged linear relation between their scope and the rate of innovation – insights which, however, do not solve the issue of IPRs scope in a conclusive way.

ECONOMICS AND IPRS: A HETERODOX APPROACH

The previously mentioned heterodox economic theories which developed the idea of competition as a dynamic process have not always elaborated an express conception of what IPRs are and should be. However, whereas the Schumpeterian and the Austrian doctrines stress the appropriability function of IPRs, by emphasizing – as the present orthodox approach does – that they serve to incentivize innovators across time periods,[140] the evolutionary doctrine points to the opposite direction. Therefore, in the light of an antitrust action aimed to give a new shape to dominant firms' IPRs, the evolutionary approach becomes crucial, because it shows that not every economic theory teaches that broad and strong IPRs increase the rate of innovation.

For evolutionary scholars intellectual goods stem from knowledge. Knowledge – which they deem the engine of change and economic growth – originates by applying to sheer information the cognitive and procedural 'routines' that are to a large extent tacit and embedded in human organizations. Thus, knowledge is something more than information: it is specific to each agent that develops it; it is strongly dependent on the unique features

where the alleged fair use was undertaken in good faith. See, e.g., *Car-Freshner Corp. v. S.C. Johnson & Son*, 70 F.3d 267 (2nd Circ. 1995).

[138] In the US it is shielded by fair use. See, e.g., *Sony Computer Entertainment, Inc. v. Connectix Corp.*, 203 F.3d 596 (9th Circ. 2000); *Sega Enterprise, Ltd v. Accolade, Inc.*, 977 F.2d 1510 (9th Circ. 1993).

[139] Consider, for instance, that the Article 6 of Council Directive 91/250/EEC of 14 May 1991 on the legal protection of computer programs rules over the conditions that must be met in order to reproduce freely the contents of a computer program, when such a reproduction is necessary to achieve the interoperability with an independently created computer program.

[140] As to the Schumpeterian approach, see footnote 58 ff. and the accompanying text. As to the Austrian approach see, e.g., Kallay, *supra* note 61, at 24–5 and 104 (however, observing that Austrian economists would not recommend too broad IPRs, fearing both a block to the process of competition and a too-intrusive presence of the government in the economic life).

of each applied routine;[141] and – because of these two factors – it does not spill over easily to other agents as information.[142]

Therefore, for evolutionary economics intellectual goods are more excludable and more rivalrous than orthodox economics would suggest.[143] As long as knowledge is complex, cumulative, tacit, and difficult to replicate,[144] intellectual goods are not pieces of pure information and IPRs should not be conceptualized as appropriability and allocative tools, but as means that contribute to explain and disseminate such a kind of knowledge among people, in the hope that this would help to foster economic and cultural progress.

In particular, as to the appropriability issue that is so dear to other economic theories, evolutionary economics does not only agree with the fact, which some orthodox scholars and empirical studies noticed, that in some industries too much appropriability blocks further innovation and causes a waste of resources,[145] but also highlights that appropriability does not hinge on the scope and enforceability of IPRs. Rather, it claims for limited, 'quite open' IPRs, because it believes that appropriability rests on team-embodied knowledge, that is to say, on firms' ability to both replicate effectively those routines that lead to successful innovations and to leverage them in other markets.[146]

In the extreme, evolutionary economics considers that what affects the

---

[141] Giovanni Dosi, Luigi Marengo and Corrado Pasquali, 'How much should society fuel the greed of innovators? On the relations between appropriability, opportunities and rates of innovation' 4–5 (2006), available at ideas.repec.org/p/ssa/lemwps/2006-17.html.

[142] See Michael Polanyi, *Personal knowledge. Towards a post critical philosophy* (1958) (noticing that in some industries knowledge is not easy to codify and transmit but is instead sticky and 'tacit').

[143] See, e.g., Giovanni Dosi, Luigi Marengo, and Corrado Pasquali, 'Knowledge, Competition and Innovation: Is Strong IPR Protection really needed for More and Better Innovations?', 13 *Mich. Telecomm. Tech. L. Rev.* 471, 479 (2007) (arguing that 'knowledge can be misleadingly identified with information. When this occurs, there is a deletion of any reference to cognitive and procedural devices, whose role is to transform raw information into 'useful knowledge'.').

[144] See, e.g., Giovanni Dosi, Luigi Marengo, Corrado Pasquali and Marco Valente, 'Appropriability, Patents, and Rates of Innovation in Complex Products Industries' 5–6, (2009) LEM Papers Series 2009/05, Laboratory of Economics and Management (LEM), Sant'Anna School of Advanced Studies, Pisa, Italy.

[145] Even inside the frame of mainstream economics, it can be argued that, since patent regimes grant many benefits to the patentee, capitalist economies may over-invest in R&D and innovation and thus duplicate the resources spent in R&D. In such a scenario, and especially when rewards are skewed heavily to the early finishers, innovations' social returns may be less than the cost of the overall investment. In other words, prospects of a quick and great success may lead to 'patent races' that result in welfare-decreasing over-investment.

[146] See, e.g., Gabriel Szulanski, 'Appropriability and the challenge of scope: banc one routinizes replication', in *The nature and dynamics of organizational capabilities* 69 (Giovanni Dosi, Richard R. Nelson, and Sidney G. Winter eds., 2000).

pace and direction of innovation is not the possibility to fully benefit from the profits that flow from inventions and creative works, but the opportunities that each body of knowledge – also named technological paradigm[147] – provides.[148] In such a scenario, IPRs are no longer neutral to the rate and direction of change as they are for the other economic theories: by denying access to intellectual goods, i.e. to some pieces of knowledge, they set the opportunities available to innovators and, hence, affect innovation's speed and course.

In summary, by shifting the focus of the analysis on knowledge and the characteristics of learning processes,[149] evolutionary economics calls attention to IPRs scope and distribution. As to IPRs scope, it recalls that broad IPRs do not only produce the static inefficiencies, such as higher prices, that mainstream economics reckons, but also dynamic inefficiencies in terms of constraints to future innovation,[150] especially when it comes to complex industries and system innovations.[151] As to IPRs distribution, evolutionary economics considers that it can seriously determine the total and sub-optimal level of innovation, because once an innovator took an innovative path, to abandon it is very difficult,[152] especially when products' complexity is high.[153] Therefore, evolutionary economics invites scholars to resize the role that IPRs are called to play in incentivizing the

---

[147] Giovanni Dosi, 'Technological paradigms and technological trajectories: A suggested interpretation of the determinant and direction of technological change', 11 *Res. Pol'y* 147–8 (1982) (arguing that a technological paradigm concerns problem-solving activities). Broadly speaking, according to evolutionary economics a paradigm encompasses: (i) the definition of the relevant problems that are to be solved; (ii) the definition of the specific knowledge necessary to the solution of those problems; (iii) a set of procedures to reach points (i) and (ii); (iv) frames of shared knowledge about 'how to do things'; and (v) basic templates of artifacts and systems, which over time are progressively modified and improved.

[148] Dosi, Marengo, Pasquali, *supra* note 141, at 7 and 16 (arguing that opportunities are the fundamental determinants of innovation rate and trajectories, since they represent 'the width, depth and richness of the sea in which incumbents and entrants go fishing for innovation').

[149] Luigi Marengo & Simonetta Vezzoso, 'Dynamic inefficiencies of intellectual property rights from an evolutionary/problem-solving perspective: some insights on computer software and reverse engineering' 2 (2006), available at www.ssrn.com; and Sampsung X. Shi, 'Knowledge and Its Inventors/Carriers in Evolutionary Economics: Towards A Relational Theory of Authorship and Copyright 2' (2008), available at www.ssrn.com.

[150] Robert P. Merges and Richard R. Nelson, 'On limiting or encouraging rivalry in technical progress: the effects of patent scope decisions', 25 *Journal of economic behavior and organization* 1, 2 (1994) (distinguishing two different trade-offs about patent scope: that between the incentives for invention, and dead weight losses due to monopoly; and that between today's inventions and tomorrow's inventions); Roberto Mazzoleni and Richard R. Nelson, 'The benefits and costs of strong patent protection: a contribution to the current debate', 27 *Research Policy* 273, 280 (1998).

[151] Dosi, Marengo, Pasquali, Valente, *supra* note 144, at 6.

[152] Dosi, Marengo, Pasquali, *supra* note 143, at 477–8.

[153] Dosi, Marengo, Pasquali, Valente, *supra* note 144, at 22–3.

production of inventions and creations. It claims, first, for 'weaker', 'quite open' IPRs, which would be good at encouraging knowledge dissemination across individuals and time periods,[154] and which should not prevent the development of complementary products, follow-on innovations and derivative works. Second, evolutionary economics seems to ask for a more reasonable distribution of IPRs, arguing that their allocation can affect future industries' development. Third, by remarking that knowledge, opportunities, paths, and paradigms are specific to each industry, evolutionary economics questions the universal nature of IPRs, even claiming that they represent an 'unfortunate juridical category for the regulation of an issue that should be essentially one of finely tuned industrial policy'.[155]

THE LEEWAY FOR POLICY CHOICES IN THE IP WORLD: A SCOPE FOR IPRS

Some pieces of knowledge may affect both innovation and competition. They affect innovation when they represent the 'bricks' of new products and processes, whether these innovations are labeled inventions or creative works. They affect competition when they represent competitive advantages, that is to say, what makes new products and processes preferable to consumers and producers.

Since IPRs, such as patents and copyrights, govern the access to these pieces of knowledge, IPRs affect innovation and competition further on: they establish who owns those 'innovative bricks' and competitive advantages, and what the boundaries of such ownership are and will be, even across time. In other words, IPRs distribute among economic agents the incentives and the opportunities to innovate and compete. They distribute incentives because, since they morph those pieces of knowledge in proprietary resources, they make economic agents believe that their efforts in innovative and creative activities – activities that, in addition, could smite rivals – will be rewarded. They distribute opportunities because they establish who can use those pieces of knowledge in order to develop new products and new processes, which perhaps will be able either to strengthen

---

[154] Paul David, 'Intellectual Property Institutions and the Panda's Thumb: Patents, Copyrights, and Trade Secrets in Economic Theory and History', in *Global dimensions of Intellectual Property Rights in Science & Technology* 19, 54–7 (Mitchell B. Wallerstein, Mary E. Mogee and Roberta A. Schoen eds., 1993); Paul David, 'Does the Economy Need All the Old IPR Institutions? Digital Information Goods and Access to Knowledge for Economic Development', Address at the Wider Conference on The New Economy in Development (May 11, 2002).

[155] Dosi, Marengo, Pasquali, Valente, *supra* note 144, at 22–3.

the already possessed competitive advantages, or to fill in the competitive gap by displacing the existing competitive advantages.

Yet, when policy-makers define IPRs scope – that is, who can access those pieces of knowledge and how broad and lasting such exclusive access is – they cannot rely on a unique economic theory because, although policy makers may believe that IPRs should boost both innovation and competition, economics cannot state what the optimal scope of IPRs should be in order to fulfill these aims. Neither does it establish which firm is in the best position to hold IPRs, whether dominant firms or their rivals.

In particular, the scope of IP protection undergoes the same time-consistency problem that torments the optimal duration of temporary monopolies: economists do not know how to provide enough returns and incentives to the production of innovations, on the one hand, and how to promote their quick social diffusion and, hence, a prompt erosion of innovators' exclusive power, on the other hand.[156] Indeed, economic theory supplies different, equally plausible, and empirically founded arguments as to the proper balance between creating and disseminating intellectual goods.

Therefore, the distribution of the incentives to invent and create is more than an issue of fact and theories: it is an issue of beliefs and, hence, a policy question.[157] Not by chance, those who question recent IP reforms

---

156 Better, this time-consistency issue involves any appropriability tool. For instance, it can as well regard property rights in general. Any time a property right is granted, non-owners suffer a kind of disadvantage: for instance, the same trade-off described in the text can concern a firm that has invested in a main infrastructure that later turns out to be a crucial competitive advantage for all other firms in the industry. In such a scenario, the choice whether to curb the property right upon the infrastructure follows the usual pattern of conflicting arguments: on the one side, the owner's competitors could greatly benefit from the use of that infrastructure, thus pushing the government to reshape the property right; on the other hand, if the owner anticipates such a governmental decision, it will not invest in the infrastructure as it knows that it will not appropriate all the advantages that flow from it. Indeed, in this vein, it is common to state that intellectual properties and tangible properties do not urge different issues and, therefore, do not ask for a different antitrust treatment. In other words, defining ownership always implies giving non-owners a competitive disadvantage: either from the outset, as they cannot exploit the property, or later in a courtroom, when they are punished for the violation of the property. Yet, the reason why intellectual property rights create so much debate is that, first, as they do not suffer any scarcity problem (see footnotes 110 ff. and the accompanying text), it is more likely that they are perceived as the artificial outcomes of government choices, and that, as such, they are easily questionable. Second, it happens that IPRs more than common property rights tend to cover significant competitive advantage, which the other firms desire and governments deem important for the progress of the whole society. Third, as IPRs deal with innovation, it can be argued that any antitrust action that faces it has to consider directly its dynamic consequences. See, in this regard, Chapter 5. For the analogy between traditional and intellectual property rights see, e.g., Drexl, *supra* note 15, at 49; and Mark A. Lemley, 'Property, Intellectual Property, and Free Riding', 83 *Tex. L. Rev.* 1031 (2005), where there are further references.

157 See, in this regard, Merges & Nelson, *supra* note 89, at 843–4 and 873 (observing that empirical-historical examination of the course of technical advance in several industries

that have increased IPRs holders' prerogatives,[158] ask antitrust law to remedy against this IP failure,[159] on the grounds of what they believe is the 'right balance' between creating and disseminating intellectual goods.

NO GENERAL YARDSTICK TO MEASURE THE OPTIMAL SCOPE OF DOMINANT FIRMS' IPRS: TWO NEW RESEARCH QUESTIONS

As Chapters 2 to 6 exemplify by enforcing Section 2 and Article 102 in order to forbid monopolists' behaviors involving IPRs, antitrust rules may end up curbing the scope of the market monopolies and IPRs in question.

Yet, how can such an action successfully restore the 'correct' scope of these market monopolies and IPRs if there is no general and *a priori* economic answer as to their optimal duration and broadness? Current economic theories cannot portray conclusively how long market monopolies should last in order to promote competition and innovation over time, and how strong IP protection should be in order to optimally distribute the incentives and the opportunities to compete and innovate over time.

Therefore, dominant firms' practices involving IPRs require the economic reasoning to be driven just to its unsettled edges,[160] where there

---

shows that the efficiency gains from the pioneer's ability to coordinate are likely to be outweighed by the loss of competition for improvements to the basic invention. In particular, they wrote that Kitch's theory for pioneers – the so-called prospect theory – ignores the limits on cognitive capacity and the tendency to focus on past experience; they both are characteristics of other models and of organizational behavior as we know it. Once a firm develops and becomes competent in one part of a 'prospect,' it may be very hard for it to give much attention to other parts, even though in the eyes of others, there may be great promise there. Consequently, one might expect that many independent inventors will generate a much wider and more diverse set of explorations than when the development is under the control of one mind or organization.).

[158] Indeed several scholars, lamenting the increasing enlargement of IPRs and, in particular, of copyrights, claim a consequently more aggressive antitrust action as a response to it, as if antitrust law could work as a kind of 'second tier regulation' for IPRs. See Steven D. Anderman, 'The Competition Law/IP "Interface": An Introductory Note', in *The Interface Between Intellectual Property Rights And Competition Policy I, II* (Steven D. Anderman ed., 2007). After all, Article 8(2) of the Agreement on Trade Related Intellectual Property Rights (hereinafter, TRIPS) states that 'appropriate measures, provided that they are consistent with the provision of this agreements, may be needed to prevent the abuse of intellectual property rights by right holders').

[159] For the same approach, see Paul A. Geroski, 'Intellectual Property Rights and Competition Policy', in *Perspectives on Innovation* 455, 456 (Franco Malerba & Stefano Brusoni eds. 2007).

[160] Alan Devlin & Michael Jacobs, 'Antitrust Divergence And The Limits of Economics' 25–6 (2009), available at www.ssrn.com (arguing that 'grave epistemological limitations

seem to be two available alternatives. Either, economic thinking is able to suggest to antitrust law, from an *ex post*, case-by-case perspective, what the optimal scope of market monopolies and IPRs is. Or, the antitrust judgments about dominant firms' practices involving IPRs have to be premised upon policy justifying principles.

The following chapters deal with these issues.

---

necessarily frustrate any attempts to resolve the tension between the short and long run, particularly when short and long run competitive effects are in seeming opposition to one another. [. . .] the indeterminacy underlying the trade-off between the long and short run is sufficiently severe that economics alone cannot lead to a complete confluence of ideas.')

2. Section 2 and Article 102(b): the antitrust roots of the antitrust-IP interface

SET THE STAGE FOR THE FOLLOWING CHAPTERS

In order to examine whether, when and why Section 2 of the Sherman Act and Article 102 of the TFEU can serve to curb dominant firms' IPRs, it is useful to describe the main features of these two provisions. First, this chapter discusses the many policy variables that, absent an economic yardstick to measure the duration and broadness of market monopolies, affect the enforcement of Section 2 and Article 102. Then, it describes not only their apparent content, not only what the economic theory suggests as to the standard for judging monopolistic behaviors, but also the aims and the analytical methodology that US and EU antitrust authorities have historically wanted, and now want, to pursue and endorse in enforcing these rules.

In this way the chapter establishes that nowadays US and EU antitrust authorities prohibit dominant firms' conduct that strengthen market power and harm consumer welfare, by profitably reducing market output, raising market price and degrading the quality and variety of their products. Afterwards, the chapter sets the stage for Chapters 3 to 6 by concluding that two questions deserve to be answered in connection with dominant firms' practices involving IPRs: from a legal perspective, what protecting innovation (say also, consumer welfare over the long-run) has meant to the US and EU antitrust authorities dealing with these practices and, from the economic perspective, what the economic models suggest as to the impact that these practices produce on competition and innovation.

JUDGING DOMINANT FIRMS' CONDUCT: BACKGROUND POLICY CHOICES

As Chapter 1 explained, the present economic thinking does not suggest where to strike the optimal balance between the benefits and costs of monopolies: it does not establish how long market monopolies should last. Accordingly, antitrust legislators do not focus their attention on market monopolies,[1] but on monopolistic behaviors, in an effort to detect which among them should be prohibited: whether any of them, or those that prolong market power, or those that prolong market power *improperly*.

Yet, since Section 2 and Article 102 provide little guidance in this regard,[2] over time antitrust authorities have addressed dominant firms' lawful behaviors as those that result from 'superior products', 'business acumen', or 'historical accident',[3] or those that consist in 'normal methods of industrial development',[4] 'undistorted competition', 'proper means', or 'competition on the merits'.[5] Yet, it is readily apparent that

---

1 Neither Section 2 nor Article 102 forbid monopoly as such: the two jurisdictions are consistent with the economic thinking and admit temporary monopolies. For the US experience, see *Standard Oil of New Jersey v. United States* 221 U.S. 1, 50 (1911), where the Court underlined that Section 2 concerns the process of monopolization and not the concept of size as such. For the EU experience, see Case 322/81, *NV Nederlandsche Banden Industrie Michelin v. Commission*, [1983] ECR 3461, § 10 (hereinafter *Michelin I*) where the ECJ stated, 'A finding that an undertaking has a dominant position is not in itself a recrimination'. Then, for a comprehensive explanation of the several reasons why prosecuting a monopoly would be a mistake, see 2B Phillip E. Areeda & Herbert Hovenkamp, *Antitrust Law: An Analysis of Antitrust Principles and their Application* ¶¶ 634–8 (2007). Even if the authors gave such a detailed explanation in connection to Section 2, nothing hinders to use it in connection with Article 102. Further, it is also true that after the Second World War, the European economy was characterized by a significant number of legal monopolies and by several public undertakings with a dominant position. Therefore, the framers of the EC Treaty decided that it would be less traumatic to tolerate the existence of these monopolies and highly concentrated markets rather than to prohibit them.

2 As noticed in Chapter 1, competition rules are poorly defined, indeed. See, e.g., Daniel J. Gifford & Robert T. Kudrle, 'European Union Competition Law and Policy: How Much Latitude for Convergence with the United States?', 48 *Antitrust Bull.* 727, 770 (2003); Jason M. Sullivan, 'Note, European Antitrust Enforcement: A Distinct Prosecution or a More Principled Approach?', 15 'Transnat'l L. & Contemp. *Probs.'* 457, 467 (2006); and Thomas E. Kauper, 'Section Two of the Sherman Act: The Search for Standards, 93 *Geo. L. J. 1623, 1623* (2005) (observing that: 'over its 114-year history, Section Two of the Sherman Act has been a source of puzzlement to lawyers, judges and scholars, a puzzlement derived in large part from the statute's extraordinary brevity').

3 See *United States v. Grinnell Corp.*, 384 U.S. 563, 570–71 (1966).

4 See *Standard Oil Co. v. United States*, 221 U.S. 1, 75 (1921).

5 See *LePage's Inc. v. 3M*, 324 F.3d 141, 147 (3d Cir. 2003) and, for the EU experience, Case 85/76, *Hoffmann-La Roche & Co. v. Commission*, February 13, 1979 [1979] ECR 461, § 6 (hereinafter *Hoffmann-La Roche*) where the ECJ stated that an abuse is a conduct 'which, through recourse to methods different from those governing normal competition in products or services on the basis of transactions of commercial operators, has the effect of hindering the maintenance of the degree of competition still existing in the market or the growth of that competition'; and *Michelin I*, § 10, where the ECJ added that, 'irrespective of the reasons for which it has such a position, the undertaking concerned has a special responsibility not to allow its conduct to impair genuine undistorted competition on the common market'. Consider, further, that article 3(1)(g) of the TFUE states that one of the Treaty's goals is 'a system ensuring that competition in the internal market is not distorted'.

all these qualifications are vague:[6] they lack clarity, consistency, and economic rigor and, more importantly, they cannot define the scope of Section 2 and Article 102 in practical terms.[7]

In order to face this issue, numerous policy matters should be solved,[8] by establishing – as hinted in Chapter 1 – (i) 'the interests' that antitrust law should protect;[9] and (ii) the set of enforcement rules that antitrust authorities should employ.[10] Consider, for instance, a dominant firm

---

[6] See, e.g., Einer R. Elhauge, 'Defining Better Monopolization Standards', 56 *Stan. L. Rev.* 253, 263 (2003) (arguing that for decades the monopolization doctrine has used and still uses vacuous labels that provide no meaningful and standard guidance about which conduct will be condemned); Kauper, *supra* note 2, at 1624; and Harry First & Andrew I. Gavil, 'Re-framing Windows: The Durable Meaning of the Microsoft Antitrust Litigation', 2006 *Utah L. Rev.* 641, 648–9 (2006). Further, for the same judgment in respect to Article 102, see Richard Whish, *Competition Law* 189 (2009); and Robert O'Donoghue & Jorge A. Padilla, *The Law and Economics of Article 82* 177–8 (2004).

[7] Indeed, nowadays the clash between these two provisions represents the most problematic area of transatlantic competition law. See Diane P. Wood, 'The U.S. Antitrust Laws in a Global Context', 2004 *Colum. Bus. L. Rev.* 265, 272 (2004); and William J. Kolasky, 'What Is Competition? A Comparison of the U.S. and European Perspectives', 49 *Antitrust Bull.* 29, 40 (2004).

[8] See, e.g., Timothy J. Brennan, 'Saving Section 2: Reframing US Monopolization Law', in *The Political Economy of Antitrust* 417, 418–19 (Vivek Ghosal & John Stennek eds. 2007) (arguing that monopolization cases 'differ from both collusion and merger cases in being controversial at the more fundamental level of whether such cases should even been considered'); and Joseph Angland, 'The Justice Department's Section 2 Report: In Search of a General Theory of Exclusionary Conduct', *The Online Magazine for Global Competition* 6 (2008) (arguing that 'dominant firms' unlawful behaviors do not exist in nature and the role of antitrust law is not that of finding them.').

[9] Indeed, as seen in Chapter 1, away from perfect competition the protection of allocative efficiency and total welfare, on the one hand, does not necessarily imply the protection of consumer welfare, on the other hand. Further, to preserve short-run efficiency and welfare does not necessarily entail boosting dynamic efficiency.

[10] Affirming a one-to-one relationship between the antitrust objectives, on the one hand, and the antitrust analytical tools, on the other hand, risks being over-simplistic. Indeed, any *ex post* exercise to frame what happens in the real world into a coherent and consistent system of ideas is never exhaustive and complete. Therefore, advising antitrust authorities to enforce antitrust law consistently with the goals that they want to fulfill is different from assuming that in practice they have always done so. Better, establishing a certain connection between a class of objectives and a class of analytical tools is different from affirming that the use of one of those tools implies necessarily the pursuit of one of those related goals, and vice versa. In other words, whether by looking at the past or by looking at the future, to suppose that all competition law judgments and decisions in both jurisdictions have been adopted (or will be adopted) by reference to a single principle or policy would be too naïve. Some of those cases, indeed, were highly fact-specific; others were not well-reasoned. Moreover, as the recent debate about the Ordoliberal root of Article 102 shows (see footnote 83 and the accompanying text), even a unique historic and philosophical explanation of past interpretations can be contested. See, in this regards, Whish, *supra* note 6, at 192–3: John Temple Lang, 'Anticompetitive Non-Pricing Abuses Under European and National Antitrust Law', in 2003 *Fordham Corporate Law Institute* 235–40 (Barry E. Hawk ed. 2004); and John Temple Lang & Robert O'Donoghue, 'Defining Legitimate Competition: How to Clarify Pricing Abuses Under Article 82 EC', 26 *Fordham International Law Journal* 83 (2002).

launching a new and better product tying it to the good that it has already monopolized.[11] Such a launch may produce several effects: namely, it may: (a) allow the dominant firm to shield its market power; (b) force the dominant firm's existing rivals to lose market share and, in some cases, exit from the market; (c) prevent the dominant firm's potential rivals from entering the market; (d) affect consumers, who suffer both coercion and a negative wealth transfer but, at the same time, benefit from the spread of a new and better product; (e) affect society as a whole, as it faces harm to allocative efficiency but, meanwhile, enjoys an increase in dynamic efficiency due to the innovation (though the monopoly power's persistence could impair future innovative process as well).

As said above, without a clear hierarchy of what interests antitrust law should protect – whether allocative efficiency, or consumer welfare, or dominant firms' rivals, or fairness and consumers' free choice, or a just distribution of wealth, or else dynamic efficiency[12] – it is almost impossible to determine whether any such behavior is lawful or unlawful. In particular, evaluating dominant firms' behaviors is unworkable without defining two specific policy issues. The first question is whether antitrust authorities should set a ceiling[13] on what dominant firms can appropriate,[14] or whether dominant firms *deserve*[15] to fully appropriate[16] all the benefits

---

11 Such a contract is said to be a contractual tying, i.e., an arrangement whereby the dominant firm forces consumers to buy a product (the tied one) together with the monopolized good (the tying product). See Chapter 4 for further details.

12 See Robert H. Bork, *The Antitrust Paradox* 50 (2d ed. 1993) (arguing that, 'antitrust policy cannot be made rational until we are able to [state] what [. . .] its goals [are]').

13 This issue begs a deeper analysis about what should be the proper role of antitrust authorities. Recall from the Introduction that, often in discussion of the differences between competition law and regulation, the former has been compared with a surgical intervention apt for ablating specific illnesses, while the latter has been conceived as the steady administration of medicine to treat a chronic disease. See, in this regard, Frederic M. Scherer & David Ross, *Industrial Market Structure and Economic Performance* 12 (1990).

14 To put this issue another way, consider that finding the limits of what dominant firms can appropriate is a way of establishing to what practical extent antitrust authorities do not prohibit dominance as such: if the dominance is legitimate, striking one or more of the advantages that flow from dominance means vanishing monopoly, at least in part. As a confirmation of this, consider that the analysis of the criteria that the EU competition authorities employed in enforcing Article 102 urged the idea that, sometimes, EU antitrust authorities prohibited monopolies as such. See Per Jebsen & Robert Stevens, 'Assumptions, Goals and Dominant Undertakings: The Regulation of Competition under Article 86 of the European Union', 64 *Antitrust L. J.* 443 (1996).

15 Interestingly, when it comes to a firm that has reached a dominant position, an issue of fairness arises almost automatically: whether, once it has been established that the firm obtained its market power legitimately, the firm must be rewarded for its success by enjoying the benefits that flow from the dominance. This issue of fairness can be then 'translated' in economic words by playing 'the appropriability argument' – see Chapter 1 and the following footnote.

16 Referencing back to what Chapter 1 explained about the importance of rewarding winning firms, for a detailed discussion of the appropriability issue in connection to

that flow from their market position and their competitive advantages,[17] such as the chance to charge non-marginal prices,[18] the possibility of entering new markets by leveraging their monopolized customer base, or the ability to be the exclusive owner of an essential resource. The second question is whether dominant firms should behave as the trustee for their rivals and customers, or should compete as aggressively as non-dominant ones, by continuing to search for competitive advantages though these could strengthen their power further.

Furthermore, the examination of any monopolistic behavior, such as the previously exemplified conduct of tying, would remain impractical without establishing guidelines for the enforcing system; for instance, whether antitrust authorities should employ a form-based or an effect-based approach. The former approach links the illegal nature of the regarded conduct to the presence of certain formal elements, such as the tying clause,[19] while the latter derives the illegal nature of a practice from the effects that it is sup-

---

monopolistic practices, see Richard M. Brunell, 'Appropriability in Antitrust: How Much is Enough', 69 *Antitrust L. J.* 1, 2 (2001) (arguing that 'appropriability arguments have commonly been employed in connection with conflicts between patent policy and antitrust, typically to support the view that patent policy should trump antitrust. Increasingly, however, incentive arguments like those used in the patent context are being used to justify limitations on antitrust enforcement within the domain of antitrust itself. The evils of monopoly in the 'old economy' are giving way to the virtues of monopoly in the 'new economy,' as monopoly profits are said to drive the innovative process.'); and Massimo Motta, *Competition Policy* 39 (2004) (observing that 'if firms were not able to appropriate the results of their investments – whether they be advertising outlays, capacity, R&D expenditures or other – they would not invest at all, with the result that consumers would not benefit from lower costs, higher quality goods, new product varieties and so on.').

17 Thanks to a competitive advantage, a firm can both acquire a dominant position and strengthen it. Yet, the policy issue behind these two scenarios is the same, namely whether firms that succeed in smiting their rivals should be allowed to enjoy the benefits that derive from their victory, whether it happenened before or after the firm reached a dominant position.

18 See Steven D. Anderman, 'The Competition Law/IP "Interface": An Introductory Note', *in The Interface Between Intellectual Property Rights and Competition Policy* 1, 6 (Steven D. Anderman ed. 2007) (arguing that US and EU antitrust laws accept that IPRs' prices can include a return which reflects the reward/incentive function of IPRs as well as the up-front investments risk of their owners). In general, in 'Verizon Communication, Inc. v. Law Offices of Curtis v. Trinko', *LLP*, 540 U.S. 398, 407 (2004) (hereinafter *Trinko*) the US Supreme Court has made clear that the mere possession of lawful monopoly power, and the concomitant charging of monopoly prices, is not only lawful, it is an important element of the free-market system. In support of this thesis, see, e.g., Michael Katz & Howard Shelanski, '"Schumpeterian" Competition and Antitrust Policy in High-Tech Markets' (2005) available at http://ssrn.com/abstract=925707; and Dennis W. Carlton & Ken Heyer, *Appropriate Antitrust Policy Towards Single-Firm Conduct* 3 (2008), available at http://ssrn.com/abstract=1111665 (stating clearly that 'the prospect of monopoly pricing (albeit, with the static deadweight loss that generally accompanies it) provides a critically important incentive for welfare-enhancing investment and innovation, and so antitrust should permit simple monopoly pricing').

19 See Femi Alese, *Federal Antitrust and EC Competition Law Analysis* 205, 211 (2008) (arguing that in such instances, the effects of such agreements or any objective justifica-

posed to produce according to the economic model employed to explain the facts in question. To be sure, these two kinds of examinations involve similar investigative analysis: in order to enforce the law, antitrust authorities must ascertain whether the observed facts can be brought into a specific framework that they consider unlawful. The difference is that, while the form-based approach's framework is a catalog of formal elements, like particular contractual terms,[20] the bricks of the effects-based approach are the effects of the practice, such as its consequences in terms of allocative, productive and dynamic efficiencies; or its short-term compared to long-term outcomes; or else its actual, compared to, its potential results. Therefore, referring back to the example of a dominant firm that launches a new product by tying it with the monopolized product: where the form-based approach would focus on the existence of the tying clause, the effects-based approach would look at the economic theories that show the conditions under which the above-mentioned effects on market power, rivals' viability, and dynamic efficiency occur, and whether these conditions happen in the case in question.

Now, the form-based approach is generally deemed clear, easily administered, inexpensive, but often inconsistent with markets' functioning.[21] In contrast, the effects-based approach is generally considered as more reliable and more theoretically 'correct' from an economic standpoint, but more complex, more risky, and more costly to administer.

Yet, a clarification is due: the effects-based approach does not require either antitrust authorities to 'measure' the effects that occur in each specific case,[22] or firms to monitor continuously the effects that their practices produce. Rather, it asks antitrust authorities to *typify* unlawful practices in line with what the economic theory teaches, that is to say, in accordance

---

tions for them are hardly given a second look, particularly if the practice has been shown to eliminate competition in the products concerned).

20 Whish, *supra* note 6, at 197–8.

21 See, Ginevra Bruzzone, Marco Boccaccio, *Identifying infringements of competition rules: the role of economic and legal thinking*, paper presented to the VIII Conference 'Antitrust Between EC Law and National Law' 10, Treviso, 22–23 May 2008, available at http://www.emagazine.assonime.it/upload/Identifying%20infringements%20def.pdf; Ariel Ezrachi, The Commission' guidance on Article 82 EC and the Effects Based Approach – Legal and Practical Challenges, *in Article 82 EC: Reflections on its recent evolution* 51, 53 (Ariel Ezrachi ed., 2009); and Orin Dayagi-Epstein, The evolution of the Notion of Consumer Interest in Light of the Modernization of Article 82, *in Article 82 EC: Reflections on its recent evolution* 67, 73 (Ariel Ezrachi ed., 2009).

22 Indeed, see Ginevra Bruzzone, Marco Boccaccio, 'Impact-Based Assesment and Use of Legal Presumptions in EC Competition Law: The Search for the Proper Mix', 32 *World Competition* 465, 469 (2009) (arguing that, 'an impact-based approach does not necessarily require the quantification of consumer harm, with reference to the effect of the conduct on output and prices, but can also be based on qualitative evidence').

with a plausible and consistent theory of the harm that in addition has to fit the facts in questions.[23] Therefore, it is true that according to the effects-based approach, on the one hand, *behaviors with the same form* may be legal in some cases, but illegal in others, and, on the other hand, *behaviors with diverse forms* are to be judged in the same way in those scenarios where they produce the same effects. But, since the 'cases' and 'scenarios' to be considered are those that economic theories explain in advance – although these economic explanations may vary over the years – and that, hence, firms can know from the outset, the effects-based approach does not increase legal uncertainty:[24] it only offers a different conduct's categorization.[25]

Then, as this discussion about accuracy, administrability, and legal certainty shows, legal standards have to satisfy several requirements in relation to which antitrust authorities can endorse different approaches, as indeed the competition authorities of United States and European Union have partially done. For instance, to promote efficiency and technological progress by lowering the risk of investing in business transactions (some of which overtime may prove to be unlawful), antitrust authorities should seek to establish clear and easily administrable legal standards that enhance business certainty.[26] After all, plain legal rules help to promote uniformity and equality, especially when, as happens in the EU jurisdiction, several different administrative and judicial bodies enforce competition law. Moreover, legal rules that can be easily applied are crucial when judges

---

[23] In this regard, see, Ioannis Lianos, Categorical thinking in Competition Law and the 'Effects-Based' approach in Article 82, *in Article 82 EC: Reflections on Its Recent Evolution* 19, 21 (Ariel Ezrachi ed., 2009) (arguing that, 'an effects-based approach does not reject the need for categorical thinking. The identification of a theory of consumer harm involves a process of categorization of the practice as falling within the boundaries of a specific theory, e.g. raising rivals' cost, leveraging, predation, maintenance of monopoly strategy, a two sided market situation. Specific effects will follow from the classification of the practice as falling within a specific antitrust theory').

[24] See Ezrachi, *supra* note 21, at 53 and ff. (arguing that the 2009 Communication is not only affected by 'internal ambiguity', but also surrounded by 'external uncertainty' which arises from the way in which European communitarian and national courts will endorse the economic, effects-based approach). See European Commission, *Guidance on the Commission's Enforcement Priorities in Applying Article 82 of the EC Treaty to Abusive Exclusionary Conduct by Dominant Undertakings*, OJ 2009, C45/7 (hereinafter, 2009 Communication). See, further, Liza Lovdahl Gormsen, *A Principled Approach to Abuse of Dominance in European Competition Law* 164–74 (2010).

[25] See Lianos, *supra* note 23.

[26] It can be stated, indeed, that firms can even walk away from lawful enterprises if, given the vague scope of antitrust liability, they fear that the relevant behaviors risk violating antitrust law. See OECD, 'Guidance to Business on Monopolization and Abuse of Dominance' 7 (2007), available at http://www.oecd.org/dataoecd/50/33/40880976.pdf (arguing for the importance of clear rules when it comes to 'companies, and particularly companies with large market shares and with cross-border activities'); and William Blumenthal, 'Clear Agency Guidelines: Lessons from 1982', 68 *Antitrust L. J.* 5 (2000).

and jurors are asked to enforce antitrust law, as happens especially in the US.[27] Further, given that any business conduct entails costs, and antitrust authorities themselves are subject to financial constraints, clear standards that are easily administered can greatly reduce enforcement costs. [28]

Yet, antitrust authorities cannot employ clear, easily administrable, and cheap standards at the expense of accuracy: competition law enforcement would be nonsense if antitrust legal standards let harmful behaviors go unpunished and found harmless practices illegal.[29] It is almost impossible to set a perfectly balanced legal standard, that minimizes both the likelihood of under-deterrence (i.e., allowing bad behaviour to continue, or false positive mistakes) and over-deterrence (i.e., punishing innocent behaviour, or false negative mistakes).[30] Therefore, in setting their standards antitrust authorities must choose where to set the benchmark: whether the couple false negatives/over-deterrence is to be preferred to the couple under-deterrence/false positives.[31] As Chapter 1 hinted, those who trust market forces and the Schumpeterian creative destruction as being able to wear away and displace dominance can afford a more lenient approach and, hence, sustain 'hands off' rules that increase the risk of underdeterrence. Those who, on the contrary, do not think that market power can be easily

---

27 See, e.g., Dennis W. Carlton, 'Using Economics to Improve Antitrust Policy', 2004 *Columbia Business Law Review* 283 (2004).

28 For instance, per se rules best serve this aim especially in private suits, *if and only if* experience and economics suggest that the regarded practices are certainly unlawful so that there is no point in wasting court or regulatory resources in investigating their effects. See, in this regard, O'Donoghue & Padilla, *supra* note 6, at 183–4. Likewise, other judicial rules such as market-share screens, presumptions, and burden of proof schemes, are all tools that competition authorities can use to save resources when they know that the relevant behaviors are not always harmful.

29 See, e.g., Richard A. Posner, 'An Economic Approach to Legal Procedure and Judicial Administration', 2 *Journal of Legal Studies* 399 (1973).

30 The term 'false positives' (or Type I errors) is used to address the cases of unlawful practices that go unpunished, while the term 'false negatives' (or Type II errors) serves to indicate the cases of lawful practices that are wrongly found to be illegal. In particular, it has been argued that the gravity of false negatives increases as long as both the remedies are strong and the regarded practice involves innovation. See, in this regard, Hendrik Bourgeois, 'The Chilling Effects of Article 82 Enforcement', *in International Antitrust & Policy: Annual Proceedings of the Fordham Corporate Law Institute* 2008 349 (Barry E. Hawk ed. 2009) (fully discussing and questioning the theoretical reasons and the empirical evidence for believing that false positives may result in chilling effects on competition).

31 See First & Gavil, *supra* note 6, at 649. Further, see Giovanni Immordino & Michele Polo, 'Judicial Errors and Innovative Activity', CSEF Discussion Paper no. 196 (2008) (given that deterrence works by affecting the initial incentive to invest in research, they argue that 'Type-I errors, through over-enforcement, discourage innovative effort while type-II errors (under-enforcement) spur it'. Therefore, they show that the *ex ante* expected welfare effect of innovations should shape the optimal policy design: when innovations are *ex ante* welfare improving, laissez-faire should be chosen; when instead innovations are welfare decreasing, law enforcement should limit them.).

eroded, perhaps because of its public origin and some market features such as network and tipping effects, endorse a stricter attitude and so sustain a more interventionist approach that increases the risk of over-deterrence.[32]

In sum, there are several policy variables that influence the US and EU approaches towards dominant firms' conduct.

THE APPARENT CONTENT OF SECTION 2 AND ARTICLE 102

Section 2 covers the offenses of 'monopolization' and 'attempt to monopolize', whereas Article 102 deals only with the so-called 'abuse of dominant position' offense. All of them require proof of two objective elements:[33] the structural component – whether called monopoly power, dangerous probability of acquiring monopoly power, or dominance – and the behavioral component – whether named exclusionary, anticompetitive conduct,[34] or abuse. Instead, only the offense of attempt to monopolize

---

[32] See, e.g., Lovdahl Gormsen, *supra* note 24, at 7 (2010); Andrew I. Gavil, 'Exclusionary Distribution Strategies by Dominant Firms: Striking a Better Balance', 72 *Antitrust L. J.* 3, 61 (2004). Not by chance, indeed, the approach to this issue is often affected by the likely disbelief in monopolists' merits – whether because of the path dependence theory or because the monopolist has benefited from public funds. See, in this regard, David Evans, 'How Economists Can Help Courts Design Competition Rules: An EU and US Perspective', 28 *World Competition* 93 (2005). Further, see Joseph Drexl, 'Real Knowledge is to Know the Extent of One's Own Ignorance: On The Consumer Harm Approach in Innovation-Related Competition Cases' 4 (2009), available at www.ssrn.com (arguing that, 'How much risk a given society is ready and willing to take belongs to the domain of politics and cultural perceptions and may therefore also vary significantly between the different jurisdictions. Competition policy does not constitute an exception in this regard.').

[33] Indeed, consider that in *Hoffmann-La Roche*, § 91, the ECJ has defined the notion of abuse by stating that, 'the concept of abuse is an objective concept'. Nevertheless, sometimes officers and judges did consider the subjective element. In Commission decision 2002/405, COMP/E-2/36.041/PO Michelin, OJ 2002 L143/1 (hereinafter *Michelin II*), for instance, the Commission decided that the intent to exclude was sufficient to show that the conduct actually had such an effect. However, in the recent AstraZeneca judgment the Court of First Instance clarified that, 'The fact . . . that the concept of abuse of a dominant position is an objective concept and implies no intention to cause harm . . . does not lead to the conclusion that the intention to resort to practices falling outside the scope of competition on the merits is in all events irrelevant, since that intention can still be taken into account to support the conclusion that the undertaking concerned abused a dominant position, even if that conclusion should be primarily be based on an objective finding that the abusive conduct actually took place'. See CFI, Astrazeneca, 1 July 2010, case T-321/05, § 359, available at http://curia.europa.eu/.

[34] By and large, the term 'anticompetitive' and 'exclusionary' are used as synonyms in order to address the behavioral component of the offense, see 3 Phillip E. Areeda & Herbert Hovenkamp, *Antitrust Law: An Analysis of Antitrust Principles and their Application* ¶ 650a (2008). Yet, the book prefers to use the tern 'exclusionary' for practices that strengthen

requires evidence of a subjective element: the firm's specific intent to monopolize.[35]

Regarding the *structural element* of the three offenses, it must be acknowledged that the concepts of monopoly power and dominance are very similar.[36] They both address – sometimes in an equally misleading way[37] – one firm's ability to price substantially above the competitive level and to persist in doing so for a significant period without erosion by new entry or expansion by the fringe.[38] Moreover, neither of the two offences requires the absolute absence of competition.

In practice, however, monopoly power and dominance have been applied in different manners: to put it simply, given that neither of the two jurisdictions infers monopoly power automatically from the possession of a commanding market share,[39] it can be stated that with low market shares EU antitrust authorities are more willing than their US counterparts

---

market power by harming rivals, and the term 'anticompetitive' for the exclusionary behaviors that further harm consumer welfare.

[35] See *Spectrum Sports, Inc. v. McQuillan*, 506 U.S. 447, 456 (1993). Nevertheless, as the subjective element does not really belong to the European experience, and even in the US experience its weight depends on the ideology of the different antitrust schools, this chapter follows the view that antitrust authorities would do well to avoid considering the subjective element and, hence, does not deal with it. However, for a recent discussion of the element of intent in monopolization cases see, e.g., Marina Lao, 'Aspen Skiing and Trinko: Antitrust Intent and Sacrifice', 73 *Antitrust* L. J. 171 (2005); and Ronald A. Cass & Keith N. Hylton, 'Antitrust Intent', 74 *S. Cal. L. Rev.* 657 (2001).

[36] See, e.g., R. Hewitt Pate, 'The Common Law Approach and Improving Standards for Analyzing Single Firma Conduct', in *International Law Policy: Fordham Corporate Law* 2003 195, 202 (Barry E. Hawk ed. 2004); Robert E. Bloch et al., 'A Comparative Analysis of Article 82 and Section 2 of the Sherman Act', 7 *Business Law International* 148–53 (2006); Gregory J. Werden, 'Identifying Single-Firm Exclusionary Conduct: From Vague Concepts to Administrable Rules', 33rd Annual Conference on International Antitrust Law & Policy, Fordham Corporate Law Institute, New York, September 14–15, 2006, 3–5.

[37] For instance, in *United States v. E. I. du Pont de Nemours & Co.*, 351 U.S. 377, 391 (1956) the Supreme Court described market power as 'the power [. . .] to exclude competitors' and in *Hoffman-La Roche*, § 38 the ECJ stated that a dominant position is 'a position of economic strength enjoyed by an undertaking which enables it to prevent effective competition being maintained on the relevant market'. Instead, exercising market power means charging supra-competitive prices that normally will attract new rivals to enter the market. Therefore, market power is not exclusionary in itself.

[38] Such a definition is not so common in the US and EU case law. Yet, for the US experience, *AD/SAT v. Associated Press*, 181 F.3d 216, 227 (2d Cir. 1999) and *United States v. Microsoft Corp.*, 253 F3d 34, 50 (DC Circ 2001). Rather, in the EU jurisdiction, before what the Commission has recently stated in its 2009 Communication, supra note 24, § 11 the notion of dominance has generally been described using the concept of independence, that is, stating that dominance is the power of a firm to behave to an appreciable extent independently of its competitors, its customers and ultimately of consumers.

[39] See, e.g., *American Council of Certified Podiatric Physicians & Surgeons v. American Board of Podiatric Surgery, Inc.*, 185 F.3d 606, 623 (6th Cir. 1999); and 2009 Communication, *supra* note 24, §§ 9–18 (hereinafter, 2009 Communication).

to find a dominant position.[40] Yet, the 'monopolization offense' covers also the practices that result (or are likely to result) in the acquisition of monopoly power, no matter how small the firm's market share may be at the time of the relevant conduct.[41] Furthermore, Section 2 lowers the market share requirement when it deals with the 'attempt to monopolize offense': indeed, attempts are commonly deemed practices that, if uninterrupted, would probably produce the degree of market power that would constitute a monopoly.[42]

In summary, one could observe that in effect US courts and EU institutions *run the same risk* of punishing harmless conduct:[43] as long as monopoly power is necessary either to put in place an exclusionary practice, such as in the case of predatory pricing, or to make it harmful – that is to say, to make its harmful effect happen or likely to happen – such as in the cases of practices that involve different markets, like tie-ins and refusals to deal,[44] US courts and EU institutions run the same risk of prohibiting a conduct in the absence of dominance, making a false negative mistake.

Actually, the two jurisdictions try to face such a risk by establishing a connection between the structural and the behavioral requirements. Especially when it comes to multi-market situations, US courts try to find a cause-effect relation between the practice and the acquired monopoly power or, at least, to verify whether the behavior is reasonably capable of making a significant contribution to the creation of monopoly power.[45]

---

[40] Indeed, in the US, courts dismiss monopolization claims against entities with a market share of less than 50 per cent. Moreover, firms with market shares well in excess of 50 per cent have been found not to possess monopoly power because their power over price was insufficiently durable. See, e.g., *Western Parcel Express v. United Parcel Service of America, Inc.*, 190 F.3d 974, 975 (9th Cir. 1999); *Tops Markets, Inc. v. Quality Markets, Inc.*, 142 F.3d 90, 99 (2d Cir. 1998); *Colorado Interstate Gas Co. v. Natural Gas Pipeline Co. of America*, 885 F.2d 683, 695-96 (10th Cir. 1989). Instead, in its 2009 Communication, *supra* note 24, at § 14, the European Commission stated that low market shares are generally a good proxy for the absence of substantial market power, because experience suggests that dominance is not likely if the undertaking's market share is below 40 per cent in the relevant market. However, the Commission also observed that there might be specific cases below this threshold where rivals are not in a position to constrain effectively the conduct of a dominant undertaking.

[41] See, e.g., *Berkey Photo v. Eastman Kodak*, 603 F.2d 263, 275 (2d Cir. 1979) (stating that, 'unlawfully acquired power remains anathema even when kept dormant'), and 3B Phillip E. Areeda & Herbert Hovenkamp, *Antitrust Law: An Analysis of Antitrust Principles and their Application* ¶ 802f (3d ed. 2008).

[42] See Areeda & Hovenkamp, *supra* note 41, at ¶¶ 804 and 807.

[43] See, for a concurring opinion, see, e.g., Ronald W. Davis & Jennifer M. Driscoll, 'The Urge to Convergence – The New EU Discussion Paper on Abuse of a Dominant Position', 20 *SPG Antitrust* 82, 83 (2006).

[44] See, in this regard, the in-depth reasoning of Ekaterina Rousseva, *Rethinking Exclusionary Abuses in EU Competition Law* 73–9 (2010).

[45] See, e.g., Areeda & Hovenkamp, *supra* note 41, at ¶806. Moreover, in order not to strike harmless conduct, US courts recognize that: (i) a conduct that is legal for a monopolist

Likewise, although scholars have often struggled with this idea[46], EU authorities have somehow established that there must be a close link[47] between the dominant position and either the conduct put in place, or its harmful effects.

Turning to the *behavioral element* of the three offenses, and referencing forward to the following sections for the legal standard to apply in order to detect unlawful monopolists' conduct, it must be recalled that the offenses of monopolization and the attempt to monopolize unquestionably deal – almost solely[48] – with exclusionary behaviors,[49] though the wording of Section 2 does not establish it expressly. Likewise, the wording

---

is also legal for a would-be monopolist – see *Olympia Equip. Leasing Co. v. W. Union Tel. Co.*, 797 F.2d 370, 373 (7th Cir. 1986); (ii) practices that are only marginally illegal when performed by a firm with monopoly power are surely legal when endorsed by an undertaking without such a power – see, e.g., *Transamerica Computer Company, Inc. v. IBM*, 698 F.2d 1377, 1382 (9th Circ. 1983) (observing that 'conduct that does not constitute 'willful acquisition or maintenance of monopoly power' (thus precluding establishment of monopolization offense) cannot constitute the 'predatory or anticompetitive conduct' required to establish the offense of attempt to monopolize'); and *California Computer Products, Inc. and Century Data System, Inc., v. IBM*, 613 F.2d 727, 737, nt. 11 (9th Circ. 1979) (stating that 'the same conduct may provide a basis for the monopolization offense and yet be excluded as a basis for the attempt to monopolize. This is so since a defendant's monopoly power or lack thereof is part of the reasonableness calculus; conduct reasonable for other firms is not necessarily reasonable for the monopolist.'); and (iii) a practice that is illegal for a monopolist may be legal for a firm that lacks monopoly power – see *United States v. Dentsply Int'l, Inc.*, 399 F.3d 181, 187 (3d Cir. 2005) (stating that 'behavior that otherwise might comply with antitrust law may be impermissibly exclusionary when practiced by a monopolist'). Further on this topic, see Chapter 5 and the US history of the leverage monopoly theory.

46 See, Rousseva, *supra* note 44, at 73 (arguing that using the case law of the European Court of Justice to draw the conclusion 'that no causal link between dominance and abuse is needed is too far-reaching and . . . contrary to the very essence of Article 82'). See, also, Whish, *supra* note 6, at 198; Jurian Langer, *Tying and Bundling as a Leveraging Concern under EC Competition Law* 49 (2007); O'Donoghue, Padilla, *supra* note 6, at 215–7; John Vickers, 'Abuse of Market Power', *in Handbook of Antitrust Economics* 419 (Paolo Buccirossi ed. 2008); Thomas Eilmansberger, 'How To Distinguish Good from Bad Competition under Article 82 EC: In Search of Clearer and More Coherent Standards for Anti-Competitive Abuses', 42 *Common Market Law Review* 129, 141–2 (2005); Mark Furse, *Competition Law of the EC and UK* 230 (2004); Luca Sanfilippo, 'Abuse of Freedom of Conduct: Neighbouring Markets and Application of Article 86', EBLR 6 (1995); and Pierre Vogelenzang, 'Abuse of Dominant Position in Article 86: The Problem of Causality and Some Application', 13 CMLR 61, 1976.

47 See Advocate General Colomer in Case C-333194P, *Tetra Pak II*, at 57.

48 Indeed, a few behaviors that are not anticompetitive are covered by Section 2, such as mergers, business torts, and unfair tactics. See Areeda & Hovenkamp, *supra* nota 34, at ¶¶ 650a, 651d and 651g.

49 In connection with the monopolization offense, see *Trinko* at 407, where the court stated 'the possession of monopoly power will not be found unlawful unless it is accompanied by an element of anticompetitive conduct'. In relation to the attempt to monopolize offense, see, e.g., *Taylor Publishing Co v. Jostens*, 216 F.3d 465 (5th Circ. 2000), where the court describes the practice using the definition of anticompetitive behavior that Areeda and Hovenkamp provide for the monopolization offense.

of Article 102 does not define the notion of abuse. To be sure, the word abuse suggests – as said before when speaking about the causation requirement – a pure form of public powers' '*ex post* control' that is triggered only after a firm has obtained monopoly power, no matter how. Moreover, the four examples of abusive practices listed by the same Article 102 help to understand the provision's scope.[50] From reading letters (a) and (c) indeed it is clear that Article 102 catches practices that Section 2 does not cover, such as exploitative behaviors,[51] and secondary-line discriminatory abuses.[52] Instead, the abuses enumerated at letters (b) and (d)[53] represent the abuses that naturally correspond to Section 2's anticompetitive conduct.[54] Therefore, it should not come as a surprise that this and the

---

50 See Whish, *supra* note 6, at 188 (arguing that the list of abuses is not exhaustive).

51 Article 102(a) prohibits expressly the abuses of dominant position that consist in 'directly or indirectly imposing unfair purchase or selling prices or other unfair trading conditions'. As is well known, the existence of exploitative abuses should not be emphasized, since nowadays the European Commission is no longer focused on the application of Article 102(a). See, indeed, Pate, *supra* note 36, at 204 (arguing that, 'the rare excessive prices cases that the EU has pursued in the last few years have been part of a broader enforcement action directed primarily at otherwise exclusionary practices'). However, this provision gives a hint at least in connection to the past European conception of the antitrust action. The will to punish excessive prices, indeed, reveals: (i) the absence of trust in the market and the possibility that extra profits induce the entrance of other firms; and (ii) the double idea that the European Commission, as well as national authorities and courts, are entitled and able to fix the proper price. For a deep description of the abusive practices, see O' Donoghue & Padilla, *supra* note 6, at 603–658. In order to understand how the US perspective is different, it is enough to consider footnote 18 and the accompanying text. By the way, according to some scholars, in Europe there can be a legitimate interest to prosecute these practices at least where they are not self-correcting, namely where the entry barriers are high or even insuperable, as it happens in particular in newly liberalized sectors, where entry barriers remain high and supracompetitive profits will therefore not automatically attract new entrants. Notice how this reasoning is connected to the appropriability issue discussed before and to the existence of innocent monopolies.

52 Discriminatory conduct may harm consumer welfare, but in practice the Commission has never paid attention to distinguishing between primary line and secondary line discriminations, prohibiting even harmless behaviors. Indeed, Article 102(c) forbids abuses that consist in 'applying dissimilar conditions to equivalent transactions with other trading parties, thereby placing them at a competitive disadvantage', so that the rule does not distinguish between rivals and customers as the passive parties of the offense. Besides, Article 102(c) has sometimes been applied to punish direct and indirect discrimination on a national basis, 'notwithstanding the absence of any effect on the structure of competition'. See Commission decision of July 20, 1999, *1998 Football World Cup*, OJ L 5/55, § 100. For a comprehensive description of discriminatory abuses, see O'Donoghue & Padilla, *supra* note 6, 552–92.

53 See John Temple Lang, 'Anticompetitive Abuses Involving Intellectual Property Rights', in *European Competition Law Annual*: 2003, *What is an Abuse of Dominant Position*? 590 (Claus-Dieter Ehlermann & Isabela Atanasiu eds. 2003) (stating that Article 102(d) represents only a specific example of conduct limiting competitors' access to markets, so that its application is also limited to cases where authorities and courts ascertain harm to consumers' welfare).

54 See, in contrast, René Joliet, *Monopolization and Abuse of Dominant Position* (1970) (concluding, by considering in isolation the wording of Article 102, that Article 102 was only

following chapters deal with exclusionary conduct which indeed belongs to the intersection between the scopes of the US and EU provisions.

THE ECONOMIC PERSPECTIVE: STANDARDS FOR DETECTING DOMINANT FIRMS' UNLAWFUL BEHAVIORS

When economists have been called upon to suggest a legal standard for sorting out legal from unlawful dominant firms' conduct, they have put forward several alternatives, such as the 'profit sacrifice test', the 'no economic sense test', the 'equally efficient firm test', and various welfare tests.[55]

The 'profit sacrifice test' asks whether the dominant firm foregoes a more profitable course of action in order to undertake the regarded behavior.[56] It does not, however, explain how to appreciate such a sacrifice: whether it should consist of a dominant firm preferring an irrational practice instead of a rational behavior, or whether it should address a dominant firm disregarding the most profitable conduct in favor of another rational

---

intended to regulate the exercise of monopolistic market power vis-à-vis consumers, purchasers, and suppliers, and did not cover practices directed against actual or potential competitors). Yet, in *Continental Can* the ECJ took a wider approach and recognized for the first time that 'the list [in Article 102] merely gives examples, not an exhaustive enumeration of the sort of abuses of a dominant position prohibited by the Treaty. As may further be seen from letters (c) and (d) of Article 86(2) [102(2)], the provision is not only aimed at practices which may cause damage to consumers directly, but also at those which are detrimental to them through their impact on an effective competition structure, such as is mentioned in Article 3(f) [3(1)(g)] of the Treaty.'. See, alternatively, Eugene Buttigieg, 'Consumer Interests and the Antitrust Approach to Abusive Practices by Dominant Firms', EBLR 1191, 1197 (2005) (arguing that in so doing, the court enhanced Article 102's effectiveness as an instrument of consumer protection because, unless exclusionary practices are checked as well, in the long run consumers will be confronted with fewer and fewer alternatives to choose from, so that the damage done to the competitive structure of the market will inevitably lead to harm to the consumer). This is the reason why the Commission chose to study first exclusionary rather exploitative abuses – see 2009 Communication, *supra* note 24, at §§ 6–7.

[55] In connection to them, see, e.g., Steven C. Salop, 'Exclusionary Conduct, Effect on Consumers, and the Flawed Profit-Sacrificed Standard', 73 *Antitrust L. J.* 311 (2006); Werden, *supra* note 36; R. Hewitt Pate, 'Exclusionary Conduct: Refusals to Deal and Bundling and Loyalty Discounts', Testimony before the Antitrust Modernization Commission (September 29, 2005); Douglas Melamed, 'Exclusionary Conduct under the Antitrust Laws: Balancing, Sacrifice and Refusals to Deal', 20 *Berkeley Tech. L. J.* 1247 (2005); Robert Pitofsky, 'Past, Present and Future Antitrust Enforcement at the Federal Trade of Commission', 72 U. *Chi. L. Rev.* 209 (2005); Herbert Hovenkamp, 'Exclusion and the Sherman Act', 72 *U. Chi. L. Rev.* 147 (2005); and Gavil, *supra* note 27; Mark R. Patterson, 'The Sacrifice of Profits in Non-Price Predation', 18 *Antitrust* 37 (2003).

[56] See Janusz Ordover & Robert Willig, 'An Economic Definition of Predation Pricing and Product Innovation', 91 *Yale L. J.* 8 (1981); and Vickers, *supra* note 46, at 423–6.

practice. Further, the test does not clarify whether the sacrifice should be appreciated in the short-run or in the long-run, though there are several behaviors, such as innovative activities, that increase profits and enhance total welfare in the long run, but that do entail significant up-front losses in the short run,[57] that is to say that require short-run sacrifices aimed to vanish in the long run. Besides, the test does not explain whether the behaviors that result from the sacrifice – however defined – should be held unlawful without any further inquiry. If they should, the test could risk entailing high enforcement costs pushing antitrust authorities to pursue every 'silly' behavior, even when it does not harm total welfare. Indeed, some behaviors can be even welfare-increasing though they are irrational for a single firm.[58] On the other hand, the test risks being under-inclusive because there are behaviors that can harm total welfare but do not entail any sacrifice for the firm, either in the short or the long run.[59] In summary, the profit sacrifice test has a great limit: as it does not focus on the harm to total welfare, it can be either over-inclusive or under-inclusive.[60] Nevertheless, by assessing the intent of the dominant firm in an objective way,[61] the test has the merit of establishing a safe harbor for rational behaviors. This is not a trivial result, rather is it fully consistent

---

[57] See Herbert Hovenkamp, 'The Harvard and Chicago Schools and the Dominant Firm', in *How the Chicago School Overshot the Mark* 109, 115 (Robert Pitofsky ed. 2008) (arguing that 'product innovations are always costly to the defendant, and their success may very well depend on their ability to exclude rivals from the market, but neither of these factors is or should be decisive in subsequent antitrust litigation. All innovation is costly, and many successful innovations succeed only because consumers substitute away from rivals' older versions and toward the innovator's version'. In summary, the sacrifice test does not adequately allow recognition of sacrifices that will, however, produce efficiencies, new and better products, and new processes.).

[58] See Dennis W. Carlton, 'The Relevance for Antitrust Policy of Theoretical and Empirical Advances in Industrial Organization', 12 *Geo. Mason L. Rev.* 47, 51 (speaking about advertising: it, indeed, can result from an irrational choice of a single firm but produce a positive benefit to consumers. Such a concrete observation contradicts the invisible hand theory, according to which the maximization of static social welfare happens via firms' profit maximizing choices.).

[59] See Hovenkamp, *supra* note 57, at 115 (observing that 'other practices, such as improper infringement suits, are often costly to the defendant in the short-run, whether or not they are anticompetitive. Indeed, the improper patent infringement suit is likely to be most costly to the dominant firm when the infringement defendant has the resources to defend it; and may not be particularly costly when the infringement defendants are nascent firms who are easily excluded from the market'); and O'Donoghue & Padilla, *supra* note 6, at 186–7.

[60] This test would work perfectly if two neoclassical hypotheses were true, namely, if there was always a unique best action for any firm and if the maximization of social welfare could occur only via firms' profit maximizing behaviors. In such a scenario, indeed, whichever action does not coincide with the best strategy would be at the same time irrational and welfare-decreasing.

[61] See Vickers, *supra* note 46, at 426.

with the idea that monopolists must be allowed to be self-interested and profit-maximizers as non-dominant firms are.[62]

Likewise, the 'no economic sense test', also called the 'but for test', asks whether the dominant firm's conduct would be profitable, or would make business sense, but for its propensity to eliminate or lessen competitive constraints. In particular, it holds unlawful not any departure from short-run profit-maximizing behaviors, but only that peculiar course of conduct that, among the several options available to the dominant firm at the time of the action, makes sense in the light of rivals' exclusion. But, again, as such a test does not focus on the practice's impact on total welfare it risks being both under-inclusive and over-inclusive. On the one hand, indeed, there are profitable and rational behaviors that harm total welfare;[63] on the other hand, there are practices that entail losses and do not make any business sense but do not impair total welfare, such as risky innovative activities. Then, as well as the 'profit sacrifice test', the 'but for test' has the merit of moving the debate on dominant firms' conduct towards an objective assessment of profit maximizing and economically rational practices.[64]

The 'as-efficient competitor test', instead, asks whether the dominant firm is acting so as to exclude rivals that are as efficient as it is.[65] This test is premised upon the correct and, hence, sharable idea that, as markets must work in order to select efficient firms, monopolistic practices that drive inefficient rivals out of the markets are to be held lawful because they are 'physiological', inherently consistent with markets' proper functioning.[66] In other words, such a test is an excellent antidote against any policy aimed at preserving dominant firms' rivals as such. Yet, the test in question works well with pricing behaviors such as predatory pricing and package rebates, but does not fit non-price conduct as it lacks a proper benchmark for it. Further, the 'as-efficient competitor test' does not fit well with dominant

---

62 See, in this regard, Hovenkamp, *supra* note 57, at 114 (arguing that monopolists cannot serve as trustees for their rivals); Richard A. Edlin & Joseph Farrell, 'The American Airlines Case: A Chance to Clarify Predation Policy', in *The Antitrust Revolution* 502, 523 (John E. Kwoka & Lawrence J. White, eds. 2003); and Elhauge, *supra* note 6, at 253.

63 See Hovenkamp, *supra* note 57, at 115–16 (considering that 'supplying false information or failing to disclose important information to a government official or standard setting organization need not cost any more than supplying truthful information, but can create monopoly under appropriate circumstances').

64 See O'Donoghue & Padilla, *supra* note 6, at 188.

65 See Richard A. Posner, *Antitrust Law* 194–5 (2d ed. 2001) (arguing that his proposed definition of exclusionary conduct would require the plaintiff to show that the defendant has monopoly power and that the challenged practice is likely to exclude from the defendant's market an equally or more efficient competitor. Then, the defendant can rebut by proving that although it is a monopolist and the challenged practice exclusionary, the practice is, on balance, efficient.).

66 O'Donoghue & Padilla, *supra* note 6, at 190.

firms' practices that cast upon firms costs that are inversely proportional to firms' initial competitive advantages, such as the first mover advantage, and scale or scope economies.[67]

As to the category of welfare tests, it regards all the standards that theoretically require antitrust authorities to make a two-step analysis articulating in a phase where they map all the possible effects that a practice can produce on welfare according to both the applied economic models and the available information;[68] and in a phase where they try to strike a balance among them in order to understand whether the effects that are welfare-increasing prevail over those that make welfare dwindle, or vice versa. Then, total welfare tests differ from consumer welfare tests according to whether the regarded effects concern total welfare or consumer welfare; while according to the kind of rules used to strike the balance among welfare effects, it is likely to distinguish among several standards. Namely, whereas some tests could require behavior to be held lawful when efficiency simply outweighs any inefficiency,[69] other tests, by acknowledging that welfare effects cannot be measured,[70] suggest a more detailed proportionality inquiry.[71] Else, other tests propose a kind of 'market structure variant', focusing on the existence of entry-barriers, and ask whether the regarded conduct creates artificial barriers to entry without any discerning benefits for consumers, or without resulting in the lesser harmful means to reach those benefits.[72] In summary, welfare tests have the merit of urging

---

[67] Hovenkamp, *supra* note 57, at 116–17; Einer Elhauge, 'Why Above-cost Price Cuts to Drive Out Entrants are Not Predatory', 112 *Yale L. J.* 681 (2003); and Posner, *supra* note 65, at 238.

[68] O'Donoghue & Padilla, *supra* note 6, at 191–2.

[69] See for a discussion of the topic Gavil, *supra* note 32, at 63.

[70] Areeda & Hovenkamp, *supra* note 34, at ¶ 651.b1; and O'Donoghue & Padilla, *supra* note 6, at 193.

[71] Areeda & Hovenkamp, *supra* note 34, at ¶ 651.a, (arguing that 'we define monopolistic conduct as acts that: (1) are reasonably capable of creating, enlarging or prolonging monopoly power by impairing the opportunities of rivals; and (2) that either (2a) do not benefit consumers at all, or (2b) are unnecessary for the particular consumer benefits claimed for them, or (2c) produce harms disproportionate to any resulting benefits. In addition, the practice must be reasonably susceptible to judicial control, which means that the court must be able to identify the conduct as anticompetitive and either fashion an appropriate deterrent or an equitable remedy likely to improve competition.'). See, further, Gavil, *supra* note 32, at 61–4 (calling this test '*the disproportionality test*' and observing that it is in line with the traditional monopolization analysis both requiring the harm to outweigh the good *significantly* and assuming that any doubts in connection to the balance would be resolved in favor of the monopolist).

[72] See Alese, *supra* note 19, at 206–208 (arguing that this approach could be applicable to exclusive agreements, refusals to supply, and contractual and technological tying). Such a test is premised on the idea that a monopolist should not be allowed to limit its rivals' market opportunities. Therefore, whereas behaviors that produce 'Stigler-alike' barriers to entry are inherent in the notion of proper competition and, hence, cannot be forbidden, practices that

antitrust authorities to distinguish clearly the species of the regarded conduct's effects, whereas in earlier cases authorities generally did not identify them. These tests are, however, very difficult to apply but for structuring them with the help of safe harbors, presumptions, burden of proof and standard of proof rules.[73]

US AND EU ANTITRUST LAW'S PAST AND PRESENT OBJECTIVES IN DEALING WITH DOMINANT FIRMS' CONDUCT

Over the years antitrust law has constantly reflected the current political concerns and values.[74] Indeed it can be acknowledged with a certain degree of simplification that both US courts and EU antitrust institutions have enforced competition rules regarding monopolies for pursuing a variety of aims, somewhat overlapping,[75] somehow divergent.[76] For

---

create barriers that change the existing market conditions putting monopolists' rivals at a disadvantage must be held unlawful. Such an approach, being focused on the entry mechanism, offers a platform for considering dynamic market inquiries. Yet, there are so many different ways of understanding and conceptualizing the dynamic of markets that focusing only on entry barriers will not be always correct.

[73] See, Bruzzone, Boccaccio, *supra* note 22; Andrew I. Gavil, William E. Kovacic, & Jonathan B. Baker, *Antitrust Law in Perspective: Cases, Concepts and Problems in Competition Policy* 76–7 (2008); Robert W. Crandall & Clifford Winston, 'Does Antitrust Policy Improve Consumer Welfare? Assessing the Evidence', 17 *J. Econ. Perspectives* 3 (2003); and Jonathan B. Baker, 'The Case for Antitrust Enforcement', 17 *J. Econ. Perspectives* 27 (2003).

[74] See Whish, *supra* note 6, at 19; and Gavil, Kovacic & Baker, *supra* note 73, at 163.

[75] Consider that the origins and purposes of the Sherman Act have been the subject of a long-running and intense debate. See, e.g., Robert H. Bork, 'Legislative Intent and the Policy of the Sherman Act', 9 *J. L. & Econ.* 7, 714 (1966) (identifying efficiency as the Sherman Act framers' overriding purpose); Robert H. Lande, 'Wealth Transfers as the Original and Primary Concern of Antitrust: The Efficiency Interpretation Challenged', 34 *Hastings L. J.* 65, 93–6 (1982) (responding to Bork's position, arguing that preventing wealth transfers was the Sherman Act framers' primary purpose). Other commentators have emphasized additional historical, legal, social, and economic factors that may have influenced the Sherman Act's drafters. For example, Professor Rudolph Peritz has described the Sherman Act as the product of a factional conflict between those adhering to two differing, recurring 'rhetoric' of competition, reflecting comparatively greater emphasis on equality and liberty, respectively. See generally Rudolph J. R. Peritz, *Competition Policy in America 1888–1992: History, Rhetoric, Law* (1996). Professor James May has emphasized the influence of the economic and political vision at the heart of contemporary 'laissez-faire constitutionalism,' which strongly encouraged a belief that antitrust law simultaneously could protect economic opportunity, efficiency, competition, fair distribution, and political liberty, through a process of largely nondiscretionary adjudication. See, generally, James May, 'Antitrust in the Formative Era: Political and Economic Theory in Constitutional and Antitrust Analysis, 1880–1918', 50 *Ohio St. L. J.* 257 (1989). For additional perspectives

instance, though during different periods, both the US and the EU public debate over dominant firms' conduct pivoted around the aim of protecting small businesses (in the EU words, SME) against the 'dictatorship' of big, concentrated, and vertical integrated businesses.[77] In particular, such a favor for small business' welfare and, hence, for dominant firms' rivals – a favor that remains an important source of political support in the public arena – has been fed not only by lobbying activity,[78] but also by a skein of ill-founded fears, economic theories, and high political ideals:[79] from a general laissez faire alarm about bigness as such,[80] to the economic misconception that good market performances rest only

---

on the Sherman Act and its origins, see William H. Page, 'Ideological Conflict and the Origins of Antitrust Policy', 66 *Tul. L. Rev.* 1 (1991); Edward O. Correia, 'Antitrust and Liberalism', 40 *Antitrust Bull.* 99 (1995); Thomas C. Arthur, 'Farewell to the Sea of Doubt: Jettisoning the Constitutional Sherman Act', 74 *Cal. L. Rev.* 263 (1986); John J. Flynn, 'The Reagan Administration's Antitrust Policy, "Original Intent" and the Legislative History of the Sherman Act', 33 *Antitrust Bull.* 259 (1988); and Eleanor M. Fox, 'The Politics of Law and Economics in Judicial Decision Making: Antitrust as a Window', 61 *N.Y.U. L. Rev.* 554 (1986).

[76] In connection to the legislative history of Section 2, see Herbert Hovenkamp, 'The Marginalist Revolution in Legal Thought', 46 *Vand. L. Rev.* 305 (1993) (arguing that such a story does not point consistently in favor of any of the possible objectives that antitrust law can pursue. In particular since, on the one hand, economics was not highly sophisticated when the framers drafted the Sherman Act and, on the other hand, politicians hedge their statements, the modern distinctions between the possible aims of antitrust law cannot be carried back to the end of the nineteenth century). Instead, in connection to the legislative history of Article 102, see Pinar Akman, *Searching for the long-lost soul of article 82 EC* (2007), http://ssrn.com.

[77] See Hans B. Thorelli, *The Federal Antitrust Policy: Origination of an American Tradition* 84, 227 (1955).

[78] For the US experience, see, e.g., 1 Phillip E. Areeda & Herbert Hovenkamp, *Antitrust Law: An Analysis of Antitrust Principles and their Application* ¶ 100b (3d ed. 2006), where there are more references. For the EU experience see, instead, Claus-Dieter Ehlermann & Laraine L. Laudati, (eds.) *European Competition Law Annual 1997: Objectives of Competition Policy* (1998).

[79] Interestingly, indeed, see Lovdahl Gormsen, *supra* note 24, at 47 and 58 (concurring both with the idea that the 'practical fall-out' of the Ordoliberalism doctrine (see footnote 83) overlaps with the structuralist approach of the first Harvard School (see footnote 81), and with the idea that, however, the Ordoliberalism doctrine has a well-developed political-philosophical flavor of which the Harvard school lacks).

[80] See. e.g., Peritz, *supra* note 75, at 302; Ian S. Forrester, *Article 82:* 'Remedies in Search of Theories?', *Fordham Int'l L. J.* 919, 920 (2005); Gunnar Niels & Adriaan Kate, 'Introduction: Antitrust in the U.S. and the EU – Converging or Diverging Paths?', 49 *Antitrust Bull.* 1, 11 (2004); and Gifford & Kudrle, *supra* note 2, at 759. Further, see Patrick Van Cayseele & Roger Van den Bergh, 'Antitrust Law', in *Encyclopedia of Law and Economics* 467 (Boudewijn Bouckaert & Gerrit De Geest, eds. 1999) (arguing that the importance given to competition as a process of rivalry taking place between large and small competitors in open and accessible markets links the Sherman Act to classic economics' favor for laissez faire).

with non-concentrated markets,[81] to the Jeffersonian-Jacksonian[82] as well as Ordoliberal[83] concern that economic power concentration would impair open and free markets, personal independence, political pluralism, and democracy.[84] In particular, according to this worldview, striking

---

[81] As seen in Chapter 1, the structural approach of the first Harvard School, which clearly arises in *United States v. Aluminum Co. of Am.*, 91 F.Supp. 333 (1950), pivoted around the idea that small business can guarantee good market performances in terms of prices, quantity, quality, variety and innovation. Yet, such a postulate does not hold either when it comes to scale economies and innovation (see Chapter 1), or when it comes to distinguishing between dominant firms' behaviors that *both* harm competitors *and* improve market performances in terms of prices, quantity, quality, variety and innovation, on the one hand, and monopolists' practices that harm competitors *without* improving those market performances. See, in this regard, footnote 131.

[82] Indeed, both the Jeffersonian and the Jacksonian democracies defended small-, local-, and individually- owned enterprises in contrast to large, absentee-owned, and possibly corrupt big firms. In other words, they urged a deconcentrated society, where small businesses could enjoy equality-enhancing opportunities and preserve their free and independent decision-making. Hence, boosting inter-firm rivalry, guaranteeing free market access, and fighting economic power concentrations – even in the form of mergers and cartels – was crucial. Indeed, consider that US antitrust decisions abound with statements suggesting that antitrust laws are 'as important to the preservation of economic freedom and our free-enterprise system as the Bill of Rights is to the protection of our fundamental personal freedoms'. See *United States v. Topco* 405 U.S. 596, 610 (1972). See, e.g., Areeda & Hovenkamp, *supra* note 78, at ¶¶111.a and 111.e; E. Thomas Sullivan, *The Political Economy of the Sherman Act: The First One Hundred Years* (1990); Donald I. Baker & William Blumenthal, 'Ideological Cycles and Unstable Antitrust Rules', 31 *Antitrust Bull.* 323, 324–25 (1986); and Arthur Schlesinger Jr., *The Cycles of American History* 220–23 and 242 (1986).

[83] The role that the Ordoliberal School played in the drafting of Article 102 has generally been derived from the circumstances where the treaty was drafted and because of the people involved, though this origin has never been articulated in any formal Community document or decision. See, in this regard, O'Donoghue & Padilla, *supra* note 6, at 4; David J. Gerber, 'Law and the Abuse of Economic Power' in *Europe*, 62 *Tulane L. Rev.* 85 (1998); id., *Law and Competition in Twentieth-Century Europe. Protecting Prometheus* 264 (2001); Wernhard Möschel, 'Competition Policy from an Ordo Point of View', in *German Neo-liberals and the Social Market Economy* 146 (Alan Peacock and Hans Willgerodt, eds. 1989); Katalin J. Cseres, *Competition Law and Consumer Protection* 82 (2005); Eilmansberger, *supra* note 46, at 132; Eleanor M. Fox, 'We Protect Competition, You Protect Competitors', 26 *World Competition* 149 (2003); Michal S. Gal, 'Monopoly Pricing as an Antitrust Offense in the U.S. and the EC: Two Systems of Belief About Monopoly?', 49 *Antitrust Bull.* 343, 364 (2004). Moreover, several scholars have noticed that the traces of the Ordoliberal school can be found in many early decisions such as, among the non-pricing abuses, Joined Cases 6 & 7/73, *Istituto Chemioterapico Italiano SpA and Commercial Solvents Corp v. Commission*, March 6, 1974, [1974] ECR 223 and Case 22/78, *Hugin Kassaregister AB and Hugin Cash Registers Ltd v. Commission*, March 31, 1979, [1979] ECR 1869. See, e.g., Liza Lovdahl Gormsen, 'Article 82: Where are We Coming from and Where are We Going to?', 2 *Comp. L. Rev.* 5, 7–8 (2006); James S. Venit, 'Article 82: The Last Frontier – Fighting Fire with Fire?', 28 *Fordham Int'l L. J.* 1157 (2005); Duncan Sinclair, 'Abuse of Dominance at a Crossroads – Potential Effect, Object and Appreciability under Article 82 EC', 8 *E.C.L.R.* 491, 494 (2004), and J. Bruce McDonald, 'Section 2 and Article 82: Cowboys and Gentlemen' (2005), available at www.usdoj.gov/atr/public/speeches/210873.htm.

[84] Consider that for Adam Smith competition was 'a simple system of natural liberty', meaning an absence of restraint and, in particular, restraints of free entry into industries.

dominant firms' restrictions of small business opportunities and choices[85] guaranteed democratic freedom, political stability, and social order.[86]

Further, over the years, US courts and EU antitrust institutions have enforced Section 2 and Article 102 in the name of both fairness and justice, as if the antitrust provisions were rules against unfair competition,[87] and equity and redistribution, so as to allow wealth transfer in favor of consumers – another very appealing argument for sustaining antitrust enforcement in public debates.[88]

Differently, only Article 102 has served as a complement to the rules governing the creation of the European common market, in order to

---

Moreover, Marshall labeled competition as 'economic freedom'. Therefore, it should not come as a surprise if this kind of political conception of competition has often been entrenched with the idea of competition as a process. In other words, stating that antitrust law should protect economic agents' freedom is not far from stating that it should protect rivalry.

[85] Treating small firms favorably does not necessarily mean acting against the protection of consumer welfare, unless it entails artificially helping small firms to survive when they are not operating at an efficient scale. Interestingly, as Chapter 5 shows, nowadays the European Commission seems to favor small and medium-sized firms, assuming that they more likely to innovate. In accord, O'Donoghue & Padilla, *supra* note 6, at 22.

[86] In connection to the Ordoliberal root of Article 102, see Akman, *supra* note 76, at 33 (arguing that from the analysis of the *travaux préparatoires* it arises that Article 102 does not result from the Ordoliberal thinking for two reasons, at least. First, a truly Ordoliberal rule would have prohibited dominant positions as such, would have envisaged their divestiture and would have provided the control of conduct only for those dominant undertakings which cannot be divested. Instead the drafters and, in particular, the German delegation, supposedly influenced by Ordoliberalism, although they had a *tabula rasa*, chose to forbid only dominant firms abusing their power – and that against the true 'Ordoliberal' proposal of the French delegation that wanted to prohibit dominant positions themselves. Second, looking at the words of the drafters, Article 102 was intended to protect dominant firms' customers rather than dominant firms' competitors. In other words, the drafters did not perceive harming rivals as synonymous with harming competition. Indeed, their suggestion was that if rules protecting competitors were to be included in the Treaty, this had to be done separately from the rules on competition, under rules for 'unfair competition'.). Given the *travaux préparatoires*, hence, it is likely that the original soul of Article 102 has been partially misunderstood during the earlier enforcement of the provision: the drafters were concerned with productive inefficiency and the 'quiet monopoly life' typical of monopolies. For a detailed analysis of the 'Drafting History, Ideologies and Major Players' in the process of Article 102's development, see Rousseva, *supra* note 44, at 9-57.

[87] See, e.g., Louis B. Schwartz, '"Justice" and other Non-Economic Goals of Antitrust', 127 *U. Pa. L. Rev.* 1076 (1979); and Carl Kaysen & Donald F. Turner, *Antitrust Policy: An Economic and Legal Analysis* 16 (1959).

[88] See, e.g., Lande, *supra* note 75; and Herbert Hovenkamp, 'Distributive Justice and the Antitrust Laws', 51 *Geo. Wash. L. Rev.* 1 (1982). Using antitrust for protecting consumers is questionable. Arguably, since everybody is a consumer, a real populist approach would have promoted consumer welfare. Indeed, US populism did care about consumer welfare, as it believed that preventing injuries to competitors was the way to prevent injuries to consumers. The weakness of such an argument is that the link between rivals exiting in the short run, and over-competitive prices in the long run, is not to be taken for granted. See, in this regard, Areeda & Hovenkamp, *supra* note 78, at ¶100.b, where there are further references; and Robert Pitofsky, 'The Political Content of Antitrust', 127 *U. Pa. L. Rev.* 1051 (1979).

prevent dominant firms from using their power for partitioning the internal market along national boundaries and for limiting competition across borders.[89] Indeed, European competition policy was enacted in the immediate aftermath of World War II as a means toward a new integrated and prosperous legal order,[90] where centuries of rivalries and bloody conflicts could be substituted by a broader and deeper community.

Finally, nowadays the two jurisdictions seem to agree – at least, this is what appears from the public statements – in considering the 'protection of consumer welfare' as the aim of Section 2 and Article 102. In particular, they both recognize that, *absent a clear model of rivalry*, to protect the process of competition requires focusing on the *results of this process*, that is to say, on the impact that economic models suggest that firms' behaviors are expected to produce on welfare.[91]

In fact, it is since the advent of the Chicago School that US courts started focusing on practices that harm consumer welfare,[92] recently

---

[89] Indeed, see Hans von der Groeben, 'The Role of Competition in the Common Market', in *American Bar Association, Proceedings of the Conference on Antitrust and the European Communities* 14, 18 (1963), arguing that EC competition policy had three purposes: (i) preventing firms or member states from erecting barriers to trade to replace those dismantled by the EC; (ii) promoting integration; and (iii) safeguarding an economic and social order based on freedom for businessmen, consumers, and workers. Further see Ivo Van Bael, Jean-Francois Bellis, *Competition Law of the European Community* (2004); Giuliano Marenco, 'The Birth of Modern Competition Law in Europe', in *European Integration and International Coordination: Studies in Transnational Economic Law in honour of C.D. Ehlermann* 2001 (Armin von Bogandy et al. eds. 2002); James B. Kobak, Jr., 'Running the Gauntlet: Antitrust and Intellectual Property Pitfalls on the Two Sides of the Atlantic', 64 *Antitrust L. J.* 341, 352 (1996); Jebsen & Stevens, *supra* note 14, at 449, and Forrester, *supra* note 80, at 929 (arguing that 'the analysis of many competition questions in Europe is distorted by the unique significance attached to market integration under our competition law. Pursuing the civil religion by honoring cross-border trade more than other economic activity is a well-established phenomenon.').

[90] Indeed, Article 102 encompasses several of the founding political, economic, and social aims of the EC Treaty, which aimed at creating a 'new legal order of international law'. See Case 26/62, *NV Algemene Transport en Expeditie Onderneming van Gend & Loos v. Netherlands Inland Revenue Administration*, [1963] ECR 95.

[91] See, in this regard, Bruzzone, Boccaccio, *supra* note 21, at 13 (arguing as to the EU approach that it is 'based on two pillars: competition has to be seen as a rule of conduct (rivalry, process, competition on the merits) and, at the same time, the rules establishing the boundaries between unlawful and legitimate business conduct have to be formulated considering the external impact that the conduct [. . .] would have on the market.'); and Dayagi-Epstein, *supra* note 21, at 76 (arguing for the cumulative nature of the two requisites: harm to competitive process and harm to consumer welfare).

[92] See, e.g., Douglas H. Ginsburg, 'An Introduction to Bork' (1966), 2 *Competition Pol'y Int'l* 225, 230 (2006) (observing that the Supreme Court has endorsed allocative efficiency as the fundamental value underlying the antitrust law); Terry Calvani & Craig Sibarium, 'Antitrust Today: Maturity or Decline', 35 *Antitrust Bull.* 123 (1990); and Lawrence A. Sullivan, 'Antitrust, Microeconomics, and Politics: Reflection on Some Recent Relationships', 68 *Cal. L. Rev.* 1, 2 (1980) (explaining how efficiency became a crucial objective in the US jurisprudence).

US courts have reaffirmed that to be condemned as anticompetitive, a monopolist's conduct must harm the competitive process and thereby harm consumers.[93]

As to the EU experience, it is with its 2009 Communication,[94] titled *Guidance on the Commission's Enforcement Priorities in Applying Article 82 of the EC Treaty to Abusive Exclusionary Conduct by Dominant Undertakings*,[95] that the Commission has definitely declared that Article 102 has to be intended as a tool for protecting consumer welfare.[96] Better, in the 2009 Communication the Commission states expressly with economic jargon that it wants to prosecute those practices that, by impairing effective access of actual or potential competitors to supplies or markets, allow monopolists to profitably increase price, reduce output, and reduce consumer choice.[97] In other words, now the European Commission deems

---

[93] *United States v. Microsoft*, 253 F.3d 53, 58 (D.C. Circ. 2001) and *Rambus Inc. v. FTC*, 522 F.3d 456, 463 (D.C. Cir. 2008).

[94] This document has been elaborated in order to fix the Commission's enforcement priorities and to explain its practice, so to 'provide greater clarity and predictability as regards the general framework of analysis which the Commission employs in determining whether it should pursue cases concerning various forms of exclusionary conduct and to help undertakings better assess whether certain behavior is likely to result in intervention by the Commission under Article 82' – § 2. Nevertheless, the document represents a piece of soft law as it is not 'intended to constitute a statement of the law and is without prejudice to the interpretation of Article 82 by the Court of Justice or the Court of First Instance of the European Communities.' – § 3. Moreover, EU courts remain free to 'adapt the approach set out in [the] Communication to the extent that this would appear to be reasonable and appropriate in a given case' (§ 8).

[95] The debate concerning the reform of Article 102 started with the so-called 2005 Discussion paper, DG *Competition Discussion Paper on the application of Article 82 of the Treaty to exclusionary abuses*, Brussels, December 2005, available at www.europa.eu.int. Indeed, there the DG Competition stated its firm intention to modify Article 102's purpose, referring to 'the protection of competition on the market as a means of enhancing consumer welfare and of ensuring an efficient allocation of resources', and clarifying that, 'this means that it is competition, and not competitors as such, that is to be protected'. 'The purpose of Article 102 is not to protect competitors from dominant firms' genuine competition based on factors such as higher quality, novel products, opportune innovation, or otherwise better performance' – see §§ 4 and 54. See, e.g., Victoria Mertikopoulou, *DG's* 'Competition Discussion Paper on the Application of Article 82 of The EC Treaty to Exclusionary Abuses: The Proposed Economic Reform From a Legal Point of View', 28 *ECLR* 241 (2007). Further, see EAGCP, 'An Economic Approach to Article 82', available at http://ec.europa.eu/comm/competition/antitrust/art82/index.html for the economic document upon which the Discussion paper premised upon.

[96] For a discussion of how the pursuit of consumer welfare has characterized the early and recent EU case law see Lovdahl Gormsen, *supra* note 24, at 69.

[97] See 2009 Communication, *supra* note 24, §§ 11 and 19. By reading this formulation, which looks at the harm to rivals as a vehicle for producing other effects on the market, it can be stated that the EU approach has now totally disregarded the protection of competitors as such. Indeed, in the 2009 Communication, the Commission has clarified that: (i) dominant firms are 'entitled to compete on the merits' despite having 'a special responsibility not to allow [their] conduct to impair genuine undistorted competition on the common market'

harm to consumer welfare as the outcome of a bad-functioning, distorted rivalry – so dear to the framers of the treaty[98] – and, therefore, chooses it as a workable and administrable standard for judging dominant firms'

(§ 1); (ii) it intends to prevent dominant firms from excluding their competitors by other means than competing on the merits; and (iii) dominant firms' competitors 'who deliver less to consumers in terms of price, choice, quality and innovation will leave the market' (§ 6). Therefore, with these statements the Commission has (finally) given a new look to the old fashioned 'special responsibility slogan' that has characterized the EU experience since the 1970s. Now this slogan does not serve to limit dominant firms' ability to compete as if they were their rivals' trustee; it does not serve to give dominant firms' competitors an alibi for their inefficiencies; but rather it serves to only specify that some unilateral conduct can be harmful only when endorsed by monopolists. Indeed, the CFI and the ECJ address what should be the behavior of a dominant firm stating that, 'dominant undertakings have a special responsibility not to allow their conduct to impair genuine undistorted competition on the common market. This special responsibility also means that the onus is on such companies to behave in a way [that] is proportionate to the objectives they seek to achieve. This implies that a conduct [that] may be permissible in a normal competitive situation may amount to an abuse if carried out by dominant firms'. For this text-book quotation, see the recent case of AstraZeneca, June 15, 2005, http://ec.europa.eu/comm/competition/antitrust/cases/decisions/37507/en.pdf, § 325. Some scholars therefore have observed that Article 102 cast upon dominant firms a kind of affirmative duty not to exclude competitors. See, e.g., Eleanor M. Fox, 'Abuse of Dominance and Monopolization: How to Protect Competition without Protecting Competitors', in *European Competition Law Annual: 2003 What Is an Abuse of Dominance Position?* 69, 70 (Claus-Dieter Ehlermann & Laraine L. Laudati, eds. 2006) and other scholars that, indeed, deem such an approach as a result of the Ordoliberal school, such as Ekaterina Rousseva, 'The Concept of 'Objective Justification' of an Abuse of a Dominant Position: Can It Help to Modernize the Analysis under Article 82 EC?', 2 *Comp. L. Rev.* 27, 30 (2006); and Bloch et al., *supra* note 36, at 141. Nevertheless, an even more descriptive interpretation of the 'slogan' is conceivable, as the CFI seemed to believe in T-191/98, *DSR-Senator Lines GmbH v Commission*, ECR 1999 II-02531, § 1460. After all, similar descriptive statements addressing the different treatment reserved to firms with monopoly power also characterized the US case law. See, e.g., *United States v. Dentsply Int'l, Inc.*, 399 F.3d 181, 187 (3d Cir. 2005) and *LePage's Inc. v. 3M*, 324 F.3d 141, 151-152 (3d Cir. 2003).

[98] Indeed, one of the Treaty's aims is 'a system ensuring that competition in the internal market is not distorted'. See further footnotes 83, 84, 86 and accompanying text. Because of whether the Ordoliberal school, or the concern for economic growth, EU competition law has often been sensitive to the dynamic aspects of competition and, hence, to operative market conditions. In other words, it has valued openness, access, absence of barriers, rivalry and the competitive structure of markets as mechanisms to produce economic welfare, competitiveness, innovation, and market integration. See Akman, *supra* note 76, at 1 (arguing that from the reading of the *travaux préparatoires* of the EC Treaty, the boosting of economic growth and productive efficiency was the main concern that has influenced the drafting of Article 102); David J. Gerber, 'The Future of Article 82: Dissecting the Conflict 8', paper presented at the 12th Annual Competition Law and Policy Workshop, Robert Schuman Centre EUI, Florence (2007), available at http://www.eui.eu/RSCAS/Research/Competition/2007(papers).shtml (arguing that 'the goal of reducing competitive distortion was specifically intended to improve the capacity of the competitive process to generate economic benefits'); and Eleanor M. Fox, *The Efficiency Paradox, in How the Chicago School Overshot the Mark. The Effects of Conservative Economic Analysis on U.S. Antitrust* 77, (R. Pitofsky ed. 2008). Nevertheless, the European Commission has never elaborated a test for assessing how well the process of competition works.

behaviors.[99] After all, EU antitrust institutions have recently affirmed that article 102 covers not only behaviors that may prejudice consumers directly (see the so-called exploitative abuses), but also practices that indirectly harm them by impairing the effective competitive structure.[100] Further, in the EU jurisdiction the importance of consumer welfare has some pedigree in the wording of Article 102(b), which speaks of 'prejudice to consumers', [101] and in Article 120 of the TFUE, which claim for the pursuit of 'an efficient allocation of resources'.[102]

In sum, although US antitrust authorities look for actual harm to consumer welfare, while EU antitrust authorities hunt for potential harm to consumer welfare, and although the Reagan and Bush administrations have discouraged interventions against practices that do not *clearly* harm consumer welfare, [103] the two antitrust jurisdictions[104] now recognize that

---

[99] In other words, in the 2009 Communication, *supra* note 24, the Commission establishes a relationship between the concept of 'competition as a rivalry' and the concept of 'competition as a state of affairs', by deeming consumer harm a consequence of the described twofold circumstance: (i) harm to effective access of actual or potential competitors to supplies or markets; and (ii) price increase, output reduction, and the restriction of consumer choice. See, e.g., Phillip Lowe, 'Consumer Welfare and Efficiency: New Guiding Principles of Competition Policy?', 27 March 2007, the 13th International Conference on Conmpetition and 14th European Competition, 2; and Girogio Monti, *EC Competition Law* 22 (2007) (arguing in favor of the focus upon the outcomes of the competitive process).

[100] See ECJ, case C-95/04 P, *British Airways v. Commission*, 2007 ECR I-2231, § 106 and CFI, case T-201/04, *Microsoft v. Commission*, 2007 ECR II-3601, § 664.

[101] See 2009 Communication, *supra* note 24, at §§ 11 and 19. That said, it must be acknowledged that in the 2009 Communication the Commission also clarified that Article 102 'is particularly important in the context of the wider objective of achieving an integrated internal market', id., at § 1. Thus, it is true that the process of market integration has made several steps forward so that the will to create a common market may be less urgent than it was in the past, leaving room to pursue other objectives. LarsHendrik Röller & Oliver Stehmann, 'The Year 2005 at DG Competition: The Trend towards a more Effects-based Approach', 29 *Review of Industrial Organization* 281, 282 (2005).

[102] Indeed, Commissioner Neelie Kroes has frequently specified that consumer welfare is the standard that the Commission applies for assessing antitrust rules' infringements, and that innovation is one of the objectives of competition policy. See Neelie Kroes, 'European Competition Policy: Delivering Better Markets and Better Choices' (2005), SPEECH/05/12, http://europa.eu.int. Moreover, Commissioner Monti summarized the Treaty as acknowledging 'the fundamental role of the market and of competition in guaranteeing consumer welfare, in encouraging the optimal allocation of resources, and in granting to economic agents the appropriate incentives to pursue productive efficiency, quality, and innovation'. See Mario Monti, 'European Competition Policy for the 21st Century', speech at The Fordham Corporate Law Institute, 28 Annual Conference on International Antitrust Law and Policy, October 20, 2000, available at http://www.europa.eu.int/comm/competition/speeches/. See Damian Chalmers et al., *European Union Law, Text And Materials* 936-937 (2006) (commenting about the importance of Commissioners' personalities).

[103] See, e.g., William F. Shughart II, 'The Fleeting Reagan Antitrust Revolution', 45 *Antitrust Bulletin* 271 (2000); Gary Minda, 'Antitrust at Century's End', 48 *S.M.U. L. Rev.* 1749, 1769 (1995) (arguing that the Chicagoan influence has unleashed ideological warfare against the other goals of competition law to the point that even antitrust as such has been

such harm is an indication that the competitive process has been, or is likely to be, impaired. They end up pursuing *at the same time*,[105] *the same objective* – that is, the protection of consumer welfare – which incidentally does not happen to be the one that economists suggest,[106] perhaps because of its political appeal.

In the past, instead, the described multi-tasking conception of antitrust law has caused a twofold problem of inconsistency: inconsistency over time inside each jurisdiction, so that in each jurisdiction it happens that present antitrust authorities take decisions that no past authority would have endorsed; and inconsistency over time and across the Atlantic Ocean, so that it happens that EU antitrust authorities have taken some decisions that US competition authorities would have not concurred with.[107]

---

questioned); Robert H. Lande, 'The Rise and (Coming) Fall of Efficiency as the Ruler of Antitrust', 33 *Antitrust Bulletin* 429 (1988); Eleanor M. Fox, Lawrence A. Sullivan, 'Antitrust – Retrospective and Prospective: Where Are We Coming From? Where Are We Going?' 62 *NYUL Rev.* 936 (1987). See, further, Deborah A. Garza, 'A Comparative Analysis of the Clinton Antitrust Program and Suggestion of Changes to Come', 15 *Antitrust* 64 (2001) (arguing that the Clinton administration had a post-Chicagoan approach with less faith in the market and greater confidence in the ability of government to correct perceived 'market imperfections'.). Given that the same reasoning about the swings of the US antitrust policy can be replicated as well for the Bush-Obama administrations, what is however important to recall is that, as seen in Chapter 1, the differences between the Chicagoan and post-Chicagoan approaches do not regard the objectives of antitrust law but the 'enforcing energy'.

104 *Contra* Drexl, *supra* note 32, at 2.

105 In particular, as nowadays EU antitrust law is experiencing a change toward the protection of consumer welfare that approaches the revolution that US competition law experienced in the mid-to-late 1970s with the advent of the Chicago School, it has been argued that the US antitrust authorities have seemed to supply the 'right answers' to competition problems or, at least, this phenomenon has given to US institutions the opportunity to argue against EU institutions that 'we thought that before you, and now we know that it doesn't work' – see for this opinion, David J. Gerber, 'Competition Law' chapter in the *Oxford Handbook of Comparative Law* 1 (2005), http://ssrn.com. Further, for the idea that EU antitrust institutions are following their US counterparts, see Stephen Martin, 'The Goals of Antitrust and Competition Policy' 6 and 72 (2007) http://ssrn.com (arguing that 'U.S. antitrust began serving a range of goals, some economic in a narrow sense and some rooted more in political economy. As the U.S. economy matured, antitrust minimized its political and social goals and emphasized pursuit of good market performance in strictly economic senses; so, in the fullness of time, one might then expect, will EU competition policy.'). To be sure, Martin also suggested another explanation for the differences between the US and the EU approaches – an explanation that focuses on the relationship between public power and private power that the conclusions discusses.

106 If economists were called to fix competition law's objectives, they would use antitrust rules to protect total welfare. Indeed, aiming at guaranteeing such a variable rescues the enforcement activity from any distributive concern – which, on the contrary, is a good argument in the political arena. Moreover, by playing again the appropriability argument, it can be maintained that protecting total welfare tends to favor long-run efficiency gains and innovation, by guaranteeing firms higher short-run profits. See Dennis W. Carlton, 'Does Antitrust Need to be Modernized?', 21 *The Journal of Economic Perspectives* 155, 157–9 (2007).

107 See, e.g., Lovdahl Gormsen, supra note 24, at 82; Whish, supra note 6, at 23; Paolo Buccirossi, 'Introduction', in *Handbook of Antitrust Economics X* (Paolo Buccirossi ed. 2008);

US AND EU LEGAL STANDARDS FOR DETECTING DOMINANT FIRMS' UNLAWFUL CONDUCT

Though earlier US decisions on dominant firms' unilateral conduct tended to focus on intuitions that lacked a clear economic foundation,[108] to assert that US courts have enforced competition law disregarding economic analysis would be a mistake. Since *United States v. Addystone Pipe & Steel Co.*,[109] indeed, they have abandoned alternative interpretative tools, such as the Sherman Act drafters' intent and common law rules, to rely upon economic concepts and theories. Thus, the reason why some earlier decisions sound, however, at odds with what today authorities would decide could be just that the past economic thinking was not really sophisticated or,[110] at least, reached conclusions that the present economics has overcome.

In applying such economic analysis to Section 2 cases US courts, after abandoning the structuralist 'small-business-friendly' approach that culminated in *Alcoa*,[111] have endorsed several of the above-mentioned economic tests. For instance, the sacrifice test has been enforced in some refusal to deal cases such as *Aspen*,[112] and *Trinko*,[113] and in predatory pricing cases such as *Brooke Group*.[114] The equally efficient test has been applied in

---

Roger Van den Bergh, 'Modern Industrial Organization versus Old-Fashioned European Competition Law', 17 *European Competition Law Review* 75 (1996) (arguing that in the 1990s European competition law was at the same stage of development as American antitrust law was in the 1960s). Indeed, when the Treaty of Rome was enacted the US Supreme Court was applying antitrust law to protect the viability of small and middle-sized businesses, to preserve the freedom of action of independent business people, and to disperse economic and political power. See in this last regard Eleanor Fox, 'Monopolization and Dominance in the United States and the European Community: Efficiency, Opportunity and Fairness', 61 *Notre Dame L. Rev.* 981, 983 (1986).

108 O'Donoghue & Padilla, *supra* note 6, at 178–9 (arguing that courts did not ask whether dominant firms have the incentive or ability to engage in harmful practices for harming consumer welfare; and they failed to consider whether, and to what extent, those business practices result from efforts to achieve efficiencies). The case of the leverage theory is paradigmatic. In this regard, see Chapter 5.

109 85 Fed. 271 (6th Circ. 1898).

110 See, e.g., Herbert Hovenkamp, 'The Sherman Act and the Classical Theory of Competition', 74 *Iowa L. Rev.* 1019 (1989); and Rudolph Peritz, *supra* note 75, *passim* (arguing that US courts did apply economics before the New Deal).

111 *United States v. Aluminum Co. of America*, 148 F. 2d 416 (2d Cir. 1945).

112 *Aspen Skiing Co. v. Aspen Highlands Skiing Corp.*, 472 U.S. 585, 610–11 (1985).

113 *Trinko, passim*. Actually, the Supreme Court majority opinion did not expressly refer to the sacrifice test, yet it justified past cases in which a duty to deal was imposed on the basis that the defendant was foregoing a more profitable course of conduct in refusing to deal.

114 Brooke Group, note 2; *A.A. Poultry Farms v. Rose Acre Farms*, 881 F.2d 1396, 1400–1401 (7th Cir. 1989), cert. denied, 494 U.S. 1019 (1990) (advocating recoupment test).

LePage's.[115] In *Microsoft*[116], instead, the court used a kind of consumer welfare test, articulated in the following prongs: the plaintiff, who bears first the burden of proof, must demonstrate that the monopolist's conduct harms the competitive process and thereby harms consumer welfare; then, it turns to the defendant to offer a justification for its conduct by explaining, for instance, that it allows the achievement of efficiency gains, or better and new products or production processes. If the monopolist shows that its conduct is indeed a form of competition on the merits, then the burden shifts back to the plaintiff to rebut that claim. Therefore, if the monopolist's justification stands unrebutted, then the plaintiff must demonstrate that the conduct's harm to consumer welfare outweighs the benefits that the very same conduct entails.[117]

Turning instead to the EU approach, it must be recalled that over time antitrust authorities have not always explained firms' behaviors by

---

[115] *LePage's, Inc. v. 3M*, 324 F.3d 141, 155 (3d cir. 2003) (en banc), cert. denied, 542 U.S. 953 (2004). See, also, *Barry Wright Corp. v. ITT Grinnell Corp.*, 724 R2d 227, 232 (1st cir. 1983) (noting that an 'avoidable' or 'incremental' cost test for predatory pricing is irrational because it would be less costly for the defendant to halt production; and moreover, 'equally efficient competitors cannot permanently match this low price and stay in business'); and *MCI Communic. Corp. v. AT&T*, 708 R2d 1081, 1113 (7th Circ. 1983), cert. denied, 464 U.S. 891 (1983); *Borden, Inc. v. FTC*, 674 Fad 498, 515 (6th Circ. 1982) vacated on other grounds, 461 U.S. 940 (1983); and *Ortho Diagnostic System, Inc. v. Abbott Laboratories*, 920 F. Supp. 455, 466–7 (S.D.N.Y. 1996) (stating that 'below-cost pricing, unlike pricing at or above that level, carries with it the threat that the party so engaged will drive equally efficient competitors out of business, thus setting the stage for recoupment at the expense of consumers').

[116] *United States v. Microsoft Corp.*, 253 F.3d 34, 58–9 (D.C. Cir. 2001), cert. denied, 534 U.S. 952 (2001).

[117] In 2008 the DOJ issued a Report, titled *Competition and Monopoly: Single-firm Conduct under Section 2 of the Sherman Act*, available at http://www.usdoj.gov/atr/public/press_releases/2008/236975.htm, now already withdrawn, as stated at http://www.usdoj.gov/atr/public/press_releases/2009/245710.htm, suggesting the so-called 'disproportionality test' as the general standard. Under it, a monopolists' conduct should have been condemned if it was likely that its negative effects substantially outweighed its positive effects. In other words, the DOJ proposed a consumer welfare test 'with a foot placed firmly on the defendant's side of the scale', and perhaps this is the reason why the Obama administration chose to withdraw it. See Angland, *supra* note 8, at 6; and Ronald W. Davis, 'The Antitrust Division's Report on Section 2: Firm Foundations for Enforcement or a Bridge to Nowhere?', 23 *Antitrust* 42, 48 (2008). In suggesting this test, hence, it seemed that the DOJ's leading concern was reducing the possibility of false positives, as it arose from the fear that short-run static effects – more readily identified and quantified – would be given more weight than long-run dynamic effects. In other words, it seemed that the DOJ was more worried about the risk of over-deterrence than about that of under-deterrence. Kovacic, the FTC chairman, however, expressed caution about the idea that 'US antitrust doctrine and policy today expose dominant firms to significant, systematic risks attributable to over-inclusive liability rules'. See, in this regard, the statements of the FTC's commissioners, available at http://www.ftc.gov/opa/2008/09/section2.shtm. Further, what seemed clear is that the DOJ was worried about long-run positive effects and not about long-run negative effects.

wondering whether they were efficiency-enhancing, profit-maximizing, or welfare-increasing, but rather discussing whether they were fair and equitable; whether they guaranteed economic pluralism and, hence, political stability; or else, whether those behaviors impaired the creation of the common market.[118] Moreover, in the past, EU competition authorities used to analyze dominant firms' practices according to the above-mentioned form-based approach.[119] Such a kind of analysis, on the one hand, prevented authorities from judging in the same way practices that do produce the same effects, but that have different phenotypes;[120] on the other hand, it was ill-suited for giving room to the positive effects that a practice can produce. In particular, EU antitrust institutions have often combined the form-based approach with the choice not to consider behaviors' objective justifications, which dominant firms put forward, so ending the endorsement of a very formal perspective.[121]

---

[118] See Gerber, *supra* note 98, at 6, (arguing that, 'the concepts of fairness and economic freedom have been used, for example, to provide means of identifying distortions of the competitive process and assessing the extent of such distortions. If conduct causes harm to a competitor using methods that are considered 'unfair' in the marketplace, this may indicate that the conduct is not 'competition on the merits' and, therefore, that it could have a distorting effect on the competitive process'. But then the author cushioned the role of these two concepts by stating that 'the concept [of fairness] is not a 'test' for actually determining that conduct distorts competition; it is rather an indicator of potential distortion. [. . . and analogously] the concept [of economic freedom] is insufficiently precise on its own terms to identify conduct as abusive, but it can indicate situations in which further analysis must be used to determine the extent of harm which the conduct poses for the competitive process.').

[119] See, e.g., Lovdahl Gormsen, *supra* note 24, at 59 (discussing about the lack of efficiency analysis); James Kavanagh, Neil Marshall, Gunnar Niels, 'Reform of Article 82 EC – Can the law and economics be reconciled?', in *Article 82 EC: Reflections on Its Recent Evolution* 1, 3 (Ariel Ezrachi ed., 2009) (arguing that lack of consideration for a consistent economic theory of consumer harm morphed dominance into a short-cut to inter-anticompetitive effects); and Whish, *supra* note 6, at 2 (arguing that 'in the early days the role of economics was not particularly emphasized'. Competition law developed in a fairly formalistic way. From the middle of the 1990s onwards the position has changed, 'not least as a result of eminent economists being appointed to some of the most influential positions in institutions entrusted with the application of competition law').

[120] Think, for instance, of price and non-price vertical restraints: from an economic standpoint, they work in the same manner, but competition authorities have always been willing to punish the former more severely than the latter.

[121] To be sure, the objective justification is not a novelty stemming from the 2009 Communication: the ECJ and the CFI have acknowledged its application since the 1970s with the *Sirena* and *Deutsche Grammophon* cases. The 2009 Communication has, however, the merit of stating clearly that an objective justification can come under two forms, that of the 'necessity defence,' born with *Hilti* and *Tetra Pak II*, and that of 'meeting competition,' born with *Irish Sugar*. See, in this regard, Almudena Arpon de Mendivil y de Aldama, 'Exclusionary Conduct and Consumer Welfare: Effects in Competition, Justifications and Efficiencies. What is the Right Balance?', in *International Antitrust & Policy: Annual Proceedings of the Fordham Corporate Law Institute* 2008 1 (Barry E. Hawk ed. 2009); and for a detailed discussion of past experience see, e.g., Katarzyna A. Czapracka, 'Where Antitrust

Nevertheless, in the 2009 Communication, the Commission established that from now on it will base itself on a sound economic, effect-based,[122] analysis on how and whether the reduction in rivalry[123] is likely to lead to consumer-welfare harm.[124]

In particular, the Communication describes the general – but adaptable – two-step consumer welfare test that it will apply to establish whether a particular dominant firm's conduct is unlawful. First, after having established that a firm holds a dominant position, the Commission has to show, based on cogent and convincing evidence,[125] that the allegedly abusive

---

Ends And IP Begins – On The Roots Of The Transatlantic Clashes', 9 *Yale J. L. & Tech.* 44 (2007); Rousseva, *supra* note 97, *passim*; Paul-John Loewenthal, 'The Defence of 'Objective Justification' in the Application of Article 82 EC', 28 *World Competition* 455 (2005); and Philip Lowe, 'DG Competition's Review of the Policy on Abuse of Dominance', in *International Antitrust & Policy: Annual Proceedings of the Fordham Corporate Law Institute* 2003 170 (Barry E. Hawk ed. 2004).

[122] See Kavanagh, Marshall, Niels, *supra* note 119, at 8–9 (arguing that in the 2009 Communication the Commission 'open[ed] the door' to a new effects-based approach by giving consideration to: (i) the degree of dominance; (ii) the degree of foreclosure, (iii) the 'as-efficient' competitor test for pricing abuses; and (iv) the objective justification).

[123] 2009 Communication, *supra* note 24, §§ 16–17.

[124] After all, since the 1990s, European competition law has been undergoing a fundamental reform. Such a change started with the adoption of the so-called Umbrella Regulation No. 2790/1999 on vertical agreements, where the Commission abandoned its form-based approach to embrace the economic-based approach. It continued, following the same line of reform, with the adoption of the Guidelines on the Application of Article 81(3) EC and the new Merger Regulation in 2004. Further, such an approach has been recently implemented in Article 102 cases, such as *Microsoft*. Yet, what is lacking so far is a document that provides guidance on how the Commission articulates such an economic-effects-based approach to exclusionary conduct under Article 102. Competition Commissioner Mario Monti, indeed, announced that 'in making this revision, we have shifted from a legalistic-based approach to an interpretation of the rules based on sound economic principles'. Indeed, already in the 2005 Discussion Paper, the DG Competition stated that 'to establish such a market distorting foreclosure effect it is in general necessary not only to consider the nature or form of the conduct, but also its incidence, i.e. the extent to which the dominant company is applying it in the market, including the market coverage of the conduct or the selective foreclosure of customers to newcomers or residual competitors,' – see Discussion paper, *supra* note 95, § 59. Further on this topic see, e.g., David B. Sher, 'The Last of the Steam Powered Trains – Modernizing Article 82', 5 *E.C.L.R.* 243 (2004); Vickers, *supra* note 46, 415–16; Sven Völcker, 'Developments in EC Competition Law in 2003: An Overview', 41 *Common Market Law Review* 1027, 1048 (2004) (contending that the law on Article 102 'currently lacks a coherent overall approach and remains largely untouched by the increasing focus on economic analysis that has characterized the development of the law and practice under Article 81'). Further, indeed, Article 81(3) provides that a restrictive agreement may escape prohibition if it contributes to improving the production or distribution of goods or promoting technical or economic progress with, *inter alia*, allowing consumers a fair share of the resulting benefit. In addition, Article 2(1) of the Merger Regulation 134/2004 states that, in appraising a merger, the Commission shall take into account, *inter alia*, 'the interests of the intermediate and ultimate consumers, and the development of technical and economic progress provided it is to consumers' advantage and does not form an obstacle to competition'.

[125] The identification of likely consumer harm can rely on (i) qualitative and, where possible and appropriate, quantitative evidence; (ii) direct evidence of any exclusionary strategy,

conduct is *likely* to increase market price, reduce market output, reduce consumer choice, and/or limit innovation. In particular, the Commission assumes that the stronger the dominant firm's market share, the higher the *likelihood* that a practice may lead to these effects. The Commission is thus willing to take into account not only short-term effects (typically price and output effects), but also medium- and long-term effects on innovation, though they are very difficult to assess.[126]

The second step requires the dominant firm to rebut this finding of a likely negative effect by showing that its behavior is likely to create efficiencies which leave the consumers better off overall.[127] As for the potential justifications on which a dominant firm may rely, the Commission states that a dominant undertaking may show that its conduct either is objectively necessary and proportionate, on the basis of factors external to the dominant firm (such as health and safety reasons), or produces substantial efficiencies which outweigh any negative effects on consumer welfare. Regarding this option, the Commission states that the dominant firm must show to a 'sufficient degree of probability' and 'on the basis of verifiable evidence' that: (a) efficiencies have been/are likely to be realized as a result of its conduct; its conduct is indispensable; (b) the likely efficiencies will outweigh any likely negative effects on competition and consumer welfare; (c) and its conduct does not eliminate effective competition, i.e., does not eliminate most sources of potential competition.

---

such as internal documents and evidence of concrete threats of exclusionary action; as well as (iii) direct evidence of actual foreclosure. If the conduct has been in place for a sufficient period of time, the market performance of the dominant firm and its competitors may provide direct evidence about anticompetitive foreclosure: the market share of the dominant firm may have risen; actual competitors may have been marginalized or may have exited, or potential competitors may have tried to enter and failed.

[126] See 2009 Communication, *supra* note at 24, at §§ 20 and 21. Here the Commission explained that the assessment of these effects will usually be made by comparing the actual or likely future situation in the relevant market (with the dominant firm's conduct in place) with an appropriate counterfactual, such as the simple absence of the conduct in question or with another realistic alternative scenario, having regard to established business practices.

[127] Id., at §§ 27–30. After all, Article 102 does not expressly foresee the possibility of 'exempting' abusive behaviors because of the efficiencies they entail when, on the contrary, both Article 101 and the merger regulations consider efficiencies. Thus, for economic reasons and for the sake of consistency, the analysis of efficiencies must be reflected in the analytical framework concerning Article 102.

USE ECONOMICS FOR FORBIDDING DOMINANT FIRMS' CONDUCT THAT STRENGTHEN MARKET POWER AND HARM CONSUMER WELFARE: WHAT ABOUT THE LEGAL PROTECTION OF INNOVATION?

This chapter has started by stating that in order to detect unlawful monopolistic behaviors antitrust authorities have to decide what interests to protect and what kind of analysis to endorse. The above sections, then, have shown that *nowadays* both US and EU antitrust authorities are willing to enforce competition law in order to protect consumer welfare and to describe dominant firms' behaviors by using the economic effects-based approach, though they still diverge in choosing the standard to apply in order to detect monopolists' unlawful conduct. Three clarifications are hence due.

First, it has not always been like that: it can be argued that, as to the antitrust objective and analytical method, EU competition institutions have now achieved the conclusions that US antitrust authorities have elaborated almost 30 years before. Therefore, provided that this does not mean that the past EU case law has to be deemed wrong,[128] the following chapters will not disregard such a divergence in dealing with the reasons why the US and EU approaches towards monopolistic conduct involving IPRs have been partially different.

Second, when it comes to dominant firms' conduct it is not very clear what 'protecting consumer welfare' means and will mean. As seen in Chapter 1, it does not mean that antitrust authorities want to change market structures and firms' behaviors in order to maximize consumer welfare, because this would amount to a regulatory approach that antitrust authorities do not want to endorse. If consumer welfare is deemed as a 'market health warning light' that signals whether a market enjoys low prices, high-quality products, and a wide selection of goods,[129] to 'protect consumer welfare' means to prohibit firms' behaviors that worse (or risk to worse) markets' performances, trying not to strike down those business practices that enhance them.

In order to discuss this last topic consider the traditional EU distinction between exploitative and exclusionary monopolistic behaviors, as described in paragraph 3: whereas the former practices – which US authorities do not prosecute and that EU antitrust authorities prohibit under the letters a)

---

[128] See Sher, *supra* note 124, at 243; and Eilmansberger, *supra* note 46, at 131. In other words, it cannot be taken for granted that when EU antitrust institutions actually found such a close link US courts would have done otherwise. See, in this regard, Herbert Hovenkamp, *The Legal Periphery of Dominant Firm Conduct* 20 (2007), available at https://ssrn.com.

[129] See Lovdahl Gormsen, *supra* note 24, at 88.

and c) of Article 102 – are just aimed at extracting surplus from clients and customers, sometimes the latter behaviors – which indeed belong to the intersection between Section 2 and Article 102 – may alter the existing market constraints and, hence, strengthen dominance. Therefore, although both exploitative and exclusionary conduct can reward the legitimate monopolist for its efforts – meaning that the monopolist may use both of them for appropriating the benefits that flow from its dominance and from its further competitive advantages – only exclusionary conduct can produce an additional countervailing effect by sheltering and prolonging market power at the expense of potential and actual rivals. Therefore, one could argue that it should be for preventing such negative effect that antitrust authorities should enforce Section 2 and Article 102(b). In other words, one could argue that given what was said in Chapter 1 as to the 'rewarding role' of market monopolies, antitrust authorities should allow dominant firms to behave so as to appropriate the advantages that flow from their positions and their next competitive advantages just as long as their practice does not strengthen market power:[130] in order to spur competition and innovation, antitrust authorities should prohibit only monopolistic practices that prolong market monopolies.

Yet, even this approach – under which, hence, the legitimacy of Article 102(a) and (c) should be questioned – does not appear fully correct. Indeed, several practices that consist of acts of fierce competition produce the mentioned exclusionary effect: they do strengthen and prolong market power.[131] Consider, for instance, a practice called 'brand proliferation', which addresses the case of a firm that offers to the market a complete spectrum of brands,[132] thus leaving rivals no profitable market niches to

---

[130] In accord, see Carlton & Heyer, *supra* note 18, at 1–2 (using the term 'extraction' and 'extension' behaviors to address respectively exploitative and exclusionary conduct and arguing that 'we subscribe strongly to the view that an essential element of appropriate antitrust policy is to allow a firm to capture as much of the surplus that, by its own investment, innovation, industry or foresight, the firm has itself brought into existence'. They observe, however that 'a policy that goes further, and which permits all unilateral conduct regardless of competitive effects (perhaps on grounds that 'even more profit will generate even more innovation') is considered [. . .] overly lenient, inconsistent with widely accepted presumptions in favor of inter-firm competition, and unwise, at least under the current state of economic knowledge').

[131] See Lovdahl Gormsen, *supra* note 24, at 89 (arguing that 'prohibiting conduct where firms are seeking to use their economic power to undermine the market's competitive structures, without considering whether such behaviors is likely to harm consumer welfare, may be viewed as nothing more than protecting smaller competitors from aggregation of economic power').

[132] On this topic, see the following seminal papers, Frederic M. Scherer, 'The Welfare Economics of Product Variety: An Application to the Ready-to-Eat Cereals Industry', 28 *The Journal of Industrial Economics* 113 (1979); Richard Schmalensee, 'Entry Deterrence in the Ready-to-Eat Breakfast Cereal Industry', 9 *The Bell Journal of Economics* 305 (1978); Donald

exploit. True, under specific conditions such a practice strengthens market power by reducing entrance profitability in a credible way and,[133] hence, by deterring rivals' entry. But, if the monopolists' brands satisfied consumers' needs and wants,[134] forbidding such a practice would stifle the monopolist's efforts to keep on searching for competitive advantages and,[135] in addition, would leave consumers disappointed.

Therefore, but for stating – as indeed the EU antitrust institutions seemed to have done with the past 'special responsibility' slogan[136] – that dominant firms have to act as the trustee of their rivals, i.e. but for stating that once a firm has reached a dominant position it cannot keep on competing fiercely[137], antitrust law cannot strike a conduct just because it prolongs market monopoly. For the regarded behavior to qualify as illegal a second requirement is needed and, looking at the objectives that nowadays competition authorities want to pursue, the harm to 'consumer welfare' can well represent this second requirement.

A. Hay, 'Sequential Entry and Entry-Deterring Strategies in Spatial Competition', 28 *Oxford Economic Papers* 240 (1976).

[133] Indeed, as repositioning new brands is costly, the chance that the incumbent would change its strategy after the entrance is impracticable. For the related economic literature see Chapter 3.

[134] A different issue is what should be the optimal level of product differentiation in the market. If antitrust authorities wondered about it, they would act as social planners and, hence, this topic is beyond the aims of the book. On the other hand, more brands generally imply higher average industry costs because, by making rivalry pivot around product differentiation, they entail additional expenses, such as new inventory holding, new product design, more advertising, and more complexity in the assembly process. See, e.g., Barry L. Bayus & William P. Putsis, 'Product Proliferation: An Empirical Analysis of Product Line Determinants and Market Outcomes', 18 *Marketing Science* 137 (1999); and Kelvin Lancaster, 'The Economics of Product Variety: A Survey', 9 *Marketing Science* 189 (1990).

[135] See *In Re Kellogg Co.*, 99 FTC 8, 269 (1982), where the FTC charged the four largest US companies producing ready-to-eat breakfast cereals that 'proliferating brands, differentiating similar products and promoting trademarks through intensive advertising result in high barriers to entry into the market'. Further, in the 1970s, the FTC brought several other cases under Section 5 focusing precisely on the special characteristics of particular brands of goods that made them uniquely desirable to consumers. See, e.g., *In re Borden, Inc.*, 92 FTC 669 (1978), aff'd, 674 F.2d 498 (6th Cir. 1982), vacated, 461 U.S. 940 (1983) (arguing for the special appeal of ReaLemon over other reconstituted lemon juice products); and in *re General Foods Corp.*, 103 FTC 204 (1984) (claiming a special dominance of Maxwell House brand coffee on the East Coast). Nevertheless, as these cases were not prosecuted under Section 2, the chapter does not deal with them. After all, as these offenses are very difficult to assess. Thus, using Section 5 and its modest remedies it is not a mistake: it reduces the risk of over-deterrence.

[136] See previous footnote 79 and the accompanying text.

[137] See in this renard, Rousseva, *supra* note 44, 72 (arguing that the notion of special responsibility 'goes beyond the distinction between types of behavior dominant and non-dominant firms are allowed to adopt. Indeed, it has benne extended in general to any and all conduct of dominant undertaking, as a result of which, whenever there is a finding of dominance, there is a significant likelihood that an abuse will also be ascertained').

And, in accordance with what was said in Chapter 1 in relation to the costs that monopolies cast upon the whole of society, protecting consumer welfare cannot mean but to prevent firms from: (i) profitably reducing market output and raising market price; and (ii) degrading the quality and variety of their products.[138] In other words, protecting consumer welfare should mean asking monopolists to compete on the merits, to offer good performances and, hence, accept that they prolong and strengthen their market power *only* via those meritorious behaviors that fierce competitors generally endorse.[139] For instance, with brand proliferation this can happen: a monopolist can shelter and reinforce its power, by improving the quality and variety of its supply and without decreasing the output available on the market. Among other things, the following chapters disclose whether, over the years, US and EU authorities have endorsed such approach that requires dominant firms' behaviors to be prohibited when they both strengthen market monopoly and harm consumer welfare.

But, what about innovation? That is to say, what about the legal protection of consumer welfare over the long run? Indeed – an this is the third clarification needed – just because of what Chapter 1 explained, it is difficult to understand what antitrust authorities should do when, for instance, it happens that a dominant firm's behavior harms allocative efficiency, but increases dynamic efficiency or harms the development and spread of

---

[138] In this light, therefore, it is just the economic meaning of the term 'consumer welfare' that induces to spur behaviors that entail low prices, high quality and variety. See, *contra*, Eugene Buttigieg, *Competition Law: Safeguarding the Consumer Interest. A Comparative Analysis of US Antitrust Law and EC Competition Law* 1 (2009) (who instead prefer to use the notions of 'consumer interest' and 'consumer well-being' for addressing the concerns for prices, service quality, and choice).

[139] Differently, protecting consumer welfare does not mean protecting competitors, even small ones: indeed, the number of competitors is relevant as long as it really affects business performances; if a dominant firm produces at marginal costs, without depriving its supply of quality, and keeps on innovating, no antitrust concern should arise. In other words, the harm to dominant firms' rivals cannot be chosen as the *discrimen* to tell legitimate competition from unlawful dominant firms' conduct simply because, as it characterizes both, there would be no logic in using it to distinguish one kind of practice from the other. See, in this regard, Bruzzone, Boccaccio, *supra* note 21, at 9 (arguing that 'a market structure objective, which takes the plurality of competitors as a direct target without considering the impact of a given choice on efficiency and consumers, risks being translated into an indefinite rule of evaluation', which does not distinguish between fierce competition and harmful competition), Likewise, protecting consumer welfare does not imply supporting consumer protection: it does not entail taking direct action against monopolistic behaviors that aim just at exploiting market power and, in this way, maybe offend consumers with high prices or with tying products and services in distribution. These behaviors, indeed, can be simply deemed to be practices whereby dominant firms appropriate the benefits that flow from their (deserved) monopoly power without changing the existing competitive constraints. Analogously, protecting consumer welfare does not require pursuing equity via a fair distribution and (re) distribution of wealth: for these objectives other pieces of legislation can be easily employed.

innovation without impairing static efficiency. For instance what if, on the one hand, a dominant firm does harm allocative efficiency by refusing to share its IPRs with rivals but, on the other hand, increases dynamic efficiency by using them in its follow-on innovations?[140] Else, what if stolen patents reduce the incentives to innovate by undermining the proprietary regime but do not harm short-run consumer welfare?[141]

In this regard, it must be recalled that nowadays both US and EU antitrust institutions seem to be aware of the impact that innovation produces on economic growth and, hence, appear willing to give a lot of attention to innovation. For instance, in 2007 in the shared Report named *Antitrust Enforcement and Intellectual Property Rights: Promoting Innovation and Competition*, both the DOJ and the FTC agencies concurred in observing that antitrust law must promote innovation. At least officially, they acknowledged that antitrust law must contribute to promote a market-based economy that increases economic growth and maximizes wealth and prosperity, by ensuring that new proprietary technologies, products, and services are bought, sold, traded, and licenses issued in a competitive environment.[142] Likewise, in the 2009 Communication the European Commission focuses on practices that do not only allow dominant firms to be in a position to profitably increase prices, reduce market output, and reduce consumer choice, but that also permit dominant firms to limit

---

[140] It has been argued that a possible solution is that currently applied in both the US and the EU in connection to the efficiency defense for mergers that harm allocative efficiency. This is the proposal of Timothy J. Brennan, 'Should Innovation Rationalize Supra-Competitive Prices? A Skeptical Speculation' 26–8, prepared for the Pros and Cons of High Prices Seminar Swedish Competition Authority/Konkurrensverket Stockholm, Sweden, November 9, 2007 (arguing that, in order to rule out simple assertions that 'dynamic trumps static', defendants should be allowed to invoke dynamic efficiencies, 'but also be required to show that they are 'unlikely to be accomplished' but for the practice and 'substantiate' those claims so they are not 'vague or speculative'').

[141] See Joseph F. Brodley, 'The Economic Goals of Antitrust: Efficiency, Consumer Welfare, and Technological Progress', 62 *N.Y.U. L. Rev.* 1020, 1035–6 (1987); and John J. Flynn, 'Antitrust Policy, Innovation Efficiencies, and the Suppression of Technology', 66 *Antitrust L. J.* 487, 496–7 (1998).

[142] Report, at 1. Further, see Thomas Barnett, 'Maximizing Welfare through Technological Innovation' 6, 8 and 16 (2007), available at http://www.usdoj.gov/atr/public/speeches/227291.pdf (arguing that 'if antitrust policy is to achieve its long-term goal of increasing consumer welfare, it also needs to foster the conditions that shift the supply curve 'out.' [. . .] antitrust enforcers must be careful not to pursue immediate, static efficiency gains at the expense of long-term, dynamic efficiency improvements, since the latter are likely to create more consumer welfare than the former'). Yet, for a voice out of the chorus, see Brennan, *supra* note 140, at 4 (stating 'a speculation that the recent focus on innovation and the concern that antitrust may stand in its way may be exaggerated, rests on a simple intuition. One need not weaken antitrust to promote innovation; policy makers could turn multiple instruments available to influence the rate of innovation. The most notable tool is the length and breadth of intellectual property (IP) rights').

innovation.[143] After all, the limitation to technical development has an express pedigree in Article 102(b).

Yet, these general political statements do not help in establishing what protecting consumer welfare over the long run means in practical terms. The following chapters contribute to reveal a possible stream of legal answers to these questions, by describing how in the past US courts and EU antitrust institutions have enforced Section 2 and Article 102 regarding practices involving IPRs.

IPRS AND THE ANTITRUST RULES REGARDING MONOPOLISTS: TWO APPROPRIABILITY TOOLS WITH DIFFERENT PERSPECTIVES BUT THE SAME OBJECTIVES

IPRs and the antitrust rules regarding dominant firms can be viewed as appropriability tools that govern the present and future distribution of incentives and opportunities to compete and innovate.[144] Indeed, as seen in Chapter 1, IPRs fix the extent to which firms can enjoy the rewards that flow from their innovations and the extent to which they can keep on innovating; and, as seen in this chapter, Section 2 and Article 102(b) establish the limits to which monopolists can appropriate the benefits that derive from their dominant competitive advantages and the limits to which they can keep on searching for competitive advantages.

From this standpoint, the main differences between IPRs and the antitrust rules regarding monopolists seem to be that they address different subjects and act upon different levels: whereas the IP rules address any kind of firm and establish the boundaries of ownership for intellectual goods, Section 2 and Article 102(b) address only dominant firms and govern their behaviors which, among the others, can be aimed at both procuring those intellectual goods and exploiting them, sometimes within, sometimes beyond their proper boundaries.

The following chapters discuss the scenarios when these two

143 See 2009 Communication, *supra* note 24, §§ 11 and 19.

144 True, broadly speaking it can be stated that whereas IP laws do provide rewards for an important type of procompetitive behavior that is innovation, antitrust law does not attempt to create an affirmative incentive for procompetitive behaviors inasmuch as it does not promise any specific recompense or legal acknowledgment for rivals who do not violate competition rules. See in this regard R. Hewitt Pate, 'Competition and Intellectual Property in the US: Licensing Freedom and the Limits of Antitrust' (2005), available at http://www.eui.eu/RSCAS/Research/Competition/2005 (papers).shtml. Nevertheless, as long as temporary monopolies are conceived as a form of reward to incentivize further competition and innovation, the same conception of competition law changes.

appropriability tools are combined, and inquire whether such combination allows promoting both competition and innovation.

After all, antitrust and IP laws pursue the protection of both. Antitrust law both looks at firms' behaviors that may worsen short-run markets' performances and regards innovation, because 'today's competition' affects present and future innovation which, in turn, influences 'tomorrow's competition'. Analogously, both patent and copyright laws are aimed at promoting the creation and dissemination of inventions and creative works and are concerned with competition, since IPRs – at least, some of them – may represent competitive advantages, that is to say, input that affect present and future market competition. Therefore, the idea of an inherent conflict between these two pieces of legislation has to be rejected.[145] Furthermore, even from a more theoretical standpoint, it is acknowledged that on the one hand, today's transatlantic competition law aims at safeguarding consumer welfare over the short and long run[146]. On the other

---

[145] See, e.g., Herbert Hovenkamp, Mark D. Janis & Mark A. Lemley, 1 *IP and Antitrust. An Analysis of Antitrust Principles applied to Intellectual Property Law* § 1.3a (2009); Dan Eklof, The *Microsoft Case* – at the heart of the IP/antitrust intersection, in *Article 82 EC: Reflections on its Recent Evolution* 97 (Ariel Ezrachi ed., 2009); Olav Kolstad, 'Competition Law and Intellectual Property Rights – Outline of an Economics-Based Approach', in *Research Handbook on Intellectual Property and Competition Law* 6 (Josef Drexl ed., 2008); Paul A. Geroski, 'Intellectual Property Rights and Competition Policy', in *Perspectives on innovation* 455, 456 (Franco Malerba & Stefano Brusoni eds. 2007) (arguing that this conclusion stems from the idea that 'competition is more conducive to innovation – or to certain particularly valuable types of innovation – than monopoly'); Lucas Peeperkorn & Emil Paulis, 'Competition and Innovation: Two Horses Pulling the Same Cart', in *On The Merits: Current Issues In Competition Law And Policy* (Paul Lugard & Leigh Hancher eds. 2005); Philip Lowe &Lucas Peeperkorn, 'Intellectual Property: How Special is it for the Purposes of Competition Law Enforcement?' (2005), available at http://www.eui.eu/RSCAS/Research/Competition/2005(papers).shtml; Mark A. Lemley, 'Property, Intellectual Property, and Free Riding', 83 *Tex. L. Rev.* 1031 (2005); Willard K. Tom & Joshua A. Newberg, 'Antitrust and Intellectual Property: From Separate Spheres to Unified Field', 66 *Antitrust L.J.* 167 (1997); Ward Bowman Jr., *Patent And Antitrust Law: A Legal and Economic Appraisal* (1973); and Paul Goldstein, 'The Competitive Mandate: From Sears to Lear', 59 *Cal. L. Rev.* 971 (1971). Further, consider U.S. Department of Justice and Federal Trade Commission, *Antitrust Enforcement and Intellectual Property Rights: Promoting Innovation and Competition* 1–2, available at http://www.ftc.gov/reports/innovation/P040101PromotingInnovationandCompetitionrpt0704.pdf (stating that antitrust law and intellectual property can be 'properly perceived as complementary bodies of law that work together to bring innovation to consumers: antitrust laws protect robust competition in the market place, while intellectual property laws protect the ability to earn a return on the investment necessary to innovate'). See U.S. Department of Justice and Federal Trade Commission, *Antitrust Guidelines for the Licensing of Intellectual Property* § 1.0 (1995), (establishing that, 'the intellectual property laws and the antitrust laws share the common purpose of promoting innovation and enhancing consumer welfare'). After all, some courts have already recognized it. See. e.g., *Atari Games Corp. v. Nintendo of Am.* 897 F.2d 1572, 1576 (Fed. Circ. 1990) (stating that competition and patent laws 'are actually complementary, as both are aimed at encouraging innovation, industry and competition').

[146] See previous footnotes 142 ff. and the accompanying text.

hand, IP laws seek to defend both dynamic efficiency, by encouraging the spreading of intellectual goods,[147] and static efficiency,[148] because patents and copyrights (no differently from what are well-known regulations)[149] are supposed to answer a specific kind of market failure, although they may allow their holders to charge prices that do not equal marginal costs.

Therefore, since dominant firms' practices involving IPRs can be investigated by looking at the effects that they produce upon these two variables: static and dynamic efficiency, the following chapters portray economic theories as applied to some dominant firms' practices involving IPRs looking at when they can strengthen monopoly power and harm consumer welfare, not only over the short but also over the long run. In other words, the following chapters employ an economic, effects-based approach in order to asses the practices that rest at the heart of the IP/Antitrust intersection, without opting *a priori* for IP immunity, or antitrust enforcement.[150]

---

[147] See, in this regard, Rudolph J. R. Peritz, 'Competition policy and its implications for intellectual property rights in United States', in *The Interface Between Intellectual Property Rights and Competition Policy* 125, 188 (Steven D. Anderman ed., 2007) (arguing how the antitrust analysis of innovation has always been set into a static scenario). Yet, such an issue does not concern the interface between antitrust and IP laws, but is clearly inherent to the sole antitrust realm.

[148] See Janusz A. Ordover, 'Economic Foundations and Considerations in Protecting Industrial and Intellectual Property', 53 *Antitrust L. J.* 503 (1984-1985) .

[149] See Herbert Hovenkamp, *The Antitrust Enterprise* 249 (2005)

[150] On the two opposite views and the arguments supporting them, see Eklof, *supra* note 145, at 100–102.

3. Ownership of IPRs

CONCERNS ABOUT ALLOWING MONOPOLISTS TO HOLD IPRS

IP laws are very 'democratic': they allow any kind of firm, dominant firms included, to hold IPRs. After all, IP laws deal with ownership of resources and not with the likely consequences that monopoly power – however strengthened by IPRs – may produce in markets. Further, whatever the rationale supporting IPRs,[1] policy-makers do not contradict any of them by allowing monopolists to hold IPRs. For instance, there is no apparent reason why monopolists should be prevented from owning the fruits of their labor that result in inventions and creative works; likewise there is no apparent reason why society as a whole would welcome the benefits that monopolists' innovations produce less than the advantages that any other firm's intellectual goods produce.

Nevertheless, once outside the IP perspective, one might question whether, under at least some economic models, letting dominant firms own IPRs might both strengthen their market power and harm consumer welfare. Consequently, one could ask if US courts and EU antitrust institutions have ever forbidden or restricted dominant firms from developing and acquiring IPRs[2] – for example, by adopting different standards for

---

[1] In this regard, see the book's introduction.

[2] For simplicity's sake, this chapter avoids making any distinction between the act of innovating – that is, developing and acquiring either an invention or a creative work – and the acts of patenting and copyrighting them – that is, the act of procuring an IPR upon those innovations. Further, it must be acknowledged that some of the anticompetitive strategies here described do not pivot around the mere procurement of IPRs, but around dominant firms' ability to capture the advantages that flow from their inventions and creative works. Therefore, what is explained here could be applied, all differences considered, to other appropriability tools. See, for instance, Richard J. Gilbert & David M.G. Newbery, 'Preemptive Patenting and the Persistence of Monopoly', 72 *Am. Econ. Rev.* 514, 515 (1982) (clarifying that 'the existence of patent rights is neither necessary nor sufficient for [the sleeping patent strategy to work]. The crucial element is that the rewards from acting first must be sufficiently large relative to the gains to subsequent investors. Patents provide a vivid example where the award goes only to the first firm.'). Therefore, as hinted in the previous chapter, given the scope of Section 2 and Article 102 a better inquiry should be whether allowing a dominant firm to keep for itself the benefits of its inventions and creations can both strengthen its market power and harm consumer welfare. In this vein, indeed, see Frederic M. Scherer,

detecting monopolistic unlawful conduct. On the surface, indeed, there might be many concerns. For instance, a monopolist might deliberately incur excessive and, therefore, welfare decreasing R&D expenses, just in order to develop a weak innovation that, by excluding rivals, allows the monopolist to strengthen its dominance and, therefore, forces society to bear the extra costs that monopolies entail in terms of price, quality and variety. Or, dominant firms might develop and acquire one or more IPRs – even IPRs ultimately demonstrated to be invalid[3] – in order to keep

---

'Comments on Patents, Sleeping Patents, and Entry Deterrence', in *Strategy, Predation and Antitrust Analysis* 287, 287–8 (1981) (arguing that it is misleading to use 'concepts as 'patenting,' 'R.& D.,' and 'innovation' as if they were interchangeable, and as if getting a patent – as distinguished from developing a superior new product or process – were the main objective of business enterprises. [. . .] [I]f (because of first-in advantages, other barriers to imitation, or the hot breath of competition) the innovation would be made without patent protection' the discussion about preemptive patents 'advance[s] our understanding little because of unduly restrictive or unrealistic assumptions.'). Nevertheless, as IPRs are one of the most widespread appropriability tools, arguing about monopolists that procure IPRs is a good proxy for discussing monopolists that appropriate the benefits that flow from their intellectual goods.

3 The benefits that should come with patents are completely thrown out when the related technologies do not deserve to be protected. In other words, given the costs that patents may bring (see Chapter 1), invalid patents do not entail any countervailing benefits. After all, as long as the quality of the patent system and the goodness of its requirements are reliable, it does not seem totally reckless to assume that consumers are not supposed to gain from an intellectual good that does not comply with those requirements. Yet, the real issue that arises when speaking about the procurement of invalid patents is whether their mere ownership might truly impair competitors' opportunities and reduce consumers' welfare, even when the patentee does not enforce its exclusive rights. On the one hand, one could argue that there are no anticompetitive effects when either the monopolist' rivals are not interested in using the fraudulently patented innovation, or the patentee does not defy their use of it. In that case, indeed, other firms tend to behave as if the invalid patent does not exist. See, e.g., Herbert Hovenkamp, Mark D. Janis, & Mark A. Lemley, *IP and Antitrust: An Analysis of Antitrust Principles Applied to Intellectual Property Law* § 11.2e (affirming that 'it is not the fraudulent patent itself that gives rise to antitrust problems, but the use of the patent to affect the market in some way'); and Neil A. Smith, 'Fraud upon the Patent Office as a Violation of the Sherman Antitrust Law', 53 *J. Pat. and Trademark Off. Soc'y* 423, 434–5 (1971) (stating that 'it is not the mere existence of the patent – however fraudulently it has been obtained – which brings antitrust liability to its owner; it is the owner's assertion or enforcement of the patent which brings on antitrust liability'). On the other hand, however, one could object that the validity of the relevant patent is pointless for the preemptive and suppressing strategies, such as sleeping patent strategies, to work effectively as tools for strengthening market power and harming consumer welfare. For instance, given that rivals cannot be sure about the invalidity of a patent and considering that ascertaining it entails significant trial costs, even the mere existence of invalid patents may decrease entrance profitability, create rational fear in entry decisions, impose litigation risks, deter customers and business partners from contracting with new entrants, and may even harm innovation efficiency by pushing the patentees' rivals to invent around the patent. And in these cases it is just the invalidity of the regarded patents that implies the absence of the usual benefits that each innovation that does not amount to mere shame entails and, hence, implies in turn harm to consumer welfare. See, in this regard, Christopher R. Leslie, 'The Anticompetitive Effects of Unenforced Invalid Patents', 91 *Minn. L. Rev.* 101 (2006); Ian Ayres & Paul Klemperer, 'Limiting Patentees' Market Power Without Reducing Innovation Incentives: The Perverse Benefits of Uncertainty and Non-Injunctive

them from their rivals and, therefore, to stifle rivals' growth, suppress new technologies, and redirect the industry's innovative path in their favor.[4]

This chapter examines some monopolistic practices involving IPRs that can strengthen market power – either by working as non-price predatory tools,[5]

Remedies', 97 *Mich. L. Rev.* 985, 1019 (1999); Mark A. Lemley, 'Property, Intellectual Property, and Free Riding', 83 *Tex. L. Rev.* 1031, 1060 (2005). As a whole, from an economic standpoint, it would not be a mistake to require antitrust authorities to prosecute invalid patents, but not every invalid patent: only invalid sleeping patents that monopolists either use inside the frame of preemptive strategies, or in order to suppress new technologies.

[4] Other practices may entail the suppression of innovations. Namely: (a) mergers; (b) restrictive intellectual property licensing agreements that discourage customers from switching to rivals' competitive technologies; and (c) timing announcements of innovations that deter rivals from developing and marketing competing products and customers from switching to them – i.e., the so-called *vaporware*. Think, for instance, of the following US cases: (sub a) *Telectronics Proprietary v. Medtronic*, 687 F. Supp. 832, 844 (S.D.N.Y. 1988), *Crucible v. Stora Kopparbergs Bergslags AB*, 701 F. Supp. 1157, 1162-1163 (W.D. Pa. 1988), and *Great Lakes Chem. Corp.* 103 F.T.C. 467 (1984); (sub b) *United States v. United Shoe Machinery Corp.* 347 U.S. 521 (1954) and *United States v. Microsoft Corp.*, 56 F.3d 1448 (D.C. Cir. 1995); and (sub c) *United States v. AT&T*, 524 F. Supp. 1336 (D.D.C. 1981). On these topics see, further, Eugene Crew, 'Foreword: Symposium on Antitrust and the Suppression of Technology in the United States and Europe: Is There a Remedy?', 66 *Antitrust L. J.* 415 (1998); Joel M. Cohen & Arthur J. Burke, 'An Overview of the Antitrust Analysis of Suppression of Technology', 66 *Antitrust L. J.* 420, 426 (1998); Yee Wah Chin, 'Unilateral Technology Suppression: Appropriate Antitrust and Patent Law Remedies', 66 *Antitrust L. J.* 441 (1998); John J. Flynn, 'Antitrust Policy, Innovation Efficiencies, and the Suppression of Technology', 66 *Antitrust L.J.* 487 (1998); Jack Kaufmann, 'Afterword: Symposium on Antitrust and the Suppression of Technology in the United States and Europe: Is There a Remedy?', 66 *Antitrust L. J.* 527 (1998); Richard Dunford, 'The Suppression of Technology as a Strategy for Controlling Resource Dependence', 32 *Admin. Sci. Q.* 512, 513 (1987); Robert C. Fellmeth, 'Suppression and Other Antitrust Concerns', in *Legal Aspects Of Solar Technology* 197 (John H. Minon & William H. Lawrence eds. 1981); Henry Etzkowitz, 'Solar Versus Nuclear Energy: Autonomous or Dependent Technology?', 31 *Soc. Probs.* 417 (1984); Gerald Sobel, 'The Antitrust Interface with Patents and Innovation: Acquisition of Patents, Improvement Patents and Grant-Backs, Non-Use, Fraud on the Patent Office, Development of New Products and Joint Research', 53 *Antitrust L. J.* 681, 682 (1984); Bruce W. Kaufman et al., 'Suppressing Technology: The Automobile Air Pollution Case', 3 *Antitrust Law and Economics Review* 111 (1970); and George E. Frost, 'Legal Incidents of Non-Use of Patented Inventions Reconsidered', 14 *Geo. Wash. L. Rev.* 273 (1946).

[5] Firms can compete by charging different prices and/or supplying better and new products. Therefore, it should not come as a surprise that predatory practices may consist in both pricing and non-pricing strategies. Generally, antitrust scholars deem non-price predation less expensive and risky than price predation. It is less costly because it does not require that short-run profits be sacrificed on a large volume of sales that is typical of predatory pricing, and because the possibility of making credible commitments to deter entry (or induce exit) is far greater with non-price variables than with price. It is less risky because, as this chapter shows, its anticompetitive goal may be harder to detect, as there could be efficient reasons to justify these non-price strategies. On this topic, see Steven C. Salop, 'Strategy, Predation, and Antitrust Analysis: An Introduction', in *Strategy, Predation, and Antitrust Analysis* 1, 13–14 (Steven C. Salop ed. 1981) (arguing that non-price methods in general, inputs market in particular, are often more cost-effective and more likely to succeed than is simple price predation); Steven C. Salop & David Scheffman, 'Raising Rivals' Costs', 73 *Am. Econ. Rev.* 267 (1983); Terry Calvani, 'Non-Price Predation: A New Antitrust Horizon', 54

or as non-price preemptive strategies[6] aimed at credibly[7] deterring rivals' entry[8] by raising their costs[9] – and explores whether these practices can also harm consumer welfare. In particular, the chapter deals with the case

---

Antitrust L. J. 409, 410–11(1985). Further, among the predatory strategies, non-price predatory practices are the more suitable to use as strategies for raising rivals' costs. Indeed, see David T. Scheffman & Richard S. Higgins, 'Twenty Years of Raising Rivals' Costs: History, Assessment, and Future', 12 *Geo. Mason L. Rev.* 371 (2003) (arguing that the acronym 'RRC' is a shorthand for non-price predation).

[6] To be clearer, suppose markets are 'spaces' of products and processes in which firms want to live. For instance, markets can be depicted as either 'geographic spaces', in which firms have to choose where to locate their plants; or as 'capacity spaces', where firms behave according to the quantity of products that the market can absorb and firms can produce; or else as 'variety spaces', where firms decide products' qualities – both physical or intangible qualities, created even via trademarks and advertising. Dominant firms' conduct involving IPRs, and especially trademarks and patents, may allow monopolists to anticipate their rivals – especially their potential competitors– in occupying the 'spaces' available for new and different products and processes, so leaving them without enough space for growth. See, as to the seminal paper about markets' spatial analysis, Harold Hotelling, 'Stability in Competition', 39 *Economic Journal* 41 (1929) (studying where firms will locate their plants under specific assumptions). Then consider that firms can build preemptive strategies that work as entry deterrence devices, and that are also known as species of non-price predation, on several competitive variables, such as: (i) product design – see Chapter 4; (ii) legal tools – see Chapter 6; (iii) investments in excess production capacity – see, e.g., B. Curtis Eaton & Richard G. Lipsey, 'The Theory of Market Preemption: The Persistence of Excess Capacity and Monopoly in Growing Spatial Markets', 46 *Economica* 149 (1979); (iv) excessive advertising – see, e.g., William S. Comanor & Thomas A. Wilson, 'The Effect of Advertising on Competition: A Survey', 17 *J. Econ. Lit.* 453 (1979); (v) R&D investments, regardless of whether the monopolist succeeds in achieving a patent – see, e.g., Avinash Dixit, 'The Role of Investment in Entry-Deterrence', 90 *Economic Journal* 95 (1980); and Richard J. Gilbert, 'Patents, Sleeping Patents, and Entry Deterrence', in *Strategy, Predation, and Antitrust Analysis* 205, 236 (Steven C. Salop, ed. 1981); (vi) R&D investments in complementary markets – see, e.g., Joseph Farrell & Michael Katz, 'Innovation, Rent Extraction, and Integration in Systems Markets' (2000), available at http://ideas.repec.org/f/pka210.html; and Jay P. Choi, *Informational Leverage and the Endogenous Timing of Product Introductions* (1996), available at http://ideas.repec.org/p/clu/wpaper/1996_03.html. Strategic investments and patent preemption generally represent components of the monopolist's overall strategy, although investments can be so effective in preventing entry as to make preemptive patenting unnecessary. For an initial analysis of the several competitive variables that can be used in a preemptive strategy see, e.g., Thomas S. Gruca & D. Sudharshan, 'A Framework for Entry Deterrence Strategy: The Competitive Environments, Choices, and Consequences', 59 *Journal of Marketing* 44 (1995); Richard J. Gilbert, 'Mobility Barriers and the Value of Incumbency', in 1 *Handbook of Industrial Organization* 475 (Richard Schmalensee & Robert Willig eds., 1989).

[7] Two conditions must be met for a strategic conduct to be successful, namely: advantage and commitment. First, the strategizing firm must have an advantage over its rivals otherwise they could easily replicate its practices with the same expenses. Such an advantage can consist of a 'natural information advantage' that derives from the incumbent's longer experience in the industry, in some market feature that favors the market's asymmetric structure (such as network and lock-in effects), or else in a 'strategic advantage' that (paradoxically) arises from the incumbent's having greater irreversible costs committed to the market than its rivals. Usually, indeed, as the incumbent is already established in the industry, it has already sustained sunk industry-specific costs from which accrues the incumbent's rational and, hence,

of 'isolated predatory innovations',[10] 'patent accumulation', and 'sleeping patent' strategies – all practices that antitrust scholars usually consider under the rubric of 'rent-seeking strategies'.[11] Further, the chapter considers the case of 'suppressed patents', and discusses whether even this practice may strengthen market power and harm consumer welfare.

---

credible incentive to protect its position against new entrants. See Salop, *supra* note 5, at 14–22. See further Massimo Motta, *Competition Policy* 411 (arguing that nowadays the interest in dominant firms' exclusionary behaviors has increased because, given the liberalization processes, markets have acquired an asymmetrical structure that gives incumbents strong incentives to exclude potential rivals). Second, the dominant firm must show a commitment to its strategy, i.e., that it will keep on applying it regardless of its competitors' actions. See Dennis W. Carlton & Jeffrey M. Perloff, *Modern Industrial Organization* 350, 352 (2005); and A. Michael Spence, 'Competition, Entry, and Antitrust Policy', in *Strategy, Predation, and Antitrust analysis* 45, 51–60 (Steven C. Salop ed. 1981). From this perspective, entry deterrence strategies, by occurring before the entrance, may appear as nothing more than empty menaces unless the incumbent does commit itself to do what it threatens to do after the entrance. See, in this regard, Frederic M. Scherer & David Ross, *Industrial Market Structure and Economic Performance* 380–81 (1990), (stating that to make their threats credible, incumbents must turn them into commitments. The distinguishing feature of a commitment to deter entry is that, if entry actually occurs, it is in the incumbent's self-interest to enforce the threat. In particular, such a commitment must be durable, irreversible, and clear). In particular, see Thomas C. Schelling, *The Strategy of Conflict* 22 (1960), (observing that entry deterrence strategies 'rest on the paradox that the power to constrain an adversary may depend on the power to bind oneself [. . .] with some voluntary but irreversible sacrifice of freedom of choice'). Therefore, in order to make their strategies credible, firms must act so that potential competitors look to current behavior as indicative of future market conditions: investing in patents is a good way of doing it.

8 Broadly speaking, dominant firms are interested in getting rid of the actual and potential competitors. Hence, a conduct is said to be 'exclusionary' when it either forces a monopolist's competitors to exit from the market in which the incumbent firm is primarily active, or prevents them from entering further into that market. Thus, the theory of strategic behaviors has been applied to explain both competition among existing firms and entry deterrence. See, Steven C. Salop, 'Strategic Entry Deterrence', 69 *The American Economic Review* 335 (1979). Entry deterrence strategies are fully consistent with what Judge Bork called 'artificial barriers to entry' – see Robert H. Bork, *The Antitrust Paradox* 195–6 and 311 (1978) – as they explain how incumbent firms can operate to make entry more difficult than it was for them. In order to understand why preemptive strategies work well as entry-deterrence practices, assume that by occupying the available market space the dominant firm reduces the profitability of both growth and entry into the market. Actual rivals, having already invested in the incumbent's market, do not lose the chance to recoup their initial investment just because the market's profitability decreases. Instead, as potential entrants are generally uncertain about the eventual success of their investments, even a small decrease in entrance profitability can make their investment decisions change. This is the reason why pre-emptive strategies work well as entry-deterrence tools.

9 The raising rivals' costs theory teaches that certain behaviors are more easily explained as devices not for excluding rivals and potential competitors, but rather for making their viability in the market more expensive. From an economic standpoint, the distinction between raising rivals' costs practices that harm actual rather than potential competitors is quite pointless, as it is not crucial whether the raised costs are those of production or of entry. Yet the US antitrust practice shows that conduct directed against actual competitors is more easily prosecuted than that directed against potential entrants. See, for a more detailed discussion of the topic, Herbert Hovenkamp, 'Antitrust Policy after Chicago', 84 *Mich. L. R.* 213, 263 (1985).

Then the chapter turns to an analysis of the US and EU case law, in order to show that US courts and EU antitrust authorities have never deemed the mere procurement of IPRs illegal, except for a very narrow stream of *easy-administrable* cases regarding monopolists who obtained their IPRs from the market via either acquisitions or exclusive licenses. Indeed, legal scenarios where antitrust authorities question simple procurement of IPRs are much rarer than economists have imagined. As a consequence, the chapter concludes that, when it comes to the procurement of IPRs, US courts and EU institutions converge in not paying much attention to economic thinking and to the sophisticated economic models that show the specific conditions under which mere ownership of IPRs can strengthen market power and harm consumer welfare.

THE ECONOMIC PERSPECTIVE: ISOLATED PREDATORY INNOVATIONS

The term 'isolated predatory innovation' can be used to address the case of a mono-product monopolist that, by incurring wasteful R&D expenses, develops a not-cost-justified new version of its monopolized good in order, first, to crush its rivals and strengthen its dominant position and, then, thanks to some market hurdles,[12] to recoup its expenses with a consistent pricing strategy,[13] according to the usual two-period frame of predatory strategies.[14]

[10] For simplicity's sake this chapter uses the term 'isolated predatory innovation' to indicate the case of a mono-product monopolist that develops a new version of the monopolized good inside the frame of a predatory strategy. Actually, the well-known expression 'predatory innovation' can equally address such a situation and the case of a multi-product. For this second scenario see Chapter 4, where the relevant predatory innovation is said to be a 'system predatory innovation'.

[11] As seen in Chapter 1, rent-seeking literature focuses upon incumbent firms' outlays in taking sales away from their rivals so as to shelter their dominant positions and deems such a phenomenon as a part of the social costs of monopoly. See, e.g., Keith Cowling & Dennis C. Mueller, 'The Social Costs of Monopoly', 88 *Econ. J.* 727 (1978).

[12] See Janusz A. Ordover & Robert Willig, 'An Economic Definition of Predation: Pricing and Product Innovation', 91 *Yale L. J.* 8, 9–12 and 22–7 (1981).

[13] In formulas, given $B(\iota)$ the private benefits that come with the innovation (ι), and $C(\iota)$ the costs in R&D sustained for developing (ι), an innovation is produced when $B(\iota) > C(\iota)$. Therefore, an innovation results from an irrational but strategic choice when it entails an indirect benefit $X(\iota)$ that changes the innovation's pay-off so that, whereas $B(\iota) < C(\iota)$, $B(\iota) + X(\iota) > C(\iota)$. In particular, in this scenario such innovation is said to be anticompetitive when $X(\iota)$ consist of the private benefits that, at least, equal the harm to allocative efficiency.

[14] Firms compete both on prices and on product quality. Therefore, it should not come as a surprise if predation may result from both pricing strategies and strategies about product changes.

It has been argued that such conduct produces a negative impact on consumer welfare both because it entails a waste of resources, as do other kinds of rent-seeking conduct that monopolists endorse in order to defend their position, and because it allows, given some market features, dominant firms effectively to strengthen such a position, reduce market output, increase market price, and cast upon society the costs that monopolies can impose.

Nevertheless, this outcome should not be assumed, because it is likely that, unless an innovation amounts to mere sham,[15] it will produce more public than private benefits.[16] In other words, even an innovation developed inside a predatory scheme may better satisfy consumer preferences, and tend to engender further good innovations, feed economic progress, and so produce a positive effect on consumer welfare, productive efficiency, and dynamic efficiency.[17] Second, when it comes to fact-finding, it is very difficult to investigate the R&D investments of a firm in order to find out their predatory nature,[18] and – as happens with each predatory strategy – it is not so simple to ascertain in advance whether a market will lend itself to such two-period behavior.

---

[15] See, Richard J. Gilbert, 'Holding Innovation to an Antitrust Standard', 3 *Competition Policy International* 47 (2007) (arguing that innovation is itself exclusionary, and concludes that the high costs of deterring beneficial innovation suggest that innovation should be legal unless a 'sham,' i.e., has no plausible efficiencies.)

[16] Studies show that the social return to investment in R&D is higher than the private return, which suggests that policies that promote innovation can pay large dividends for society. See, e.g., Zvi Griliches, 'The Search for R&D Spillovers', 94 *Scandinavian Journal of Economics*, 29 (1992).

[17] In other words, say $CW(\iota)$ the effects that the innovation produces on consumer welfare, on the basis of what is said in the text it is understood that a predatory innovation that does not amount to a mere sham entails a twofold impact on CW: say $\Delta CW(\iota)<0$, as it helps in prolonging the effects of the dominance, and $\Delta CW(\iota)>0$, because it represents an innovation. It is apparent that, as these effects cannot be measured, making the sum between these effects is more a matter of policy and faith, than an issue of algebra.

[18] The Ordover-Willig model did recognize the innovations' welfare-increasing effects that follow from the superiority of the new product. Simply, perhaps taking inspiration from the Areeda-Turner reasoning about predatory investments – see Philip Areeda & Donald F. Turner, 'Predatory Pricing and Related Practices under Section 2 of the Sherman Act', 88 *Harv. L. Rev.* 697, 720 (1975) – it supposed that the socially wasteful R&D investments outweighed them. Such a strong assumption about the innovation's total welfare impact allowed Ordover and Willig to shift the focus of their analysis from the assessment of the anticompetitive nature of the innovation – which they derived from the existence of overwhelming socially wasteful investment – to the happening of its exclusionary effect, that is, the most natural consequence to show because even procompetitive innovation implies an exclusionary effect. Perhaps, without the assumption about R&D expenditure, they would have studied whether the exclusionary innovation was further able to harm consumer welfare via the intertemporal strategic conduct and the recoupment test underlying every predatory behavior. See further Janusz A. Ordover, Alan O. Sykes, & Robert D. Willig, 'Predatory Systems Rivalry: A Reply', 83 *Colum. L. Rev.* 1150 (1983).

Therefore, though economic thinking has conceived anticompetitive innovations that are, in and of themselves, anticompetitive, arguably antitrust authorities are less able and willing to base enforcement actions on this economic analysis.

PATENT ACCUMULATION

Patent accumulation, which in cumulative industries is one of the quintessential business practices that, together with cross-licensing and patent pools agreements, allow firms to navigate the patent thicket successfully, consists in collecting all the patents available in a specific field, even when they are relatively weak, so as to cover even minor variations of existing technologies.[19] Therefore, given that a mass of patents tends to turn into something much larger than the sum of its parts,[20] what is peculiar to this business behavior is not that the firm is procuring one or more new patents, but that the firm is adding these new patents to a collection of patents that it already controls, thus leaving no room for competitors' innovations.

Patent accumulation hence may work as a pre-emptive entry-deterrence strategy to protect monopoly power and, in this manner, it may well lower consumer welfare by allowing dominant firms to keep on charging over-competitive prices.[21]

---

[19] See, in this regard, Daniel L. Rubinfeld & Robert Mannes, 'The Strategic Use of Patents: Implications for Antitrust', in *Antitrust, Patents and Copyright. EU and US Perspective* 85, 88 (François Leveque & Howard Shelanski eds. 2005); Carl Shapiro, 'Navigating the Patent Thicket: Cross Licenses, Patent Pools, and Standard Setting', in *Innovation Policy and the Economy* 119 (Adam B. Jaffe, Josh Lerner, & Scott Stern eds. 2001); Sri Krishna Sankaran, 'Patent Flooding in the United States and Japan', 40 IDEA, *The Journal of Law and Technology* 393 (2000); and David J. Teece, 'Profiting from Technological Innovation: Implications for Integration, Collaboration, Licensing and Public Policy', in 15 *Research Policy* 285, 290 (1986) (arguing that patent thicket may grant to the patent holder the time necessary to identify the right design before being eclipsed by imitators).

[20] Carl Kaysen & Donald F. Turner, *Antitrust Policy, An Economic and Legal Analysis* 165 (1965).

[21] See Salop, *supra* note 5, 51. Yet, this conclusion is not so meaningful if the first best solution is abandoned, and market imperfections are accepted. See, in this regard, Janusz A. Ordover & Garth Saloner, 'Predation, Monopolization, and Antitrust', in 1 *Handbook of Industrial Organization* 537, 590 (Richard Schmalensee & Robert D. Willing, eds. 1989) (arguing that 'when perfect competition is not attainable, and the market is not fully contestable, there is no presumption that more firms in the market is preferable to fewer firms. Consequently, rules which restrict the ability of firms to deter entry in the first place may stimulate undesirable entry.'); and Gilbert, *supra* note 6, at 479 and 528 (observing that 'mobility constraints are welfare decreasing relative to a first-best allocation of economic resources. But we do not live in a first-best world. Mobility barriers arise for reasons of technology and consumer tastes and need not impair efficiency in an imperfectly competitive economy.

Yet, usually, monopolists acquire this mass of patents just one by one and, as stated above in the discussion about isolated predatory innovations, each new procured patent that does not amount to a mere sham produces a positive effect on dynamic efficiency and consumer welfare. Therefore, as a matter of prosecution, antitrust authorities should find a way to judge the welfare effects of the accumulation and prohibit it only when the newly achieved patent is a blatant sham.[22] For instance, antitrust authorities could strike down the overall accumulation of patents when subsequent procurements happen in a short time – as EU authorities do in sham litigation cases.[23] In such a scenario, indeed, antitrust authorities could assume that all the procurements belong to a single anticompetitive strategy. Alternatively, antitrust authorities could impose – as they used to do in vertical integration cases[24] – a certain number of patents above which the monopolist is banned from making subsequent patent procurements.

In either case, prohibition on patent accumulation would be difficult to administer based on the effects that such a practice produces on consumer welfare.[25] In addition, such a prohibition would remain complicated to enforce by studying the effects that patent accumulation produces on the industry's innovative path because it is unknown whether such an accumulation changes the innovative path for the worse. On the one hand, especially in cumulative industries, patent accumulation increases the costs that innovators sustain in inventing around existing patents; in getting a license for them,[26] and in organizing their research and development in

---

Indeed, there are many circumstances where welfare is strictly improved by impeding entry into an industry.').

22 In formulas, say CW ($\Sigma\iota$) the effect that patent accumulation produces on consumer welfare, antitrust authorities can find themselves in the position of comparing two factors, that is to say CW ($\Sigma\iota$) <0 and CW (ι) > 0, which actually cannot be compared.

23 See Chapter 6, for discussions about *California Motor Transport Co. v. Trucking Unlimited*. 404 U.S. 508, 510 (1972) and European Commission, Decision of 21 May 1996, Case IV/35.268, *aff'ed* in CFI, Case T-111/96, *ITT Promedia NV v. Commission of the European Communities*, [1998] ECR II-2937.

24 See, in this regard, Louis Kaplow, 'The Patent-Antitrust Intersection: A Reappraisal', 97 *Harv. L. Rev*. 1815, 1867–68 (1984).

25 For an analogous reasoning referred to the brand proliferation strategy see Frederic M. Scherer, 'The Welfare Economics of product Variety: An Implication to the Ready-To-Eat Cereals Industry', 28 *The Journal of Industrial Economics* 113, 132–3 (1979); and, see Richard Schmalensee, 'Entry Deterrence in the Ready-to-Eat breakfast Cereal Industry', 9 *The Bell Journal of Economics* 305, 319 (1978).

26 Indeed, as the patent thicket creates a considerable uncertainty for competitors as to whether their technologies infringe some patents, a patentee can exploit this uncertainty by extracting concessions from rivals, especially high royalties. See FTC, 'FTC 2003 Report on Patents and Competition, Executive Summary' 7 (2003) available at www.ftc.gov/os/2003/10/innovationrpt.pdf; and Steven C. Carlson, 'Patent Pools and Antitrust Dilemma', 16 *Yale Journal on Regulation* 359 (1999). In some cases, besides, if it is not possible to obtain a license for an essential patent, on the one hand, the dominant firm's basic patent evergreens and

light of them,[27] so that it 'locks-up' a particular technology. On the other hand, where there is no evident benchmark for distinguishing the proper number of patents, and the 'right' innovative path is unknown, it is difficult to conclude that dominant firms' patent accumulation establishes an innovative path that is worse than the path that small firms would otherwise create.[28]

In summary, when it comes to patent accumulation, as with isolated predatory innovations, economic theory achieves results that antitrust authorities can arguably disregard because they are too sophisticated and difficult to apply.

SLEEPING PATENT STRATEGIES

To understand the logic of a sleeping patent strategy,[29] it is necessary first to analyze the private costs and benefits that each innovative activity entails.

The costs that firms sustain to procure patents vary according to how firms achieve them. When a firm chooses to develop the patent internally,

---

tends to snowball on, and hence changing the industry's innovative path; on the other hand, other firms' incentives to innovate decrease. See, in this regard, Alexandre Almeida & Aurora A.C. Teixeira, 'Does Patenting Negatively Impact on R&D Investments? An International Panel Data Assessment' (2007), available at www.ftc.gov/os/2003/10/innovationrptsummary.pdf; Robert M. Hunt, *When Do More Patents Reduce R&D?* (2006), available at http://ideas.repec.org/e/phu40.html; and Michael Heller & Rebecca Eisenberg, 'Can Patents Deter Innovation? The Anticommons in Biomedical Research', 280 *Science* 698 (1998); (referring to this problem as the 'tragedy of gatekeepers'); and Kaysen & Turner, *supra* note 20, at 165.

[27] In particular, if the monopolist's innovation becomes the quintessential innovation that any other firm has to confront, it could happen that some firms choose not to invest anymore in that industry. See, in this regard, Shapiro, *supra* note 19.

[28] Motta, *supra* note 7, at 456–7 (arguing that 'while it is theoretically possible that an incumbent over invests in advertising, R&D, or capacity, or that it introduces new brands, or engages in product proliferation for the purpose of strategically deterring entry or forcing exits of small rivals, it would seem difficult to suggest any rule that allows identifying such behavior in practice.').

[29] Consider that a sleeping patent is sometimes referred to as a 'paper patent'. On this topic, see, e.g., Dayton R. Stemple, 'Nonuser of Paper Patents', 34 J. *Pat. Off. Soc'y* 23 (1952). Instead, a sleeping patent is different from a *patent troll*, which is a company (or a person) who acquires the ownership of a patent without the intention of actually using it to produce a product, but who either licenses the technology, or sues a person believed to already have incorporated the technology in a product without permission – according to a scheme that is usually addressed to as the 'patent hold up' phenomenon. In this regard, see, e.g., Marcus Reitzig et al., 'On Sharks, Trolls, and Other Patent Animals – "Being Infringed" as a Normatively Induced Innovation Exploitation Strategy', (2006), http://ssrn.com/abstract=885914; and James F. McDonough III, 'The Myth of the Patent Troll: An Alternative View of the Function of Patent Dealers in an Idea Economy', 56 *Emory L. J.* 189 (2006).

the costs are equal to the R&D investment it undertakes.[30] Instead, when a firm purchases an innovation or obtains a license for it, the costs are respectively equal either to the purchase price of the invention or to the stream of royalties that the firm has to pay to the patent holder.[31]

The benefits that the achievement of a patent produces are twofold. A firm may improve its reputation if it patents a breakthrough technology and, at least in civil law countries, individual inventors acquire the moral right to be recognized as inventors.[32] Yet, firms derive most of the advantage that flows from patents by being the first to market the patented innovations,[33] whether directly or through licensees.[34] After all, whereas not all jurisdictions recognize patents' 'moral soul', they all consider patents as tools intended to reward the commercialization of inventions, so patent-holders can really recoup the investments they made in innovations, thanks to the exclusive right of making, using, offering for sale, or selling the invention. Procuring a patent thus entails expected benefits equal to the stream of income that the firm expects to gain from either producing and selling the innovation, or granting a licensee the right to do it.[35]

---

[30] R&D investments as such may also work as preemptive devices, regardless of whether the monopolist succeeds in achieving a patent. The amount of R&D investments, indeed, can signal to rivals the monopolist's commitment not to leave market-space to them. Not by chance, in the *Alcoa* case Justice Hand observed that 'drastic expenditures of research and development with knowledge or intent to preempt and dominate an industry' may represent an offense under Section 2 of the Sherman Act, *United States v. Aluminum Co. of America*, 148 F. 2d 416 (2d Cir. 1945). Further, see, e.g., Dixit, *supra* note 6; and Gilbert, *supra* note 6, at 236. Strategic investments and patent preemption generally represent components of the monopolist's overall strategy, although investments can be so effective in preventing entry as to make preemptive patenting unnecessary.

[31] In formulas, as arguably R&D expenditures are built in the price and royalties required for the marketing of the innovation, the chapter does not distinguish between these alternatives and names C (π) the costs of procuring the patent.

[32] In formulas, say BR [h (π)] those 'reputational benefits'.

[33] Besides, see Scherer & Ross, *supra* note 7, at 627 (observing that the first mover has a head start in the race down the learning curve, so gaining costs advantages which may be used to deter entry and enjoy supra-normal profits).

[34] In particular, as the value of intellectual goods does not decrease the more people utilize them IP non-exclusive licenses are probably the most profitable tool to extract profits. As Judge Easterbrook recently wrote, 'intellectual property can be used without being used up; the marginal cost of an additional user is zero', *Wallace v. IBM*, 467 F.3d 1104, at 1107 (7th Circ. 2006). Moreover see Edmund W. Kitch, 'Elementary and Persistent Errors in the Economic Analysis of Intellectual Property', 53 *Vand. L. Rev.* 1727, 1740 (2000) (remarking that IPRs may easily arise in the hands of persons or firms who are not in the best position to exploit them, so that the simple IPRs' transferability not only allows inventors to really capitalize on inventions, but also allows the system to work).

[35] Say σB [m (π)] those expected benefits. For sure, such benefits are only 'expected' – i.e., they happen according to a specific probability, say σ – as the monopolist cannot know from the outset whether consumers will like the innovation. In particular, the expected benefits can be higher in case of patent thicket, because patent accumulation may produce positive externalities.

Hence, a first conclusion to bear in mind in order to understand sleeping patent strategies is that, in accordance with industrial organization models, firms innovate when the benefits that they expect to derive from a patent exceed its costs.[36]

Consider further that, especially when the innovation is internally developed,[37] a firm making such a calculation takes a gamble about the innovation's profitability – a bet that a monopolist addresses several times during the development period: from the decision to invest in R&D, to the decision to market the patented innovation. In the economic world a monopolist would ultimately develop and market its innovations if it expects the benefits to exceed the costs whenever it asks itself this question.[38]

Now sleeping patent strategies occur when a monopolist consciously procures a patent though it knows from the outset that its costs will outweigh its benefits – an outcome that is particularly probable because the monopolist has decided from the beginning that it will not use the patent,[39] but will allow it to stay dormant or 'asleep'. Assuming that firms are rational agents, such behavior is understandable only if it is *strategic* – i.e., only if the monopolist knows from the commencement that procuring a sleeping patent will bring additional advantages that outweigh the patent's costs.[40]

Broadly speaking, these additional advantages may arise when firms use patents as 'bargaining chips' in tech-transfer agreements and to signal likely streams of future profits to financial markets.[41] But, from

---

36 In formulas, when $BR\ [h\ (\pi)] + \sigma B[m\ (\pi)] > C\ (\pi)$. The chapter equalizes, for simplicity's sake, the costs of procuring a patent to the cost of marketing it. After all, 'intellectual property is characterized by heavy fixed costs relative to marginal costs. It is expensive to create but once created the cost of making additional copies is low', Richard A. Posner, 'Antitrust in the New Economy' 3 (2000), available at www.ssrn.com.

37 Arguably, the decision-making process that leads to the purchase of an innovation or to the conclusion of a licensing agreement is less time-consuming and risky than the process that leads to the internal development of the innovation and so is less prone to be reviewed. Indeed, in the former case the monopolist can benefit from an already crafted and patented innovation.

38 For simplicity's sake, assume that the monopolist makes the abovementioned calculus only twice: before achieving the patent and before marketing the innovation. Say t_0 the moment before achieving the patent, and t_1 the moment before marketing the innovation, a monopolist eventually develops and markets the innovation when, in t_0, $BR[h(\pi)] + \sigma B_0[m(\pi)] > C_0(\pi)$ *and* in t_1, $BR[h(\pi)] + \sigma B_1[m(\pi)] > C_1(\pi)$.

39 Indeed, if $\sigma B_0[m(\pi)] = \sigma B_1[m(\pi)] = 0$ it is really likely that even from the outset, i.e. even in t_0, $B_0R\ [h\ (\pi)] < C(\pi)$.

40 Name $AA(\pi)$ these additional advantages, sleeping patent strategies occur when, in t_0 $BR[h(\pi)] + AA(\pi) > C(\pi)$, with $\sigma B_0[m(\pi)] = \sigma B_1[m(\pi)] = 0$

41 Adam Jaffe, 'The US Patent System in Transition: Policy Innovation and the Innovation Process', 29 *Research Policy* 531 (2000); Bronwyn H. Hall & Rosemarie H. Ziedonis, 'The Patent Paradox Revisited: Firm Strategy and Patenting in the US Semiconductor Industry',

the antitrust standpoint, sleeping patents become dangerous strategic tools when they serve as means for entry deterrence, for blocking rivals' innovations, or for infringement and counter-infringement suits against rivals. In these cases, indeed, sleeping patents allow the dominant patentee to protect its monopoly power and, hence, to keep on charging over-competitive prices.

For instance, suppose that a dominant firm has monopolized a specific technology and realizes in advance that a new technology, substitutable for the monopolized one, could displace or, at least, harm its monopoly. In such a scenario, then, in order to prevent its rivals from using the new technology and so gaining market shares to its detriment, the monopolist decides in advance to win the race to patent the new technology, though that race entails wasteful investments that make the technology not cost-justified.[42] Such a monopolistic strategy can succeed and rivals can be barred from gaining shares in the monopolized market, thus leaving the monopolist free to maintain its power when,[43] for instance, the incumbent

---

32 *Rand Journal of Economics* 101 (2001). There is a rich literature about firms that, realizing that patents can be easily monetized into licensing fees and damages, have undertaken formalized business plans both to acquire critical patents in particular fields and to leverage value from asserting those patents. In other words, several scholars have recognized that patentees, who take financial advantage of the patent rules that should serve the overarching goals of innovation, act in contravention to the underlying values of the patent system. See, e.g., Amy L. Landers, 'Liquid Patents', 84 *Denver University L. Rev.* 199 (2006) and Robert P. Merges, 'Of Property Rules, Coase, and Intellectual Property', 94 *Colum. L. Rev.* 2655, 2659 (1994). Consider, for instance, the additional advantages that could come from using the patent as a '*legal bargaining chip*' during either the negotiation of cross-licensing agreements, infringement suits, or the access to external finance. See, e.g., Bronwyn Hall & Rose Marie Ham, 'The Patent Paradox Revisited: Determinants of Patenting in the US Semiconductor Industry', *1980–94*, NBER Working Paper Series, no. 7062 (1989); Heller & Eisenberg, supra note 26; Wesley M. Cohen, Richard R. Nelson, & John Walsh, 'Protecting their Intellectual Assets: Appropriability Conditions and Why U.S. Manufacturing Firms Patent (or Not)', NBER Working Paper Series, no. 7552 (2000).

[42] Indeed, the monopolist is interested in undertaking such a patent race as, with entry, it will lose (at least) half of its profits (passing from a monopoly to a duopoly). In other words, to preserve its dominance the incumbent may offer a greater sum for the new patent – even when it does not incur R&D expenses but buys the patent from the inventor – than anyone else.

[43] In the 1980s, a central concern of the industrial organization literature was to determine if markets dominated by a leading producer tend to remain that way, though rivals' entry is possible. For instance, Gilbert & Newbery, *supra* note 2, 514, 'inquir[e] whether institutions such as the patent system create opportunities for firms with monopoly power to maintain their monopoly power', and understand that a firm may sustain its monopoly power through patent preemption. See, further, John Vickers, 'Pre-Emptive Patenting, Joint Ventures, and the Persistence of Oligopoly', 3 *International Journal of Industrial Organization* 261 (1985); Stephen Salant, 'Preemptive Patenting and the Persistence of Monopoly: Comment', 74 *Am. Econ. Rev.* 247 (1984); Jennifer F. Reinganum, 'Uncertain Innovation and the Persistence of Monopoly', 73 *Am. Econ. Rev.* 741 (1983); Drew Fudenberg et al., 'Preemption, Leapfrogging and Competition in Patent Races', 22 *The European Economic Review* 3 (1983); Larry S.

faces only one or a small number of potential competitors;[44] the reward from investing in the R&D expenses necessary for achieving the new invention is relatively certain;[45] or the target sleeping patent contains a drastic innovation.[46]

In summary, though it is uncertain how frequent monopolists procure pre-emptive sleeping patents,[47] a sleeping patent strategy may decrease consumer welfare because of the resources wasted to achieve the patent, the lack of the social benefit that usually accompanies the marketing of an innovation because the innovation is kept idle, and the over-competitive prices that the monopolist continues to charge.

Moreover, when the sleeping technology also blocks monopolists' rivals from producing follow-on innovations,[48] this strategy prevents the whole society from enjoying not only the technology that remains idle but also these further innovations, leaving the dominant firm in position to control

---

Karp & Jeffrey Perloff, 'The Optimal Suppression of a Low-Cost Technology by a Durable-Good Monopoly', 27 *Rand Journal of Economics* 346, 359 (1996); and Mark Lemley, 'The Economics of Improvement in Intellectual Property Law', 75 *Tex. L. Rev.* 989, 1066 (1997); Ka Man Chan & Yue Kuen Kwok, 'Asymmetric Preemptive Patenting Races and Sleeping Patents' (2007), available on www.ssrn.com. For a discussion of these models, see Richard Gilbert, 'Looking for Mr. Schumpeter: Where Are We in the Competition-Innovation Debate?', in *Innovation Policy and the Economy* 159, 168-175 (Adam B. Jaffe, Josh Lerner & Scott Stern eds. 2006).

44 See, e.g., Gilbert & Newbery, *supra* note 2, at 522–5 and Richard J. Gilbert & Steven C. Sunshine, 'Incorporating Dynamic Efficiency Concerns in Merger Analysis: The Use of Innovation Markets', 63 *Antitrust L. J.* 569, 578 (1995). Indeed, there is a trade-off between the probability that the preemptive patenting strategy succeeds and the number of potential entrants: as it increases, the likelihood that one or more of them will discover either a way to 'invent around' the patent, or a patentable opportunity that does not fall under the preempt patent increases as well.

45 Recall, indeed, that in order to apply the pre-emptive strategy the incumbent undertakes wasteful R&D expenses. Thus, if even achieving the invention was not sufficiently certain, the dominant firm's choice would be totally unjustifiable. See Gilbert & Sunshine, *supra* note 44, at 578; Fudenberg et al., *supra* note 43, at 10–21; and Reinganum, *supra* note 43, at 741 and 745–6.

46 Indeed, the more drastic the future innovation is, the greater is the likelihood that the new innovation will cannibalize the monopolized one, thus producing the well-known 'replacement effect'. Therefore, the more drastic the innovation, the greater the monopolist's incentives are to preempt that new and drastic innovation.

47 The view among mainstream economists is that preemptive patenting is uncommon. See, e.g., Gilbert, *supra* note 6, at 211, 239–57, 269; Gilbert & Newbery, *supra* note 2, at 514; Reinganum, *supra* note 43, at 746. Yet, some recent empirical studies show the contrary. See, e.g., Marco Ceccagnoli, 'Appropriability, Preemption, and Firm Performance' (2007), available at www.ssrn.com and Cohen, Nelson, & Walsh, *supra* note 41. Both papers suggest that entry deterrence is a key driver of higher profits.

48 A technology is said to be *blocking* (so that the related patent is said to be blocking as well) if inventing around it is 'either not commercially practicable, or will not produce a commercially viable product', Ian Simmons, Patrick Lynch, & Theodore H. Frank, '"I Know It When I See It": Defining and Demonstrating "Blocking patents"', 16 *Antitrust* 48, 49 (2002). Moreover, consider Shapiro, *supra* note 19, at 120 and 123.

the innovative path.[49] Therefore, in such a scenario consumer welfare also dwindles because of the harm to dynamic efficiency.

Yet, once again for antitrust authorities it would be complicated to administer a prohibition of sleeping patent strategies, at least because distinguishing a sleeping patent strategy from permitted behaviors requires antitrust authorities to examine whether the dominant firm has an objective justification for its lack of commercialization. For instance, a monopolist could choose not to commercialize a technology only after its development, if it then realizes that its marketing would be not cost-justified,[50] because of (a) lack of a current demand; an unexpected prohibitive increase in production costs; a sudden lack of financing; inability to develop a marketable product to embody the innovation; or (b) the rapid development of other more promising inventions; or (c) the fact that the technology lacks commercial applications within the area of the patent owner's expertise, perhaps because of the lack of complementary assets or because of the poor fit of the project with the firm's general sales strategy; (d) compatibility problems in industries where interoperability and critical mass are crucial; or (e) the wish not to de-skill or displace workers; and a 'bureaucratic' interest in preserving the status quo.[51] Indeed, in these cases of non-cost-justified inventions, it is rational for the monopolist not to market the innovation, though it has previously and rationally patented it. As a matter of fact, this latter scenario involves a patent that is not developed, used or marketed as strategic sleeping patents are: the difference is that the choice not to market the patent does not belong to a preemptive scheme – i.e., a scheme aimed at preventing a new invention from competing against the monopolized product – but stems from one or more of several reasons.[52] Therefore, since the monopolist is doing nothing more

[49] Making this hypothesis means assuming that 'the right incentive to innovate' is upon the potential competitor, rather than upon the monopolist. In other words, the crucial hypothesis is that another firm would have commercialized the invention. Indeed, as said before, this assumption requires thinking of antitrust authorities as social planners who know who is in the best position to innovate.

[50] In formulas this scenario occurs when, in t_0 $BR[h(\pi)] + \sigma B_0[m(\pi)] > C_0(\pi)$ *but* in t_1 $BR[h(\pi)] + \sigma B_1[m(\pi)] < C_1(\pi)$.

[51] For an overview of those non-use objective justifications, see, e.g., Joseph Rossman & Barkev S. Sanders, 'The Patent Utilization Study', in '*Nurturing New Ideas: Legal Rights and Economic Roles*' 106, 135 (L. James Harris ed. 1969); Helen Weeds, 'Sleeping Patents and Compulsory Licensing: An Options Analysis' 4, (1999) at 21, available at http://privatewww.essex.ac.uk/~hfweeds/sleeping%20patents.pdf; and Teece, *supra* 19.

[52] See Karp & Perloff, *supra* note 43, at 355 (observing that in the absence of anticompetitive justifications, a rational monopolist has a strong incentive to adopt a new technology so that the choice not to use it must find rational economic justifications). This is true even when the relevant phenomenon consists not in suppressing but in delaying the use of the innovation. Indeed, there are several models where, giving the possibility to shape the timing of R&D investments according to either technological and market uncertainty, a potentially

than paying for the risk of having bet at the outset on the patent's profitability, striking down such a sleeping patent would discourage monopolists' incentives to innovate.

SUPPRESSED PATENTS

In contrast to the scenarios mentioned above is the situation in which a monopolist patents a cost-justified innovation but does not market it, though its commercialization would be rational and beneficial for the whole society. The monopolist does this because it can benefit more by keeping the innovation idle than by marketing it.[53] To give an example: suppose that, after having developed an innovation, the monopolist realizes that it could be used as a base for rivals' future innovations that could displace both the monopolized technology and the monopoly itself. In order to block such follow-on innovations and thus to protect its market power, the monopolist chooses to keep the patent idle.[54]

Now, such behavior could harm dynamic efficiency, as it deprives the whole society of the benefits that would follow from both the use of the patented innovation and the development of the technology's improvements.

Yet, virtually all behaviors relating to innovation may to some extent be

---

profitable technology is left unexploited for some lapse of time and not for anticompetitive reasons. See Weeds, *supra* note 51, (affirming that any compulsory license in a changed facts scenario would be counterproductive. Indeed, 'it may be rational for a firm to carry out research at times when market profitability is below the level that would induce exploitation of the new technology. The intuition for this result lies in a trade-off between two potential costs facing the firm. By carrying out research while conditions are not sufficiently favorable to induce market entry, the firm incurs the costs of research to gain an investment option that may not be exercised for an extended period of time. During this period it bears an opportunity cost given by the risk-free return on this investment. If, on the other hand, the firm delays research until conditions improve, it is likely that the discovery will not be achieved until some time after market entry would have been desirable. During this period the firm forgoes the product market profits which it would have earned had it been in a position to enter the market immediately.').

[53] In formulas, that scenario occurs when, in t_0 $BR[h(\pi)] + \sigma B_0[m(\pi)] > C_0(\pi)$ *and* in t_1 $BR[h(\pi)] + \sigma B_1[m(\pi)] > C_1(\pi)$ *but* $AA(\pi) > \sigma B_1[m(\pi)] > C(\pi)$. The suppression of technology phenomenon can be analogized to the case of a monopolist who delays the technology's introduction so as to stifle future incentives to innovate by eliminating or minimizing research competition.

[54] See, e.g., William L. Baldwin & G. L. Childs, 'The Fast Second and Rivalry in Research and Development', *S. Econ. J.* 18–24 (1969); Scherer & Ross, *supra* note 7, at 407–38; Gilbert, *supra* note 6, 205–300; and Gilbert & Newbery, *supra* note 2, at 517–24; and Heller & Eisenberg, *supra* note 26, at 699–700 (arguing that 'when owners have conflicting goals and each can deploy its rights to block the strategies of the others, they may not be able to reach an agreement that leaves enough private value for downstream developers to bring products to the market.').

said to suppress technology.[55] Further, for antitrust authorities it could be difficult to prove that the absent commercialization of an innovation impairs economic growth or technological development of an industry. In summary, it seems complex to elaborate a reliable way to detect true acts of technological suppression.

THE US AND EU LEGAL APPROACHES: THE MERE PROCUREMENT OF PATENTS

Neither courts nor the competition authorities of US and EU apply competition law to prosecute the mere procurement of patents. Today, in the United States, such immunity has a twofold basis. First, applying Justice Hand's teaching,[56] the Second Circuit noted in *Berkey Photo v. Eastman Kodak* that 'because [. . .] a monopolist is permitted, and indeed encouraged, by § 2 to compete aggressively on the merits, any success that it may achieve through 'the process of invention and innovation' is clearly tolerated by the antitrust law'.[57] There is also a procedural basis, because

---

[55] Even the simple unilateral choice to invest in a particular product/process may entail a related decision not to develop alternative products/processes, indeed. See Cohen & Burke, *supra* note 4, at 427. Therefore, some scholars have concluded – in a paradoxical way – that a real case of technology suppression is a 'unicorn'. See, e.g., Armen Alchian & William R. Allen, *Exchange and Production: Competition, Coordination, and Control* 326 (1983) (referring to patent suppression as 'a commonplace of modern folklore'). Yet, some old empirical studies have estimated that approximately 40 to 90 per cent of issued patents are not used or licensed by the patentee, such as Peter Meinhardt, *Inventions, Patents and Monopoly* 189 (1946); Barkey S. Sanders, 'Patterns of Commercial Exploitation of Patented Inventions by Large and Small Corporations', 8 *Pat., Trademark, & Copyright J. Res. & Educ.* 51, 63 (1964); and Roger L. Beck, 'Competition for Patent Monopolies', 3 *Res. L. & Econ.* 91, 98 (1981). Yet, one should make a distinction between data regarding non-used innovations, and data concerning non-used good innovation. Numerous anecdotes have been told about suppressed innovations, such as safer cigarettes, electric lamps, solar energy, and pain control devices, and alternative vehicles. For a brief description of those anecdotes, see Kurt M. Saunders & Linda Levine, 'Better, Faster, Cheaper Later: What Happens When Technologies are Suppressed', 11 *Mich. Telecomm. Tech. L. Rev.* 23 (2004), and Kurt M. Saunders, 'Patent Nonuse and the Role of Public Interest as a Deterrent to Technology Suppression', 15 *Harv. J.L. & Tech.* 389 (2002) and the related references.

[56] See *United States v. Aluminum Co. of Am.*, 148 F.2d 416, 430 (2nd Circ. 1945), where the court stated that 'a single producer may be the survivor out of a group of active competitors, merely by virtue of his superior skill, foresight and industry. In such cases a strong argument can be made that, although the result may expose the public to the evils of monopoly, the Act does not mean to condemn the resultant of those very forces which it is its prime object to foster [. . .] the successful competitor, having been urged to compete, must not be turned upon when he wins.'. To be sure, whereas recognizing that 'superior skill, foresight, and industry' could vindicate some dominant firms, Justice Hand assumed that Alcoa's 90 per cent market share was so great as to exclude such a defense.

[57] 603 F.2d 263 (2nd Circ. 1979). Further, see *United States v. Grinnell Corp.*, 384 U.S. 563 (1966). Likewise see *Intergraph Corp. v. Intel Corp.*195 F.3d 1346, 1354 (Fed. Cir. 1999),

the mere act of applying for a patent is simply 'an act of 'petitioning' an administrative agency (the PTO)',[58] and therefore it enjoys, pursuant to the so-called '*Noerr-Pennington* doctrine',[59] immunity from antitrust liability even when it produces anticompetitive effects.

In the EU jurisdiction, the ECJ did grant immunity to the procurement of patents, stating that the mere existence of these rights cannot be prohibited by Article 102. In reaching this conclusion the ECJ, although it probably believed that firms procuring new patents do not distort genuine competition, relied expressly on Article 345 of TFEU that establishes that, since the existence of IPRs is a matter solely of national law, EU institutions do not have jurisdiction over matters relating to the granting of patents and IPRs, in general.[60]

Therefore, looking back at the policy issues that Chapter 2 discusses, it seems that whereas US courts rejected the idea that dominant firms have to act as their rivals' trustee, because of their lack of jurisdiction EU courts did not take an explicit position on the matter. Either way, though for different reasons, the general principle in force in both jurisdictions is that a dominant firm is free to innovate and obtain patents even when permitting such a practice in effect shelters market power, by excluding rivals, and happens to harm consumer welfare under, for instance, the conditions of the above described economic models.[61]

Having said that, it is nevertheless worth speculating whether this principle should still apply when looking at more extreme cases; namely, the case of a dominant firm that fraudulently procures its patents; does not use them; or acquires them – whether sleeping or not – from the market.[62]

---

where the court stated 'product superiority and the ensuing market position, flowing from a company's research, talents, commercial efforts, and financial commitments, do not convert the successful enterprise into an illegal monopolist under the Sherman Act'. To be sure, the *Berkey-Kodak* case involved a multi-product firm. Berkey, the plaintiff, alleged that the defendant, Kodak, used its innovative capacity in film to gain a competitive advantage in cameras by innovating in such a way that only Kodak's newest model camera would be capable of using Kodak's newest, and presumably much-desired, film.

[58] See *Medimmune, Inc. v. Genentech, Inc.*, No. CV 03-2567 MRP, slip op. at 18 (C.D.Cal. Dec. 24, 2003), aff'd, 427 F3d 958 (Fed. Cir. 2005).

[59] See Chapter 6 for a more detailed discussion of this doctrine, which offers protection against antitrust law to actions that involve the access to public powers.

[60] Case 24/67, *Parke, Davis and Co. v. Probel, Reese, Beintema-Interpharm and Centrafarm*, February 29 1968, [1968] ECR 55, 72. The same dichotomy of existence-exercise was applied in connection with copyright, in Case 78/70 *Deutsche Grammophon Gesselschaft mbH v. Metro-SB-Großmärkte GmbH & Co. KG.*, June 8 1971, [1971] ECR 487, § 11 and – even if this subject goes beyond the boundaries of this chapter – in connection with trademarks, in Case 40/70, *Sirena Srl v. Eda Srl and Others*, February 18 1971, [1971] ECR 69, § 5.

[61] It is likely that the same conclusion can be drawn from *Astrazeneca* judgment, General Court, case T-321/05 (2010), available at http://curia.europa.eu.

[62] It is apparent that these three scenarios are different from those that the economic

THE FRAUDULENT PROCUREMENT OF PATENTS

It is manifest that the practice of a dominant firm fraudulently procuring a patent is inconsistent with the aims of patent statutes, which indeed provide remedies against such a practice both in the US and in the EU Member States.[63] And, just as there is no social merit in permitting a firm to cheat the patent office, it is equally clear that such a practice should be subject to Section 2 and Article 102 if it helps to maintain or strengthen a firm's dominance and to harm consumer welfare. Yet, the US case law exempts the mere procurement of a fraudulent patent from violating antitrust law. The reasoning is as follows: on the one hand, the existence of a fraud bars the application of the Noerr-Pennington immunity, because the patent's petition is a sham that does not deserve to be protected against antitrust law.[64] On the other hand, as the so-called *Walker Process* doctrine teaches,[65] the application of Section 2 rests with the knowing *enforcement* of the invalid patent and the mere procurement of a patent does not satisfy such condition.[66] In other words, as the Federal Circuit held in *Unitherm Food Systems v. Swift-Eckrich*, courts lack jurisdiction if the patentee has done nothing but obtain a patent in a manner that the plaintiff believes is fraudulent.[67]

---

models suggest. Indeed, as the final paragraph of this chapter will explain, this is one of the differences between the economic thinking and the legal rules.

63 Neither the US courts nor the European Commission consider the existence of those remedies a good reason not to apply competition law. The US Supreme Court, stressing the deterrent effect of the antitrust remedies, held that the 'paramount interest in seeing that patent monopolies spring from backgrounds free from fraud' is well served by treble damages. See *Walker Process Equip., Inc. v. Food Machinery & Chemical Corp.*, 382 U.S. 172, at 177 (1965). In particular, consider that Justice Harland held that, 'to recover damages for Sherman Act monopolization knowingly practiced under the guise of a patent procured by deliberate fraud, cannot well be thought to impinge upon the policy of the patent laws to encourage inventions and their disclosure.' – id. at 179–180. The European Commission, besides being sensitive to the theme of deterrence, claimed that 'the fact that other laws and remedies prohibit misleading representations or provide for remedies against them is irrelevant where the objective of competition enforcement is not to penalize such misconduct per se, but rather to prevent the anticompetitive effects of such misconduct in the marketplace. Such anticompetitive effects must fall within the scope of competition law, and the fact that otherwise prohibited means may have been used to achieve them cannot be decisive for the application of competition law.' – See *AstraZeneca* (COMP/A. 37.507/F3), 15 June 2005, http://ec.europa.eu/comm/competition/antitrust/ cases/decisions/37507/en.pdf (hereinafter, *AstraZeneca*), § 744.

64 Indeed, as Chapter 6 explains, the 'Noerr-Pennington' immunity does not apply when the petition is a mere sham used to cover an attempt to interfere directly with the business relationships of a competitor. Arguably, to obtain a patent by cheating the PTO could be considered as a sham.

65 See Chapter 6 and *Dippin' Dots, Inc. v. Mosey*, 476 F.3d 1337 (Fed. Circ. 2007) for a clear and recent restatement of the doctrine.

66 *Walker Process Equip., Inc. v. Food Machinery & Chemical Corp.*, 382 U.S. 172, at 179 (1965).

67 375 F.3d 1341, 1358 (Fed. Circ. 2004). Several years before, the same court held in *FMC*

Therefore, although the Supreme Court has never specifically articulated such an 'enforcement requirement', US antitrust courts prosecute patents as fraudulently obtained only when they have been enforced, at least at a minimum level.[68]

In the EU jurisdiction, instead, the issue of the fraudulent procurement of a patent has never arisen. However in the *AstraZeneca* decision the Commission deemed as illegal the mere fraudulent procurement of a series of supplementary protection certificates (hereinafter, SPCs), i.e., certificates aimed to extend the patent's term.[69] This case does not appear to be at odds with the US case law or – more importantly – with the idea that the antitrust action must rest with the effects that a dominant firm's conduct produces on the market. First, since the privilege to ask for SPCs arises only after obtaining a patent,[70] *AstraZeneca* is simply the case of the abusive enforcement of one of the licit administrative procedures that are available to a patentee. Not by chance, indeed, the Commission analogized AstraZeneca's conduct to a case of sham litigation, where the abuse of the

---

Corp. v. Manitowoc Co., 835 F.2d 1411, 1418, footnote 16 (Fed. Circ. 1987) that, the 'mere procurement of a patent, whatever the conduct of the applicant in the procurement, cannot without more affect the welfare of the consumer and cannot in itself violate the antitrust laws'. Moreover, see *California Eastern Laboratories, Inc. v. Gould*, 896 F.2d 400, 403 (9th Cir. 1990), where the Court affirmed a district court dismissal of a *Walker Process* claim because the plaintiff did not allege that the defendant 'actually attempted to enforce the patents'. As a whole, hence, federal courts have never seriously considered whether mere ownership of invalid patents can distort competition; rather they have simply assumed that it cannot.

[68] Suing for infringement clearly constitutes enforcement, so do threatening to sue, and sending cease and desist letters. See, e.g., *Agron, Inc. v. Lin*, 72 U.S.P.Q.2d 1714, 1720 (C.D. Cal. 2004); *OpenLCR.com, Inc. v. Rates Tech., Inc.*, 112 F. Supp. 2d 1223, 1228-33 (D. Colo. 2000); *Arcade, Inc. v. Minn. Mining & Mfg. Co.*, No. CIV-1-88-141, 1991 WL 185155, at 3 (E.D. Tenn. July 2, 1991), *aff'd*, 1 F.3d 1253 (Fed. Cir. 1993).

[69] The marketing of a drug follows a specific public authorization that authorities such as the Food and Drug Administration (FDA) and the Public Health Departments of the European Member States generally grant some years after the procurement of the related patent. Therefore, in order not to erode the period during which the pharmaceutical firm can, as a matter of fact, exploit the economic value of its exclusive right, both the US and EU patent systems grant to pharmaceutical patents extra-time protection in the form of SPC. These certificates are available to US patentees pursuant to 35 U.S.C. § 156, and to EU patentees under Article 3 of Regulation (EEC) No 1768/92. During the period covered by an SPC, generic drug producers are not entitled to enter into the market. Enforcement issues relating to the infringement and the validity of SPCs are also dealt with by national courts in accordance with national law. But, as said before, nothing prevents the Commission from analyzing some of those practices as anticompetitive, when the other requirements of Article 82 are satisfied. In the *AstraZenaca* decision, the Commission mentioned the judgments whereby some national courts invalidated the SPCs – see § 602.

[70] Pursuant to Article 3 of Regulation (EEC) No. 1768/92, an SPC can be granted 'if, in the Member State . . . a) the product is protected by a basic patent in force'. Thus, the *AstraZeneca* argument, according to which the decision would not respect the dichotomy between the ownership and the enforcement of IPRs, does not seem sound, even regardless of the Commission's arguments.

judicial procedure consists of the unlawful enforcement of a valid patent.[71] Second, the certificates concerned were connected to an already fully enforced patent. Since producers of cheaper generic products cannot enter the relevant market as long as a patent lasts, the anticompetitive nature of any behavior whose purpose is to delay the duration of a patent, and thus the entrance of such competitors to the market, is apparent: it prolongs the dominance and its costs without producing any countervailing benefit; it impairs rivals' opportunities without improving market performance.[72] Third, even if the Commission did not discuss explicitly – as a US court probably would have done – whether the patentee used the fraudulently acquired SPCs, the patentee did actually assert their validity in national courts.[73] Thus, it is also conceivable that a US court would have considered the minimum enforcement requirement satisfied.

As a whole, the fraudulent procurement of a patent alone does not represent an antitrust violation in the US or in the EU, despite the theoretical possibility that dominant firms might also use invalid patents either to build up their preemptive strategies or to suppress new technologies. Antitrust authorities have decided not to follow the economic models mentioned above and they choose not to use competition law and its remedies as an additional sanction to what IP regimes already provide for fraudulent procured patents.

THE NON-USE OF PATENTS

Early in the twentieth century, when US courts were split over the lawfulness of patent non-use,[74] the US Supreme Court recognized in *Continental*

[71] In the decision, the Commission did not challenge the validity of the patent – as it is not supposed to do pursuant to Article 345 – and due to some national invalidity the claims ended with settlement in favor of the dominant firm. See *AstraZeneca*, §§ 87–96.

[72] See *AstraZeneca*, §§ 112–38. Further, see CFI, *Astrazeneca*, 1 July 2010, case T-321/05, § 362, available at http://curia.europa.eu/, where the court stated that 'the mere possession by an undertaking of an exclusive right normally results in keeping competitors away'.

[73] *AstraZeneca*, §§ 231, and 727–40, where the Commission reported that *AstraZeneca* both sued a number of generics firms that entered into the German market following the patent's expiry, and used its invalid patent to build its defenses in other national courts. In this regard, the Commission wrote that, 'AZ's conduct of its defense before the national courts concerned was simply the continuation of the pattern of misleading representation initiated by AZ well before the competitors instituted proceedings, and not the cause of the costs and delays suffered by them. In addition, the German court proceedings were crucial as far as the maintenance of AZ's SPCs (including their duration) in other countries was concerned.' – see § 738.

[74] Indeed some courts held that, pursuant to patent doctrine, the infringement of a non-used patent awarded only damages to the patentee, and not the injunction. See, e.g., *Electric Smelting & Aluminum Co. v. Carborundum Co.*, 189 F. 710 (C.C.W.D. Pa. 1900);

Paper Bag Co.[75] – a patent case – that a patent holder is under no obligation either to use the invention itself or to license the invention to others. In particular, the Supreme Court held that it was reasonable for a patentee to use existing equipment embodying old technology rather than to sustain the expenses of changing or altering the old machines to craft new machines using new patents. The Court stated that, as to the suggestion that competitors were excluded from the use of the new patent, such exclusion had to be deemed the very essence of the right conferred by the patent, since it was the privilege of any owner of property to use or not use it, without question of motive.[76]

Some years later, in *Special Equipment Co. v. Coe*[77] – another patent case – the Supreme Court upheld the patentee's privilege not to use its patents in a specific scenario, namely, when the patentee had kept the patent sleeping in order to protect another of its patented technologies. In particular, in discussing Justice Douglas' dissenting opinion,[78] the majority observed

---

Dorsey Harvester Revolving Rake Co. v. Marsh, 7 F. Cas. 939, 945 (C.C.E.D. Pa. 1873). That remedy was a form of compulsory licensing with judicially determined damages as the royalty. Further, even recently in *Allied Research Products v. Heatbath Corp.*, 300 F. Supp. 656, 657 (N.D. Ill. 1969) the court refused to award injunctive relief, and in *Kearns v. Chrysler Corp.*, 32 F.3d 1541, 1551 (Fed. Cir. 1994) the Federal Circuit has stated in dicta that entitlement to injunctive relief is 'discretionary', and this though Section 271(d) (4) of the US Patent Act, '[n]o patent owner otherwise entitled to relief for infringement [. . .] shall be denied relief or deemed guilty of misuse [. . .] by reason of his having [. . .] refused to license or use any rights to the patent'.

75 210 U.S. 405 (1908). Other decisions follow the *Continental Paper Bag* principle, upholding non-use of patents as within the rights of the patentee, see, e.g., *Crown Die & Tool Co. v. Nye Tool & Mach. Works*, 261 U.S. 24, 35 (1923); *Motion Picture Patents Co. v. Universal Film Mfg. Co.*, 243 U.S. 502, 514 (1917), where the Court stated that 'under the patent system, a patent owner clearly had the right to withhold his patent[ed] machine from public use'; *Lewis Blind Stitch Mach. Co. v. Premium Mfg. Co.*, 163 F. 950, 954 (8th Cir. 1908), where the court stated that 'during the life of his monopoly, a patentee is under no obligation to use or place upon the market [. . .] his invention'; and *United Shoe Mach. Corp. v. O'Donnell Rubber Prods. Co.*, 84 F.2d 383, 386 (6th Cir. 1936), where the court held that 'whatever may be the policy of patent laws elsewhere, it has long been settled that, in the United States, exclusion of competitors is the very essence of the right conferred by a patent, and it is the privilege of any owner of property to use or not to use it without question of motive'. In a more recent case – *Dawson Chemical Co. v. Rohm & Haas Co.*, 448 U.S. 176, 215 (1980) – the Supreme Court is representing a 'long-settled view that the essence of a patent grant is the right to exclude others from profiting by the patented invention'.

76 210 U.S. 405, at 429. The Court did, however, acknowledge that some forms of non-use could be directed at wrongful purposes and that such non-use might merit revocation of exclusionary patent rights. Although the Court did not expressly identify these situations at the time, several of these reasons have since developed as new and evolving technology continues to challenge the foundation of patent rights in U.S. law.

77 324 U.S. 370 (1945).

78 Justice Douglas argued that the choice to keep a patent idle is inconsistent with the constitutional purpose of the patent clause, which is to promote the progress of science and the useful arts. Thus, he stood for invalidating a non-used patent when the patentee 'has employed or plans to employ the patent not to exploit the invention but to suppress it in

that patents do not grant to their holders the obligation to use the invention, because they already possess the right to use it.[79] Besides, in order to further justify its opinion, the Court observed that it was not supposed to second guess what the Congress had decided about compulsory licenses, arguing further that Congress has frequently been asked to change the policy of the statutes but, nevertheless, has always avoided providing for either forfeiture or compulsory licensing if the patentee does not use the patent. In this regard, indeed, the Court stated that it had no occasion to consider during the suit whether a better rule governing the grant of patents could be devised than that prescribed by Congress.[80]

In the same year as the *Special Equipment* judgment, the Supreme Court declined again to prosecute patent non-use discussing an antitrust case, i.e., *Hartford-Empire Co. v. United States*.[81] There the Court eliminated the provisions of a decree that would have prohibited the patentees from obtaining new patents covering improvements on previously patented machines if they were not intended to be used.[82] Thus the Supreme Court,

---

order to protect another patent or otherwise', as 'in that way the constitutional objective will be more nearly realized – the product of the inventive genius of the human mind will be put to work in the economy.' – id., at 384. His reasoning was: 'It is a mistake [. . .] to conceive of a patent as but another form of private property. The patent is a privilege 'conditioned by a public purpose.' [. . .] The public purpose is 'to promote the Progress of Science and useful Arts.' The exclusive right of the inventor is but the means to that end. That was early recognized by this Court. [. . .] But the *Paper Bag* case marked a radical departure from that theory. It treated the 'exclusive' right of the inventor as something akin to an 'absolute' right. It subordinated the public purpose of the grant to the self-interest of the patentee. The result is that suppression of patents has become commonplace. Patents are multiplied to protect an economic barony or empire, not to put new discoveries to use for the common good. It is difficult to see how that use of patents can be reconciled with the purpose of the Constitution 'to promote the Progress of Science and the useful Arts.' Can the suppression of patents which arrests the progress of technology be said to promote that progress? It is likewise difficult to see how suppression of patents can be reconciled with the provision of the statute which authorizes a grant of the 'exclusive right to make, use, and vend the invention or discovery.' [. . .] I think it is time to return to the earlier, and I think the true, philosophy of the patent system. We should not pass on to Congress the duty to remove the private perquisites which we have engrafted on the patent laws' (internal citations omitted).

79 Id., at 378.

80 'Congress was aware that an unpatented invention could be suppressed and the public thus deprived of all knowledge or benefit of it. It could have concluded that the useful arts would be best promoted by compliance with the conditions of the statutes which it did enact, which require that patents be granted only for a limited term upon an application fully disclosing the invention and the manner of making and using it. It thus gave to the inventor limited opportunity to gather material rewards for his invention and secured to the public the benefits of full knowledge of the invention and the right to use it upon the expiration of the patent.' – id., at 379.

81 323 U.S. 386 (1945).

82 In particular, discussing paragraph 52 of the decree, which dealt with the problem of suppressed or unworked patents, the Court noticed that 'it enjoins every defendant from applying for a patent 'with the intention of not making commercial use of the invention

relying again on the legislature's choice not to require compulsory licensing in cases of patent non-use,[83] confirmed that an inventor of technology should be allowed to patent an innovation even if it intends not to use it. The Court observed that a patent holder is not in the position of a 'quasi-trustee' for the public or under any obligation to see that the public acquires the free right to use the invention, since the patentee has no obligation either to use it or to grant its use to others. In particular, the Court stated that the only obligation imposed by the statute to patent owners is that of disclosing the invention when the patent has expired.[84]

In summary, US courts have never held monopolists that did not use patents liable of antitrust violation, because as patentees they were under no obligation to use them. In other words, by flattering their approach on what IP doctrines establish antitrust courts have eliminated any conflict between competition law and IP law. They have negated the former and enforced the latter, by disregarding economic models that teach how sleeping patents can strengthen market power, harm consumer welfare, and affect innovation.

The EU institutions, in contrast, have never dealt with a claimant accusing a dominant firm of abusing its power by non-use of its internally developed patents. Nevertheless, Article 102(b) expressly mentions abuses of dominance consisting in 'limiting . . . technical developments to the prejudice of consumers'.

PURCHASING PATENTS OR OBTAINING A LICENSE FOR THEM

Patent sales and licenses represent not only a crucial device to reward patentees for their up-front investments, but also a vehicle to spread innovations among different firms that are, or might be, in the market. Indeed,

---

within four years' from issue of the patent and makes the failure commercially to use the invention prima facie proof of the absence (*sic*) of such intention. This provision is also legislative rather than remedial. Unless we are to overturn settled principles the paragraph in question must be eliminated.' – id., at 432.

83 The Court observed that 'a party seeking a right under the patent statutes may avail himself of all their provisions, and the courts may not deny him the benefit of a single one. These are questions not of natural but of purely statutory right. [. . .] No court can disregard any statutory provisions in respect to these matters on the ground that in its judgment they were unwise or prejudicial to the interests of the public.' – id., at *United States v. American Bell Telephone Co.*, 167 U.S. 224, 247 (1897).

84 Id., at 432–3. The Court in *Hartford-Empire* did not specifically ascertain that the patentee was a monopolist. Yet, in those years Hartford succeeded in tying up the entire glass container industry by purchasing and internally developing all of the important patents relating to the relevant technology.

given that such a 'trade' would leave the patent in the hands of its most efficient user,[85] IP regimes protect and encourage IP sales and licensees, making no distinction depending on whether their nature is exclusive or not nor depending on the market position of the firm that receives the IPR.

In *Tetra Pak I (BTG License)*[86] – a case about an exclusive patent license – EU case law provides its rule to govern a monopolist taking part in this 'trade of patents'. In that case, a dominant firm became the exclusive licensee of a technology that was directly connected – or '*related*', using the word suggested by some US scholars[87] – to the business in which the firm had its dominant position. The exclusive nature of the license allowed the dominant firm to prevent potential and actual rivals from using the patented technology as a springboard to challenge its monopoly power. Further, at the time, the patented technology was one of the few alternatives – and a very efficient one, indeed – to the techniques that the dominant firm employed. Therefore, the Commission concluded that the acquisition of an exclusive license for a superior technology was abusive, since it was aimed at protecting and strengthening the firm's dominant position, to the detriment of potential and actual rivals.

According to the CFI, which upheld the Commission's decision, the decisive factor in finding that acquisition of the exclusive license constituted an abuse lay quite specifically in the fact that at the material time the right to use the process protected by the license was the only one technically capable of giving an enterprise the means of competing effectively with the dominant firm.[88]

In fact, the competitive perils connected to an IPR license in favor of a dominant firm are two: the connection between the licensed IPR and

---

[85] For instance, generally the owners of basic innovations are in the best position to exploit their improvements and, equally, inventors may not have the capacity to develop and market their innovations so that they need to sell/license them.

[86] See *Tetra Pak I* (88/501/EC), July 26, 1988, OJ 1988 L 272/27. This single case goes back to the years before the first European Merger Regulation entered into force, and hence does not find any counterparts today. The dominant firm had monopoly power in the market for machines designed to fill board cartons under aseptic conditions; it obtained an exclusive license for a patented process to sterilize board cartons.

[87] See Hovenkamp, Janis, & Lemley, *supra* note 3, ¶ 14.3a (describing 'a 'related' patent as any patented product or process that is a substitute for or an improvement upon the monopolized product, a component thereof, or the process used in producing it.').

[88] Actually, it could be argued that even the acquisition of an exclusive license for a related equivalent/inferior technology could produce anticompetitive effects. See, in this regard, Hovenkamp, Janis & Lemley, *supra* note 3, ¶ 14.3a. Perhaps, the CFI meant this when it wrote 'for . . . applying Article 8[2], the circumstances surrounding the acquisition, and in particular its effects on the structure of competition in the relevant market, must be taken into account'. For the statements quoted here and in the text, see Case T-51/89, *Tetra Pak Rausing SA v. Commission*, 1990 ECR II-309, § 27.

the monopolized product, and the exclusive nature of the license.[89] Since antitrust authorities' aim to prevent dominant firms from strengthening their positions, there is no reason to prosecute the acquisition either of an IPR that does not threaten the dominant firm's monopoly, or of a related IPR that is still available to each actual and potential rival of the dominant firm. Interestingly, in *Tetra Pak I* the remedy agreed to by the dominant firm was to renounce its exclusive right to the superior technology.

The US approach to exclusive patent licenses is not very different. For instance, in *In re Biovail Corp.*,[90] the dominant firm agreed not to acquire and enforce patents that represented improvements to its basic patented drug and that, hence, could help it in prolonging its monopoly power. In such a case, the acquisitions not only perpetuated the life of the basic patent, but also perpetuated the life of second-generation patents and produced the effects of accumulation. Further, in two combined judgments – *Automatic Radio Mgs. Co. v. Hazeltine Research, Inc.*[91] and *United Shoe Machinery*[92] – the Supreme Court stated that, even if the mere accumulation of patents, no matter how many, is not in itself illegal,[93] a firm is nevertheless liable when it obtains exclusive rights from patentees when it could just as easily have obtained non-exclusive rights.[94] In other words, while a dominant firm should be allowed to procure as many patents as it pleases through its own internal research and development, it is guilty of monopolization when it acquires exclusive rights over technologies developed by other firms.[95] Indeed, in *SCM Corp. v. Xerox Corp.*,[96] the Court indicated that, whereas firms without monopoly power may externalize the innovative process, acting more as investors than as innovators, monopolists cannot do so, at least, they cannot if two conditions are present: first, if the innovation brings, at the moment of its acquisition, a significant

---

[89] See Hovenkamp, Janis, & Lemley, *supra* note 3, ¶14.3a (arguing 'the monopolist's acquisition of exclusive rights of any related patent can endanger competition.').

[90] 2002 WL 727033 (FTC No. 011 0094, April 23, 2002).

[91] 339 U.S. 827 (1950).

[92] 347 U.S. 521 (1954). In this case more than 2000 shoe machinery patents were accumulated. Only about 5 per cent of these had been acquired from outsiders by United Shoe.

[93] 339 U.S. 827, 834.

[94] 347 U.S. 521, 533.

[95] In this regard see also the Report of the Attorney General's National Committee to Study the Antitrust Laws 226 (1955).

[96] 645 F.2d 1195, 1205 (2nd Cir. 1981). In this case the plaintiff, SCM, claimed that the defendant, Xerox, by obtaining the exclusive rights to all the patents relating to xerography and refusing to grant licenses for plain-paper copying, willfully acquired monopoly power in a relevant market and purposely excluded SCM from that market in violation of Section 2.

market share; and, second, if the monopolist acquires an exclusive right over the innovation that it helps to create.[97]

Case law about monopolists' grantback agreements[98] concurs with this approach. Just as obtaining an exclusive license in a patent covering an improvement to the monopolist's basic patent may allow the monopolist to perpetuate its monopoly and may discourage R&D by competitive rivals, antitrust authorities may impose non-exclusive grantback clauses.[99] For instance, in *United States v. General Electric*[100] the district court established that the monopolist's decision to condition licenses to its competitors on an exclusive grantback clause, covering the development of new technology related to the one that it monopolized, represented an attempt to monopolize the market. Analogously, in *Kobe, Inc. v. Dempsey Pump Co.*,[101] the Court held that the systematic acquisition of exclusive grantbacks upon all related improvement patents constituted an attempt to monopolize. By contrast, the courts have found that nonexclusive licenses, as well as nonexclusive grantback clauses, are fully sufficient for the monopolist's needs to improve its business and to have access to improvements in its own basic technology. The monopolist does not need the right to deny rivals access to technology that it has not developed itself and which might serve to preserve its monopoly position.[102]

---

97 The judges who, dealing with the acquisitions rather than the licenses of patents, did not need to face the issue of exclusivity, recognized that 'investors [. . .] play a key role, if not an indispensable one today, in both the inventive process and the commercialization of inventions'. Therefore, in order to encourage investors to invest in developing a patented invention, courts must leave them free to enjoy the acquired patent to the end of its term as long as the patent, *when acquired*, does not confer any significant market power. id., at 1206.

98 A grantback is a clause in a patent license that obliges the licensee to convey back to the licensor any improvement patent that the licensee might develop. A grantback is exclusive when it allows only the licensor and the licensee to patent and use the improvement technology. Yet, it may be that grantback clauses forbid even the innovating licensee to patent and use its own invention, thus entailing the total transfer to the licensor of the rights that can come with the innovation. Consider that exclusive grantback conditions are deemed to be, pursuant to Article 40 TRIPs, practices that restrain competition and impede the transfer and dissemination of technology.

99 *In re Biovail Corp.*, 2002 WL 727033 (FTC No. 011 0094, April 23, 2002) where the respondent agreed not to acquire or enforce the patents upon the improving innovation related to Tiazac, in order to settle the charges of 'ever greening' its original patent.

100 82 F. Supp. 753, 901 (D.N.J. 1949).

101 198 F.2d 416, 422-27 (10th Cir. 1952), where the patentee was ascertained to have a plan to acquire all present and future patents in the industry and to obtain covenants not to compete from the sellers of the patents, to threaten suits against all who dealt with possible infringers, and to publicize the infringement suits.

102 Herbert Hovenkamp, *Innovation and the Domain of Competition Policy* 33, http://ssrn.com/abstract=1091488 (2008). Consider that licenses may be subject to challenges under the antitrust laws but not by the inventor, seller, assignor, or licensor of that patent. Indeed, US courts analyzed two cases of individuals who licensed their patents and claimed that the acquirers refused to develop and market the related innovations so as to suppress the new

As a whole, as the EU and US case law shows, even a dominant firm has the right to take part in the market of IPRs, not only in order to pursue its lawful strategies, but also for the good of both IPR holders, who will profit from the royalties, and consumers who will benefit from the fact that the dominant firm will subsequently employ the licensed IPRs, in some cases improving them.[103]

The only limitation that must be imposed on such a behavior does not flow from the fact that the traded asset is an intellectual good; rather, it flows directly from the desire to limit conduct that unnecessarily impairs rivals' opportunities.

HANDS OFF INTERNALLY DEVELOPED PATENTS: AN INITIAL CONVERGENCE BETWEEN THE US AND EU APPROACHES

Though the comparison between the US and EU antitrust experiences relating to patent procurement can be considered somewhat 'weak', because of the limited number of available cases, the above analysis leads to the following conclusions, incorporating some topics discussed in the previous chapters.

First, there exist some economic models that, by employing a case-by-case approach, try not only to give a new shape to dominant firms' IPRs, but also question the right of these firms to hold patents. Yet, even the economic models discussed above about isolated predatory innovations, patent accumulation, sleeping patents, and suppressed technologies,

---

technologies and avoid paying them royalties. In both cases, the pleas were rejected for lack of antitrust injury and standing. See *McDonald v. Johnson & Johnson*, 722 F.2d 1370 (8th Cir. 1983), where the plaintiffs alleged that a pharmaceutical firm acquired from them a company that made innovative pacemakers and nerve stimulators with the intent to cause this business to 'languish' for the benefit of the firm's pharmaceuticals business (parts of which treated the same ailments as the acquired company's products). The plaintiffs claimed that Johnson & Johnson had monopoly power in the relevant market and willfully failed to commercialize intellectual property acquired from the plaintiffs with the intent and result of injuring competition in that market. Moreover, see *Alling v. Universal Mfg. Corp.*, 5 Cal. App. 4th 1412, 1430 (Ct. App. 1992), where the plaintiff alleged that the defendant acquired from him a license for technology that permitted the manufacture of more energy efficient fluorescent lights and then intentionally suppressed this technology in favor of its own traditional technology.

[103] See, for this argument, 3 Phillip E. Areeda & Herbert Hovenkamp, *Antitrust Law: An Analysis of Antitrust Principles and Their Application*, ¶ 704d (2008) (arguing further that, whereas prohibiting a firm from buying someone else's 'traditional' assets, such as a plant, does not stop the firm from building its own plant, preventing a monopolist from obtaining a patent could ruin it, as the monopolist is not free to produce the patented innovation by itself).

acknowledge that detecting these strategies is very difficult.[104] Moreover, prosecuting non-used patents would entail a cumbersome burden of proof.[105] Therefore, it seems that US and EU antitrust authorities prefer to set their case law relying on different non-economic reasons. For instance, the cases discussed here show that, generally, the antitrust authorities of both jurisdictions allow monopolists to strengthen their market power via patents. Therefore, it can be stated that US and EU antitrust authorities chose to permit dominant firms to continue to search for further competitive advantages, though it must be acknowledged that the EU side of this result is somehow affected by the fact that the EU antitrust authorities are not entitled to question patents' procurement.

Second, as to the choice of whether or not to prosecute invalid patents, US courts and – as far as it can be derived from the *AstraZeneca* case – EU antitrust institutions establish one simple principle: they are willing to prosecute invalid patents if and only if they violate competition law. In other words, these authorities clarify that antitrust sanctions are not available as 'extra remedies' for IP violations. In this vein, the enforcement requirements introduced by the US courts could be interpreted as a means to prevent just such an over-reaching use of competition law. Therefore, at least from this perspective, it can be affirmed that harm to dynamic efficiency – the harm which is supposed to follow from a mere breach of IP law – cannot represent a stand-alone basis for antitrust enforcement. Also, in taking this path, therefore, is clear that US and EU antitrust authorities chose to disregard the economic models that show that even non-used invalid patents can strengthen market power and harm consumer welfare.

However the contrast between economic thinking and US and EU legal rules about the mere procurement of patents disappears when the two jurisdictions converge in paying attention to the anticompetitive effects, that follow from a dominant firm acquiring a patent from the market. Indeed, US courts and EU institutions change their approach towards obtained patents whether the related inventions have been internally developed or obtained from others in the market.

This approach could stem from the idea that prosecuting an internally developed patent creates a dangerous risk of false positives that could seriously affect firms' incentives to innovate. Indeed, given that investing in innovation is risky, and given that firms should be encouraged to invest

---

104 See Gilbert & Newbery, *supra* note 2, at 525 (stating that, 'preemption would be very hard to identify in any practical situation, because it is difficult to distinguish product development that is the result of superior foresight and technological capabilities from development that is motivated by entry deterrence'). See, further, Flynn, *supra* note 4, at 496–7.

105 See Areeda & Hovenkamp, *supra* note 103, at ¶ 705b.

in innovation, US and EU antitrust authorities seem to believe that they cannot afford to run the risk of prohibiting a patent that has resulted from an internal process of development. Therefore, it is not by chance that the only prohibition granted – i.e. the prohibition regarding the acquisition of an exclusive license for a related patent – asks for the application of a 'soft remedy' – the elimination of the exclusivity condition – that does not jeopardize the patent itself or the investments in it.

Further, looking in depth at the US case law about idle technologies, another justification arises to explain why US courts do not prosecute sleeping patents: US judges did not want to oblige monopolists to share their sleeping patents, since the Congress has never required that they do so.[106] US antitrust courts thus show, first, consideration of what IP statutes state and, second, significant respect for the idea that the legislative and the judiciary powers have to remain separate.

As a whole, the attitudes of the two jurisdictions towards the mere IPR ownership seem very careful, and sensitive towards emerging innovation.

The following chapter explores whether this attitude changes when the patentable innovation involves a system of products, i.e. the monopolized good joined together with other products – say, auxiliary products – that acquire special value when (and because) pooled together.

---

[106] Actually, over the past century in the US three broad categories of compulsory licenses have arisen. See, e.g., Kirby W. Lee, 'Permitted Use of Patented Inventions in the United States: Why Prescription Drugs Do Not Merit Compulsory Licensing', 36 *Ind. L. Rev.* 175 (2003).

4. Predatory system innovations

SEVERAL BEHAVIORS FOR ONE CONCERN: ALLOWING MULTI-PRODUCT MONOPOLISTS TO CREATE INCOMPATIBILITY VIA INNOVATION

As Chapter 3 has shown by looking at some mono-product monopolists' behaviors, even the mere ownership of an IPR can generate some concerns, at least from the economic standpoint. This chapter completes the picture by discussing the effects that the procurement of an IPR can produce when the monopolist in question is a multi-product firm[1] and,[2] hence, when its practices involving IPRs affect not only the monopolized market but secondary markets as well.[3] In particular, from the phenomenological

[1] The book uses the distinction between mono-product and multi-product firms for simplicity's sake though it is not always very simple to strike. Indeed, just the discussion about innovations that put together products that were previously sold separately and the so-called 'separate product requirement' (see footnotes 68 and 80 and the accompanying text) shows how it is complex differentiating markets across time.

[2] Once again, as clarified in Chapter 3, it must be acknowledged that some of the anti-competitive strategies here described do not pivot around the mere procurement/ownership of IPRs, but around dominant firms' ability to capture the advantages that flow from their innovations. Therefore, what is explained here could be applied, *ceteris paribus*, to other appropriability tools.

[3] Usually the term 'primary market' addresses the market where the monopolist has its dominant position – i.e., the monopolized market – while the term 'secondary market' serves to indicate other markets where the monopolist acts. It should not come as a surprise that a mono-product monopolist acts only in its primary market, whereas a multi-product dominant firm acts in several markets, the primary, and the secondary ones. Antitrust scholars distinguish between secondary markets that are 'vertically related' to the primary market and secondary markets that are 'horizontally related', or 'collaterally related' to it. In the former case, firms interact in the positions of buyers and sellers; in the latter case, instead, firms interact directly with the same group of end-users, so that the competitive conditions in one market affect the competitive conditions in the other. See Patrick Rey & Jean Tirole, 'A Primer on Foreclosure' 1 (2006), available at http://idei.fr/doc/by/tirole/primer.pdf. For instance, a producer of toys and the chain of stores that distribute them act in two vertically-related markets; differently, a producer of cameras and a producer of films – and, more generally, the producers of complementary goods – act in two horizontally-related markets. However, consider 3B Phillip E. Areeda & Herbert Hovenkamp, *Antitrust Law: An Analysis of Antitrust Principles and their Application* ¶775 (2008) (arguing that 'the distinction between vertically-related and collaterally-related markets is not always clear, not always stable, and not always important for antitrust purposes'). In this regard see also Steven C. Salop, 'Strategy, Predation, and Antitrust Analysis: An Introduction', in *Strategy, Predation, and Antitrust Analysis* 1, 13 and

standpoint, the chapter regards the following scenario: consider a 'system product', that is to say, a product made of different parts, i.e., a main component and several others auxiliary elements.[4] Say that a multi-product monopolist is the only firm that produces the main component, while competing with other firms in the production of the auxiliary parts. Posit that the monopolist develops and markets a new version of its monopolized main component, which is no longer compatible from a technological standpoint with its rivals' auxiliary elements. In this scenario, the monopolist's rivals can claim that the 'System Innovation' harms their market positions. In fact, US and EU antitrust authorities have actually dealt with several claims, of differing forms, but equivalent in the effects that they produce, complaining that the monopolist has developed one of the following:[5]

25–30 (Steven C. Salop ed., 1981) (arguing that even complementary products can be seen as inputs in the production of system product).

4 In connection to the concept of compatibility see, e.g., Nicholas Economides & Lawrence J. White, 'Networks and compatibility: Implications for Antitrust', 38 *European Economic Review* 651 (1994); Richard J. Gilbert, 'Symposium of Compatibility: Incentives and Market Structure', 40 *The Journal of Industrial Economics* 1 (1992); Nicholas Economides, 'Desirability of Compatibility in the Absence of Network Externalities', 79 *American Economic Review* 1165 (1989); Carmen Matutes & Pierre Regibeau, 'Mix and Match Product Compatibility without Network Externalities', 19 *Rand Journal of Economics* 221 (1988); id., 'A Selective Review of the Economics of Standardization. Entry Deterrence, Technological Progress and International Competition', 12 *European Journal of Political Economy* 183 (1996); Michael L. Katz & Carl Shapiro, 'Technology Adoption in the Presence of Network Externalities', 94 *Journal of Political Economy* 822 (1986); id., 'Product Compatibility Choice in a Market with Technological Choices', 38 *Oxford Economic Series* 146 (1986); id., 'Network Externalities, Competition, and Compatibility', 75 *American Economic Review* 424 (1985); Joseph Farrell & Garth Saloner, 'Installed Base Compatibility: Innovation, Product Preannouncement, and Predation', 76 *The American Economic Review* 940 (1986); Joseph Farrell & Garth Saloner, 'Standardization, Compatibility and Innovation', 16 *Rand Journal of Economics* 70 (1985); and, for a literature survey, see Stanley M. Besen & Joseph Farrell, 'Choosing How to Compete: Strategies and Tactics in Standardization', 8 *Journal of Economic Perspective* 117 (1994).

5 Though every firm can manipulate compatibility, only a dominant firm can be interested in using incompatibility as an anticompetitive device. Indeed, if a firm without market power introduces a new product that is supposed to be combined with others but that cannot work with them, the firm will lose customers as they will prefer the rival's product that lets them enjoy the benefits of the system. In particular, see Economides, *supra* note 4, at 1165 (arguing that the existence of different competitive characteristics is a motive to prefer incompatibility to compatibility: firms that have the same size and are similar in other competitive characteristics prefer the latter). Moreover, see Joseph Farrell, Hunter K. Monroe & Garth Saloner, 'The Vertical Organization of Industry: Incompatibility versus Compatibility', 7 *Journal of Economics and Management Strategy* 143 (1998) (showing that firms may prefer incompatibility with cost, or quality, heterogeneity); Michael Katz & Carl Shapiro, 'Systems Competition and Network Effects', 8 *Journal of Economic Perspectives* 93, 110 (1994) (stating 'if one firm has a distinctly superior overall package, including its product offering, its installed base, and its reputation, that firm is likely to prefer incompatibility and may in fact spend resources to block compatibility'); Matutes & Regibeau, *supra* note 4, at 221; and

- an innovative version of the monopolized product, but closed its interface, thus preventing competitors from knowing what they needed to make their 'old' auxiliary products work with the 'new' monopolized one;[6]
- an innovative system product where the monopolist physically integrated all the products that previously sold separately – i.e., the monopolized as well as the auxiliary goods – thus leaving their rivals' 'old' auxiliary components without technologically equal access to the 'new' version of the monopolized main component;[7] or
- an innovative version of the monopolized product that is technically incompatible with all rivals' auxiliary goods, so conditioning – via what is called a 'technological tying'[8] – the sale of their

---

Vincenzo Denicolò, 'Compatibility and Bundling with Generalist and Specialist Firms', 2 *The Journal of Industrial Economics* 177 (2000).

[6] In order to close the interface the monopolist can either acquire an IPR on that interface, or exploit the fact that the interface is too complicated to be understood by its rivals without its help. Indeed, that was the case when Microsoft introduced its new version of the operating system for networks without disclosing the information necessary to interoperability – a case that the EU Commission prosecuted with Commission Decision of March 24, 2004, relating to a proceeding under Article 82 of the EC Treaty (Case COMP/C-3/37.792 Microsoft), C(2004)9 final (Brussels 21.4.2004) (hereinafter '*Microsoft IV*'). See footnote 73. Similarly, consider a producer of durable goods who refrains from communicating the technical specifications to manufacturers of spare parts covered by IPRs, preventing them from building their components compatible with the monopolized good. For instance, the EU *Cicra* and *Volvo* cases as well as the US *Kodak*, *Data General*, and *Xerox* cases were all about integrated firms, producing two or more complementary goods whereof one was a durable good, such as an automobile or a photocopier. In all these cases, when the firms decided to change their business strategy, stopping to supply to independent service providers their durable goods' spare parts, the independent service providers complained because they were not able to make their old spare parts to work together with the new durable goods. See Case 53/87, *Consorzio Italiano della Componentistica di Ricambio per Autoveicoli (CICRA) and Maxicar v. Régie nationale des usines Renault*, October 5 1988, 1988 ECR 6039; Case 238/87, *Volvo AB v. Erik Veng (UK) Ltd.*, October 5 1988, 1988 ECR 6211 and *Image Technical Servs., Inc. v. Eastman Kodak Co.* 125 F.3d 1195, 1202 (9th Cir.1997); *Data General v. Grumman Systems Support* 36 F.3d 1147 (1st Cir. 1994), (hereinafter, also '*Data General*'); and *Independent Service Organizations Antitrust Litigation*, 203 F.3d 1322 (2000). These are all refusal to deal cases because, as Chapter 5 explains, different practices with different phenotypes can produce the same effects.

[7] As it happened, for instance, when IBM integrated in new versions of its CPUs several functions previously sold separately. See, e.g., *Telex Corp v. IBM*, 367 F.Supp. 258, 347 (N.D. Okla 1973), *rev'd on other grounds*, 510 F.2d 894 (10th Cir.1975). See footnotes 58 and ff. and the accompanying text.

[8] It is common to say that the term 'tying' identifies a special case of bundling. Bundling is the practice of selling two (or more) separate products together in a package. Economic theory distinguishes the case of pure bundling (also referred to as package tie-in), which occurs when the products are available only together either in fixed proportions (A-B, 2A-2B, 3A-3B) or variable proportions (A-2B, A-3B, A-4B), from the case of mixed bundling (also referred to as commercial tying), which happens when the products are available both separately and together, but the sum of their singular prices is superior to the bundle price. Therefore, it is correct to state that the word 'tying' addresses a special case of mixed bundling

own compatible auxiliary products to the purchase of the 'new' monopolized main component.[9]

Recalling that antitrust scholars bring all these cases under the rubric of 'predatory innovations', the chapter begins by discussing whether dominant firms' System Innovations may strengthen market power and harm consumer welfare. In so doing, the chapter reflects the literature about 'horizontal foreclosure'. In fact, this industrial organization theory looks at the case of a monopolist, which controls a specific product and which, via different types of behaviors,[10] prevents its competitors from using it, although they would have needed to sell the monopolized product together with their own products to the same end-consumers.[11] The chapter continues by considering whether US courts and EU antitrust authorities properly assessed these System Innovations. It finds that, except for two cases when the EU institutions obliged dominant firms to share their outstanding System Innovations with their rivals, in the US and the EU antitrust authorities employ sophisticated rules to evaluate System Innovations.[12]

---

when, given A and B, the items for sale are B and the package A+B, so that the acquisition of B is conditional on the purchase of A, and A is not sold on a stand-alone base. For this classification, see Barry Nalebuff, 'Bundling, Tying and Portfolio Effects' (2003), available at www.berr.gov.uk/files/file14774.pdf. The tie may result either from an agreement – also referred to as 'contractual tying' – or from a technological species of incompatibility – also referred to as 'technological tying'. As explained by Frank H. Easterbrook, 'An Economical and Legal Analysis of Physical Tie-Ins', 89 *Yale L. J.* 769 (1980), several factors distinguish the former from the latter. For instance, while the time period of a tying arrangement is defined by the initial parties and is potentially permanent, a technological tie lasts only as long as it takes a competitor to develop a compatible product. Further, with a technological tie, the disposal of the bundled good may be costly or even impractical, while with a contractual bundle, there is at least the possibility of getting rid of the unwanted part of the bundle. See, further, Pranvera Kellezi, Rhetoric or reform: Does the law of tying and bundling reflect the economic theory?, in *Article 82 EC: Reflections on Its Recent Evolution* 147 (Ariel Ezrachi ed., 2009); and Jurian Langer, *Tying snd Bundling As s Leveraging Concern Under EC Competition Law* 4-6 (2007).

9 For instance, in one of the cases of the Microsoft saga, Microsoft was charged with the allegation of having comingled its operating system Windows with its browser Internet Explorer in a way that prevented other browsers from working well with Windows. See, e.g., *United States v. Microsoft Corp.*, 253 F.3d 34 (D.C. Circ. 2001) (hereinafter, '*Microsoft III*'). See footnotes 61 and ff. and the accompanying text.

10 Consider that also refusals to deal can produce the effects discussed in this chapter. Yet, since their legal history deserves a specific treatment, the book deals with them in Chapter 5.

11 See, Rey, Tirole, *supra* note 3; and Janusz A. Ordover & Garth Saloner, 'Predation, Monopolization, and Antitrust', in 1 *Handbook of Industrial Organization* 537, 563 (Richard Schmalensee & Robert D. Willing, eds. 1989).

12 To be sure, as the following discussion will show, in the relevant cases here discussed IPRs did not play a significant role. The existence of patents and copyrights does not help in appreciating the inherent value of the regarded System Innovation. Nor does it give any hint in connection to the likely harm that such innovation could cause to allocative and dynamic efficiencies. Indeed, Harry First, 'Microsoft and the Evolution of the Intellectual Property Concept', *Wis. L. Rev.* 1369, 1383–4 (2006), discussing the US *Microsoft* case observed that,

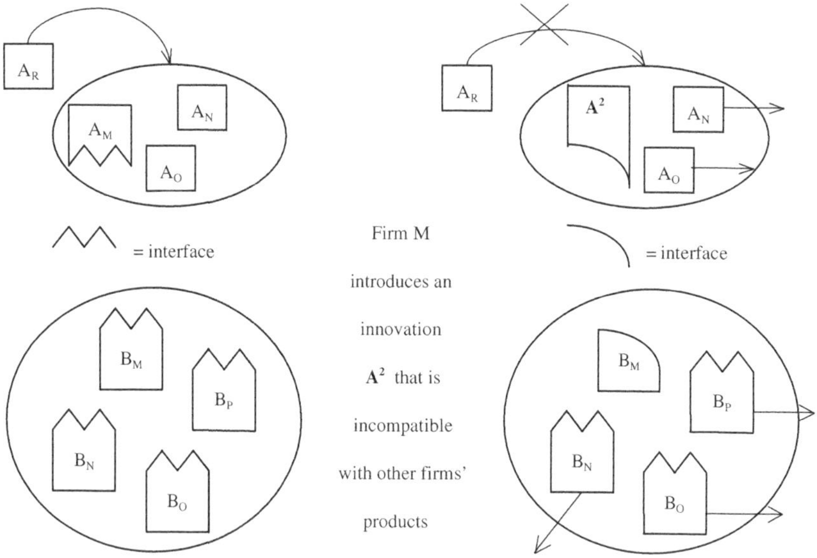

Figure 4.1 Closing the interface

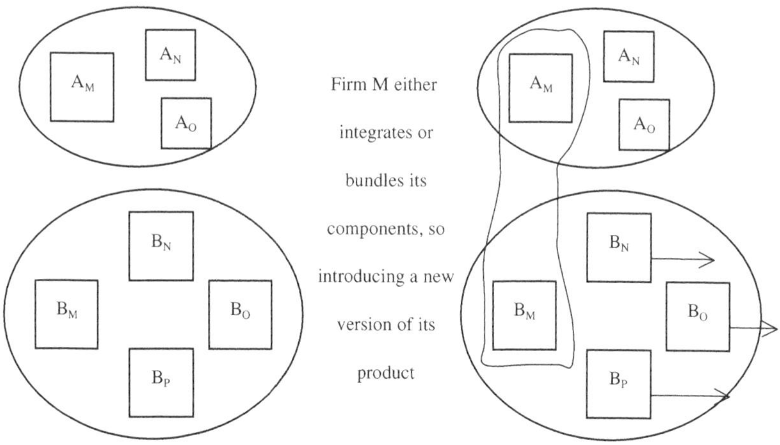

Figure 4.2 Physical integration and bundling

THE ECONOMIC PERSPECTIVE: THE IMPACT OF MONOPOLISTS' SYSTEM INNOVATIONS ON CONSUMER WELFARE

From the economic standpoint, innovations that do not amount to simple manipulations and that entail and rely on incompatibility produce, beyond the usual increase in dynamic efficiency, several efficiency gains, especially via physical integrations and tech-ties.[13] These efficiencies,[14] which are welfare-increasing by definition, do not stem from pursuing the 'Cournot effect'[15] alone, but also from a better risk allocation;[16] from the possibility

---

'the court of appeals' balancing approach had little to do with the scope of the actual IPRs that Microsoft might have had [. . .] the question for the court was whether [. . .] Microsoft's conduct constituted an exclusionary practice under section 2 of the Sherman Act. [. . .] product quality of Windows was a sufficiently strong justification to make Microsoft's conduct, on this point, not unreasonable and, therefore, not a violation of the antitrust laws'.

13 For a detailed discussion of the economics of tying, see Langer, *supra* note 8; Richard J. Gilbert & Michael H. Riordan, 'Product Improvement and Technological Tying in a Winner-Take-All Market', 15 *The Journal of Industrial Economics* 113 (2007); Nalebuff, *supra* note 8; and Bruce H. Kobayashi, 'Does Economics provide a reliable guide to regulating commodity bundling by firms? A Survey of the Economic Literature', *1 Journal of Competition Law & Economics* 707 (2005).

14 See, e.g., Alan Devlin, 'A Neo-Chicago Perspective on the Law of Product Tying', 44 *Am. Bus. L.J.* 521 (2007); Daniel E. Gaynor, 'Technological Tying', available at *www.ftc.gov/be/workpapers/wp284.pdf* (2006); David S. Evans & Michael Salinger, 'Why Do Firms Bundle and Tie? Evidence from Competitive Markets and Implications for Tying Law', 22 *Yale J. Reg.* 37 (2005); David S. Evans & A. Jorge A. Padilla, 'Designing Antitrust Rules for Assessing Unilateral Practice: A Neo Chicago Approach', 72 *U. Chi. L. Rev.* 27 (2005); and Stefan Stremersch & Gerard J. Tellis, 'Strategic Bundling of Products and Prices: A New Synthesis for Marketing', 66 *J. Mkt'g* 55 (2002). They all elaborated their results looking at competitive secondary markets. Nevertheless, the same efficiencies can result even when secondary markets have an oligopolistic structure. See, in this regard, Patrick Rey, Paul Seabright, & Jean Tirole, 'The Activities of a Monopoly Firm in Adjacent Competitive Markets: Economic Consequences and Implications for Competition Policy' (2001), available at http://ideas.repec.org/p/ide/wpaper/660.html.

15 A monopolist that acts in secondary markets can take over them, in order not to see the sales of its monopolized product decrease because of the mark-up that its vertical or horizontal rivals may charge. Vertical rivals will charge this additional mark-up upon the same monopolized good; horizontal rivals upon the auxiliary goods that have to be sold with the monopolized good. The Cournot effect addresses this second case and, indeed, it premises upon the idea that the monopolized and auxiliary products are complements that have value only when used together. In summary, the so-called 'Cournot effect', whose explanation goes back to Antoine A. Cournot, *Researches into the Mathematical Principles of the Theory of Wealth* (1838) is nothing more than the horizontal equivalent of the double marginalization issue that is typical of vertical relations. See, Nalebuff, *supra* note 8; Michael L. Katz & Joseph Farrell, 'Innovation, Rent Extraction, and Integration in System Markets', 48 *Journal of Industrial Economics* 413 (2000); and Nicholas Economides & Steven C. Salop, 'Competition and Integration among Complements, and Network Market Structure', 40 *Journal of Industrial Economics* 105 (1992).

16 See, e.g., Joseph G. Sidak, 'Debunking Predatory Innovation', 83 *Colum. L. Rev.* 1121, 1135 (1983).

of controlling product quality and goodwill reputation,[17] and from the ability to make cost savings. Integrations and tech-ties, especially, may reduce searching costs, and the costs of production, distribution, and transactions.[18]

Yet, in specific situations, monopolists can employ System Innovations within a strategy that strengthens market power and may produce a negative effect on consumer welfare. In particular, System Innovations can work as predatory tools as well as isolated innovations,[19] or serve as monopoly leveraging strategies.[20] In this last regard, a clarification is due.

Traditionally,[21] courts used the so-called 'leveraging monopoly theory'

---

[17] Assume that the monopolist cannot prevent its monopolized product from working with its rivals' components, and suppose that the system fails to satisfy consumers' needs. As consumers may be unable to understand why the system fails, it is possible that the monopolist will bear the risk of being held responsible for the failure, even when the failure results from the low quality of its rivals' products. In such a situation, therefore, creating incompatibility (maybe via technological-tying and integration) can be a proper way to fight both the asymmetry of information that affects consumers and the risk that rivals' products will ruin the system's performance.

[18] See e.g., Jean Tirole, 'The Analysis of Tying Cases: A Primer' 15 (2004), available at http://www.ssrn.com/; Yannis Bakos & Eric Brynjolfsson, 'Bundling Information Goods: Prices, Profits, and Efficiency', 45 *Mgmt. Sci.* 1613 (1999) (observing that integration is possible not only because its costs are low, but also because the industry of microprocessors has developed products that are more and more powerful); and Steven Davis, Jack MacCrisken & Kevin Murphy, 'Integrating New Features into the PC Operating System: Benefits, Timing, and Effects on Innovation', available at http://www.chipar.com/papers/integration.pdf; and David J. Teece, 'Profiting from Technological Innovation: Implications for Integration, Collaboration, Licensing and Public Policy', 15 *Research Policy* 285, 295 (1986).

[19] See Janusz A. Ordover & Robert Willig, 'An Economic Definition of Predation: Pricing and Product Innovation', 91 *Yale L. J.* 8 (1981) (just considering the case of a dominant firm that purposely redesigns its monopolized product so that it is incompatible with its rivals' complementary products and concluding that such an innovative system will be predatory if it results from R&D expenditures that are socially wasteful and if, thanks to the created incompatibility coupled with a specific post-innovation pricing strategy, it drives competitors out of the market so as to allow the dominant firm to extract monopoly profits. Indeed – they argued – when monopolists knowingly and intentionally invest in these socially undesirable innovations, they cannot do anything different from having a predatory intent, i.e., pursuing the innovations' exclusionary effects so to acquire/increase dominance in the complementary market. This strategy cannot work for software, as the price of the bundle between the operating system and one of its compatible software programs is as expensive as the operating system without the software. Therefore, a predatory pricing strategy is not possible.); and Janusz A. Ordover, Alan O. Sykes, and Robert D. Willig, 'Predatory System Rivalry: A Reply', 83 *Columbia Law Review* 1150 (1983).

[20] The book does not consider the case when System Innovations work as devices for escaping the monopolized market price regulation. See, in this regard, Mark Armstrong, 'The Theory of Access Pricing and Interconnection', in 1 *Handbook of Telecommunication Economics* (Martin E. Cave, Sumit K. Majumdar, & Ingo Vogelsang eds. 2002); and Jean-Jacques Laffont & Jean Tirole, *Competition in Telecommunications* (2000).

[21] In the United States the leveraging monopoly theory has experienced a changing fortune. Nowadays, the Supreme Court observed that such a theory cannot work as a stand-alone source of antitrust liability. See *Verizon Communication, Inc. v. Law Offices of Curtis*

to explain why a monopolist is interested in using some practices, such as tying,[22] in order to exclude rivals from a secondary market and why society is interested in prohibiting such a behavior. Indeed, according to this theory – mainly, an intuitive one[23] – two monopolies create more monopoly profits than one does. Thus, on the one hand, it is logical for dominant firms to be interested in enlarging their power across markets, in order to create multiple over-competitive prices. On the other hand, the

---

v. Trinko, LLP, 540 US 398, 415 nt. 4 (2004) (hereinafter, also '*Trinko*'). Yet, in the past the leveraging monopoly theory has been deemed as a free standing monopolization claim. See in this last regard, *United States v. Griffith*, 334 US 100, at 107 (1948) (stating that Section 2 could be enforced for prohibiting 'the use of monopoly power, however lawfully acquired [. . .] to gain a competitive advantage'); and *Berkey Photo Inc. v. Eastman Kodak Co.*, 603 F. 2d 263, at 275 (2nd Circ. 1979) (holding that, 'a firm violates § 2 if [it uses] its monopoly power in one market to gain a competitive advantage in another, albeit without an attempt to monopoly the second market'). Further, for a detailed description of the 'wave-like' history of the leveraging theory in the US jurisdiction see 3 Phillip H. Areeda & Herbert Hovenkamp, *Antitrust law: An Analysis of Antitrust Principles and their Application* ¶652 (2008) and Jennifer M. Clarke-Smith, 'The Development of The Monopolistic Leveraging Theory and its Appropriate Role in Antitrust Law', 52 *Cath. U. L. Rev.* 279 (2002). As to the application of the leveraging monopoly theory in the European Union, consider that Article 102 not only does not require a causal link between the monopolized market and the other secondary markets, but also casts upon dominant firms a 'special responsibility' (see Chapter 2). Therefore, the EU antitrust authorities have often qualified as abusive those behaviors whose effects concerned a market different from the monopolized one, without ascertaining whether such a behavior actually created a dominant position in the secondary market. They looked just at the risk of a further monopolization. For the same opinion, see Alexandros Stratakis, 'Comparative Analysis Of The US And EU Approach And Enforcement Of The Essential Facilities Doctrine', 27(8) *E.C.L.R.* 434, 436 (2006), (arguing that the most striking difference between the US and EU experiences as to multi-product monopolists that act across primary and secondary markets is the treatment of leveraging. '[In the United States] [t]he 'Berkey Photo formula' for dispensing with the need to show an attempt to monopolize or actual monopolization in the second market was heavily criticized by a number of cases, attacked by the US Government, and finally buried by the Supreme Court with a footnote [in Trinko]. On the contrary, under EU competition law, market power in the downstream market, although being relevant, is not an essential element of the relative analysis.').

[22] Actually – to be more correct – the great majority of the antitrust cases involving a multi-product monopolist, such as exclusive dealing agreements, mergers, incompatibility choices, physical integrations, tie-ins, and refusals to deal, tend to follow a recurring pattern that pivots around three elements. Namely: (i) a dominant firm that acts in the monopolized market and in at least one secondary market; (ii) its actual and potential rivals act (or would like to act) in one or both of the two markets; and (iii) a resource that the dominant firm either starts providing for itself whereas in the past it acquired it from the market (the term 'vertical integration' serves to address this case); or begins supplying to the market whereas in the past it did not offer it at all; or does not share with any other firm. Thus, it should not come as a surprise that in such a scenario monopolists' actual and potential rivals complain of a loss of business stemming from any of the choices that the monopolists made in relation to the resource. If the dominant firm starts providing the resource for itself or supplying it to the market, rivals claim that their own products, which are substitutes for the resource, have no market; if the dominant firm does not share the resource, rivals complain once again that, without that resource, their goods have no market.

[23] See Langer, *supra* note 8, at 18.

whole society is clearly interested in forbidding practices that entail multiple dead-weight losses and, hence, in forbidding monopolists from exploiting their dominance in a way that allows them to acquire a competitive advantage in further markets.[24]

Nevertheless, the Chicago School questioned this theory by showing that a monopolist can exercise its power only once.[25] According to the Chicago School, dominant firms are indeed able to monopolize secondary markets, but – and this is the theory's critical point – they do not expand their power across markets to acquire more monopoly profits but for neutral or procompetitive reasons,[26] since in the short run a monopolist

---

[24] In this vein, therefore, the adoption of the leveraging monopoly theory would require answering 'no' to the policy question whether dominant firms could be allowed to appropriate all of the advantages that flow from their temporary monopolies so to reward them of the efforts and investments done in order to smite their rivals. See, in this regard, Chapter 2.

[25] See, e.g., Robert H. Bork, *The Antitrust Paradox* (1978), and Richard A. Posner, *Antitrust Law* (1976).

[26] The efficiencies mentioned above are a clear example of the procompetitive reasons why a firm decides to tech-tie. A further reason, which actually produces ambiguous effects on consumer welfare, is price discrimination. Consider a classic patent tying that occurs when the tying product (such as a copy machine) is patented, the tied product is an unpatented commodity (meaning a product marketed in a really competitive market) used as an input (such as ink or cartridge) for the system product (the patented machine plus the ink and the cartridge), and the sale of the patented product is conditioned on the purchase of the unpatented product. In such a situation, the tying allows the multi-product monopolist to mimic the effect of a non-linear (two tariff) pricing strategy, which charges a flat and low price for the monopolized product, and an over-competitive price for the tied goods. In this way, indeed, the monopolist succeeds in both reaching many consumers, even those that do not value the system highly, and earning monopoly profits from the consumers who use the monopolized product a lot and, hence, value it most. In other words, the price of the durable tying good is assumed to cover fixed costs; the price for compatible goods should cover the variable expenses and so reflect consumers' willingness to pay for the durable good. Metering cannot work with complements that are used only in fixed proportions, such as Internet Explorer and the Windows operating system. Further, in order to charge over-competitive prices for the tied products, the monopolist has not acquired a significant market power in the secondary markets (which, indeed, remain commodity markets) but has shifted a part of its power to make prices upon the tied goods. See, e.g., Sreya Kolay & Greg Shaffer, 'Bundling and Menus of Two-Part Tariffs', 51 *J. Ind. Econ.* 383 (2003); Kobayashi, *supra* note 13, 13–15; Michael A. Salinger, 'A Graphical Analysis of Bundling', 68 *J. Bus.* 85 (1995); Preston R McAfee, John McMillan, & Michael D. Whinston, 'Multiproduct Monopoly, Commodity Bundling, and Correlation of Values', 104 *Quarterly Journal of Economics* 371 (1989); Richard Schmalensee, 'Gaussian Demand and Commodity Bundling', 57 *Journal of Business* 211 (1984); id., 'Commodity Bundling by Single Product Monopolies', 25 *J. L. & Econ.* 67 (1982); William J. Adams & Janet L. Yellen, 'Commodity Bundling and the Burden of Monopoly', 90 *Quarterly Journal of Economics* 475 (1976); and George J. Stigler, *US v. Loew's Inc.*: 'A Note on Block Booking', 1963 *Supreme Court Review* 152 (1964). As to the most well-known cases where tie-ins have been used as metering devices but have been, however, forbidden as species of patent misuses aimed at unlawfully extending the 'patent power' see, e.g., *Motion Picture Patents Co. v. Universal Film Manufacturing Co.*, 243 US 502 (1917); *Carbice Corp. of America Patent Development Corp.* 283 US 27 (1931); and *Mercoid Corp. v. Mid-Continent Investment Co.*, 320 US 661 (1944). Afterwards, US courts have translated this approach

can earn just one single total maximum amount of monopoly profits. In other words, according to this theory a monopolist that gains control over a secondary market cannot reap additional monopoly profit from it without losing consumers and, hence, does not create more economic damage than the original monopoly alone.[27]

The Chicago critique relied on several assumptions, however. Namely, that: (i) the secondary market is a competitive market, with constant returns to scale, so that firms are not interested in increasing their sales to realize economies;[28] (ii) the scenario studied is static;[29] (iii) consumers are interested in acquiring the monopolized product and the auxiliary good in a fixed one-to-one proportion;[30] and (iv) consumers are perfectly informed.[31] Thus, by relaxing these hypotheses, the Chicagoan critique breaks down in a variety of settings, so that its conclusion does not apply so broadly.[32]

The post-Chicago economic literature, has identified several specific situations when a dominant firm is interested in enlarging its power across secondary markets for exclusionary reasons and, more exactly, either to deter entry into the secondary market or to defend its monopoly in the primary market.[33]

---

from the kingdom of patent misuse to that of the violations that Section 1 of the Sherman Act and Section 3 of the Clayton Act provide for. See, in this regard, *International Salt Co. v. United States*, 332 US 392 (1947).

[27] This is the reason why integration of successive monopolies reduces market prices. Franklin M. Fisher, 'Innovation and Monopoly Leveraging', in *Dynamic Competition and Public Policy: Technology, Innovation, and Antitrust Issues* 138, 142 (Jerry Ellig ed. 2001).

[28] See Louis Kaplow, 'Extension of Monopoly Power through Leverage', 85 *Colum. L. Rev.* 515, 536 (1985).

[29] See Kaplow, *supra* note 28, at 524–30 (explaining that, inside the frame of a long-term analysis, dominant firms become interested in enlarging their power across markets for an anticompetitive reason: for changing the market structure in their favor). In particular, if the core of the Chicago fixed-sum monopoly argument is that in the short-run firms cannot maximize their monopoly profits by enlarging monopoly power across markets, in a long-term frame it may be rational for a firm to earn less than full monopoly profits today in the hope of greater gain tomorrow. Yet, this interpretation, though correct, does not help antitrust authorities: it leads the analysis inside the frame of predation, though predation is very hard to distinguish from lawful competition. See, in this last regard, Richard N. Langlois, 'Technological Standards, Innovation, and Essential Facilities. Toward a Schumpeterian Post-Chicago Approach', in *Dynamic Competition and Public Policy: Technology, Innovation, and Antitrust Issues* 193, 200–202 (Jerry Ellig ed. 2001).

[30] See Christian Ahlborn, David S. Evans & Jorge A. Padilla, 'The Antitrust Economics of Tying – A Farewell to Per Se Illegality', 49 *Antitrust Bull.* 287 (2004).

[31] See Roger J. Van den Bergh & Peter D. Camesasca, *European Competition Law and Economics — A Comparative Perspective*, 278–85 (2001).

[32] See, for the law literature, Robin Cooper Feldman, 'Defensive Leveraging in Antitrust', 87 *Geo. L. J.* 2079, 2087 (1999).

[33] See Rey & Tirole, *supra* note 3, at 11 (explaining that 'horizontal foreclosure is an act of predation; as other predatory behaviors, it reduces the predator's current profit and is

As to the first stream of scenarios, that is, deterring rivals' entry into the secondary market, it has been shown that a multi-product monopolist,[34] which faces only a limited degree of competition in the secondary market,[35] is inclined to tech-tie[36] its monopolized good to certain auxiliary non-complementary goods.[37] In this way, the monopolist can reduce the profits that its rivals could make by entering the secondary market and,[38] thereby, deters their entry.[39] By credibly committing itself to sell the products only as a bundle, the dominant firm obliges itself to a very aggressive pricing policy if entry occurs – an aggressive pricing policy that is the rational implication of the tying because, had it faced competition in the adjacent market, the dominant firm would lose sales in both the primary and secondary market. Crucial for this theory to work is that consumers have to value highly the monopolized good and cannot prefer the rival's auxiliary products to those of the dominant firm. Otherwise, consumers would not buy the bundle and this would make the rivals' entry easier.[40] Analogously, several economic models have proved that the deterrent effect can stem from tie-ins of complementary goods as well, when the monopolized product is not essential; or if the monopolized product has an inferior alternative;[41] or else when potential rivals cannot enter the secondary market because, as a result of the bundle, they do not have enough scale.[42] Further economic models have shown that, when the would-be rivals of the dominant firm must enter the two markets together via a double innovation in order to compete, and the dominant firm bundles the two

meant to lower the competitors' profitability, with the ultimate goal of inducing their exit and ultimately recouping the lost profit.'); Langer, *supra* note 8, at 21; and Thomas A. Piraino, 'An Antitrust Remedy for Monopoly Leveraging by Electronic Networks', 93 *Nw. U. L. Rev.* 1 (1998).

[34] Indeed, without such power the undertaking does not have the bargaining leverage required to impose a bundle on its customers.

[35] Monopoly is a necessary but not a sufficient condition for competitive harm from vertical integration to occur; and if the secondary market is competitive, vertical integration as such is rarely anticompetitive.

[36] Indeed, such a tie represents a credible commitment because of the expenses that a technological tie requires.

[37] Indeed, consider that the one-monopoly profit theorem (i.e., the Chicago critique) holds when the two products are complements sold in fixed proportions.

[38] To be sure, the more aggressive competition should not decrease the incumbent's profits more than the rival's profits, otherwise the tie is not profitable anymore.

[39] See Michael D. Whinston, 'Tying, Foreclosure, and Exclusion', 80 *Am. Econ. Rev.* 837, 845 (1990); Andrea Lofaro & Derek Ridyard, 'Beyond Bork: New Economic Theories of Exclusion in Merger Cases', 23 *European Competition Law Review* 153 (2002); and Matutes, Regibeau, *supra* note 4.

[40] Fisher, *supra* note 27, at 142 and 148 (discussing this conclusion just looking at the US IBM cases).

[41] See Massimo Motta, *Competition Policy* (2004).

[42] See Barry Nalebuff, 'Bundling as an Entry Barrier', 119 *Quart. J. Bus. Econ.* 159 (2004).

complementary goods together, the bundle not only produces an entry-deterrence effect but also reduces the incentives to innovate.[43] In such a scenario, indeed, the tying may represent a commitment by the dominant firm to have an aggressive R&D policy in the tied market and, hence, may discourage rivals' R&D investments in that market.[44]

As to the second stream of scenarios, that is, defense of monopoly in the primary market, other economic models have shown that dominant firms may use tying to protect their original monopoly from products that are complementary to current products that may develop into substitutes for the monopolized good. In a setting with oligopolistic secondary markets, when entry into one market is made dependent on the success of entry into a secondary market, the dominant firm may foreclose the secondary market to producers of compatible products, preventing the rivals from entering the primary market and thus displacing its original monopoly.[45] The underlying idea is that, given a bundling, an entrant that is unable to offer the bundle will find its potential market limited to the few customers who like its single product and are not interested in the other products in the bundle, knowing from the outset that it will enjoy reduced profits.[46]

---

43 See Jay P. Choi & Christodoulos Stefanadis, 'Tying, Investment, and the Dynamic Leverage Theory', 32 *Rand Journal of Economics* 52 (2001). Further, for other models where the tying makes the prospect of recouping an investment less certain and, therefore, reduces the rivals' incentives to innovate, see Farrell, Katz, *supra* note 15; and Jay P. Choi, 'Informational Leverage and the Endogenous Timing of Product Introductions' (1996), available at http://ideas.repec.org/p/clu/wpaper/1996_03.html. Besides, for a specific case where bundling is a means through which a firm can commit to more aggressive R&D investment in the secondary market, see Jay P. Choi, 'Tying and Innovation: A Dynamic Analysis of Tying Arrangements' (1998), available at http://ssrn.com.

44 See, e.g., James F. Ponsoldt & Christopher D. David, 'A Comparison between U.S. and E.U. Antitrust Treatment of Tying Claims against Microsoft: When should the Bundling of Computer Software be Permitted', 27 *Nw. J. Int'l L. & Bus.* 421 (2007).

45 See Dennis W. Carlton & Michael Waldman, 'The Strategic Use of Tying to Preserve and Create Market Power in Evolving Industries', 33 *Rand Journal of Economics* 194 (2002) (considering as an example a computer (primary good) and a printer (complementary good). Their model shows that bundling can be profitable for the monopolist in such a setting, supposing that the alternative producer faces entry costs for both the primary and complementary markets or that there are network effects for the complementary good rather than costs. By bundling, the monopolist stops the alternative producer from selling any complementary units in the first period, which reduces the alternative producer's chances of returning to the complementary market. In turn, this reduction can stop the alternative producer from entering either the primary or complementary markets in the second period, allowing the monopolist to preserve its primary market monopoly). Further, see Ahlborn, Evans & Padilla, *supra* note 30 (arguing that Waldman and Carlton model's validity depends on strong assumptions, such as that entry into the bundled good market is very costly). See, besides, Feldman, *supra* note 32, at 2088–90.

46 For example, to compete against Microsoft Office, an entrant with a superior word-processing program might only be able to persuade customers who care about word processing and not about presentation software or spreadsheets.

In particular, such a deterrent effect will be most significant in industries subject to network effects, where firms need a sufficient mass of customers to consider entrance profitable.[47] Yet, it occurs as well in industries where consumers prefer to mix and match, because rivals or entrants will be at a competitive disadvantage in supplying their product to consumers, by being deprived of equal access to the required complementary product.[48]

The problem with all the post-Chicagoan models that explain how a monopolist's System Innovations can strengthen market power is that they do not show whether they also harm consumer welfare.[49] Therefore, striking a proper balance among the manifold effects that follow from dominant firms' System Innovations is complex, because the analysis is highly fact-specific, and difficult to implement, and because these effects are difficult to 'measure'.[50] To begin with, the magnitude of the welfare-increasing impact that any good innovation entails rests with the nature of the good innovation and with a prognostic judgment about the market's technological development.[51] Moreover, in performing an analysis of how and

---

[47] See, Whinston, *supra* note 39 (explaining how bundling may create foreclosure even when it is known that the practice will come to an end: given network externalities, indeed, in the competitive market for complementary products a monopolist's rival having no sufficient market today due to the tie may want to exit even if the tie will come to an end, since there will be little demand for its product tomorrow in the absence of an installed base).

[48] See, e.g., Carmen Matutes & Pierre Regibeau, 'A Selective Review of the Economics of Standardization. Entry Deterrence, Technological Progress, and International Competition', 12 *European Journal of Political Economy* 183, 189 (1996).

[49] In the Whinston model, the results on social welfare are ambiguous since, even if consumers are not better off, and exit happens, it is also possible that the efficiency produced by tying outweighs the anticompetitive effects that the exit produces. After all, the Whinston model does not take into account efficiencies, whereas when making an overall assessment the efficiencies should be weighed against the possible anti-competitive effects of foreclosing the adjacent market. See, e.g., Jay P. Choi, Gwanghoon Lee & Christodoulos Stefanadis, 'The Effects of Integration on R&D Incentives in Systems Markets', 5 *Netnomics* 21 (2003) (arguing in relation to their model that the welfare implications of tie-ins are ambiguous since in the short-run they reduce prices, but in the longer run they increase one firm's R&D incentives to innovate and reduce those of its rivals, bringing to attention the issue that Chapter 1 illustrated, about which kind of firms – whether incumbents or rivals – are in the best position to innovate). See Fisher, *supra* note 27, at 157–8 (arguing that perhaps the most harmful effect of Microsoft's actions was the strong message they sent that innovations that interfered with Microsoft's monopoly in operating systems would not be tolerated).

[50] See Kobayashi, *supra* note 13, at 32; Daniel L. Rubinfeld, 'Antitrust Enforcement in Dynamic Network Industries', 43 *Antitrust Bull.* 859, 881 (1998); Evans & Salinger, *supra* note 14, 51 (commenting on the Carlton-Waldman model, stating that 'the new models rest, however, on very restrictive assumptions. [. . .] As it currently stands, the literature represents a significant scholarly contribution which, with further work, might yield useful policy insights. The existing literature by itself, though, does not give the antitrust authorities or the courts much practical guidance on how to determine whether a particular tie harms consumer welfare.').

[51] It may be argued that major innovations produce noteworthy increases of social welfare; but sometimes it is hard to distinguish between major product change improvements

when System Innovation might harm consumer welfare and innovation, antitrust courts and authorities are not always well-equipped to verify the specific economic model. Therefore, although the economic thinking seems to suggest to antitrust authorities the need to strike a balance between all the goods that may come with System Innovations and the harm that dominant firms' System Innovations may sometimes cause, it is questionable whether US courts and EU antitrust institutions are able to do this.[52]

The following section addresses this question by analyzing US and EU case law.[53]

THE LEGAL PERSPECTIVE: THE US NET PLUS STANDARD

An examination of US cases shows that US courts have faced several instances where the relevant innovation represented either a major cost-saving step or a brilliant and significant improvement – for example, the launch of a revolutionary new type of camera,[54] or the integration in one single computer of several features and functions previously supplied separately.[55] In other words, in these cases US courts scrutinized innovations

---

and mere product differentiation representing simple redesign of the pre-existing product, without deliberating on the inherent technological nature of the innovation – an inquiry that many lawyers are not well-equipped to make. In this regard, it is notable that even the existence of a patent or of a copyright cannot be used as a proxy of the quality of the innovation, as patents are granted even to minor inventions and copyright follows from mere creation and, in some cases, the combination between creation and fixation. Moreover, it is speculation to anticipate both the extent to which an innovation generates further innovation and the benefits yielded by those subsequent innovations. To perform such a judgment, indeed, one should estimate both the innovations that might subsequently be developed and the innovations that would have been developed in the absence of this new innovation, so as to conclude whether the innovations that belong to the former kind are superior to the latter.

52 See Herbert Hovenkamp, 'The Antitrust Movement and the Rise of Industrial Organization', *68 Tex. L. Rev.* 105 (1989).

53 For the legal literature about Systems Innovations and, in particular, about System Innovations in the form of tie-ins see beyond what quoted above, e.g., Ahlborn, Evans & Padilla, *supra* note 30; David S. Evans, Jorge A. Padilla & Michele Polo, 'Tying in Platform Software: Reasons for a Rule-of-Reason Standard in European Competition Law', 25 *World Competition* 509 (2002); Joseph G. Sidak, 'An Antitrust Rule for Software Integration', 18 *Yale Journal on Regulation* 1, 15–20 (2001) (arguing that the costs of integration are very low); and Aryeh S. Friedman, 'Law and the Innovative Process: Preliminary Reflections', 1986 *Colum. Bus. L. Rev.* 1 (1986).

54 See See, e.g., *Berkey Photo v. Eastman Kodak*, 603 F.2d 263 (2nd Cir. 1979).

55 See, e.g., *California Computer Products, Inc. and Century Data System, Inc., v. IBM*, 613 F.2d 727 (9th Cir. 1979) (although the plaintiff claimed IBM made design changes on certain of its central processing units (CPUs), disk drives and controllers that were of no technological advantage and solely for the purpose of frustrating competition from plug-compatible manufacturers, the court held that technological changes comprised significant

whose value was outstanding – i.e., innovations that, thanks to their inherent quality, seem to produce a clearly positive impact on consumer welfare by increasing dynamic efficiency. Therefore, these courts stopped their examination as if the inherent quality of the regarded innovations was enough to outweigh any likely anticompetitive effects, whether static or dynamic. Indeed, these courts quickly rejected any plea of anticompetitive innovation. For instance, they stated that a monopolist has the right to redesign its products to make them more attractive to buyers and has no duty to act as the trustee of its competitors by helping them to survive or expand.[56] Other states that challenge in courts the monopolist's innovation sometimes permit rivals to avoid new rounds of reverse engineering and reduces the dominant firm's incentive to innovate.[57]

On the other hand, US courts have also faced cases where the challenged technological changes either deliberately caused a deterioration of the product, or represented nothing more than manipulations aimed at creating incompatibility[58] – i.e., cases where the inherent quality of the innovation was so low that its impact on consumer welfare was negative or, at least, not positive. In these cases, therefore, the courts shifted their respective focus to identifying the innovation's anticompetitive rationale, though they reached different levels of economic rigor. For instance, in *C.R. Bard v. M3 Systems*,[59] the jury relied on the subjective element of

---

innovations); *ILC Peripherals Leasing Corp. v. IBM*, 448 F.Supp. 228 (N.D.Cal.1978) and *ILC Peripherals Leasing Corp. v. IBM*, 458 F.Supp. 423 (N.D.Cal. 1978) (holding that the plaintiff failed to prove that certain interface changes were predatory) both *aff'd per curiam sub nom. Memorex Corp. v. IBM*, 636 F.2d 1188 (9th Cir. 1980); *Telex Corp v. IBM*, 367 F.Supp. 258, 347 (N.D. Okla 1973), *rev'd on other grounds*, 510 F.2d 894 (10th Cir.1975) (despite allegations that IBM undertook predatory behaviors by introducing 'technological obsolescence hence through mid-life kickers' and by tying peripheral products, including memories and control units, to its CPUs, the trial court's conclusion that practices made available improved devices at the earliest practicable time and represented technological advancements upheld; IBM found not to be dominant).

56 613 F.2d 727, 744 (9th Cir. 1979).

57 458 F. Supp. 423, 443 (N.D. Cal 1978).

58 See, e.g., *In re IBM Peripheral EDP Devices Antitrust Litigation*, 481 F.Supp. 965 (N.D.Cal. 1979), *aff'd Transamerica Computer Company, Inc. v. IBM*, 698 F.2d 1377 (9th Cir.. 1983) where the plaintiffs, who were manufacturers of peripheral computer equipment, such as keyboards and printers compatible with IBM PCs, brought suit for antitrust violations when IBM redesigned its CPU and made it incompatible with any peripheral product not made by IBM. The courts found lawful all but two design changes – System 370, Models 115 and 125 – that unreasonably restricted competition as they allowed operating just short of the speed that would have enabled peripherals to attach (481 F.Supp. 965, 1006–1008 and 698 F.2d 1377, 1383). Notwithstanding such a negative judgment about these two innovations IBM was not condemned because it lacked monopoly power and because the court established that the plaintiff did not suffer any damages.

59 157 F.3d 1340 (Fed. Circ. 1998), where the plaintiff alleged that Bard had modified its biopsy gun and needles not for improving the operation of the gun, but for the purpose of preventing use of its rivals' needles so that they did not fit the gun without an adapter. The

the offense: after having considered evidence showing that the innovation was never intended to be an improvement,[60] it found – actually, without explanation – that Bard had launched its innovation in order to raise rivals' entry costs into the secondary market. In contrast, in *Microsoft III* [61] the court carefully elaborated the strategic effects of Microsoft's innovation. In particular, seeming to evoke a leveraging theory, the court maintained that Microsoft's technological changes – i.e., the integration of Internet Explorer in Windows,[62] and the development of a Microsoft version of Java that was incompatible with other comparable programs available on the market[63] – produced a foreclosure effect to the detriment of Netscape and Sun Microsystems. These changes, prevented Netscape and Sun Microsystems from developing a way to bypass Microsoft's operating system. In other words, the Court concluded that Microsoft

---

plaintiff contended that Bard's design changes were anti-competitive, pointing to documents from Bard showing internal discussions of anti-competitive aims.

60 In other words, the subjective element was crucial. Indeed, given the unpredictability of innovation, it is impossible to infer its anticompetitive nature from the fact that it is not a significant improvement.

61 The literature about the *Microsoft* case is huge. See, e.g., Stan J. Liebowitz & Stephen E. Margolis, 'Network Effects and the Microsoft Case', in *Dynamic Competition and Public Policy* (Jerry Ellig ed., 2001); Franklin M. Fisher, 'The IBM and Microsoft Cases: What's the Difference', 90 *Am. Econ. Rev.* 180 (2000); Franklin M. Fisher, Daniel L. Rubinfeld, *United States v. Microsoft: An Economic Analysis*, in *Did Microsoft Harm Consumers? Two Opposing Views* 10 (David S. Evans, Franklin M. Fisher, Daniel L. Rubinfeld, and Richard A. Schmalensee eds., 2000); Richard A. Schmalensee, 'Antitrust Issues in Schumpeterian Industries', 90 *Am. Econ. Rev.* 192 (2000); Kenneth G. Elzinga & David E. Mills, 'PC Software', 44 *Antitrust Bull.* 739 (1999); Steven C. Salop & R. Craig Romaine, 'Preserving Monopoly: Economic Analysis, Legal Standards, and Microsoft', 7 *Geo. Mason L. Rev.* 617 (1999); John E. Lopatka & William H. Page, 'Antitrust on Internet Time: Microsoft and the Law and Economics of Exclusion', 7 *Sup. Ct. Econ. Rev.* 157 (1999); and John E. Lopatka & William H. Page, 'Microsoft, Monopolization, and Network Externalities: Some Abuses of Economic Theory in Antitrust Decision Making', 40 *Antitrust Bull.* 317 (1995).

62 Microsoft's integration of Internet Explorer (IE) and Windows 'prevented OEMs from pre-installing other browsers and deterred consumers from using them.' *Microsoft III*, 63–4. The integration consisted in: (i) excluding IE from the 'Add/Remove Programs' utility; (ii) co-mingling in the same files the code related to browsing to other codes, so that any attempt to delete the files containing IE would, at the same time, cripple the operating system; (iii) designing Windows so as to override the user's choice of a default browser other than IE.

63 Java is another type of middleware posing a potential threat to Windows' position as the ubiquitous platform for software development. The District Court found that Microsoft took four steps to exclude Java from developing as a viable cross-platform threat: (a) designing a JVM incompatible with the one developed by its rival (Sun Microsystems); (b) entering into contracts, the so-called 'First Wave Agreements,' requiring major ISVs to promote Microsoft's JVM exclusively; (c) deceiving Java developers about the Windows-specific nature of the tools it distributed to them; and (d) coercing Intel to stop aiding Sun in improving the Java technologies. The first of these behaviours is the one here addressed.

used those innovations to defend its original monopoly in the operating system market by acquiring a significant market power in secondary markets.

In particular, in its analysis of these technological changes, the Microsoft court used the burden of proof rule in a pivotal way, requiring Microsoft to rebut the alleged anticompetitive effects of its innovations with objective justifications regarding their superior quality. When Microsoft was unable to justify from a technical/commercial standpoint the different practices that resulted in the integration between Internet Explorer and its Windows PC operating system, the Court deemed those practices unlawful. Yet, when Microsoft could justify its choice to override the user's preference for a default browser with 'valid technical reasons'[64] and the introduction of its own version of Java, underlining its superior speed,[65] the Court did not strike these innovations. In short, while rejecting some of the claims of Microsoft rivals, the DC Circuit was quite deferential in assessing the positive side of the monopolist's innovations.

In summary, it should be acknowledged that in scrutinizing monopolists' System Innovations US courts considered whether they were 'unreasonably restrictive of competition'.[66] They compared System Innovations' inherent value against their anticompetitive effects, acting under the rule of reason approach, or the 'separate products requirement',[67] which are

---

64 Although all three acts mentioned above had anticompetitive effects, only the first two had no offsetting justification and, therefore, 'constitute[d] exclusionary conduct [. . .] in violation of § 2'. As for overriding the user's choice of internet browser, the court held the plaintiffs had neither rebutted Microsoft's proffered technical justification nor demonstrated that its justification was outweighed by the anticompetitive effect. The court therefore concluded Microsoft was not 'liable for this aspect of its product design'. See *Microsoft III*, 66–7.

65 Id., 74–5.

66 See, e.g., 613 F.2d 727, 735–736 (9th Cir. 1979); 698 F.2d 1377, 1382–1383 (9th Cir. 1983); 510 F.2d 894, 902 and 906 (10th Cir.1975); and *Caldera, Inc. vs. Microsoft Corp.*, 72 F. Supp. 2d 1295, 1323 (Utah D.C. 1995). In this way, hence, US courts rejected the per se legality rule that law scholars suggested without obliging plaintiffs to demonstrate that a design choice was entirely devoid of technological merit. See Frederic M. Scherer, 'Technological Innovation and Monopolization', AAI Working Paper 05–07, July 15, 2005, available at: http://ssrn.com/abstract=1103594 (arguing that, 'in Microsoft, Judge Jackson struggled admirably to weigh the benefits of browser integration against competitive harm, but his efforts were insufficient to convince a skeptical Court of Appeal fearful of impeding technological progress and reluctant to undertake the job on its own').

67 Indeed, when the US court addressed tying claims under Section 1, they applied the well-known per se prohibition, which is triggered when the following conditions have been met. Namely: (1) the tying and tied products are separate products; (2) there is evidence of actual coercion of consumers; (3) the firm that introduces the tying has sufficient economic power in the market of the tying product; (4) there are anticompetitive effects in the tied market; and, (5) there is involvement of a 'not insubstantial' amount of interstate commerce in the tied product market.

the specific standards of Section 2 and Section 1 tying cases, respectively.[68] They placed the burden of proof in order to ask the party that was in the best position to do so to explain the conduct. On the one hand, by employing the net-plus standard,[69] they chose to be particularly lenient in judging innovations' inherent values, as if they were following the Chicago-like approach to innovations.[70] On the other hand, in assessing the anticompetitive effects, they did not disregard considering the most recent, post-Chicagoan economic theories about the defensive leveraging monopoly.

---

[68] Now, under the 'separate products requirement', US courts focused on the tying market and asked whether the tie entailed efficiencies substantial enough to compensate consumers for the loss of choice in the tied product market. See, e.g., *Telex Corp. v. IBM*, 367 F. Supp. 258 (ND. Okla 1973). Antitrust authorities can approach differently the 'separate product requirement'. For instance, they can just focus upon the tied market and wonder whether, despite the efficiencies coming from the bundling, there is sufficient residual demand for suppliers of the standalone product to break even or operate profitably. As this second inquiry places greater emphasis on the position of competitors in the tied market and is likely to be less demanding to prove, such a threshold for the 'separate products requirement' is lower than the one employed in the US. Nevertheless, if this second way for interpreting the 'separate products requirement' is accompanied by a proper assessment of the efficiencies elsewhere, the final outcome is not very different. See, in this regard, footnote 80 and the accompanying text. For a concurring opinion, see David A. Heiner, 'Assessing Tying Claims in the Context Of Software Integration: A Suggested Framework for Applying the Rule Of Reason Analysis', 72 *U. Chi. L. Rev.* 123, 125 (2005).

[69] See Maria Lillà Montagnani, 'Predatory and Exclusionary Innovation: Which Legal Standard for Software Integration in the Context of the Competition v. Intellectual Property Rights Clash?', 37 *IIC* 304 (2006).

[70] In accord, James D. Hurwitz & William E. Kovacic, 'Judicial Analysis of Predation: The Emerging Trends', 35 *Vand. L. Rev.* 63, 127–9 (1982) (observing that 'the case law generally leaves dominant firms relatively free to conduct innovation-related activities when they are acting alone. At present, the only real danger to a dominant firm – and even this danger is remote – is that it will be held liable for a design change that cannot even [. . .] be justified as a genuine improvement, but which is made with demonstrably predatory intent. The courts' rationales for this position are that inexpert intervention might diminish a dominant firm's innovation incentive, and that no apparent manageable guidelines exist for identifying genuinely pernicious behavior. These concerns, coupled with the high value that judges attach to innovation generally, have led courts to devote relatively little attention to the frequency with which dominant firms arguably use innovation strategies for principally predatory ends.').Yet, several US antitrust scholars have suggested, regardless of the case law, a different standard. See, e.g., Frank H. Easterbrook, *Predatory Strategies and Counterstrategies*, 48 U. Chi. L. Rev. 263 (1981); and Sidak, supra note 16; and Hebert J. Hovenkamp, Mark D. Janis and Mark A. Lemley, *IP and Antitrust. An Analysis of Antitrust Principles Applied to Intellectual Property Law* § 12.2 (2009) (observing, 'we think the better rule is one of non-liability for practical reasons. Courts will find it very difficult to estimate both the *ex ante* expected cost and expected return from investment in research and development. Indeed, companies themselves probably cannot do so perfectly. And reasoning from *ex post* results is problematic, since punishing research merely because it turned out to be unsuccessful would significantly chill risk-taking research efforts. So the better approach is not to punish monopolists for making allegedly predatory investments in research.').

THE EU APPROACH: TORN BETWEEN THE REFUSAL TO DEAL DOCTRINE AND A LOOK TO THE LONG-RUN EFFECTS

Turning to EU case law, a first distinction arises in comparison to the US cases. The Commission applied the refusal to supply doctrine in two of the most important cases where it challenged the introduction of a new product under Article 102.[71] Specifically, this occurred in relation to the launch of the new integrated version of the IBM mainframe System-370 in 1984, and in connection with Microsoft's introduction of its new operating system for networks in 1999. The former case ended with the *IBM Settlement*,[72] whereas the latter development comprised the first of the two abuses contested in *Microsoft IV*.[73] In both cases, the Commission, rather than discussing (as in the US cases) whether the advantages that the

---

[71] It is noteworthy that the Commission has also followed the same approach in Article 81 cases. See, for instance, *Decca Navigator System* ([1988] OJ L/43/27, §§ 108–110; [1989] 18th Annual Report on Competition), 80–81. Here the dominant firm (Decca) developed a radio signal transmission system for which there were no substitutes. After patent coverage elapsed, Decca entered into licensing agreements and changed its signals in order to prevent competitors' unlicensed equipment from interoperating with the signaling system. The Commission initially concluded that Decca's practice of modifying the electronic signals without notice and without justification rendered competing equipment useless, so as to represent an anticompetitive agreement. The Commission subsequently archived the file when Decca voluntarily ended the agreements and the regarded practice.

[72] Commission case IV/29.479, XIV *Report on Competition Policy* 78 (1984), where the Commission focused, not only upon IBM's choice of integrating the operating system in the CPU for its most powerful range of computers, but also the IBM System/370, and the IBM's practice of not disclosing interface information about the new product until it had actually marketed it. More specifically, the Commission observed that: (i) the incompatibility created by the new IBM System-370 with non-IBM peripheral equipment would have foreclosed such complementary markets to the detriment of independent manufacturers of peripheral equipments; (ii) the non-disclosure of the IBM System-370 source code would have prevented companies from designing and preparing software that could have worked in conjunction with IBM software; and that (iii) the non-disclosure of the interface information relating to IBM's system network architecture would have affected industry efforts to develop its own standard. As part of the settlement, IBM agreed to disclose, in a timely manner, sufficient interface information to enable competing companies to attach both their hardware and software products to the IBM System-370. Further, IBM agreed to disclose adequate and timely information to rivals to enable them to interconnect their systems or networks with IBM's System-370 using a set of network protocols – the Systems Network Architecture – which IBM had developed. On this case see, e.g., Frederic M. Scherer, 'Microsoft and IBM in Europe', in 84 *Antitrust & Trade Regulation Report* 65 (2003).

[73] After Microsoft moved from the Windows NT 4.0 to the Windows 2000 generation of its operating systems for both client PCs and work group servers, Microsoft's competitors in the market for work group servers operating systems complained that Microsoft refused to supply them with the interoperability information necessary to make their own operating systems for work group servers dialogue with the Microsoft operating system for PCs. In other words, the first abuse consisted in Microsoft's refusal to disclose the technical specifications that could have allowed its competitors to develop compatible products.

innovations brought to society as a whole outweighed their anticompetitive effects, deemed the interface data needed for compatibility to be an essential facility, despite Microsoft's alleged IPRs covering that information. In other words, when faced with cases of straightforward innovations – i.e., innovations whose inherent quality was so outstanding as to produce a clear positive impact upon consumer welfare[74] – EU antitrust institutions did not stop their analyses, as the US courts did in their decisions.[75] They applied the refusal to deal doctrine, irrespective of the fact that imposing such a duty to deal meant reshaping the scope of existing IPRs.[76] After all, the link between predatory innovation and refusal to deal cases is quite apparent, because when a monopolist's System Innovation forecloses competitors from a related market, the monopolist's rivals have two choices. They can challenge the anticompetitive nature of the innovation in a public forum, as it happened in the US predatory innovation cases. Alternatively, they can try to obtain a license either for the innovation itself or for what is necessary to restore compatibility with the new product – i.e., interface information – as happened in the EU cases that the Commission chose to treat as refusal to deal cases, rather than as predatory innovation cases.

In contrast, in *Microsoft IV* and in *Microsoft V*,[77] the European Commission and the Court of First Instance evaluated the integration between Windows Media Player (WMP) and the Windows PC operating system by endorsing the same net-plus standard employed by the US courts and, to some extent, by employing the same burden of proof rule. More specifically, the assessment of this integration fell under the EU law respecting monopolistic tying, which imposes a five-prong test that resembles the US standard for Section 1 violations.[78] Indeed, in *Microsoft V* the

---

[74] Indeed, in both cases there were sufficient technological reasons to qualify the relevant changes so that claims of alleged anticompetitive nature would have been frivolous. For instance, though the quality of the regarded innovations seem to stem out as a matter of fact, it is worthwhile to consider that in *Microsoft IV* the Commission itself recognized that the Windows NT 4.0 replaced by Windows 2000 was an 'already outdated technology', id., § 583.

[75] In the US, as courts traditionally dislike imposing duties to deal and admit the obligation to disclose interface information only as a remedy to a different antitrust violation, plaintiffs prefer to claim the predatory nature of the innovation in question – a claim that regards the advantages and disadvantages that flow from the innovation and that, hence, does not really question the existence and enforcement of the IPRs that may protect the innovation. In this regard, see the following chapter.

[76] Indeed, the present EU approach towards monopolists who refuse to license their IPRs seems to use the following reasoning. As long as the enforcement of a monopolist's IPR impairs future innovation and, hence, long-term consumer welfare, the EU antitrust institutions must intervene. In this regard, see the following chapter.

[77] Court of First Instance, case T-201/04, September 17, 2007, available at http://curia.europa.eu/.

[78] The present EU standard has urged several contrasting opinions. See, e.g., Robert O'Donoghue & Jorge A. Padilla, *The Law and Economics of Article* 82 509–517 (2004)

Court of First Instance, affirming the Commission's previous decision in *Microsoft IV*, established that a tying violates the law when the following conditions are met.[79] First, the firm in question possesses a dominant position in the tying market. Second, the tie exists between two separate products.[80] Third, because of the tying, consumers suffer coercion. Fourth, there is a reasonable likelihood[81] of foreclosure effects in the tied market.[82] Fifth, the dominant firm's conduct lacks objective justifications.[83]

Under the heading of 'objective justification', the European Commission and the Court of First Instance developed the analyses that the US courts

(distinguishing among the Microsoft tests that, though more reasonable, does not allow a fair consideration of tie-ins' procompetitive effects and the 'modified per se prohibition' applied in *Hilti* and *Tetrapak II* that could be satisfied just by showing market power, separate products, and coercion – see *Eurofix-Baucol Hilti*, OJ 1988 L 65/19, affirmed in Case T-30/89, *Hilti AG v. Commission*, [1991] ECR II-1439 and Case C-53/92, *Hilti AG v. Commission*, [1994] ECR I-667; and *Tetra Pak II*, OJ 1992 L 72/1, affirmed in Case T-83/91, *Tetra Pak International SA v. Commission*, [1994] ECR II-755 and in Case C-333/94, *Tetra Pak International SA v. Commission*, [1996] ECR I-5951); Maurits Dolmans & Thomas Graf, 'Analysis of Tying under Article 82 EC: The European Commission's Microsoft Decision in Perspective', 27 *World Competition Law & Economics Review* 225 (2004) (defining *Microsoft IV*'s test as a rule of reason standard); David S. Evans & A. Jorge Padilla, 'Tying under Article 82 EC: And the Microsoft Decision: A Comment on Dolmans and Graf', 27 *World Competition Law & Economics Review* 503 (2004) (disagreeing and considering the present EU approach as still an interventionist version of the previous modified per se illegal rule).

[79] See *Microsoft IV*, § 794 and *Microsoft V*, § 859CFI.

[80] As the EU test allows for consideration of efficiencies under the 'objective justification' prong, its 'separate product requirement' serves to thresh out cases where there is so little prospect of competitive harm that no further investigation is necessary. In other words, in the EU the 'separate product requirement' set a threshold that is lower than that which the US 'separate product requirement' set forth, because the efficiencies that US courts consider under this prong in Section 1 cases can be, however, analyzed under the EU objective justification prong. See David Howarth & Kathryn McMahon, '"Windows Has Performed an Illegal Operation": The Court of First Instance's Judgment in *Microsoft v. Commission*', 29 *E. C. L. R.* 117, 127 (2008). See footnote 68 and the accompanying text.

[81] Further, see *Microsoft V*, § 868, where the Court stated that the Commission's theory of foreclosure was prospective and relied on the response of third parties (software developers and internet content providers). Such an approach is consistent with the post-Chicago view, in that this is really the only school that would find an abuse in the circumstances of the case. See Howarth & McMahon, *supra* note 80, at 128–30 (arguing that 'however, an economic rationale is impossible to extract from the judgment itself: the CFI refers to none of the economic literature and the legal test for tying can be applied without having to delve into the economics. Nor should it be the CFI's role to undertake complex economic inquiries. To the extent that the CFI has arrived at its own judgment on foreclosure, it expressly emphasized the 'competitive structure' of the market, rather than the dynamics.').

[82] In arguing in favor of the likely foreclosing effect, the Commission focused its attention on Microsoft's distributive advantage, that is to say, on the fact that Microsoft entered the market of music players easily, by exploiting Windows ubiquity.

[83] The EU law places the burden of proof on the party claiming the efficiencies, who must establish that (i) efficiencies are likely to be realized; (ii) the conduct is necessary to achieve the efficiencies; (iii) the efficiencies benefit consumers; and (iv) competition in respect of a substantial part of the products involved is not eliminated.

made under Section 2's rule of reason and Section 1's 'separate product requirement'. They observed first that Microsoft did not submit either 'substantiated evidence' that the integration would have led to superior technical product performance,[84] or 'evidence that tying of WMP is indispensable for the alleged pro-competitive effects to come into effect'.[85] Then, they rejected all the various efficiencies that the dominant company alleged the integration would have produced.[86] Third, seeming to recall a leveraging theory, they ascertained the anticompetitive effects that the integration was likely to cause,[87] affirming that, due to Microsoft's dominant position and the network effects of the industry, WMP enjoyed such an extraordinary distributive advantage that it effectively forced content providers to standardize their content on WMP.[88] Such standardization,[89]

---

84 See *Microsoft IV*, § 962 where further the Commission made an express reference to the US District Court judgment which, as said before, found that '[. . .] according to several standard programs used by Microsoft to measure system performance, the removal of Internet Explorer by the prototype program slightly improves the overall speed of Windows 98.' Afterwards, the CFI concurred, observing that Microsoft's reply to the Commission's finding was 'unsupported' – see *Microsoft V*, § 1159.

85 See *Microsoft IV*, § 963 affirmed in *Microsoft V*, §§ 1097–8.

86 See *Microsoft IV*, §§ 956–61 and 962–9 affirmed in *Microsoft V*, §§ 1097–8.

87 See *Microsoft IV*, §§ 971–2, where the Commission wrote, 'It may be true that media players *today* are not substitutes for client PC operating systems insofar as no general purpose application programs can be written using a media player's APIs only. However, 'limited purpose' application programs, in particular media applications, can be written using a media player's APIs. [. . .] The possibility cannot be ruled out that, if such a limited platform for applications became wide-spread, there would be incentives to expand the available APIs so as to allow the writing of applications which would no longer be for 'limited purposes' only. Second, middleware such as Java *in combination with* a media player could in fact *be* a general purpose platform substitute today. As such, the media player can be deemed a necessary component of a 'full-fledged' platform threat. In this sense, Microsoft has incentives to foreclose third party media players through tying.' The CFI concurred with the idea that 'by means of the bundling, Microsoft sends signals which deter innovation in any technologies in which it might conceivably take an interest and which it might tie with Windows in the future', *Microsoft V*, 1088. The Commission's choice to pay attention not to actual but to potential foreclosure effects (and, thus, to the way in which markets are likely to evolve) represents a peculiarity of the EU approach to foreclosure – a peculiarity that has been criticized. It is necessary to acknowledge that, with *Microsoft IV*, the Commission took a step forward by examining the integration's effects, rather than merely considering – as it normally used to do in cases of tying – that the tying has by its nature a foreclosure effect.

88 The CFI does not require a finding of monopoly in a second market for a leveraging violation, but the Commission was careful to show the extent to which Microsoft's conduct led to dominance. In other words, the CFI did accept the defensive leveraging monopoly argument but, at the same time, did not disregard that Microsoft was pretty close to attaining the monopoly in the secondary market as well.

89 See, indeed, Rudoph Peritz, 'Re-Thinking *US v Microsoft* in Light of the EC Case' (2001), available at http://ssrn.com/abstract=571803 (arguing that 'the EC complaint recognizes that there is more involved than a middleware threat to Windows' dominance.'). About the event that suppliers will standardize their technologies so to be compatible with the platforms when the degree of hardware differentiation is sufficiently small, see J. Church

in particular, would have led to a situation where content would have been available only for WMP, with spillover effects on competition in the market for client PC operating systems, thereby strengthening Microsoft's monopoly.[90] Finally, the Commission and the Court of First Instance concurred that the integration would have deterred innovation in the whole market to which the integrated product belongs.[91]

In summary the Commission and the Court of First Instance observed that the innovation under review produced a negative net consumer welfare effect because, on the one hand, it did not have a unique inherent value and did not produce significant efficiency; and, on the other hand, the integration harmed allocative efficiency and impaired dynamic efficiency. In reaching this conclusion both EU institutions relied on certain prognostic insights, which actually grew out of the most recent path-dependence[92] and post-Chicagoan economic theories,[93] about what future market developments could have been.

Indeed, even more recently the Commission has followed this approach both in its 2009 Communication and in *Microsoft VI*[94] – the EU case about the integration between Internet Explorer and Windows Operating System. The 2009 Communication – which establishes that a monopolist's tie-in has to be held unlawful when it involves separate products and when it is likely to produce anticompetitive foreclosure – largely reproduces the above-described Chicagoan and post-Chicagoan economic doctrines, by describing the conditions under which tie-ins may produce 'anticompetitive foreclosure' and the efficiencies that this kind of practice may entail.[95]

& N. Gandal, 'Networks Effects, Software Provision and Standardization', 40 *Journal of Industrial Economics* 85 (1992).

90 See *Microsoft IV*, § 842. The Commission used this argument also in the new case against Microsoft, arguing that 'the ubiquity of Internet Explorer creates artificial incentives for content providers and software developers to design websites or software primarily for Internet Explorer which ultimately risks undermining competition and innovation in the provision of services to consumers'. See MEMO/09/15, January 17 2009, available at http://europa.eu/rapid/pressReleasesAction.do?reference=MEMO/09/352&format=HTML&aged=0&language=EN&guiLanguage=en.

91 More exactly the Commission wrote that whereas in a competitive scenario market forces attenuate the deterrent effect that tying a software with an operating system produces on innovation as competing platforms still exist, 'this is not the case where the platform market is virtually monopolized', *Microsoft IV*, § 961. Even in the new case against Microsoft – see footnote 90 and the accompanying text – the Commission focused its attention on 'the pace of product innovation and to the quality of products which consumers ultimately obtain.' – see MEMO/09/15, *supra* note 90.

92 In this regard, see Chapter 1.

93 For a concurring opinion see Ekaterina Rousseva, Rethinking Exclusionary Abuses in EU Competition Law 249–56 (2010).

94 See MEMO/09/15, *supra* note 90.

95 See *Guidance on the Commission's Enforcement Priorities in Applying Article 82 of the EC Treaty to Abusive Exclusionary Conduct by Dominant Undertakings*, OJ 2009, C45/7, at §§ 47–62.

In Microsoft *VI* – a case that ended with a commitment decision pursuant to article 9 of Reg. 1/2003[96] – the Commission justified the alleged harm to competition looking not only at the said 'artificial' distributive advantage that Microsoft enjoyed,[97] but also at Microsoft's ability to impair future innovations. Indeed, in commenting on this case, and the subsequent separation between Windows Operating System and Internet Explorer, Commission Nieele Krooes observed that it will 'act as an incentive for web browser companies to innovate and offer people better browsers in the future'.[98]

THE SOMETIMES DIVERGENT, SOMETIMES CONVERGENT US AND EU APPROACHES TOWARDS MONOPOLISTS' SYSTEM INNOVATIONS

Except for the EU choice to evaluate some innovations under the refusal to deal doctrine, recently both US courts and EU antitrust institutions made analogous use of the net-plus standard, so that nowadays it can be argued that their assessment of dominant firms' System Innovations follows a kind of three-step analysis.

Given that an innovation that goes beyond mere tinkering with products and processes represents a key driver of economic progress and, hence, is a crucial source of enhanced consumer welfare, US and EU antitrust authorities seem to start their analysis by distinguishing such 'good' System Innovations and sham innovations. In other words, US courts and EU antitrust institutions seem to approach the cases of Predatory System

96 See IP/09/1941, December 16 2009, available at http://europa.eu/rapid/pressReleasesAction.do?reference=IP/09/1941&format=HTML&aged=0&language=EN&guiLanguage=en. There, it is explained that, 'under the commitments approved by the Commission, Microsoft will make available, for five years, in the European Economic Area (through the Windows Update mechanism,), a 'Choice Screen' enabling users of Windows XP, Windows Vista, and Windows 7, to choose which web browser(s) they want to install in addition to, or instead of, Microsoft's browser Internet Explorer. The commitments also provide that computer manufacturers will be able to install competing web browsers, set those as default and turn Internet Explorer off'.

97 See, indeed, MEMO/09/15, *supra* note 90. There, it can be read that, 'The evidence gathered during the investigation leads the Commission to believe that the tying of Internet Explorer with Windows, which makes Internet Explorer available on 90 per cent of the world's PCs, distorts competition on the merits between competing web browsers insofar as it provides Internet Explorer with an artificial distribution advantage which other web browsers are unable to match.'

98 See IP/09/1941, 16 dicembre 2009, http://europa.eu/rapid/pressReleasesAction.do?reference=IP/09/1941&format=HTML&aged=0&language=EN&guiLanguage=en.

Innovations by evaluating first the inherent quality of the patented inventions or copyrighted creative works.

In this regard, US courts have seemed very willing to recognize the positive value of innovations, perhaps in order not to discourage firms' efforts and investments in innovative activities. In so doing, therefore, they seem to state the Chicago principle, that as long as the innovation benefits the whole society, a monopolist should be encouraged to produce non-sham innovations and deserves to appropriate the advantages that flow from them, though they allow the monopolist to strengthen its dominant position. On this issue, instead, the past EU choice to oblige some monopolists to share their revolutionary System Innovations points in just the opposite direction. Further, it is at odds with what was said in the previous chapter when looking at mono-product monopolists' innovations, because it recalls the idea that dominant firms have to act as their rivals' trustee, without searching for further competitive advantages.

However – and moving to the second step of their analysis – when either US courts or EU antitrust institutions recognize the scant positive value of an innovation, or its shameful nature, they use the most recent and sophisticated post-Chicago economics to establish whether the conditions occur under which dominant firms may be permitted to employ these System Innovations to harm consumer welfare. In the Microsoft cases, indeed, the EU antitrust authorities shared with US courts the anticompetitive theory underpinning Microsoft's conduct, i.e., that Microsoft was leveraging its monopoly in the middleware over secondary markets via integrations just in order to defend it. But in so doing, whereas the DC Circuit assumed a short-run perspective in its analysis, the EU Commission and the Court of First Instance, irrespective of the risk of false positives, gave more emphasis to future and partially speculative anticompetitive effects that some economic models, such as those deriving from the path-dependence doctrine, supply.[99]

Moving to the third step of their analysis, by using a particular imposition of the burden of proof US courts as well as EU antitrust institutions have tried to strike the right balance between all the good that may come with System Innovations and the ills that, at the same time, they may sometimes cause.[100]

More in general, indeed, most cases applying the consumer welfare test can be solved at an early stage, i.e., without the need for complex balancing exercises. Sometimes, there is no material harm to consumer welfare

---

[99] After all, even in assessing the *likely* foreclosure effect the EU approach appears more tolerant of the risk of false positive than the US one.

[100] Kellezi, *supra* note 8, at 160 and 167.

– as could happen with revolutionary System Innovations. Other times, it is clear that the conduct in question is overwhelmingly harmful – as could happen with System Innovations that amount to a mere sham. Only when the examined conduct belongs to a grayer area other legal tools can operate, such as rules about the burden of proof, presumptions based on limited factual showing, and redeeming justifications[101] as the kind that, indeed, Microsoft have tried to put forward in its saga.

In summary, when IPRs ownership regards System Innovations, but for morphing the regarded case into a refusal to deal case, the analysis' spotlight shifts away from IPRs and focuses on innovations themselves, that is to say, on monopolists' right to introduce new products that somehow hinder their rivals in secondary markets. In this regard, both the US and EU jurisdictions seem willing to establish the principle that a monopolist is free to create these kind of innovations as long as they do not amount to mere manipulations because they can enhance, even a bit, consumer welfare.

The following chapters analyze what changes when the analysis' focus swings from IPRs ownership to those rights that are inherent in each IPR scope, such as the right to refuse others the proprietary intellectual goods, or the right to bring legal actions, or other specific administrative procedures, in order to defend those proprietary intellectual goods.

---

[101] Ginevra Bruzzone, Marco Boccaccio, 'Impact-Based Assesment and Use of Legal Presumptions in EC Competition Law: The Search for the Proper Mix', 32 *World Competition* 465 (2009); Andrew I. Gavil, William E. Kovacic, & Jonathan B. Baker, *Antitrust Law in Perspective: Cases, Concepts and Problems in Competition Policy* 76–77 (2008); Robert W. Crandall & Clifford Winston, 'Does Antitrust Policy Improve Consumer Welfare? Assessing the Evidence', 17 J. *Econ. Perspectives* 3 (2003); and Jonathan B. Baker, 'The Case for Antitrust Enforcement', 17 J. *Econ. Perspectives* 27 (2003).

5. Refusals to license IPRs

THE CASE FOR AN AFTER-THE-FACT, CASE-BY-CASE CONFLICT

We have previously discussed the competitive implications of IPRs ownership. This chapter turns to the case of a dominant firm that enforces one of the fundamental rights that IPRs grant,[1] namely, the right to exclude third parties from the use of the protected intellectual goods. It discusses whether economic models, on the one hand, and US and EU case law, on the other hand, have ever found such behavior harmful.

In particular, after a brief review of the economic literature about foreclosure, and the short discussion of the US and EU refusal *to deal* doctrines – which, indeed, are the logical forerunners of the US and EU refusal *to license* doctrines[2] – the chapter inquires if the standards that the

---

1 After all, as said previously, from the legal standpoint IPRs are *ius excludendi alios* and from the economic standpoint it is just the power to exclude that justifies their existence.

2 The chapter avoids any discussion of the 'essential facilities doctrine'. It is 'unnecessary', when it does not add anything to conditions that refusal to deal doctrines set forth in order to find a behavior unlawful. It is 'harmful' when, by inducing a less sophisticated economic analysis of the regarded scenario, it derives automatically the existence of competitive harm from the essential nature of the requested resource and, hence, it works as a further stand-alone base for the antitrust action, in addition to the refusal to deal doctrine. See, in this regard, 3B Phillip Areeda & Herbert Hovenkamp, *Antitrust Law: An Analysis of Antirust Principles and Their Application* ¶771c (2008); Abbott B. Lipsky & J. Gregory '*Sidak, Essential Facilities'*, 51 *Stan. L. Rev.* 1187, 1248 (1999); Richard J. Gilbert & Carl Shapiro, 'An Economic Analysis of Unilateral Refusals to License Intellectual Property', 93 *Proc. Nat'l Acad. Sci.* 12749, 12754 (1996), available at http://pnas.org/cgi/reprint/93/23/12749.pdf; David McGowan, 'Regulating Competition in the Information Age: Computer Software as an Essential Facility Under the Sherman Act', 18 *Hastings Comm. & Ent. L.J.* 771, 850–51 (1996); Phillip E. Areeda, 'The Essential Facilities Doctrine: An Epithet in Need of Limiting Principles', 58 *Antitrust L.J.* 841 (1990); Gregory J. Werden, 'The Law and Economics of the Essential Facility Doctrine', 32 *St. Louis U. L.J.* 433 (1987); and Michael Boudin, 'Antitrust Doctrine and the Sway of Metaphor', 75 *Geo. L.J.* 395, 397–403 (1986). Some scholars disagree. See, e.g., Marina Lao, 'Networks, Access, and 'Essential Facilities': From Terminal Road to Microsoft', 62 *SMU L. Rev.* 557 (2009); Brett Frischmann & Spencer Weber Waller, 'Revitalizing Essential Facilities', 75 *Antitrust L.J.* 1, 4 (2008) (proposing an 'infrastructure theory' to revitalize the doctrine, meaning that they would apply the theory, assuming other antitrust requirements are met, in cases where a monopolist refuses access to 'infrastructure,' which they define as including not only traditional infrastructure such as 'bridges, highways, ports, electric power grids, and telephone networks,' but also 'ideas, the Internet, and other assets which are vital inputs to the production of wealth at later stages of production on a

former doctrines set forth change when the refused resource happens to be an intellectual good. Then, it explains why US and EU authorities diverge as to whether to oblige dominant firms to share their IPRs and concludes that the existing differences between the two jurisdictions have their roots in a more general cultural and jurisdictional background, which is not specific to either the antitrust or the IP realm.[3] Antitrust actions against monopolists that refuse to make IP deals are premised upon some crucial – though not always stated – policy choices and, hence, illustrate the respective way in which US and EU antitrust authorities look at dominant firms' behaviors, IPRs, and the relationship between them.

ECONOMIC THINKING ABOUT REFUSALS TO LICENSE: A REMINDER

As hinted in Chapter 2 when discussing the form-based and the effects-based approaches, practices that have different phenotypes, that is, which appear different from a behavioral standpoint may, however, produce the same effects on market power and consumer welfare and, therefore, may deserve to be treated in the same manner. In contrast, practices having the same form merit to be judged in a dissimilar way when the applied economic theory states that they produce different effects in different scenarios. Likewise, on the one hand, refusals to supply proprietary resources may, despite their unique form, produce the same economic effects that behaviors with other forms entail. Indeed, various modes of conduct, such as exclusive dealings, tie-in sales, closed joint ventures, product incompatibilities, and discriminatory and monopoly pricing strategies involve either

basis disproportionate for their actual use.'); Spencer Weber Waller, 'Areeda, Epithets, and Essential Facilities', 2008 *Wis. L. Rev.* 359 (2008); Robert Pitofsky, Donna Patterson & Jonathan Hooks, 'The Essential Facilities Doctrine Under U.S. Antitrust Law', 70 *Antitrust L.J.* 443 (2002). Yet, see David W. Carlton, 'A General Analysis of Exclusionary Conduct and Refusal to Deal – Why Aspen and Kodak Are Misguided', 68 *Antitrust Law Journal* 659, 661 nt. 4 (2001) (arguing that the idea that essential facilities could address natural monopolies 'seems dubious, especially when detailed knowledge of an industry is needed to design efficient regulation. A judge or jury is not a substitute for a regulatory agency.').

[3] Regarding the role that cultural principles play in shaping competition policy see, e.g., Dieter De Smet, 'The Diametrically Opposed Principles of US and EU Antitrust Policy', 29 *E.C.L.R.* 356 (2008). A twofold premise nourishes the present conclusion about the cultural and jurisdictional factors that have affected the US and EU refusal to license doctrines: first, the list of explanatory factors that the chapter presents does not aim to be either conclusive or exhaustive. Second, as the analysis focuses on the US and EU case law developing over a long period of time, the chapter does not intend to state that the different factors it discusses to explain the divergences between the two jurisdictions play the same role, at the same time, in any case.

explicit or implicit refusals to deal.[4] On the other hand, refusals to deal may produce different consequences according to the economic conditions under which monopolists use them.

As evidence of this latter kind of situation, consider first that monopolists' refusals to license may amount to exploitative practices. Monopolists can refuse to license their IPRs in order to appropriate the advantages that flow from their dominant positions, or from the ownership of their intellectual competitive advantages.[5] Given the two-prong standard that Chapter 2 set forth to detect unlawful dominant firms' behaviors – which requires that the conduct in question strengthens market power and harms consumer welfare – this kind of 'exploitative refusals to license' should not be prosecuted pursuant to Section 2 or Article 102(b),[6] mainly because, though they may directly impair consumer welfare, they do not increase market power.

Second, monopolists' refusals to license may represent exclusionary practices that respond to the logic underpinning both horizontal and vertical foreclosure.[7] As the current leveraging monopoly theory

---

[4] Indeed, some of the most important pieces of the economic literature that regard refusals to deal look as well at the other practices mentioned in the text. See, e.g., the literature quoted in the previous chapter and, in particular, Dennis W. Carlton & Michael Waldman, 'The Strategic Use of Tying to Preserve and Create Market Power in Evolving Industries', 33 *Rand Journal of Economics* 194 (2002); B. Douglas Bernheim & Michael Whinston, 'Exclusive Dealing', 106 *J. Pol. Econ.* 64 (1998); Eric Rasmussen, 'Naked Exclusion', 81 *Am. Econ. Rev.* 1137 (1991); Janusz Ordover, Garth Saloner & Steven Salop, 'Equilibrium Vertical Foreclosure', 80 *Am. Econ. Rev.* 127 (1990); Michael Whinston, 'Tying, Foreclosure and Exclusion', 80 *Am. Econ. Rev.* 837 (1990).

[5] As to the idea that refusals to deal may consist in mere extracting practices see, e.g., 1 Herbert Hovenkamp, Mark D. Janis, Mark A. Lemley, *IP And Antitrust. An Analysis of Antitrust Principles Applied to Intellectual Property Law* § 13.1 (2009); Richard N. Langlois, 'Technological Standards, Innovation, and Essential Facilities. Toward a Schumpeterian Post-Chicago Approach', in *Dynamic Competition and Public Policy: Technology, Innovation, and Antitrust Issues* 193, 202–203 (Jerry Ellig ed., 2001); Areeda & Hovenkamp, *supra* note 2, at ¶ 771a; Keith N. Hylton, 'Economic Rents and Essential Facilities', in 1991 *B. Y. U. L. Rev.* 1243 (1991), Areeda, *supra* note 2, at 841; and David J. Gerber, 'Rethinking the Monopolist's Duty to Deal: A Legal and Economic Critique of The Doctrine of Essential Facilities', 74 *Van. L. Rev.* 1069, 1089 and 1093 (1988).

[6] True, in the sole European Union Article 102(a) prohibits exploitative behaviors. Yet – interestingly –EU antitrust institutions have never advocated this provision so to justify their enforcement actions against monopolists' refusals.

[7] See Areeda & Hovenkamp, *supra* note 2, at ¶775 (arguing that 'the distinction between vertically related and collaterally related markets is not always clear, not always stable, and not always important for antitrust purposes.'). In particular, foreclosure can occur in both horizontally and vertically related markets, with one sole difference. In horizontally related markets foreclosure can stem also from a two-period predatory strategy (see Chapter 4, for a discussion about predatory System Innovations). In vertically related markets foreclosure can work as a tool for confronting a commitment problem. Suppose, indeed, that the dominant firm owns a patent. It would like to license it to the highest number of licensees possible. Yet, potential licensees know that if everyone holds a license, the intense competition among

shows,[8] when the holder of an intellectual resource refuses it to its rivals though they would like to use it in their secondary markets – i.e. either horizontally or vertically connected markets – the refusal works as a tool to lessen competitive constraints and, hence, to strengthen market power. Yet, even when refusals allow monopoly power to spread across markets, they can produce either static efficiency, welfare increasing effects – as it happens, for instance, when the refusal is simply the practice which permits vertical integration to occur[9] – or ambiguous effects on consumer welfare. In other words, as seen in the previous chapters, economic models showing that a practice works to prolong monopoly power does not necessarily prove that the same practice also reduces consumer welfare.[10]

---

them will destroy their profits. Therefore, in order to license its patent to at least at one licensee, the monopolist must promise to limit the number of granted licenses and, better, in order to make such promise credible, the monopolist has to commit itself not to undertake further licenses than the one granted. The commitment occurs when the monopolist signs an exclusive dealing agreement with its sole licensee and refuses to license the patent to any other firm. See, e.g., Patrick Rey & Jean Tirole, *A Primer on Foreclosure* 8–9 and 12 (2006), available at http://idei.fr/doc/by/tirole/primer.pdf; and U.S. *Department of Justice & the Federal Trade Commission, Antitrust Enforcement and Intellectual Property Rights: Promoting Innovation and Competition* 24, (2007), available at http://www.ftc.gov/reports/innovation/P040101PromotingInnovationandCompetitionrpt0704.pdf.

8 Indeed, what said in the previous chapter in connection to the most recent developments of the leveraging monopoly theorem generalizes to several kinds of practices, including the refusal to license offence. See Langlois, *supra* note 5, at 200. For instance, a multiproduct monopolist may refuse to deal in order to raise barriers in secondary markets, so to protect its monopolized market against those competitors that could enter it by leveraging their market share in secondary markets; or the refusal can serve to shift the monopoly power in the secondary markets, so to make there its monopoly profits, when these profits are not available in the monopolized market. See, in this regard, Steven C. Salop, An administrable and efficient legal standard for refusals to deal and price squeezes by an unregulated, vertically integrated monopolist, available at www.ssrn.com. In sum, if the dominant firm's objective is to prevent competitors from using a specific resource, the practices that can help in fulfilling this aim are not only integrations, bundles, tie-ins, but also refusals to deal. Not by chance, 'foreclosure refers to a dominant firm's denial of proper access to an essential good it produces', no matter how such a denial has been expressed. See Rey, Tirole, *supra* note 7, at 1.

9 See, e.g., Gerber, *supra* note 5, at 1083; and Werden, *supra* note 2, 462 and ff. (listing, just in connection to refusals to deal, the potential benefits and costs of vertical integration). Indeed, vertical integration produces efficiencies that increase consumer welfare by definition; namely, especially when there is a technological interdependence between the primary and the secondary markets, vertical integration allows reducing transaction costs; correcting information/reputation problems; aligning incentives and, hence, eliminating free riding; and eliminating the 'successive monopoly' problem.

10 See, in this regard, Carlton, *supra* note 2, at 660 (arguing that economists' ability to describe when incumbents' conduct harm rivals 'should not necessarily translate into more active antitrust policy. The zeal with which economists foist these theories on antitrust practitioners must not obscure two key facts. First, the harm to a rival is not . . . harm to competition. Empirically documenting a harm to competition from various exclusionary conduct is usually quite difficult and is not necessarily an implication of the theories. [. . .] Second, economists often neglect to focus on where antitrust enforcement is likely to help or harm the economy the most.')

Therefore, Section 2 and Article 102 should not necessarily prohibit these 'exclusionary refusals to deal'.

Third, monopolists' refusals to license IPRs may both prevent monopolists' rivals to develop complementary, follow-on, or derivative innovations and permit dominant firms to control the industry's innovative path.[11] Nevertheless, showing that future innovation has been blocked or that the industry's innovative path has been changed in favor of the monopolist does not mean that harm to long-term consumer welfare is actually occurring, unless it is assumed – but, as shown in Chapter 1, this assumption is a matter of belief – that followers are better innovators than incumbents and, hence, that a refusal to license causes a breakdown in incentives to innovate.

In summary, as a matter of prosecution, the economic question at the bottom of the refusal to deal offense presents the false positives issue that previous chapters have also faced: though under specific conditions refusals to deal can constitute anticompetitive conduct, these conditions are hard to detect and, without clear means to assess the harm done (or the harm that is likely to be done), prosecutors run the risk of prohibiting behaviors that are not harmful.

THE US AND EU REFUSAL TO DEAL DOCTRINES: A QUICK COMPARISON

Let us assume that a monopolist has legally acquired a resource that then refuses to license and suppose that, perhaps, it has even acquired its property right upon the resource because of its 'superior skill, foresight, and industry'.[12]

In such a scenario, imposing on the monopolist a duty to deal for the sake of competition means creating a conflict between two pieces of legislation, namely antitrust law and property law. Moreover, such a duty to deal risks[13] stifling the dominant firm's incentive to search for competitive

---

11 See Langlois, *supra* note 5, at 194.

12 Indeed, one of the reasons why EU antitrust authorities oblige monopolists who hold IPRs to share them is that they do not always believe in the innocent nature of those IPRs, or in the innocent nature of the connected dominant positions.

13 There is no real dispute about the soundness of the arguments (here reproduced) against the imposition of a duty to deal. For a detailed description of them, see Robert O'Donoghue & Jorge A. Padilla, *The Law and Economics of Article 82* 411–14 (2004). As the subsequent footnotes will show, indeed US courts and EU institutions claim them as well. The real difference between the experiences of the two jurisdictions, therefore, is that judges and officers give a different consideration to this line of reasoning. Typically, EU institutions are more skeptical towards them.

advantages;[14] might induce a kind of laziness between firms, allowing them not to defer development of their own resources;[15] makes rivals cooperate, though 'cooperation is a problem in antitrust, not one of its obligations';[16] and forces courts to act like 'central planners',[17] although antitrust law is not supposed to substitute for regulation, and courts are ill equipped to identify the inputs to be shared, to fix their prices, and to monitor compliance with these requirements.[18]

---

[14] See, e.g., Opinion of Mr Advocate General Jacobs delivered on 28 May 1998, *Oscar Bronner*, European Court reports 1998, I-07791, § 57; and *DG Competition Discussion Paper on the Application of Article 82 of the Treaty to Exclusionary Abuses* § 213, Bruselles, December 2005, available at www.europa.eu.int (hereinafter, 'Discussion Paper'). In *Verizon Communications v. Law Offices of Curtis v. Trinko*, 540 U.S. 398, 407 (2004) (hereinafter, *Trinko*), where the court held that, as long as inputs represent a competitive advantage, compelling dominant firms to 'share the source of their advantage . . . may lessen the incentive for the monopolist, the rival, or both to invest in those economically beneficial facilities'. This case arose when a dominant firm failed to provide a rival with some elements of its network in a timely manner, notwithstanding that the rival needed them to offer new services for arguably the consumers' good. Importantly the case took place in a regulated industry – the Telecommunication Industry, where an authority was already in charge of establishing when, and under which conditions, the incumbent local telephone company had to share its network with new entrants. Though this relevant circumstance, the Supreme Court decided to verify whether Section 2 could represent a further legal source of the dominant firm's duty to deal with rivals. Its answer was negative for several reasons. Some of them are reported in this and in the following footnotes.

[15] See Discussion Paper, *supra* at note 14, § 213, and Einer Elhauge, 'Defining Better Monopolization Standards', 56 *Stan. L. Rev.* 253 (2003).

[16] See Hylton, *supra* note 5, at 1252 (arguing that 'shared access may itself be a "facilitating mechanism" for collusion', though – as usual – the incentive to cheat and the possibility of new entrants also gaining access to the resource serve to lessen the incentive to collude); *Schor v. Abbott Laboratories*, 457 F.3d 608, 610 (7th Circ. 2006). Besides, in *Trinko* the Supreme Court stated 'compelling negotiation between competitors may facilitate the supreme evil of antitrust: collusion', at 408.

[17] Such a skepticism about federal judges ability to deal with complicated economic evidence – a skepticism that reminds Justice Marshall's cautionary words in *United States v. Topco associates*, 405 U.S. 596 (1972), when he stated that Congress did not intend to leave federal judges 'free to ramble through the wilds of economic theory' – has been criticized by the same Supreme Court in some cases such as *Continental T.V., Inc. v. GTE Sylvania, Inc.*, 433 U.S. 36 (1977) and *Brunswick Corp. v. Pueblo Bowl-O-Mat, Inc.*, 429 U.S. 477 (1977). There courts showed that economics can be a very effective tool in informing antitrust decisions. Nevertheless, the present Supreme Court could be more susceptible to the idea that judges are ill-equipped to apply sophisticated economic models. At least, this is what arises from reading several judgments where the Court stresses the false-positive mistakes issue, such as *Trinko* and *Credit Suisse Securities (USA) Llc v. Billing*, 127 S.Ct. 2383 (2007).

[18] See Areeda & Hovenkamp, *supra* at note 2, at ¶770e and Valentine Korah, 'The Interface between Intellectual Property and Antitrust: The European Experience', 69 *Antitrust L. J.* 801, 832 (2002) looking mainly at regulated industries. Sharing a monopolized input, in fact, does not make the market less monopolized unless courts fix the input price and the other conditions of the deal. Because of the duty, indeed, the monopolist will reduce its output to compensate the rival's production and will charge the rival the monopoly price. Besides, even assuming that a court could define the conditions of the

Thus, it could be better to manage the refusal to deal offense with caution,[19] recalling that a general principle is in force in US and EU: even dominant firms are free to contract,[20] by choosing whether and with whom to make a deal.[21] In addition, applying the appropriability theory dear to the IP realm, it can be argued that a duty to deal, on the one hand, could lead dominant firms 'as well as enterprises that may become dominant not to invest, or to invest less, in innovative activities; and, on the other hand, could lead their competitors to enjoy a free ride on the investments made by the dominant firm, instead of investing themselves.'[22] In sum, for one or another reason in both the US and EU jurisdictions the refusal to deal doctrine is described as a list of 'certain'[23] or 'exceptional'[24]

---

deal, it would be then charged of the duty to monitor the dominant firm's behavior, which could turn out to be a very expensive routine. Further, see Steven Anderman, 'The epithet that dares not speak its name: the essential facilities concept in article 82 EC and IPRs after the Microsoft case', *in Article 82 EC: Reflections on Its Recent Evolution 87*, 90 (Ariel Ezrachi ed., 2009).

[19] See Areeda & Hovenkamp, *supra* at note 2, at ¶ 773a, (arguing that no duty to deal should be imposed unless it is proven – 'taking full account of the anticompetitive incidents of chilling desirable behaviors and of administering prices or other terms of dealing' – that it significantly improves market competition).

[20] US antitrust judges have established this principle with the so-called 'Colgate doctrine'since the first half of the twentieth century. See, indeed, *United States v. Colgate & Co.*, 250 U.S. 300, 307 (1919) (where the Court stated that, 'in the absence of any purpose to create or maintain a monopoly . . . a trader or manufacturer engaged in an entirely private business [has the right] . . . to exercise his own independent discretion as to parties with whom he will deal'); see also *Associated Press v. United States*, 326 U.S. 1, 15 (1945); *Olympia Equip. Leasing v. Western Union Telegraph*, 797 F.2d 370, 375 (7th Circ. 1986); and *Trinko* at 416 (2004). In the EU jurisdiction, instead, a clear official statement of this principle is recent and goes back to the Discussion Paper, *supra* note 14, at § 207 and to European Commission, *Communication from the Commission — Guidance on the Commission's Enforcement Priorities in Applying Article 82 of the EC Treaty to Abusive Exclusionary Conduct by Dominant Undertakings*, OJ 2009, C45/7, § 75 (hereinafter, 2009 Communication).

Nevertheless, as the freedom of contract principle is pivotal for the legal cultures of EU Member States, thinking that it did not count in the EU jurisdiction would be a mistake; on the contrary it receives a constitutional status as well as the other principles that, though not outspoken, are common to the legal culture of the Member States.

[21] In other words, US and EU antitrust law does not impose any general duty to treat customers equally and, in case, IP licensees. Better – absent some showing of monopoly leveraging – it is hard to conceive why a dominant firm would put some of its customers – that are not competitors, indeed – at a disadvantage. Therefore, if it happens, there are reasonable and not anticompetitive factors that justify the dominant firm's discriminatory choice. In summary, monopolists have no duty to protect those among their customers that are less good at satisfying their requests.

[22] See 2009 Communication, *supra* note 20, at § 75.

[23] See *Trinko*, at 408 (holding 'under certain circumstances, a refusal to cooperate with rivals can constitute anticompetitive conduct').

[24] See *Magill TV Guide/ITP, BBC and RTE* (89/205/EC), 21 December 1988, OJ 1989, L78/43, upheld in Joined Cases C76, 77 and 91/89 R, *Radio Telefis Eireann and others v Commission*, 11 May 1989, 1989 ECR I-1141, upheld in Joined Cases C241 and 242/91 P,

circumstances in which the monopolist's refusal to deal happens to be harmful.[25]

The two jurisdictions, however, do not identify the same special circumstances, and it is here that the 'great divergence' between the two arises.

The present US approach to dominant firms' refusal to deal follows from *Trinko*,[26] the conclusions of which seem to apply to all legal theories for treating refusals to deal under Section 2.[27] In *Trinko* the US Supreme Court held that a judge can oblige a dominant firm to share its proprietary resources only if two conditions occur: first, the market in question cannot be realistically capable of producing this input;[28] second, the dominant firm had already full developed and marketed the claimed good.[29]

Radio Telefis Eireann and Others v Commission, 6 April 1995, 1995 ECR I-743 (Hereinafter '*Magill TV*').

25 Hovenkamp, Janis, Lemley, *supra* note 5, at § 13.3d.

26 See *Trinko*, 540 U.S. 398 (2004). This case arose when a dominant firm failed to provide a rival with some elements of its network promptly, notwithstanding that the rival needed them to offer new services arguably for the consumers' good. Importantly, the case took place in a regulated industry – telecommunications –, where an authority was already in charge of establishing when, and under which conditions, the incumbent local telephone company had to share its network with new entrants. Through this relevant circumstance, the Supreme Court decided to verify whether Section 2 could represent a further legal source of the dominant firm's duty to deal with rivals. Its answer was negative for several reasons. Some of them are reported in the previous and following footnotes.

27 See Areeda & Hovenkamp, *supra* note 2, at ¶ 773g. To be sure – as explained by Edward D. Cavanagh, 'Trinko: A Kinder, Gentler Approach To Dominant Firms Under the Antitrust Laws?', 14 (2006) available at www.ssrn.com – *Trinko* can be read in a narrower way, considering it as a case decided in the context of a heavily regulated telecommunications industry where access to rivals' facilities is mandated by statute. Under this view, *Trinko* stands for the proposition that violations of the Telecommunications Act itself do not create separate claims for relief under the antitrust laws. Nor should a dominant firm's refusals to deal be condemned under traditional antirust principles where, as in the case of telecommunications, the industry has a heavy regulatory overlay, which includes mandated access to rivals' facilities, particularly where the regulatory authorities have already sanctioned the dominant firm for the conduct in question. In this regard, see Nicolas Economides, 'Hit and Miss: Leverage, Sacrifice, and Refusal to Deal in the Supreme Court Decision in Trinko', 10 *Vand. J. Ent. & Tech. L.* 121, 141 (2007) (arguing that, 'The Trinko Court stated that it did not want to get involved in regulatory matters, and that is understandable. However, the Court had already accepted that the savings clause of the 1996 Act allowed for antitrust law to be applied in parallel with telecommunications regulation. Therefore, nothing would prevent the Court from declaring, for example, that Verizon's degradation of service to AT&T was anti-competitive, accepting the antitrust implications and avoiding getting the courts involved in regulatory issues. There is a long tradition of court enforcement of the antitrust laws in telecommunications, despite the fact that the sector has been regulated since the 1930s.').

28 Even after *Trinko*, hence, a duty to deal could still apply to inputs that either belong to a natural monopoly, or represent both public facilities managed by third parties and structures created as a part of a regulatory regime.

29 The Court, indeed, kept on saying that the requested input 'exist[s] only deep within the bowels of Verizon; they are brought out on compulsion of the 1996 Act and offered not

Further, in *Trinko* the Supreme Court avoided any broader application or interpretation of *Aspen Skiing*[30], which conditioned the unlawfulness of the refusal to deal to and its three requirements;[31] that is to say the termination of a previous business relationship,[32] the harm to competition,[33] and the absence of any business justification.[34]

Overall, nowadays the US duty to deal doctrine is inapplicable when the refusal: (i) is not anticompetitive[35]; and (ii) is justifiable; and when satisfying the request of rivals would require the dominant firm to (iii) share a resource that the market can otherwise offer (i.e. an input that is not

---

to consumers but to rivals, and at considerable expense and effort. New systems must be designed and implemented simply to make that access possible – indeed, it is the failure of one of those systems that prompted the present complaint', at 410.

[30] *Aspen Skiing Co. v. Aspen Highlands Skiing Corp.*, 472 U.S. 585 (1985) (hereinafter, '*Aspen Skiing*'). This is the famous judgment where the owner of three of the four major ski areas in Aspen made it more expensive for the owner of the fourth ski area to continue a joint lift ticket arrangement, so that such a demand was tantamount to a refusal to continue the joint venture.

[31] Indeed, the *Trinko* Court relegated *Aspen Skiing* to 'at or near the outer boundary of Section 2 liability' at 399.

[32] After all, the existence of a previous relationship makes it easier to set the condition of a possible compulsory license. See, further, *In Re Elevator Antitrust litigation*, 502 F.3d 47, 54 (3rd Circ. 2007) (holding that the suppression of a previous business relationship represents 'the sole exception to the right of refusal to deal'). On the contrary, consider that not all courts have concurred in applying such a 'duty to continue an existing business relationship'. See, e.g., *Olympia Equip. Leasing v. Western Union Telegraph*, 797 F.2d 370, 375 (7th Circ. 1986).

[33] As seen in Chapter 2, scholars are struggling in connection with the proper test to detect anticompetitive behaviors. Some have observed that *Trinko* means that a refusal to deal is anticompetitive when it implies a short-run sacrifice for the monopolist, i.e., when the dominant firm forsakes profitable sales in order to harm its rival. Indeed, this was the test that the government proposed in its brief. See, for this opinion, Areeda & Hovenkamp, *supra* note 2, at ¶ 773g and Marina Lao, 'Aspen Skiing and Trinko: Antirust Intent and Sacrifice', 73 *Antitrust L.J.* 171 (2005). Yet, as seen in Chapter 2, such a test bring some intrinsic faults. See, e.g., Eleanor Fox, 'Is There Life After Trinko? The Silent Revolution of Section 2 of the Sherman Act', 73 *Antitrust L.J.* 153, 161 (2005) (observing that the profit-sacrifice test does not fit the facts of *Trinko* because 'there were no profits to be made from giving access to the rivals'). Further, see Economides, *supra* note 27, at 144–147. Beyond this debate, it has been noticed that 'unquestionably, the lower courts even after Trinko remain suspicious of exclusionary behavior by dominant firms and continue their search for a principled basis upon which to distinguish lawful from unlawful exclusionary behavior by dominant firms. Accordingly, *Trinko* does not mark an abrupt departure from the doctrine of prior cases but rather underscores the lack of clarity on the issue of when non-price exclusionary behavior by a monopolist is unlawful under Section 2'. See Cavanagh, *supra* note 27, 4–5.

[34] See Economides, *supra* note 27, at 141 (arguing that is holding *Trinko's* refusal as lawful, 'The Court missed the vertical leveraging issue [. . .]. That is, the application of the vertical price squeeze and [Raising Rivals' Costs] actions of a vertically-integrated monopolist that were addressed earlier in the context of competition in long-distance and the need for line of business restrictions.' Indeed, according to Economides, in *Trinko* the incumbent had the incentive to raise its rivals' costs in secondary markets in order to maintain its profitable monopoly.).

[35] As seen in Chapter 2, in *Trinko* the court applied the sacrifice test to judge the conduct anticompetitive.

indispensable);[36] or (iv) produce a good (or a combination of them) that the monopolist does not use to employ; or (v) enter in a new joint venture with its competitors.

The present EU perspective is quite different and less strict. It follows from the lines of cases: the *Commercial Solvent* and *Telemarketing* cases, on the one hand, and preliminary judgment[37] of the ECJ in *Oscar Bronner* on the other.[38] In the first two cases, the EU institutions held that a refusal to deal that interrupts an existing commercial relationship is unlawful when: (a) it is likely to eliminate competition in the secondary market; and (b) cannot be objectively justified. In *Oscar Bronner*, instead, the Court held that a refusal to deal is illegal when: (a) it is likely to eliminate all competition in the secondary market;[39] (b) cannot be objectively justified; and when (c) the claimed input is indispensable for rivals to carry on their own business, inasmuch as there are no actual or potential substitutes for that input.[40] Therefore, in *Oscar Bronner* the monopolist was obliged to enter into a new joint-venture with its rivals.

Afterwards, the 2005 Discussion Paper of the EU DG Competition distinguished the refusal-to-deal scenarios in two categories: the *Aspen*-like

---

36 Consider, indeed, that in the few *'ante-Trinko'* cases where the essential facility doctrine has been discussed in detail the courts hold that essentiality has to be ascertained from an objective standpoint, considering the viability of the market in general, and not focusing on the viability of a particular firm. See *Aldridge v Microsoft Corp*. 995 F.Supp. 728, 753 (S. D. Tex. 1998) and *Intergraph Corp. v. Intel Corp.*, 3F. Supp. 2d 1255, 1258 (N.D. Ala. 1998). In the former case the court was judging a product inprovement: the essential facility claim, indeed, was a part of a more general complaint whereby Aldridge lamented that Microsoft was denying Aldridge's products access to Microsoft's new operatying system. Indeed, Microsoft had not only integrated in its new Operating system the function that Aldridge previously sold separately, but also disabled Aldridge's function to run on top of it.

37 Comm. CE, decision December 14 1972, Commercial Solvent, GUCE L229/51; and Case 311/84, 3 October 1985, Telemarketing, [1985] ECR I-3261.

38 Case C-7/97, *Oscar Bronner GmbH & Co. KG v* Mediaprint Zeitungs- und Zeitschriftenverlag GmbH & Co. KG, Mediaprint Zeitungsvertriebsgesellschaft mbH & Co. KG and Mediaprint Anzeigengesellschaft mbH & Co. KG, 26 November 1998, [1998] ECR I-7817 (hereinafter *Oscar Bronner*). This case was about the owner of the only Austrian nationwide home-delivery network, which used that scheme to distribute its own daily newspapers, and refused the publisher of a rival daily newspaper access to its network, depriving its competitor of a means of distribution.

39 It is interesting that, here, the EU institutions referred not to 'effective competition', but to a kind of minimal degree of competition.

40 See *Oscar Bronner*, § 41. Although in his opinion Advocate General Jacobs analyzed the facts from the perspective of who aims at protecting long-run consumer welfare (see Opinion, §57), the Court did not use his economic terminology. Therefore, to understand whether the ECJ took consumer welfare in consideration is difficult to state. See Liza Lovdhal Gormsen, *A Principled Approach To abuse of Dominance in European Competition Law* 75 (2010). Yet, it is true that the Microsoft test (see footnote 110 and the accompanying text) recalls the post-Chicagoan approach.

refusals, which concern the 'termination of an existing supply relationship'; and the *Oscar Bronner*-like refusals, which concern the 'refusal to start supplying input'.[41] Then, the Discussion Paper determined that, while both categories of dominant firms' refusals are normally[42] abusive when two conditions occur – namely: (A) the refusal is likely to have a negative effect on competition; and (B) the conduct does not have any objective justification – the unlawfulness of the *Oscar Bronner*-like refusal rests with a further requirement, i.e., (C) the indispensable nature of the claimed resource.

In its 2009 Communication[43] the Commission replicates the above categorization, but not in the same degree of detail. It states that the concept of refusal to supply covers a broad range of practices – even the refusals to license that this chapter addresses separately; referencing to *IMS Health*[44] it clarifies that it is not necessary for the refused product to have been previously traded: because it is sufficient that there is demand from potential purchasers and that a potential market for the input at stake can be identified;[45] and it establishes that, regardless of the existence of a previous business relationship,[46] it intends to strike down a refusal to deal when the refusal: (A) is likely to[47] lead to the elimination of effective competition in the downstream market;[48] (B) is not objectively justified;[49] (C) relates to a product or service that is *objectively necessary* to be able to compete

---

41 Discussion paper, *supra* at note 14, § 229.

42 Unfortunately, it seems that the Discussion Paper allows an extensive interpretation of these conditions as it states that 'normally' they have to be fulfilled. See, e.g., id., §§ 218, 224 and 237.

43 2009 Communication, *supra* note 20, at §§ 9–18.

44 See, *infra*.

45 2009 Communication, *supra* note 20, §§ 77–8.

46 *Id.*, at § 83, though the Commission however clarifies that 'it is more likely that the termination of an existing supply arrangement is found to be abusive than a de novo refusal to supply'. In so doing, indeed, the Commission appears interested in protecting dominant firms' customers' specific investments and stricter in evaluating the business reasons why the previous relationship stopped being profitable for the dominant firm.

47 *Id.*, at § 84 where the Commission states that, 'the likelihood of effective competition being eliminated is generally greater the higher the market share of the dominant firm in the downstream market; the less capacity-constrained the dominant firm is relative to competitors in the downstream market; the closer the substitutability between the dominant firm's output and that of its competitors in the downstream market; the greater the proportion of competitors in the downstream market that are affected, and; the more likely it is that the demand that could be served by the foreclosed competitors would be diverted away from them to the advantage of the dominant undertaking'.

48 Therefore, if the dominant firm refuses to supply an input to a firm that acts in a market where the monopolist is not present, it would be improper to speak about a 'refusal to deal offence'. See, in this regard, Ekaterina Rousseva, *Rethinking Exclusionary Abuses in EU Competition Law* 411 (2010).

49 2009 Communication, *supra* note 20, at §§ 88–9.

effectively in a downstream market;[50] and (D) is likely to lead to *consumer harm*.[51]

Although there are points in common[52], between the case law of the two jurisdictions, and regardless of the omission in the EU experience of the *Trinko* requirement, – an omission that is not necessarily significant because EU institutions have not faced a *Trinko*-like scenario yet,[53] present US and EU refusal to supply doctrines nevertheless diverge in two main areas.[54]

First, the EU approach is more focused upon the potential rather than upon the actual anticompetitive effects of the refusal, though forecasting harms is more difficult than measuring whether they have actually occurred. In particular, the Commission assesses the likely consumer harm by engaging in a speculative balance between the negative consequences that the refusal to deal and the duty to deal could produce.

---

[50] *Id.*, §§ 82, where the Commission states that a resource is objectively necessary when it 'is capable of allowing competitors to exert a competitive constraint on the dominant undertaking in the downstream market'. In this regard see Rousseva, *supra* note 48, at 413 (arguing that, whereas in *Oscar Bronner* the relevant question was whether an input alternative to the required one would have been economically viable to create, in the 2009 Communication the relevant issue comes from *Microsoft V* – see footnote 114 and the accompanying text – and is whether the alternative input would challenge or, at least, contain the dominance). According to the author, this change together with the reference to 'the elimination of effective competition on the downstream market' shows that, while in Oscar Bronner the Commission was concerned with 'the maintenance of some minimal degree of competition', in the 2009 Communication it is concerned with the maintenance of a somehow higher degree of competition.

[51] 2009 Communication, *supra* note 20, at § 85. The Commission elaborates on the concept of the likely consumer harm arguing that 'in examining the likely impact of a refusal to supply on consumer welfare, the Commission will examine whether for the consumers, the likely negative consequences of the refusal to supply in the relevant market outweigh over time the negative consequences of imposing an obligation to supply'. Further, the Commission explains that such an outcome could result in two cases: (i) when the refusal blocks the launch of a new product or of a follow-on innovation; and (ii) in one of the cases where the leveraging monopoly theory holds, that is to say, when the monopolist that acquires monopoly power downstream and reaps monopoly profits there, in order to escape a price cap in the upstream regulated market.

[52] Prongs (ii) and (b) and prongs (iii) and (c) of the previous two lists address the same phenomena.

[53] The *Trinko* requirement, indeed, cannot be compared with the new product/new market conditions that are proper of the EU refusal to license doctrine (see, *infra*). These criteria address the development of products that the monopolist has not produced and marketed yet, but do not ask the monopolist to develop them. Up to now, in the EU dominant firms have been required to share input that they already produce and use.

[54] To be sure, till the 2005 Discussion Paper in the EU jurisdiction the indispensability requirement must be fulfilled only when a new supplying relation is to be established, as if the existence of a past business relation between the dominant firm and its rivals proved and entailed that only the dominant firm is capable of producing and marketing the requested input. Nevertheless, with the 2009 Communication this divergence disappears, though the Commission still recognizes that judging the end of a previous relationship is easier than discussing whether a new relationship has been created.

Second, the 2009 Communication, the 2005 Discussion Paper, and relevant EU judgments not only seem to assume that a duopoly of a proprietary resource is better than a monopoly,[55] but also do not suggest how to solve the administrability problem that the forced creation of a new joint-venture between the dominant firm and its rivals will produce. In this regard, whereas it is conceivable that the European Commission will find a way to establish how to share the input, asking its economists to indicate at what price and under which conditions the duty to deal should be imposed, it is more questionable that national courts will be able to do the same. On the other hand, such an argument should not be pushed too far. Indeed, courts are accustomed to setting licensing rates in other contexts (such as infringement suits), and they could do so in this context as well or, alternatively, they could send the parties back to the bargaining table.

In conclusion, the differences between the US and EU refusal to supply doctrines – differences that are independent of any IP concern but stem from a magma of policy issues that play different roles over time – are several. Beyond the diverse antitrust aims and methodologies that, as seen in Chapter 2, US and EU antitrust authorities have endorsed over the years,[56] and beyond the different considerations that US courts and EU institutions give to the leveraging monopoly theory when they assess the competitive harm that a dominant firm can cause by preventing its rivals from using an input in a related market,[57] what seems to be relevant to explain the different US and EU approaches are their divergent ideas not only about the role that public powers should have in presiding over markets' development and dominant firms' conduct, but also about the costs that interference by public powers impose.

---

[55] Indeed, one should argue that a monopolist that is obliged to share its input with its rival will still sell the input at the monopoly price, splitting the monopoly profits with the rival.

[56] Indeed, it should be recalled that some of the oldest European decisions about monopolists' refusal to supply date back to a period – now almost past – when the European competition law was highly influenced by the Freiburg school, and by a formalistic approach to the study of dominant firms' conduct. If the main concern of EU antitrust authorities was that of protecting the numbers of competitors so as to preserve economic pluralism, and if they did not pay a great deal of attention to the real efficiency consequences of a dominant firm's conduct, monopolists' rivals might well receive a more deferential treatment than the monopolist itself.

[57] In other words, in dealing with refusals to deal involving firms operating in related markets, even assessing whether allocative efficiency has been impaired is difficult, as such an inquiry requires an understanding of whether the peculiar circumstances occur under which it is rational for a monopolist to acquire or shift monopoly power in related markets. As seen in the previous chapter, only in the Microsoft saga did the Commission finally discuss expressly the leverage issue following the arguments and counter-arguments of the Chicago and post-Chicago schools. See, in this regard, *Rousseva*, supra note 48, at 106.

That said, it is worthwhile analyzing whether the above-mentioned exceptions to the freedom of contract principle still apply when IPRs appear on the scene. The following discussion will show that in such a case the US and EU doctrines diverge yet again, and in an even broader way: though IPRs are property rights indistinguishable from those that cover non-IP resources, the role that IPRs play in protecting innovation makes the refusal to license doctrines in the US and EU stricter and more lenient, respectively.

WHEN IPRS MAKE AN APPEARANCE: THE US COURTS SEEM DEFERENTIAL TO THE RULES OF THE IP WORLD

In the US, several rules about refusals to license IPRs have appeared over time:[58] from the absolute legality rule of *SCM Corp. v. Xerox Corp.*[59] and *Miller Insituform*,[60] in 1981 and 1987, respectively, to the essential facility approach that the District Court more recently applied in *Intergraph Corporation v. Intel Corporation*[61] – an approach however, that the court of appeal definitively rejected in appeal,[62] and that the Supreme Court in *Trinko* stigmatized on general grounds.[63]

Yet, recently in *In re Microsoft corp. antitrust litigation* another District

---

58 See, e.g., Michael A. Carrier, 'Refusals to License Intellectual Property after Trinko', 55 *DePaul L. Rev.* 1191 (2006); and Joseph P. Bauer, 'Refusal to Deal with Competitors by Owners of Patents and Copyrights: Reflections on the Image Technical and Xerox Decisions', 55 *DePaul L. Rev.* 1211 (2006).

59 645 F.2d 1195, 1296 (2d Cir. 1981), cert. denied, 455 U.S. 1016 (1982), (stating that 'where a patent has been lawfully acquired, subsequent conduct permissible under the patent laws cannot trigger any liability under the antitrust laws'). The court reasoned that 'the patent system would be seriously undermined, however, were the threat of potential antitrust liability to attach upon the acquisition of a patent at a time prior to the existence of the relevant market and, even more disconcerting, at a time prior to the commercialization of the patented art'. – id., at 1208.

60 830 F.2d 606, 609 (6th Circ. 1987) (stating that 'a patent holder who lawfully acquires a patent cannot be held liable under Section 2 of the Sherman Act for maintaining the monopoly power he lawfully acquired by refusing to license the patent to others'. In particular, the Court added that by terminating the exclusive license the patentee 'merely exercised his power to exclude others from using the [patented process] as was its right').

61 3F. Supp. 2d 1255 (N.D. Ala. 1998) (granting a preliminary injunction to Intergraph by concurring with its claim that Intel's chips and technical know-how were essential for its business). See also *BellSouth Advertising v. Donnelley Information* 719 F. Supp. 1551 (S.D.Fla. 1988) (holding that the non-copyrightable information of the Yellow Pages was an essential facility. Yet, the court would have reached the same result relying on the idea/expression dichotomy proper of copyright law.).

62 195 F.3d 1346 (Fed. Circ. 1999) (establishing that the essential facility doctrine has no

Court has maintained, by concurring with the opinion of several scholars that,[64] to require one company to provide its intellectual property to a competitor would significantly chill innovation,[65] quoting as confirmation the case law analyzed in the previous chapter.[66] Further, in the most recent case about a refusal to license, regarding photocopier spare parts covered by patents and copyright, the *Independent Service Organizations Antitrust Litigation* (hereinafter, '*Xerox*'),[67] the Federal Circuit endorsed a quasi per se legality rule stating that, 'a patent owner who brings suit to enforce the statutory right to exclude others from making, using or selling the claimed invention is exempted from the antitrust law, even though such a suit may have an anticompetitive effect'.

In reaching this conclusion the Court assumed the same perspective as a

---

sense when applied to firms that do not compete one against the other in the same market and, according to the Federal Circuit, Intergraph and Intel were not competitors at all).

63 *Trinko*, at 415, nt. 4.

64 See David Teece & Mary Coleman, 'The Meaning of Monopoly: Antitrust Analysis in High-Technology Industries', *Antitrust Bulletin* 801, 809 and 843–4 (1998) (arguing that antitrust intervention against dominant firms should be avoided in high-technology industries because, among other reasons, 'efforts to hobble the winner in one round of innovations will be seen as diminishing the returns available from competing in [these] high-risk environments, thereby diverting resources to other sectors of the economy displaying less risk and affording less innovation'. In other words, antitrust law cannot penalize the possibility of success through superior skill, foresight, and acumen, or just dumb luck, induces entry, investment, and unparalleled even maniacal effort). See Janusz A. Ordover & Robert D. Willig, 'Access and Bundling in High-Technology Markets', in *Competition, Innovation and the Microsoft Monopoly: Antitrust in the Digital Marketplace* 103, 104 (Jeffrey A. Eisenach & Thomas M. Lenard eds. 1998) (observing that 'due to the uncertainties of prediction and the repressing effects of long investigations and the concomitant concerns about interventions, antitrust should be applied cautiously [in high-technology markets], and only to the most certain and compelling threats to competition'); and Richard Schmalensee, 'Antitrust Issues in Schumpeterian Industries', 90 *Am. Econ. Rev.* 192, 193 (2000) (stating that 'since most software firms fail, there would be no entrants into the business if category leaders were not highly profitable'). Besides, see Timothy F. Bresnahan, 'New Modes of Competition: Implications for the Future Structure of the Computer Industry', in *Competition, Innovation and the Microsoft Monopoly: Antitrust in the Digital Marketplace* 155, 192 (Jeffrey A. Eisenach & Thomas M. Lenard eds. 1998) (observing that the investment that is arguably impaired under a restrictive regime is not only the monopolist's investment, but investment in high-tech industries in general).

65 274 F. Supp. 2d 743, 745 (D. Md. 2003). Further the Court elaborated that 'because the software development industry is dynamic and involves continuous innovation, a requirement that Microsoft disclose significant information to its competitors would be unworkable. Who would determine what information is 'significant?' At the least, the determination would have to be subject to judicial scrutiny by judges who lack the competence – either as direct decision-makers or as reviewing authorities – to decide the technical issues involved. Delay and confusion would be inevitable, and the software development process would be strangulated'.

66 See. e.g., *Berkey Photo Inc. v. Eastman Kodak Co.*, 603 F.2d 263, 281–2 (2d Cir.1979); and *ILC Peripherals*, 458 F.Supp. at 437.

67 203 F.3d 1322 (2000).

court called upon to judge a case of misuse and,[68] relying upon the concept of patent scope, underlined that a patentee's practice is unlawful only when it falls outside the boundaries of such a scope.[69] Therefore, since refusing to license an IPR represents the very heart of the exclusive right, and since Section 271(d) of the Patent Act provides patentees refusing their innovations to others with immunity from misuse,[70] the *Xerox* court held that antitrust law has no reason to strike down such a behavior. In other words, the *Xerox* court determined that since US patent and copyright laws do not impose upon IPRs holders any general duty to use intellectual property and, a *fortiori*, to make or permit others to use it, competition law cannot intervene in order to impose a duty to deal upon the IPR holder. On the other hand – the court continued – antitrust courts will refuse to permit any refusal to license that is accompanied by 'illegal tying, fraud in the Patent and Trademark Office, or sham litigation', because in those cases the patentee is enforcing its statutory powers beyond what it is entitled to do pursuant to the Patent Act.

Thus, in *Xerox* the Federal Circuit Court chose to be deferential to the IP legislation by complying with its terms, which, however, address misuse and not competition law. And, in so doing, the court foreshadowed both the institutional argument that the Supreme Court would later use in *Trinko* in connection with the role that antitrust law should have in regulated industries,[71] and the reasoning that the same Supreme Court employed in 2006, in *Illinois Tool Works v. Independent Ink*.[72]

---

[68] Patent and copyright misuses are judicial doctrines, devised as affirmative defenses against patent and copyright infringements. They both require the alleged infringer to prove that the IPR holder has wrongfully broadened the physical and temporal scope of the IPR, producing anticompetitive effects. US scholars and courts debate whether the boundaries of these misuse doctrines overlap with those of the antitrust offenses, i.e., whether to extend a patent or a copyright beyond its scope can be anticompetitive without complying with the antitrust provisions. For a detailed discussion of this topic see Hovenkamp, Janis, and Lemley, *supra* note 5, at §§ 3.1–3.6.

[69] For an analogous approach see *Atari games corp. v. Nintendo of Am.*, 897 F.2d 1572, 1576 (Fed. Circ. 1990).

[70] 'No patent owner otherwise entitled to relief for infringement or contributory infringement of a patent shall be denied relief or deemed guilty of misuse or illegal extension of the patent right by reason of his having done one or more of the following: . . . (4) refused to license or use any rights to the patent'. Moreover, in accord is the joint statement of the United States Department of Justice and Federal Trade Commission, *Antitrust Guidelines for the Licensing of Intellectual Property* 4 (1995), available at http://www.justice.gov/atr/public/guidelines/0558.htm that market power does not 'impose on the intellectual property owner an obligation to license the use of that property to others'.

[71] In *Trinko*, indeed, the Court assigned a marginal role to antitrust law as a regulator to preside over the competitiveness of the industry as it already exists. For an equivalent approach, see *Credit Suisse Securities (USA) Llc v. Billing*, 127 S.Ct. 2383 (2007).

[72] 126 S. Ct. 1281, 1291 (2006), where the Supreme Court clearly used a proviso of the Patent Act – Section 271 (d), n.5 – to reject the 'patent-equals-market power presumption'.

Now, arguably *Xerox* and *Trinko* share the same idea about 'separation of powers': if Congress has already decided how to deal with a matter, courts are not entitled to second guess that choice. In effect, in *Xerox* the Federal Circuit quoted expressly what the First Circuit established in *Data General v. Grumman Systems Support*,[73] that courts 'cannot require antitrust defendants to prove and reprove the merits of this legislative assumption in every case where a refusal to license a copyrighted work comes under attack'.

Further, *Xerox* and *Independent Ink* assign the same priority role to the IP legislation, as if what is true for the IP realm could work as a benchmark also for the interface between antitrust law and IP law.

Yet, with *Xerox* the Federal Circuit openly rejected that the presumption of legality covering this offense – a presumption that the First Circuit had introduced in *Data General* – could be rebutted considering the intent of the IPR holder, as the Ninth Circuit instead did in *Image Technical Servs., Inc. v. Eastman Kodak Co.*[74] In other words, the *Xerox* court clearly disagreed with the Ninth Circuit, which had required the monopolist to share its IP-protected photocopier spare parts and diagnostic software by finding, as a matter of fact, that the IP protection could not justify the refusal because the defendant had used it as a pretext.[75]

It stated, 'Congress amended the Patent Code to eliminate that presumption in the patent misuse context. . . . Given the fact that the patent misuse doctrine provided the basis for the market power presumption, it would be anomalous to preserve the presumption in antitrust after Congress has eliminated its foundation'.

73 36 F.3d 1147 (1st Cir. 1994), (holding that as courts cannot second guess legislative choices, the refusal to license a copyright must benefit from a rebuttable presumption of legality). In *Data General* the facts are the same concerning copyrighted diagnostic software which independent service providers used without permission. There was no evidence to rebut the presumption.

74 125 F.3d 1195, 1202 (9th Cir.1997), (hereinafter, '*Kodak*'). Both in *Kodak* and in *Xerox* plaintiffs claimed that Section 2 was violated because the defendants each had a monopoly in a relevant parts market and, by refusing to supply parts to the ISOs, they were extending their monopolies into the servicing of their equipment. A number of commentators criticized the *Kodak* judgment. See, e.g., Daniel J. Gifford, 'The Antitrust/Intellectual Property Interface: An Emerging Solution to an Intractable Problem', 31 *Hofstra L. Rev.* 363, 409 (2002); R. Hewitt Pate, 'Refusals to Deal and Intellectual Property Rights', 10 *Geo. Mason L. Rev.* 429 (2002); Peter M. Boyle et al., 'Antitrust Law at the Federal Circuit: Red Light or Green Light at the IP-Antitrust Intersection?', 69 *Antitrust L.J.* 739 (2002); Nicholas Oettinger, 'In re Independent Service Organizations Antitrust Litigation', 16 *Berkeley Tech. L.J.* 323 (2001); Michelle M. Burtis & Bruce H. Kobayashi, 'Why an Original Can Be Better Than a Copy: Intellectual Property, The Antitrust Refusal to Deal, and ISO Antitrust Litigation', 9 *Sup. Ct. Econ. Rev.* 143 (2001); Robert Pitofsky, 'Challenges of the New Economy: Issues at the Intersection of Antitrust and Intellectual Property', 68 *Antitrust L.J.* 913, 919–23 (2001); and James B. Gambrell, 'The Evolving Interplay of Patent Rights and Antitrust Restraints in the Federal Circuit', 9 *Tex. Intell. Prop. L.J.* 137 (2000).

75 More exactly, the *Kodak* court held that a 'reluctance to sell . . . patented or copyrighted parts was a presumptively legitimate business justification' but the 'presumption may

In summary, current US law addressing refusal to license IPRs reflects a split among the circuits.

That said, it must be acknowledged that beyond the courts' decisions, in 1999, with the *Intel settlement*,[76] the FTC took a different position on this issue, when it forbade Intel from using its IPRs to prevent its rivals from gaining access to its technical information. According to the FTC, the 'natural and probable effect' of Intel's refusal to share this technical information was to decrease the incentives of Intel's rivals to develop new technologies relating to microprocessors. With that settlement, hence, the FTC, despite relatively weak consumer-harm,[77] expected to promote innovation in the industry as a whole, by boosting innovation by Intel's rivals without discouraging Intel's own innovation, using a logic that is similar to that applied by the European commission in *Microsoft IV*.

Nevertheless, in their common position about monopolists refusing IP licenses both the DOJ and the FTC observed that refusals to deal should not play a meaningful part in Section 2 enforcement[78] thus suggesting that it could be wrong to treat the *Intel settlement* as a leading case.

Therefore, a future Supreme Court judgment endorsing the reasoning of *In re Microsoft corp. antitrust litigation* and *Xerox* would not be surprising. Such a conclusion comes from the fact that a number of courts followed

---

also be rebutted by evidence of pretext'. The court also held that there was sufficient evidence of pretext because the defendant refused to sell both patented and unpatented parts and was not even thinking about its patent rights when it did so. See *Kodak*, 125 F.3d at 1219, 1220.

[76] See *FTC Intel Corp.*, FTC Docket. No. 9288 (June 8, 1998) (Complaint); *Intel Corp.*, FTC Docket. No. 9288 (August 6, 1999) (Decision and Order). Indeed, whereas in 1997 Intergraph brought suit against Intel alleging patent infringement, anticompetitive practices, and antitrust violations, in 1998 the FTC brought an action against Intel alleging that the company, which had monopoly power in the microprocessor market, was entrenching its position by refusing to deal with certain competitors, and attempting to coerce licenses from these competitors by its refusal to deal. In its consent decree the FTC clarified that Intel cannot withhold 'advanced technical information', meaning the confidential product information required by the OEM to enable the incorporation of a microprocessor into the product, including the product's electrical, mechanical, and thermal characteristics; samples; fixes; and technical support for the information. See William J. Baer & David A. Balto, 'New Myths and Old Realities: Recent Developments in Antitrust Enforcement', 1999 *Colum. Bus. L. Rev.* 207, 225 (1999).

[77] The FTC, indeed, argued that explicit proof of consumer harm does not always mean evidence of immediate and actual consumer harm; potential harm has to be deemed enough when, as in the Intel case, the firms were 'reasonably capable' (Intel Corp., FTC Docket No.9288, February 25, 1999) of making a significant contribution to preserving dominance without factual evidence on reduced rate of innovation, lowered prices or restricted output. Interestingly, this approach is the same as that EU antitrust institutions use, especially when they focus their enforcing action on the effects monopolist's conduct produces on dynamic efficiency.

[78] U.S. Dep't Of Justice and Fed. Trade Comm'n, *Antitrust Enforcement and Intellectual Property Rights: Promoting Innovation and Competition* 32 (2007), available at http://www.ftc.gov/reports/innovation/P040101PromotingInnovationandCompetitionrpt0704.pdf.

Xerox's rule,[79] and from the *Trinko* minimalist approach that does not make it easier to challenge IP refusals to license,[80] and also from the use that the Supreme Court made of the Patent Act in *Independent Ink*. After all, prior to *Kodak* and *Intel*, no reported federal antitrust decision had imposed liability for the refusal to license a patent.

Nevertheless, some objections are due. First, the holding in *Xerox* is not free from criticism.[81] Second, in regulated industries (such as the telecommunication industry examined in *Trinko*) antitrust law can play a residual role, because the regulator is actually in charge of making the market work. Yet, there is no IP regulator to address the competitive problems that IPRs may create in particular market settings. Therefore, holding that even in such scenarios judges cannot 'second-guess' what the IP legislation states means either choosing to leave the existing issues unsolved, or calculating that solving those issues would be too expensive for the sake and proper functioning of the interface between antitrust law and IP law.[82]

Second, Section 271 deals with patent misuse. Assuming that what is right for patent misuse is also right for antitrust law means concurring in the idea that what is right for IP law is right also for antitrust law, and vice versa. Although it is consistent with the words of the Patent Act,[83] this is not an axiom but a hypothesis yet to be demonstrated. Arguably, indeed, had Congress intended using Section 271(d)(4) to refer to antitrust violations or claims, it could have done so explicitly. Further, courts have held that Section 271(d)(4)'s companion provision – that is section 271(d)(5), which is about conditioning a license, or sale of a patented product, on the

---

[79] See *United Asset Coverage Inc. v. Avaya, Inc.*, 409 F. Supp. 2d 1008 (N. D. Ill 2006); and *Schor v. Abbot Labs*, 378 F. Suppp. 2d 850 (N. D. Ill 2005).

[80] See Carrier, *supra* at note 58, 1209.

[81] The judgment, indeed, has been described as unnuanced, overbroad, troubling, unwise, and unfortunate. See, e.g., Simon Genevaz, 'Against Immunity for Unilateral Refusals to Deal in Intellectual Property: Why Antitrust Law Should Not Distinguish Between IP and Other Property Rights', 19 *Berkeley Technology L. J.* 741 (2004); A. Douglas Melamed & Ali M. Stoeppelwerth, 'The CSU Case: Facts, Formalism and the Intersection of Antitrust and Intellectual Property', 10 *George Mason L. Rev.* 407 (2002); Robert Pitofsky, 'Antitrust and Intellectual Property: Unresolved Issues at the Heart of the New Economy', remarks before the Antitrust, Technology and Intellectual Property Conference, Berkeley Center for Law and Technology, University of California at Berkeley, March 2, 2001, available at http://www.ftc.gov/speeches/pitofsky/ipf301.shtm; Oettinger, *supra* note 74, at 323; Pitofsky, *supra* note 74, at 913; and Gambrell, *supra* note 74, 156. Moreover, it is worthwhile remembering that the DOJ oppose *certiorari* in *Xerox*, expressing 'serious concerns about such a holding' and stating that the United States 'would not be prepared to endorse it'. See brief for the United States as *amicus curiae*, 10.

[82] See footnotes 123 ff.

[83] The wording of Section 271(d)(4), indeed, spikes of 'misuse or illegal extension of the patent right'. Thus, it is possible to refer to antitrust violations as the unlawfulness other than misuse. To be sure, the Congress might have used the phrases 'illegal extension of the patent right' and 'misuse' to describe different aspects of the doctrine of patent misuse.

purchase of some other product or the taking of some other licenses – does not immunize patentees from antitrust liability. Hence, reading the same term 'illegal extension of the patent right' to immunize patentees from antitrust liability for their refusals to license, but not for such conditioning of licenses would appear inconsistent. After all, as the First Circuit held in order to sustain the rebuttable presumption of immunity that it introduces for copyright holders' refusals to license, absent clear, express Congressional intent to immunize conduct or repugnancy between some other body of law and antitrust, a finding of immunity is unwarranted. Therefore, if the Sherman Act does not explicitly exempt patented and copyrighted materials from antitrust scrutiny, courts should be wary of creating implied exemptions.[84]

THE EU CRITERIA FOR ESTABLISHING WHETHER INNOVATION HAS BEEN IMPAIRED: THE 'NEW PRODUCT' AND 'NEW MARKET' CRITERIA

In the EU jurisdiction, similarly, there is no general obligation for an IPR holder to license its IPRs, not even when it holds a dominant position. Indeed, as recently restated in the 2005 Discussion Paper[85] and as previously acknowledged by the EU courts,[86] the very aim of granting an exclusive right is to prevent unauthorized third parties from using the IPR object. However, as the oldest EU case law shows,[87] dating back to 1980s the EU antitrust institutions have applied to IPRs the general idea that the principle of refusal to deal is subject to exceptions.[88] Early EU case law

---

84 *Data General Corp. v. Grumman Systems Support Corp.*, 36 F.3d 1147, 1185 (1st Cir. 1994).

85 Discussion paper, *supra* at note 14, § 238.

86 'The right of the proprietor of a protected design to prevent third parties from manufacturing and selling or importing, without its consent, products incorporating the design constitutes the very subject-matter of his exclusive right. It follows that an obligation imposed upon the proprietor of a protected design to grant to third parties, even in return for a reasonable royalty, a licence for the supply of products incorporating the design would lead to the proprietor thereof being deprived of the substance of his exclusive right, and that a refusal to grant such a licence cannot in itself constitute an abuse of a dominant position.' See *Volvo*, *infra* at note 51, § 8, and, similarly, *Magill TV*, § 49.

87 See the *Cicra* and *Volvo* preliminary judgments, which share the same pattern of facts as *Xerox*, *Data General*, and *Kodak* but for the durable good in question – automobiles. See Case 53/87, *Consorzio Italiano della Componentistica di Ricambio per Autoveicoli (CICRA) and Maxicar v Régie nationale des usines Renault*, October 5, 1988, 1988 ECR 6039 and Case 238/87, *Volvo AB v Erik Veng (UK) Ltd.*, October 5, 1988, 1988 ECR 6211. Since they were preliminary judgments, we do not know the outcome of the national cases, but only the criteria that the Court gave to the national courts to interpret the EU law.

88 The exceptions consist in 'conduct such as the arbitrary refusal to supply spare parts

established that a refusal to license is only unlawful when it results either in the disruption of pre-existing business relationships or in another kind of abusive conduct – an exploitative practice or an irrational discriminatory behavior.[89]

Subsequently, however, the EU institutions have endorsed a partially different approach, focusing on the effect that refusals to license IPRs can produce, not only on allocative efficiency, but also on future innovation. More precisely, in *Magill TV*, *IMS Health*, *Microsoft IV*, and *Microsoft V*, the EU institutions developed different criteria to establish how a monopolist might restrain dynamic efficiency by leveraging its exclusive IP right. To be sure, whereas in *Magill TV* and *IMS Health* the IPRs involved (copyrights) addressed rights to use the patented materials, in the Microsoft saga the object of the alleged IPRs[90] (copyrights, trade secrets and patents) was the information necessary to make the monopolized product work together with competitors' products – i.e., so-called interoperability information.

More specifically, in *Magill TV*[91] the ECJ ascertained, as it did in other, non-IP cases about 'refusals to start supplying input', that the refusal: (α) was a conduct whereby the dominant firms had excluded all competition on the secondary market;[92] (β) was not objectively justified; and (γ) concerned a product indispensable to the exercise of the monopolist's rivals' activity.[93] It thus went further, formulating a new fourth condition in order to apply the duty to deal to be applied: (δ) the new product criterion.

---

to independent repairers, the fixing of prices for spare parts at an unfair level or a decision no longer to produce spare parts for a particular model even though many cars of that model are still in circulation'. *Volvo*, § 9.

89 Indeed, reading together the judgments and the Advocate-General's opinions it is understood that the evil of the refusal to supply spare parts to independent repairers rested with its discriminatory character, and not with the exclusion of the independent repairers as such. See, e.g., Ian Forrester, 'Abuse of Intellectual Property as an Abuse of Dominance: Views across the Atlantic', 708 *PLI/Pat.* 35, 41 (2002) (underlying the importance of an additional element as a necessary requirement for the application of Article 82).

90 Indeed, though it is not sure whether IPRs protect Microsoft's interoperability codes, both the Commission and the Court of First Instance decided to deal with the case as if those IPRs really existed.

91 The facts were the following: Magill attempted to publish a comprehensive weekly television guide for the Republic of Ireland and Northern Ireland markets at a time when this product was not available to consumers. The interested television stations refused Magill the weekly programme listings necessary to realize the guide, claiming under Irish and United Kingdom legislation, copyright protection for them. Each television station used to publish its own television guide covering exclusively its own programmes. The Commission, deeming the refusal as abusive, ordered the television stations to supply third parties on a non-discriminatory and reasonable basis with the broadcasting listing. The CFI and the ECJ affirmed.

92 Indeed, this is a way – perhaps not so unquestioned – to ascertain the occurrence of the competitive harm.

93 See *Magill TV* (ECJ judgment), respectively §§ 56, 55, and 53 and the prongs (A), (B), and (C) of the above list.

Namely, the ECJ held that the refusal was also abusive because it kept the appearance of a new product that the dominant firm did not offer and for which there was a potential consumer demand.[94] After *Magill TV*,[95] EU judges endorsed an almost identical legal standard in *IMS Health*,[96] where they again imposed a joint venture between the dominant firm and its rivals operating in an alleged[97] secondary market. Again the ECJ stated that the refusal to give access to a copyrighted input[98] was abusive, as: (α)

---

[94] See *Magill TV* (ECJ judgment), § 54.

[95] Regardless of the panic created by *Magill TV*, indeed, this judgment was not followed by several decisions that imposed a duty to license. By contrast, not only the above-mentioned *Oscar Bronner* stifled the wishes for a sort of duty to deal principle, but also in the subsequent IPR case – i.e. *Tiercé Ladbroke (B)/PMU*, June 24 1993, IV/33699, rejection of denounce, not published and upheld in Case T-504/93, *Tiercé Ladbroke SA v Commission*, June 12, 1997, [1997] ECR II-923, (hereinafter, '*Ladbroke*') – the Commission rejected the analogy with *Magill TV* and, hence, the allegations of abuse. In *Ladbroke*, an operator of betting shops in Belgium complained that its French rival refused it a license for copyrighted TV pictures and sound commentaries of French horse races. The Commission and the CFI rejected the complaint since the copyrighted material was not essential for Ladbroke to operate on the market. There the court seemed to suggest that, given the other conditions for the refusal to be unlawful, the two above-mentioned were alternatives and not cumulative (§ 131). But this view has not been confirmed in *IMS Health*. See, in this regard, Forrester, *supra* note 89, at 49; Korah, *supra* note 22, at 810–11; Henrik Meinberg, *From Magill to IMS Health: The New Product Requirement and the Diversity of Intellectual Property Rights*, 28(7) E.I.P.R. 398, 401 (2006).

[96] *NDC Health/IMS Health*: Interim Measures (2003/741/EC), August 13 2003, OJ 2003, L268/69, upheld in Case T-184/01, *IMS Health v Commission*, March 10, 2005, not yet published. The citations here reproduced are taken from Case C-418/2001, *IMS Health GmbH & Co. OHG v NDC Health GmbH & Co. KG*, April 24, 2004, http://eur-lex.europa.eu. The facts are that a firm (IMS) created, with the help of some German pharmaceutical companies, a database known as the 'brick structure' to split and organize the German data about regional sales of drugs in Member States. The 'brick structure' was covered by the German copyright law as a database. IMS sued PII – its competitor in the market for the sale of the regarded data – in a German court for copyright infringement, and the court referred to the ECJ for a ruling on whether the refusal to license the brick structure was an abuse. After the ECJ's preliminary ruling, the German process ended with a declaration of invalid copyright on the database.

[97] This judgment, indeed, disregarded that the rival claiming the input operated in the market of the dominant firm. In other words, in *IMS Health*, the 'vertical element' of every, though questionable, essential facility case was bypassed by the Court affirming that, 'for the purposes of the application of the earlier case-law, it is sufficient that a potential market or even hypothetical market can be identified. Such is the case where the products or services are indispensable in order to carry on a particular business and where there is an actual demand for them on the part of undertakings which seek to carry on the business for which they are indispensable. Accordingly, it is determinative that two different stages of production may be identified and that they are interconnected, inasmuch as the upstream product is indispensable for the supply of the downstream product.' §§ 44 and 45.

[98] The ECJ left the German court to decide whether the database was actually indispensable, but it seemed to suggest it when it considers the database like a standard (§§ 28 and 38) – an interoperability standard, one could argue, after reading the *IBM settlement*, *Microsoft IV* and *Racal Decca*. On the existence of a standard, see, e.g., Kenneth Glazer, 'The IMS Health Case: a U.S. Perspective', 13 *Geo. Mason L. Rev.* 1197, 1213 (2006).

it excluded competition in the secondary market; (β) it was unjustified; and (γ) it concerned an indispensable input.[99] Moreover, the Court observed that (δ) the refusal prevented the development of a new market by blocking the advent of a new product for which there was potential consumer demand. In particular, the Court held that the new market requirement occurred because the rival firm did not intend to limit itself essentially to duplicate the goods or services already offered by the owner of the intellectual property right, but had further developed products based on the desired input.[100]

It is not surprising, therefore, that the Discussion Paper established that monopolists' refusals to license IPRs would generally be illegal when four conditions occur, namely: when the three requirements of the *Oscar Bronner*-like cases are satisfied and when 'the refusal to grant a license prevents the development of the market for which the license is an indispensable input, to the detriment of consumers'.[101] Indeed, in the Discussion Paper, the Directorate-General for Competition maintained that 'the refusal of licensing an IPR protected technology should not impair consumers' ability to benefit from innovation brought about by the dominant undertaking's competitors'[102] and – consistent with the idea expressed in *IMS Health* that the monopolist did not deserve its copyright because of the way the brick structure had been created[103] – also questioned whether the investments behind innovations leading to intellectual property rights were necessarily very significant.

MICROSOFT IV AND THE 'INNOVATION'S INCENTIVES' TEST

In *Microsoft IV*,[104] the European Commission dealt with Microsoft's refusal to share its interoperability information, that is to say, the information

[99] See *IMS Health* (the ECJ judgment), § 38.

[100] Id., § 49. Before, the idea of the advocate: 'In the balancing of the interest in protection of the intellectual property right and the economic freedom of its owner against the interest in protection of free competition, the latter can prevail only where refusal to grant a licence prevents the development of the secondary market to the detriment of consumers', § 48. Further, see Haris Apostolopoulos, 'Refusal to deal Cases Of IP Rights at the Aftermarket in the US and EU Law: Converging of both Law Systems through Speaking the Same Language of Law and Economics', 7 *Chi.-Kent J. Int'l Comp. L.* 144 (2007), discussing the difference between competition by substitution and competition by imitation.

[101] Discussion paper, *supra* note 14, § 239.

[102] Id., § 240.

[103] For the same opinion, see Glazer, *supra* note 98, at 1211.

[104] Commission Decision of March 24, 2004, relating to a proceeding under Article 82 of the EC Treaty (Case COMP/C-3/37.792 Microsoft), C(2004)9 final (Brussels 21.4.2004).

needed to make Microsoft's Operating System – i.e. Windows – work with other software and middleware. The Commission discussed the case using a standard that – contrary to what has been often noted – was very favorable to the defendant. Although the case involved the disruption of precedent levels of supply (i.e., the Aspen condition), the Commission verified that the request input was indispensable, i.e., it verified the occurrence of the Oscar Bronner condition.[105] Moreover, although it was not sure that IPRs could protect the interoperability information, the Commission referred back to the *Magill TV* set of requirements. Therefore, the Commission deemed the refusal illegal because it fulfilled all of the necessary conditions, namely that: (γ) the interoperability information was essential; (α) the refusal was likely to harm competition as such; (β) the refusal did not have any objective justification; and (δ) the refusal was preventing follow-on innovation appearing in the market.[106]

Given that this approach is quite coherent with the above mentioned post-Chicagoan models,[107] considering the object of this chapter, what is interesting about this decision is the way in which the Commission verified the occurrence of the fourth condition. It did not limit itself to ascertaining whether a new product or market could have developed, as it did in *Magill TV* and *IMS Health*.[108] Rather, it discussed whether an uncertain duty to

---

105 It goes without saying that in the US the duty to deal follows the coexistence of both conditions; the disruption of precedent levels of supply and the essential nature of the required input. Nevertheless, as stated before, that was not true for the EU jurisdiction, where the occurrence of the indispensability condition was connected only to the creation of a new joint venture between the monopolist and its rivals.

106 See, e.g., Steven C. Salop & R. Craig Romaine, 'Preserving Monopoly: Economic Analysis, Legal Standards and Microsoft', 7 *George Mason Law Review* 617, 664 (1998) (arguing that if a market is driven more by innovation than price competition, then entrants also must have an open environment in order to challenge the monopolist. An antitrust regime which is overly permissive towards defendants may reduce aggregate innovation, as innovation by entrants and small competitors is reduced by more than innovation by the monopolist increases).

107 For a concurring opinion, see Ekaterina Rousseva, *Rethinking Exclusionary Abuses in EU Competition Law* 81 and 101–102 (2010).

108 After all, at the time of the decision it had already been argued that if the Commission's main concern was about a proper distribution of the incentives to innovate, the test applied in *Magill TV* and *IMS Health* did not work so well. Indeed, according to François Lévêque, 'Innovation, Leveraging and Essential Facilities: Interoperability Licensing in the EU Microsoft Case', in *Antitrust, Patents, and Copyright* 103, 107–108 (2005), available at www.ssrn.com if the new product test aims to grasp the preliminary stages of innovations, the test applied in Microsoft works better and for at least two reasons. Firstly, incentives to innovate are a good proxy of consumers' benefits. Economic theory predicts that wherever incentives are present firms will innovate to propose valuable improvements to consumers. Secondly, the incentive-effects approach is adequate for economic theory on intellectual property: 'In any case, as a required test to apply the essential facility doctrine to intellectual property, the approach based on incentives is more economically sound than the new product condition'.

license would have reduced incentives to innovate in the whole industry, by comparing the incentives of Microsoft with those of its rivals. The answer was that, on the one hand, Microsoft's competitors were likely to develop their own products with the help of the interoperability information; and on the other hand, the new product competition between Microsoft and its rivals would have improved (rather than reduced) Microsoft's incentives to innovate.[109] As a whole, thus, the Commission showed that the duty to license would have had a positive net impact on incentives to innovate in the whole industry.

With *Microsoft IV*, the Commission turned to consider directly both the role that antitrust action can play in governing the innovative and creative process,[110] and, at the same time, how to allocate the incentives to innovate. Once again the Commission chose to allocate those incentives as it did in *Magill TV* and *IMS* – i.e. in a way that was contrary to that resulting from simply examining existing IPRs.[111] The Commission justified its approach – which it partially endorsed in the Discussion Paper as well[112] – by conceptualizing IPRs as devices in the service of the public interest.[113] Thus, as long as the Commission is supposed to intervene in the market to protect the public interest, it is also entitled to refashion the scope of IPRs.

---

[109] The absence of negative effects allowed the Commission not to make a real balance. See, on this point, Simonetta Vezzoso, 'The incentives balance test in the EU Microsoft case: a pro-innovation "economic-based" approach', 27 *E.C.L.R.* 382, 384-385 and 389 (2006).

[110] In this connection, the words of Cecilio Madero Villarejo, Head of Unit C-3 (Information Industries, Internet and Consumer Electronics), DG Competition, are very interesting: 'Innovation plays a key role in software markets and should be treated with great care. This means that the action of antitrust authorities should be careful not to diminish a dominant undertaking's incentive to innovate. It also means that antitrust enforcement has particular relevance when addressing behavior that risks stifling follow-on innovation and the development of new products'.

[111] From the outset, the Commission observed that, 'it cannot be excluded that ordering Microsoft to disclose such specifications and allow such use of them by third parties restricts the exercise of Microsoft's intellectual property rights'. Commission Decision of March 24, 2004 (Case COMP/C-3/37.792 Microsoft), C(2004)9 final (Brussels 21.4.2004), § 546.

[112] Indeed, in the Discussion Paper, the DG Competition tried to consider interoperability information as if it were not covered by IPRs, stating: 'A special case arises when an undertaking refuses to supply information in a way that allows it to extend its dominance from one market to another. . . . Even if such information may be considered a trade secret it may not be appropriate to apply to such refusals to supply information the same high standards for intervention as those described in the previous subsection [i.e. those about refusals to]' *supra* at note 14, §§ 241–2.

[113] 'The central function of intellectual property rights is to protect the moral rights in a right-holder's work and ensure a reward for the creative effort. But it is also an essential objective of intellectual property law that creativity should be stimulated for the general public good. A refusal by an undertaking to grant a license may, under exceptional circumstances, be contrary to the general public good by constituting an abuse of a dominant position with harmful effects on innovation and on consumers'. id., § 711.

MICROSOFT V AND THE 'LIMITATION TO TECHNICAL DEVELOPMENT' CRITERION

In 2007 the Court of First Instance (hereinafter, 'CFI') affirmed *Microsoft IV*,[114] showing again what the ECJ established in *IMS Health*, that is to say, that the 'exceptional conditions' established in *Magill TV* are not exhaustive.[115] Indeed, the CFI also altered somewhat the conditions that the Commission had developed *in Microsoft IV* to impose the duty to deal. Two changes are worth stressing here.

First, the Court altered – or removed it as an independent fourth condition – the innovation's incentives test, holding that it is up to the monopolist to show as an objective justification of its refusal that the duty to deal would decrease its incentives to innovate.[116] While the Commission decided to prove that a duty to deal can improve the whole industry's incentives to innovate, the CFI allowed a less defendant-friendly approach: it shifts the burden of proof to the defendant. After having established that the Commission did not make any 'manifest error'[117] in deciding that if Microsoft had a duty to deal, it would increase incentives to innovate on the past of Microsoft's rivals, CFI made it more difficult for the monopolist to cast upon Microsoft the burden of proving that the reduction of its incentives should it have a duty to deal outweighs that increase. The Court then concluded that Microsoft did not establish that if it were required to disclose the interoperability information its incentives to innovate would be reduced.[118] Hence, beyond the specific outcome of the case, it is apparent that in opting for this new distribution of the burden of the proof, the Court showed its usual distaste for dominant firms.

---

114 Court of First Instance, case T-201/04, September 17, 2007, available at http://curia.europa.eu/.

115 See Rousseva, *supra* note 48, at 103.

116 See *Microsoft V*, § 688.

117 According to the EU case law, the European Community courts can carry out only a limited review of considerations involving complex technical and economic assessments. In other words, 'although as a general rule the Community Courts undertake a comprehensive review of the question as to whether or not the conditions for the application of the competition rules are met, their review of complex economic appraisals made by the Commission is necessarily limited to checking whether the relevant rules on procedure and on stating reasons have been complied with, whether the facts have been accurately stated and whether there has been any manifest error of assessment or a misuse of powers'. Nevertheless, when dealing with economic or technical matters, the Community Courts must not 'decline to review the Commission's interpretation of economic or technical data. The Community Courts must not only establish whether the evidence put forward is factually accurate, reliable and consistent but must also determine whether that evidence contains all the relevant data that must be taken into consideration in appraising a complex situation and whether it is capable of substantiating the conclusions drawn from it'. See *Microsoft V*, §§ 87 and 89.

118 See *Microsoft V*, § 697.

The second way in which the CFI adopted the criteria of the Commission in *Microsoft IV* concerns an expansion of the applicable law. CFI held that, while both the new product and the new market criteria should be considered under Article 102(b), it also established that those criteria are not the only parameters, which determine whether a refusal to license an intellectual property right is capable of causing prejudice to consumers, within the meaning of that Article. As the wording of the provision clearly states, the Court added to the new market and new product criteria that prejudice to rivals may arise where there is a limitation of technical development.[119] According to the CFI, it was a technical development that was lost to Microsoft's rivals; hence, without the required interface specifications, they could not offer their own differentiated products.[120]

Not only had the CFI affirmed the Commission's choice to use antitrust law to restrain the innovative and creative process, by forcing the monopolist to share its proprietary resources. Not only had the CFI endorsed the idea that the monopolist was manipulating innovative paths in the industry. The CFI even widened the legal standard for showing that a restriction to innovation occurred as a result of a refusal to deal. Although the addition of a technical development criterion is plainly consistent with the wording of Article 102(b), its interpretation may become quite broad. It is apparent that any blocking of any potentially differentiated product could be deemed a restriction on innovation and, perhaps, on technical development. In this way, the CFI seems to assign significant discretionary power to the Commission.

The CFI did not show any hesitation in affirming the Commission's decision when it chose to act as a regulator which must decide what are the relevant competitive variables in a market. Indeed, the CFI concurred with the Commission's statement that the current rivalry among alternative operating systems should be played out based upon their security, reliability, ease of use and speed, rather than according to their interoperability with other products.[121] Ultimately, both in *IMS Health* and in the Microsoft saga, the EU institutions affirmed the idea that even proprietary standards have to be shared, with the aim of prompting the industry to invest its resources in directions other than searching for alternatives to the standard – though this too remains an option.[122]

---

119 Id., §§ 643 and 647.

120 The CFI, indeed, concurred with the Commission in stating that by disclosing the interface information Microsoft did not run the risk of having its products cloned. See, e.g., *Microsoft V*, §§ 655–63.

121 *Microsoft V*, §§ 650–53.

122 Suppose that the development of an industry can be depicted as if the rivalry among its firms lasts until a standard is achieved. In such a scenario, the EU Microsoft saga

In summary, the present EU approach towards monopolists who refuse to license their IPRs seems to track the following reasoning. Once the enforcement of a monopolist's IPR impairs future innovation and, thus, consumer welfare, the EU antitrust institutions must intervene. By obliging the monopolist to share its IPR, they intervene to protect the public interest by questioning, although not always expressly, that the monopolist deserves it, although their ability to express such a judgment should be discussed.

THE JURISDICTIONAL AND CULTURAL ISSUES SURROUNDING REFUSALS TO LICENSE: THE DIVISION OF POWER ARGUMENT

The analysis of the US and EU case law about monopolists who refused to license their IPRs reveals a divergent transatlantic scenario. In the US there are the premises to overrule Kodak and apply a quasi per se legality rule to refusals to license IPRs. In the EU the presence of IPRs does not change the common favorable attitude towards the refusal to deal doctrine.[123] More exactly, while in the US IPRs are deemed to be the best legislative device to govern the innovative process from an *ex ante* and generic standpoint, in the EU jurisdiction IPRs are (only) an ordinary instrument in the hands of antitrust authorities – who are also adjudicatory branches – to govern the innovative process by themselves, from an *ex post* and case-by-case perspective.[124] Therefore, while US courts do not use antitrust law to question IPRs' boundaries and to remedy alleged IPRs' failures, EU institutions use antitrust law to confront IPRs that, in their opinion, fall short of boosting innovation. In other words, regardless of the (likely) harm to allocative efficiency,[125] the EU institutions hold that enforcing antitrust law

---

teaches that: (i) when the standard has been achieved it has to be shared, though it results from the efforts of a single (dominant) firm (see above); (ii) when the standard has not yet been achieved, a dominant firm cannot use anticompetitive behaviors in order to impose its own technology as the standard. See, in this last regard, the second of the abuses alleged of Microsoft about the integration of Windows Media Player in Windows. In particular, *Microsoft V*, § 1152.

[123] See François Lévêque and Yann Ménière, *The Economics of Patents and Copyright* 94 (2004) (arguing that in this regard, therefore, 'competition law puts intellectual property on a par with other forms of property.').

[124] See, e.g., Cyril Ritter, 'Refusal to Deal and 'Essential Facilities': Does Intellectual Property Require Special Deference Compared to Tangible Property?' 28(3) *World Competition* 281 (2005).

[125] For some scholars the consumer welfare loss is clear. If consumers receive a new good or service that did not previously exist and for which there is a demand, there is a clear increase in the consumer welfare. In this regard see, e.g., John Temple Lang, 'Anticompetitive

so as to allow monopolists' rivals to develop new products, new markets, follow-on innovations, and technical changes furthers consumer welfare better than enforcing IPRs against those rivals.

There are some cultural issues that, residing in the *milieu* of judges and officers, may explain this divergent approach, such as the dissimilar interpretation of the appropriate division of power, the attitudes toward the false-positive mistakes issue, and the different *status* that the two jurisdictions assign to the IP culture – a different *status* that also shapes the jurisdictional side of the interface between the antitrust law and IP law.

As to the first argument, US case law about monopolists who refuse to license their IPRs could suggest that US courts believe that the choice not to share IP properties boosts innovation even when monopolists make that choice. Yet, in their judgments, US courts have seldom expressed such a belief,[126] though it would have been consistent with the so-called 'cowboy competition' that US courts applied.[127] Instead they offer another

---

Abuses Involving Intellectual Property Rights', (2003), available at http://www.eui.eu/RSCAS/Research/Competition/2003/200306COMP-TempleLang-sIII.pdf; O'Donoghue & Padilla, *supra* at note 13, 447; and Alexandros Stratakis, 'Comparative Analysis of the US and EU Approach and Enforcement of the Essential Facilities Doctrine', 27 *E.C.L.R.* 434, 442 (2006). For some other scholars the loss is problematic and lacks economic foundations. See Damien Gerardin, 'Limiting the Scope of Article 82 EC: What Can the EU Learn from the US Supreme Court's Judgment in Trinko, in the Wake of Microsoft, IMS and Deutsche Telekom?', 41 *C.M. L. Rev.* 1519, 1531 (2004). See Derek Ridyard, 'Compulsory Access Under EC Competition Law – A New Doctrine of 'Convenient Facilities' and the Case for Price Regulation', 25(11) *European Competition L. Rev.* 670 (2004) (arguing that, 'It would be trivially easy for NDC, the main potential licensee in the IMS case, to implement some product change that rendered its market research product "innovative" relative to that of IMS. In any event, it is hard to see a justifiable public policy rationale for this condition. If it was established that foreclosing competition allowed IMS to sustain an inefficient and abusive outcome on the market for pharmaceutical market research products, then the public policy case for allowing NDC to enter the market through compulsory licensing of the brick structure is valid even if the only "innovation" provided is a competitive price. But if the view is taken that the IMS offering was competitive, it is hard to see what role there is for intervention to force innovation through compulsory licensing, since IMS would have a normal commercial motive to boost demand for its product by promoting innovation itself.'). Among the others who have expressed doubts are Lévêque, *supra* at note 69, at 103–106, Daniel Kanter, 'IP and Compulsory Licensing on both Sides of the Atlantic – An Appropriate Antitrust Remedy or Cutback to Innovation', 27(7) *E.C.L.R.* 351, 355 (2006) and Ahlborn et al., *supra* at note 45, at 47 and 49, where the authors underline the risk that such an undetermined threshold risk could create for the patent system.

[126] Indeed, whereas the Federal Circuit opinions follow mainstream antitrust precedent more closely than the FTC's consent decree in the *Intel* case, the Federal Circuit deals with antitrust in terms that are doctrinaire on the side of intellectual property owners: the court virtually ignores the market for innovation as well as potential anticompetitive concerns. See, in this regard, James B. Kobak Jr, 'The Federal Circuit as a Competition Law Court', available at http://www.hugheshubbard.com/files/tbl_s20NewsPring%5CPDFUpload103%5C701%5CJournal_Patent_Trademark_August_2001.pdf.

[127] See, e.g., J. Bruce McDonald, 'Section 2 and Article 82: Cowboys and Gentlemen', available at www.usdoj.gov/atr/public/speeches/210873.htm.

argument, i.e., that, as courts, they are not allowed to second-guess the legislators' decisions and, in particular, the IP legislators' decision not to condition the enforceability of an IPR on the degree of market power that the IPR holder enjoys. In other words, in dealing with monopolists who refuse to license their IPRs, US courts do not consider the impact that the refusal has on dynamic efficiency. Rather, they rely on the formal 'division of power' argument, in which it is not up to the judiciary to question the choices of the legislature, even though those choices address misuse and not antitrust issues; and, in so doing, the courts affirm the belief that IPRs always enhance innovation.

On the contrary, the EU institutions have maintained clearly, both in their case law, in the Discussion Paper and in the 2009 Communication, that dominant firms' IPRs may harm dynamic efficiency by blocking the innovations of monopolists' rivals. In other words, they endorse a substantive approach to the matter though, in so doing, they take a formal position as well: they clearly do not regard that controlling the decisions of national legislatures conditions the enforceability of IPRs on the strength of market power that the IPR-holder enjoys.

This is the reason why one could argue that, had a European-dominant firm deployed the *Xerox* institutional argument, the EU institutions would have turned out to be quite insensitive to it: they would not have affirmed that national legislators' decisions about IPRs can pre-empt EU antitrust action. On the contrary, they could easily have rebutted an argument that a national law cannot interfere with a communitarian competition concern, and that only the European Commission is capable of protecting the European public interest. In this regard, hence, even if Member States were to adopt a provision equivalent to Section 271(d) of the US Patent Act, this would not be enough.[128]

Now, given this divergence, one might be inclined to think that EU institutions do not respect the Montesquieu ideals; but this would be a mistake. Rather, as the following sections shows, the more intrusive EU approach stems both from a different consideration of the hurdles and risks that public powers' interference into the economy entails, and from the national status of IPRs.

---

128 The EU institutions would change their attitude if the Commission adopted EU legislation stating that, in granting an IPR, it has already contemplated the case of a dominant firm as its holder. Then, it must be acknowledged that in the recent *Microsoft V* judgment the Court, speaking about the concept of interoperability and discussing whether the Commission had to comply with what Directive 91/250 envisaged, held that: 'In any event, it must be borne in mind that what is at issue in the present case is a decision adopted in application of Article 82 EC, a provision of higher rank than Directive 91/250'. See *Microsoft V*, § 226.

THE FALSE-POSITIVE ISSUE

As the EU practice shows, EU officers and judges are willing to endorse long-term exams of the effects that monopolists' conduct entails. In particular, in deciding whether to grant access to dominant firms' proprietary inputs, they chose to evaluate the likelihood of the advent of new products, new markets, and follow-on innovation. Even if such exams seem unavoidable when concerned with dynamic efficiency, it must be acknowledged that such analyses risk being highly speculative, especially when the antitrust action occurs in industries that are experiencing fast technological changes, so do not allow one to predict with confidence what the future winning technology will be.[129] In other words, those kinds of analyses imply a high risk of errors, both false-negative and false-positive mistakes.

Now, according to the Chicago School, whereas the market can remedy for unlawful conduct that judges fail to strike, there is no remedy against lawful behaviors that judges prohibit. Thus, in order not to produce such a harmful over-deterrence, the Chicago school suggests that antitrust authorities refrain from hunting practices that are almost unavoidably illegal.

And, in effect, nowadays the US courts seem to endorse this approach. In particular, as imposing a duty to deal forces courts and authorities to act like regulators, though they are ill equipped to perform this task, whether it is to detect the inputs to be shared, to fix their prices, or to monitor compliance with these requirements,[130] it is not surprising that those US courts, fearful of committing false-positive mistakes, are not willing to impose a duty to deal.[131]

In contrast, given the opposite EU approach to the duty to deal, it has to be inferred that EU institutions are less worried about the risk of false positives and over-deterrence.[132]

---

[129] See, e.g., Nicholas Economides, 'Public Policy in Network Industries' (2006) available at www.ssrn.com.

[130] Areeda & Hovenkamp, supra note 2, at ¶ 770.e; and Valentine Korah, *supra* at note 22, 832, looking mainly at regulated industries. Sharing a monopolized input, in fact, does not make the market less monopolized unless courts fix the input price and the other conditions of the deal. Because of the duty, indeed, the monopolist will reduce its output to compensate the rival's production and will charge the monopoly price to the rival. Besides, even assuming that a court could define the conditions of the deal, it would be then charged with the duty to monitor the dominant firm's behavior, which could turn out to be a very expensive routine.

[131] From a private point of view, besides, compulsory licenses entail the passage of something more than the mere IPR.

[132] See Ritter, *supra* note 124, at 298 (arguing that, 'some commentators have asked whether antitrust agencies are well-equipped to carry out this kind of industry-wide balancing of incentives but this is a biased formulation. The real question is: the risk of antitrust agencies erring in evaluating the need for compulsory licenses so great that we should

Two theories can serve to explain such a divergent attitude. First, because of their history of public monopolies and regulated industries, Europeans are quite comfortable with a strong presence of public powers in the market, so that they tolerate an antitrust law that sometimes encroaches into the realm of industrial policy, overseeing the market rather like a nanny.[133] As one scholar has put it, 'it is a fact that within liberal society itself one of the key divisions of political identity (and hence identification) is between these two sides: the side that fears private power more, and in order to fight it is ready to give room to the power of government; and the side that fears the expansion of government more, and is therefore more prepared to tolerate private power'.[134] Therefore, it could be that Europeans favor their institutions to be over-deterrent rather than under-deterrent, as they prefer to bear the risks of public power's mistakes rather than the risks of private power's undetected unlawful acts. This does not mean that the US does not conceive of the Sherman Act as a tool for fighting private powers: the Sherman Act triggered a substantial history of commentary and dialogue about the balance of power between the public

---

generally prefer no compulsory licenses at all?'). For a concurrent opinion see Ken Heyer, 'A World of Uncertainty: Economics and the Globalization of Antitrust', 72 *Antitrust L.J.* 375, 409 (2005) (observing 'I would . . . conjecture that differing positions [between the US and EU jurisdictions] are generally not based on differences in either the analytical frameworks being applied or the welfare standards being employed. Rather . . . varying approaches are likely the result of a combination of uncertainty and differences in underlying beliefs about the ability of imperfect government regulators (i.e., antitrust authorities) to (a) determine the net value to society of a monopolist's business practices, and (b) impose remedies that will outperform the imperfect marketplace.'). Then, at 412–13, Heyer clarifies 'How aggressive and interventionist an antitrust policy one proposes (or adopts) will depend greatly on how confident one is in the government's ability to identify correctly which type of scenario is presented, develop an efficient remedy for the ailment (if any), and weigh correctly the tradeoffs involved in potentially 'getting it wrong''. Moreover, consider Jeffrey K. Mackie-Mason, *What to do about Unilateral Refusals to License?* 5 (2006) available at www.ssrn.com, who looks at the clash between the Chicago rules and the modern economics in connection with the refusal-to-deal cases. Generally, then, it is the analysis of pricing abuses – such as predatory pricing and bundle discounts – that shows clearly this new EU tendency to use quite complicated economic theories as benchmarks for its antitrust assessments.

[133] On this topic see, e.g., Michael A. Carrier, *Of Trinko, Tea Leaves, and Intellectual Property*, Journal of Corporation Law 101, 108 (2005) and id., *supra* at note 58, 1202. After all, the concern for dynamic efficiency goes back to debate over a 'no-fault' monopoly offense. The 'hope of monopoly (with its supracompetitive returns) is an incentive to the efficient and innovative market performance that the law seeks to encourage'. See Lawrence A. Sullivan & Ann I. Jones, 'Monopoly Conduct, Especially Leveraging Power from One Product or Market to Another', in *Antitrust, Innovation and Competitiveness* 165, 66 (1992) and Phillip E. Areeda & Herbert Hovenkamp, *Antitrust Law: An Analysis of Antitrust Principles and Their Application* ¶ 112 (2006).

[134] As noticed by Giuliano Amato, *Antitrust and the Bounds of Power: The Dilemma of Liberal Democracy in the History of the Market* 4 (1997), and Heyer, *supra* at note 7, 412–13.

and private sectors.[135] Nevertheless, in the US this argument cannot be pushed too far, as the small number of monopolization cases shows.[136]

Second, it can be argued that such a mistrust towards monopolists stems from the fact that – as noted by the Discussion Paper[137] – several of the European-dominant firms are former public monopolies.[138] Therefore, it should not come as a revelation that EU antitrust institutions perceive differently any negative impact on their incentives to innovate that might arise from obliging dominant firms to share their IPRs. If US courts maintain that, had monopolists known they would have a duty to license, they would not have invested in innovation from the outset, the EU institutions can rebut that some of the monopolists' IPRs are more a windfall than a deserved reward, so that monopolists ordered to share their IPRs have no reason to recriminate. Nevertheless, that rebuttal does not apply in every case.

Yet, regardless of any historical context the US approach towards the false-positive issue is not critique-free: given the effectiveness of some monopolists' practices, the hands-off approach may seriously contribute to both the direction of determining a change in the process of competition, and the exit of rivals and new or improved products and services, as *Microsoft III* showed.[139]

---

[135] See, e.g., Harry First & Andrew I. Gavil, 'Re-Framing Windows: The Durable Meaning of the Microsoft Antitrust Litigation', 2006 *Utah L. Rev.* 641, 642-643 (2006) (arguing that, 'since the first federal antitrust law the federal government has been repeatedly cast as the policeman of national markets, dispensed to rein in overbearing private corporate power. Public power, wielded in the public interest, was conceived as the antidote to such private power'); David S. Millon, 'The Sherman Act and the Balance of Power', 61 *S. Cal. L. Rev.* 1219, 1255 (1988); and. John J. Flynn, 'Introduction, Antitrust Jurisprudence: A Symposium on the Economic, Political and Social Goals of Antitrust Policy', 125 *U. Pa. L. Rev.* 1182 (1977).

[136] See William E. Kovacic, 'The Modern Evolution of U.S. Competition Policy Enforcement Norms', 71 *Antitrust L.J.* 377, 448–60 (2003) (observing that Section 2 has been enforced in few circumstances, especially according to the administration in power).

[137] DG Discussion paper, *supra* at note 14, § 237.

[138] Margaret Bloom, 'The US and EU Move towards substantial Antitrust Convergence on Consumer Welfare Based Enforcement', *'19-SUM Antitrust'*, 18, 22 (2005).

[139] See, indeed, First, Gavil, *supra* note 135, at 722-723 (elaborating clearly that, 'the Microsoft prosecution . . . provides an answer to a question that is critical for monopolization cases: When an incumbent, dominant firm directs strategic conduct at its smaller rivals and succeeds in impairing their ability to compete, or, perhaps, totally excludes them from the market, who should bear the risk of judicial error – the predator or the prey? The answer that the Microsoft prosecution gives – which is part of this case's durable meaning – is that the emergence of a new competitive threat to an entrenched and dominant firm is a competitive moment that warrants protection. Excess caution by enforcers and courts at that moment – for fear of a "false positive" – inherently favors the incumbent at the expense of competition'). Further, see Andrew I. Gavil, 'Exclusionary Distribution Strategies by Dominant Firms: Striking a Better Balance', 72 *Antitrust L.J.* 3, 30–51 (2004); and John J. Flynn, 'Antitrust Policy and the Concept of a Competitive Process', 35 *N. Y.L. Sch. L. Rev.* 893 (1990).

THE ROLE OF THE IP CULTURE

In the US, patents, copyright, and trademarks, as well as antitrust law, are primarily matters of federal law. By contrast, pursuant to Article 345 of the TFUE,[140] in the EU jurisdiction IPRs are only a matter of national law,[141] while competition law is essentially the result of the Communitarian experience. From a comparative perspective,[142] this different distribution of governing law between IPRs and antitrust law produces at least two consequences, a substantial and a jurisdictional one,[143] which helps in explaining why the US and EU experiences about monopolists refusing to license their IPRs diverge as much as they do.

As to the substantial consequence, consider that in the US some IP doctrines, such as patent and copyright misuse,[144] and some IP principles, such as IPRs holders' freedom not to use and license their IPRs, [145] have always played a significant role in the definition of the interface between IPRs and

---

[140] It provides that the Treaty 'shall in no way prejudice the rules in Member States governing the system of property ownership', including IPRs.

[141] The ECJ stated clearly that, 'the determination of the conditions and procedures under which the protection of [European IPRs] is granted is a matter for the national rules of each Member State. It is for the national legislature to determine which products may benefit from protection, even where they form part of a unit which is already protected as such'. See *Volvo*, § 7.

[142] The use of European IPRs as devices to recreate the national divisions between Member States, so preventing the Common Market's development, is one of the 'famous differences' between the US and EU experiences that this book does not address. But that difference explains why in its first judgments the ECJ had an unduly negative attitude towards IPRs that, nevertheless, it later modified. See, in connection with patents and copyright, Case 16/74, *Centrafarm v. Winthrop* [1974] ECR 1183 and Case 15/74, *Centrafarm v Sterling Drug* [1974] ECR 1147, and in connection with trademarks, see Case 40/70, *Sirena Srl v Eda Srl* [1971] ECR 69, Case 192/73, *Van Zuylen Freres v. Hag AG* [1974] ECR 731 and Case 10/89, *SA CNL – SUCAL NV v. Hag GF AG* (*Hag II*) [1990] ECR I-3711.

[143] For a concurring opinion see, e.g., Rita Coco, 'Antitrust Liability for refusal to license Intellectual Property: a Comparative Analysis and the International Setting', 12 *Marq. Intell. Prop. L. Rev*. 1 (2008).

[144] The oldest cases about the interface between patent law and antitrust law were about a patentee which sold its patented good with an unpatented one. They were actually cases of patent misuse that, after the introduction of the Clayton Act, began to be litigated as tying cases. They had a questionable economic basis: from the presumption of monopoly power to the use of the leveraging monopoly theory.

[145] Even if it is not possible to claim a kind of cross-sectional consistency between the different US IPRs, there are some general principles that apply – at least to some extent – to each kind of US IPR. The IPRs holders' freedom not to use/license the IPRs is one of them. See Hovenkamp, Janis, Lemley, *supra* note 5, at §13.2a–b. Nevertheless, in *eBay Inc. v. Mercexchange LLC*, 126 S. Ct. 1837 (2006), the US Supreme Court reversed the Federal Circuit general rule that 'courts will issue permanent injunctions against patent infringement absent exceptional circumstances', 401 F.3d 1323, 1339 (2005). The Supreme Court held that 'a permanent injunction must satisfy a four-factor test before a court may grant such a relief'. In the future, therefore, there could be more room for the application of compulsory licenses from an IP perspective.

antitrust law. Therefore, recently US courts have deemed the content of IP legislation crucial to the solution of antitrust cases.

The present EU equilibrium between IPRs and competition law, instead, results almost entirely from the vision and ideas of competition officers and judges. And that for one thing: the European Commission and the ECJ may enforce their powers vis-à-vis Member States' courts and legislatures, thus making EU competition law prevail over national IP laws, since the EU authorities are in charge of protecting the public interest[146] and of driving the EU integration process. In addition, the absence of EU legislation about IPRs[147] and of a shared and established tradition of EU IP principles reveal the actual weakness of the IP side of the EU interface between antitrust and IP laws. For instance, although a European judge-made misuse doctrine does not exist,[148] the concept of misuse is well-known both to the national courts that apply their national IP law, and to the Commission and the ECJ that apply competition law. Since its first preliminary ruling about patents, indeed, the ECJ has held that the Commission could apply Articles 101 and 102 if the use of the patent were to degenerate into an abuse of the [national] protection.[149] But, interestingly, the ECJ elaborated this concept of the subject matter of IPRs – which shapes the boundaries of the antitrust action by working as the functional equivalent of the US 'IPRs' scope'[150] – without

---

146 Interpreting Article 295, the ECJ held that Member States' constitutions recognize that the exercise of property rights might be restricted in the public interest. See Case 44/79, *Hauer v. Land Rheinland Pfalz*, [1979] ECR 3727. Therefore, in order to legalize the application of competition law to property rights that fall under Article 295, the European Commission assumed that the application of Article 82 aims to protect the general interest in competition as a means, *inter alia*, to create the common market.

147 However, directives and regulations have been enacted in order to harmonize the IP legislation. See, e.g., Council Directive 91/250 of May 14, 1991, on the legal protection of computer programs, OJ 1991 L122/42, replaced in part, OJ 1993 L290/9; Council Regulation 1768/92 of June 1992, concerning the creation of a supplementary protection certificate for medicinal products, OJ 1992 L182/1; Council Directive 93/98 of October 20, 1993, harmonizing the term of protection of copyright and certain related rights, OJ 1993 L290/9; Council Regulation 40/94 of December 20, 1993, on the Community Trade Mark, OJ 1994 L11/1; Council and Parliament Directive 96/9 of March 11, 1996, on the legal protection of databases, OJ 1996 L77/20, and Council and Parliament Directive 98/44 of July 6, 1998, on the legal protection of biotechnological inventions, OJ 1998 L213/3. For a complete list, see Ivo Van Bael & Jean Francois Bellis, *Competition Law of the European Community* 583, nt. 1 (2005). Moreover, the great majority of the current Member States of the EU have signed the European Patent Convention of October 5, 1973.

148 The same conclusion has been reached by James B. Kobak, 'Running the Gauntlet: Antitrust and Intellectual Property Pitfalls on the Two Sides of the Atlantic', 64 *Antitrust L.J.* 341, 355 (1996). Kobak recalls the UK Patent Act, 1977, ch. 32 §44(3) as a statutory form of misuse.

149 Case 24/67, *Parke, Davis and Co. v. Probel, Reese, Beintema-Interpharm and Centrafarm*, February 29, 1968, [1968] ECR 55, 72.

150 For instance, in *Xerox*, the idea of scope of patent is pivotal in understanding which behaviors are lawful.

referring to any IP doctrine. In an analogous way, though it is likely that the US IP principle about IPR holders' freedom not to use and license their IPRs would find a counterpart in each of the 27 Member States, it also likely that there will be many differences among the national IP laws,[151] which would prevent EU institutions from deriving from the IP realm clear answers to competition issues. At the end, therefore, it is not surprising if, in the EU jurisdiction, national IP legislators' words do not receive much credit.[152]

Turning to the jurisdictional consequence, as US IPRs and antitrust law are both federal matters, federal courts are equally competent to judge antitrust law and IP law, so that a previous finding about an IPR may seriously affect the subsequent antitrust analysis, sometimes concluding it.[153] The Commission and the EU courts, in contrast, are not empowered to rule on the validity or infringement of national IPRs, so that sometimes their decisions and judgments seem jeopardized by shaky IPRs that a US federal court might have declared invalid. Therefore,[154] if the Commission had been entitled to void the copyright in *Magill TV* and *IMS Health*, it might have done so, if it had been acting as a US federal court.

This view has sparked some debate as to whether competition law should be used in order to correct the flaws within the IP system, such as overbroad copyright.[155] Some commentators object to such an

---

151 For instance, in Italy the right of a patentee not to use its invention can be limited by its competitors, who may obtain a compulsory license either when the patentee does not use the innovation, or when they have developed a dependent innovation.

152 After all, in deciding *Microsoft IV* the Commission went beyond what it has stated in the Directive about the interoperability information. See Robert J. Hart, 'Interoperability Information and the Microsoft Decision', 28 *E.I.P.R.* 361 (2006) (arguing that 'art. 6 does not open the door to unlimited de compilation and reverse engineering . . . the commission decision, hence, goes beyond the notion of interoperability set out in the directive').

153 It could be the case, for instance, of a refusal to deal based on an invalid patent. In this situation a federal court can solve the potential conflict between an antitrust duty deal doctrine and the IP exclusive right by observing that the IP is illegitimate.

154 This is the thesis of Ian S. Forrester, 'EC Competition Law as a Limitation on the use of IP rights in Europe: Is there Reason to Panic', in *European Competition Law Annual 2003: What is an Abuse of Dominant Position?* 506 (Claus-Dieter Ehlermann & Isabela Atanasiu eds. 2003) and Advocate-General Jacobs' opinion in *Oscar Bronner*, § 63. See, also, Ritter, *supra* at note 122, 286; Meg Buckley, 'Licensing Intellectual Property: Competition and Definitions of Abuse of a Dominant Position in the United States and the European Union', 29 *Brook. J. Int'l L.* 797, 821 (2004); Makan Delrahim, 'Forcing Firms to Share the Sandbox: Compulsory Licensing of Intellectual Property Rights and Antitrust' (2004), available at http://www.justice.gov/atr/public/speeches/203627.htm.

155 See William Cornish & David Llewellyn, *Intellectual Property: Patents, Copyright, Trade Marks and Allied Rights* 755 (2003) (stating that, 'In a period when intellectual property rights are being rapidly expanded, it must be wise for competition authorities to retain some ultimate means of curbing their range in egregious cases, which, in the scramble to satisfy industrial lobbies, legislatures may not have sufficiently cogitated').

approach,[156] and the EU authorities have never recognized it. Nevertheless, such a thesis has two merits: first, it allows *Magill TV* and *IMS Health* to be relegated into a niche. Second, returning to what was said above, it helps to understand that the *Xerox* institutional argument is not easy to endorse when the authorities that are in charge of the protection of competition and the creation of the Common Market – the European Commission and the ECJ – cannot trust and rely with confidence on the IP choices of national legislators.

BOOSTING INNOVATION: THE GREAT DIVERGENCE BETWEEN US AND EU ANTITRUST AUTHORITIES

The previous analysis has shown that, in dealing with cases about monopolists who refused to license their IPRs, both the US courts and the EU antitrust institutions have acknowledged that boosting innovation represents a crucial challenge, which must be enhanced by enforcement of antitrust law. However, while EU institutions struck those refusals, stating that they restricted innovation, US courts deemed them quasi per se legal, maintaining that they enhance innovation. Hence, the resulting transatlantic scenario is idiosyncratic; it being established that encouraging innovation plays a critical role in the enforcement of antitrust law regarding monopolists' refusals to license IPRs, US courts and EU institutions endorse two opposite approaches towards the IP law principle that refusals to share IP proprietary resources do not hurt innovation.

More exactly, looking at the case law about monopolists who refuse to license their IPRs, the US and EU experiences diverge significantly in two respects. EU officers may require dominant firms to share their proprietary inputs in order to support rivals' ability to make their own current products and, if possible, to generate follow-on innovations. US judges generally reject any intrusion of considerations of promoting welfare into business relationships. Moreover, when dealing specifically with incentives to innovate, US and EU competition officers and judges assign a different role to IPRs. The US is willing to preserve the *ex ante* and not a market-specific pattern of incentives created by the IP legislator, even when the IPR holder

---

156 See, e.g., Ariel Katz, 'Intellectual Property Rights and Antitrust Policy: Four Principles for a Complex World', 1 *Journal of Telecommunications & High Technology Law* 325, 351 (2002); Thomas Cotter, 'Intellectual Property and the Essential Facilities Doctrine', 44 *Antitrust Bulletin* 211, 214 and 250 (1999); Carlton, *supra* note 2, at 674; and Lipsky and Sidak, *supra* note 2, at 1218.

is a monopolist and the market in question is favorable to monopolies. The EU, in contrast, is able to make an *ex post* and case-by-case analysis of that pattern of incentives, even though in so doing they run the risk of overturning what national IP legislators chose, and of over-deterring lawful conduct.

Three sets of circumstances have combined to create such a scenario. First, economics does not offer US courts or EU institutions a reliable benchmark about the conditions under which monopolists' refusals to deal can harm dynamic efficiency.[157] Second, while EU institutions can only enforce competition law against IPRs that seem to restrain innovation, US courts can face those problematic IPRs by applying federal IP law. Third, notwithstanding the fact that the 2009 Commission's Communication to some extent fills the gap between US and EU practice about competition law's aims and methodologies, US courts and EU institutions still have a divergent approach towards some topics that affect the enforcement of antitrust law as well as shaping the interface between antitrust law and IP law.

For instance, they have a dissimilar interpretation of the division of power argument; the false-positive mistakes issue; and the role that IP culture should play in IPRs interface with competition law. EU competition authorities seem less respectful of what individual national IP legislators established, perhaps because being communitarian institutions, they enjoy a natural supremacy over national institutions. On the other hand, EU antitrust authorities cannot rely on a strong European IP doctrine to elaborate on as the US courts can do instead. Further, EU institutions seem to assert more confidence in their ability to predict future market developments and to detect a proper distribution of the incentives to innovate than US courts, regardless of any concern about administrability. Indeed, whereas US courts have never dared to impose a duty to deal, arguing that monopolist's rivals can use monopolist's properties better than their legitimate owners can,[158] the EU did embrace such a social planning perspective. In particular, in dealing with IPRs they have at time used competition law to remedy what they considered to be 'IP failures', that is, situations where invoking a supremacy of IP over antitrust would have decreased innovation incentives and undermined the 'correct' innovation path.

[157] Better, Chapter 4's debate about the reliability and enforceability of the most sophisticated versions of the leveraging monopoly theorem shows that economic models do not offer a final answer even about the conditions under which monopolists' refusals harm allocative efficiency. For the same opinion, see, e.g., Stratakis, *supra* note 125, at 436.

[158] *See* David S. Evans & Richard Schmalensee, 'Economic Aspects of Payment Card Systems and Antitrust Policy Toward Joint Ventures', 63 *Antitrust L.J.* 861, 877–8 (1995).

One might wonder whether it could be possible to deal with IPR and, hence, with dynamic efficiency without speculation about innovative paths, which entail such a high risk of false-positive mistakes and such an intrusive role by the public authorities. To put this issue in another way, one could argue that when antitrust law turns to dynamic efficiency considerations, indeterminacy drives antitrust authorities to two opposite approaches: the US 'hands off' rule and the EU 'social planning' attitude.

The following chapter confronts these and other issues in connection to another fundamental right inherent to IPRs: the right to defend them, and the advantages that they entail, via legal actions and some specific administrative procedures.

6. IP judicial and administrative processes

IP AND ANTITRUST APPROACHES TO INFRINGEMENT ACTIONS AND SOME IP ADMINISTRATIVE PROCEDURES

IPR ownership may give access to some otherwise inaccessible 'legal devices' whose existence is intrinsically connected to the architecture of IP regimes. For instance, since IPRs are exclusive rights, their holders can bring specific legal actions, named 'infringement actions', against those who embezzle their inventions and creative works.[1] Analogously, in the highly regulated pharmaceutical industry the mere ownership of a patent may involve some specific administrative procedures – such as the procurement of a supplementary protection certificate (hereinafter, 'SPC')[2] and the listing of a patented drug in the Orange Book[3] – that IP legislators created in order to govern product entrance into that industry.[4]

---

[1] Since the beginning of the XX century the US Supreme Court wrote that, 'the heart of [a patentee's] legal monopoly is the right to invoke the State's power to prevent others from utilizing his discovery without his consent' – see *Crown Die & Tool Co. v. Nye Tool & Machine Works*, 261 U.S. 24, 43 (1923). See, further, Wesley M. Cohen, Richard R. Nelson, John P. Walsh, 'Protecting their Intellectual Assets: Appropriability conditions and why U.S. Manufacturing firms patent (or not)' 25 (2000), available at http://www.nber.org/papers/w7552 (showing that, 'the threat, often implicit, of infringement suits and countersuits underpins almost all the uses of patents, whether to force participation in cross-licensing negotiations in complex product industries, to build patent fences in discrete product industries, or to protect the ability to license or commercialize a new technology in the drug and other industries [. . . so that . . .] patents appear to be used as the basis for either threatening or defending against litigation independent of whether they are considered to be effective in their more conventional applications [. . . as though . . .] they need only confer the right to sue and thus impose the costs of litigation and possible injunctive relief on rivals').

[2] As to SPC see the previous Chapter 3.

[3] In the US the Federal Food, Drug, and Cosmetic Act (FDCA – 21 U.S.C. § 301 et seq.) imposes that any company seeking approval to sell a new drug must submit a New Drug Application (NDA) to the FDA showing that the new drug is safe and effective for its proposed use. But the Drug Price Competition and Patent Restoration Act – commonly known as the Hatch-Waxman Act (21 U.S.C. § 355 et seq.) – establishes a cheaper and quicker procedure to obtain such marketing approval for a generic version of an already approved brand product. Under this scheme a company that develops generic products that are *bioequivalent* to the corresponding brand products can submit an Abbreviated New Drug Application

At least for IP legislators, these 'legal devices' are supposed to be beneficial for the whole society, except for the case when IPR holders use them in a fraudulent manner. In other words, when firms that hold IPRs knowingly and willfully misrepresent their rights, or another firm's mischief, they misuse the legal tools that support their IPRs.[5] Therefore, from the IP standpoint, there are two kinds of infringement actions and IP administrative procedures aimed at regulating entrance into an industry (hereinafter say simply 'IP administrative procedures'): valid ones, which are welcomed as structural bricks supporting IP regimes, and fraudulent ones, which in contrast deserve to be prohibited by IP enforcers.[6]

Instead, when it comes to dominant firms that either bring infringement actions[7] or enforce IP administrative procedures, one should wonder

---

(ANDA) relying on the safety and efficacy data obtained from the branded product's tests. In particular, a generic producer may seek marketing approval before the expiration of the corresponding patent listed in the *Orange Book* (the official list of *Approved Drug Products with Therapeutic Equivalence Evaluations*), if she states on factual and legal bases that the patent is invalid and/or she will not infringe it. In that case, the patentee has 45 days to initiate a patent infringement suit against the generic manufacturer. The filing of such an infringement suit triggers a 30-month stay of the FDA approval. Therefore, an incumbent may use both the fraudulent listing of an invalid patent in the Orange Book, and a non-genuine patent suit against the generic producer, so to prevent her competitors' entrance into the market.

4 Actually, it is not difficult to imagine that in several other industries there are administrative procedures that preside over firms' entrance. For example – as Lars Noah, 'Sham petitioning as a threat to the integrity of the regulatory process', 74 *N.C. L. Rev.* 1, 13 (1995) noticed – there are numerous US agencies that apply this sort of procedures. Think, for instance, of the Interstate Commerce Commission (ICC), the Federal Communications Commission (FCC), the Federal Energy Regulatory Commission (FERC), the Nuclear Regulatory Commission (NRC), the Food and Drug Administration (FDA), the United States Department of Agriculture (USDA), the old Civil Aeronautics Board (CAB), the United States Department of Commerce, and the Federal Reserve Board. Moreover, see Milton Handler & Richard A. De Sevo, 'The Noerr Doctrine and Its Sham Exception', 6 *Cardozo L. Rev.* 1, 20 (1984) (observing that '[t]he largest number of suits raising [these] issues [have] concerned the petitioning of administrative bodies'). Nevertheless, IP law is not really involved in these other industries that, thus, do not represent the focus of this chapter.

5 The chapter does not discuss when infringement actions violate IP law and, more in general, it does not discuss the US misuse doctrine. In the EU jurisdiction, indeed, a real misuse doctrine does not exist. For an examination of the former see, among others, Thomas F. Cotter, 'Misuse' (2007), available at www.ssrn.com.

6 For the term 'fraudulent actions' see Christopher C. Klein, 'The Economics of Sham Litigation: Theory, Cases, and Policy, Bureau of Economics Staff' – Report to the Federal Trade Commission 20 (1989), available at www.ftc.gov. Further, consider that most work to date focuses on so-called 'strike suits' – cases in which a plaintiff files knowing her suit is frivolous. See Robert G. Bone, 'Modeling Frivolous Suits', 145 *U. Pa. L. Rev.* 519, 523 (1997).

7 In other words, this chapter considers when the IP-defendant can countersue the IP-plaintiff, who is a monopolist, alleging that the infringement action violates the antitrust law. Indeed – as Esther H. Steinhauer, 'Is Noerr-Pennington Immunity Still a Viable Defense Against Antitrust Claims Arising From Hatch-Waxman Litigation?', 61

– as Chapter 2 explained – if these dominant firms' practices might be employed to shelter market power and harm consumer welfare, regardless of whether they are fraudulent or not.

This chapter, first, uses economics in order to understand when infringement actions and IP administrative procedures satisfy the two-pronged standard for assessing monopolists' unlawful conduct. Then, it looks at the legal rules that the US and EU antitrust authorities, respectively, endorsed in examining dominant firms' infringement actions and IP administrative procedures. It concludes that, in this area, the US and EU approaches mainly converge, in trying to guarantee legal certainty by driving under the antitrust scrutiny actions and processes that either are fraudulent, or amount to mere sham.

Food and Drug Law Journal 679, 680 (2006) noticed in speaking about the pharmaceutical industry – in the US it is now common that antitrust claims will be filed ancillary to patent litigation against the pharmaceutical patentee, either during the infringement action itself or in subsequent class action suits. This chapter does not discuss the case when antitrust countersuits are, in turn, anticompetitive, though this analysis would teach that when judges easily admit antitrust counterclaims, the incentives to protect IPRs decrease. See, indeed, David R. Steinman & Danielle S. Fitzpatrick, 'Antitrust Counterclaims in Patent Infringement Cases: A Guide to Walker Process and Sham-Litigation Claims', 10 *Tex. Intell. Prop. L.J.* 95, 96 (2001) (arguing that 'the mere threat of treble damages, coupled with the loss of patent rights, obviously raises the stakes for patent holders pursuing infringement claims'); and for a further analysis of this topic see, e.g., Christopher C. Klein, 'Strategic Sham Litigation: Economic Incentives in the Context of the Case Law', 6 *International Review of Law and Economics* 241 (1986); William F. Shughart II, 'Private Antitrust Enforcement: Compensation, Deterrence, or Extortion?', 13 *Regulation* 53 (1990); R. Preston McAfee, Hugo M. Mialon, Sue H. Mialon, 'Private Antitrust Litigation: Procompetitive or Anticompetitive?' (2005) available at http://userwww.service.emory.edu/~hmialon/PrivateAntitrustEnforcementProOrAntiCompetitive.pdf. Further, as one of the chapter's focuses is on monopolists' conduct, it does not address whether either the IP-defendant would be interested in suing or settling, or whether the achieved IP-settlement could harm consumer welfare. In other words, consider Steven C. Salop & Lawrence J. White, 'Economic Analysis of Private Antitrust Litigation', 74 *Geo. L.J.* 1001, 1116 (1986) (arguing that, 'private litigation is part of a larger overall system consisting of four distinct phases – the business conduct of potential litigants; the suing decisions of potential plaintiffs; the settlement offers of the litigants once a dispute has arisen; and the litigation strategies and expenditures of both parties if settlement cannot be reached'). The main focus of this chapter is on the suing decision of the incumbent that holds an IPR and somehow on its choice to settle in order to skip the litigation costs (see also infra notes 19 ff. and accompanying text). See for a deeper analysis of the reasons why an IP-defendant prefers settling rather than going to the court, the recent William M. Landes, 'Empirical Analysis Of Intellectual Property Litigation: Some Preliminary Results', 41 *Hous. L. Rev.* 749 (2004). While on the anticompetitive nature of IP settlements see, e.g., Daniel A. Crane, 'Exit Payments in Settlement of Patent Infringement Lawsuits: Antitrust Rules and Economic Implications', 54 *Fla. L. Rev.* 747, 748 (2002) and Timothy J. Muris, 'Generic Pharmaceuticals: Marketplace Access and Consumer Issues: Hearing Before the S. Comm. on Commerce, Science & Transportation', 107th Cong. 23–24 (2002), available at http://www.ftc.gov/os/2002/04/pharmatestimony.htm.

THE ECONOMIC PERSPECTIVE: IP ADMINISTRATIVE PROCEDURES

Broadly speaking, since governmental decisions can be powerful factors affecting market performance, firms may attempt to use governmental coercive powers against their rivals. For instance, since all sorts of government activities place some firms at an advantage over others, firms can lobby to change legislation in their favor:[8] they can secure the use of particular resources and technologies, the increase in the minimum industry wage, or the adoption of costly regulations (e.g. safety and environmental regulations). Nevertheless, the power to lobby does not rest with either monopoly power or IPRs ownership: any kind of firm can try to influence legislators,[9] in some cases acting together.

On the contrary, only incumbents in regulated industries can use a variety of administrative procedures to delay, or perhaps completely prevent, market entry by potential competitors,[10] as pharmaceutical firms that hold patented and branded drugs actually do, often using IP-specific processes, such as the listing of a particular drug in the Orange Book and the procurement of a SPC.[11]

Now, these procedures are inherently exclusionary,[12] because IP legislators themselves conceived them in order to prevent generic drug

---

[8] See, e.g., Robert H. Bork, *The Antitrust Paradox* 347–49 (1993).

[9] See, e.g., James C. Miller III & Paul Pautler, 'Predation: The Changing View in Economics and the Law', 28 *Journal of Law and Economics* 495 (1985); and Ralph Winter, 'The Use of Adjudicative Processes to Injure Competitors', in *The Political Economy of Regulation: Private Interests in the Regulatory Process* 278 (FTC Law & Econ. Conf., 1984).

[10] See, e.g., Lars Noah, *supra* note 4, at 1; Bruce M. Owen & Ronald Braeutigam, *The Regulation Game: Strategic Use of the Administrative Process* 2–5 (1978); Thomas A. Balmer, 'Sham Litigation and the Antitrust Laws', 29 *Buff. L. Rev.* 39, 39 (1980); Einer Elhauge, 'Making Sense of Antitrust Petitioning Immunity', 80 *Cal. L. Rev.* 1177, 1229 (1992); and Frank H. Easterbrook, 'Petitioning for Protection from Competition: A Comment', in *The Political Economy of Regulation* 93, 98 (FTC Law & Econ. Conf., 1984) (arguing that, 'the incumbents in an industry may have scored a political victory, the essence of which was the creation of a cumbersome administrative process that could be invoked to retard entry').

[11] *For a recent survey of the FTC's actions in the pharmaceutical industry see Overview Office Antitrust Actions In Health Care Services And Products, Health Care Services and Products Division Bureau of Competition Federal Trade Commission Washington D.C. 20580, David R. Pender, Markus H. Meier Deputy, October 2005; and EU Commission, Sector Inquiry,* on July 8, 2009 available at http://ec.europa.eu/competition/sectors/pharmaceuticals/inquiry/index.html.

[12] See, e.g., Melissa K. Davis, 'Monopolistic Tendencies of Brand-Name Drug Companies in Pharmaceutical Industry', 15 *J.L.& COM.* 357, 363–5 (1995); James Perrine, 'Defining the Sham Litigation to the Noerr-Pennington Antitrust Immunity Doctrine: An Analysis of the *Professional Real Estate Investors v. Columbia Pictures Industries* Decision' 46 *ALA. L. Rev.* 815 (1995); and Natalie M. Derzko, 'The Impact of Recent Reforms of the Hatch-Waxman Scheme on Orange Book Strategic Behavior and Pharmaceutical Innovation', 45 *IDEA* 165, 176 (2005).

companies from entering into the market before the relevant patent has expired. Further, they are very likely to harm consumer welfare because, as several empirical studies show, when generic drug producers enter the monopolized market, the market price of the patented drug falls dramatically.[13]

Therefore, since these IP administrative procedures both strengthen market power and harm consumer welfare, antitrust authorities could enforce Section 2 and article 102 against monopolists that employ them, regardless of whether they are valid or fraudulent.

Actually, as the following sections show, it does not happen, unless the procedures in question either are fraudulent or amount to mere sham. In these two scenarios, indeed, manipulated procedures do not offer any countervailing virtue – such as the protection of well-functioning IP regimes – to oppose the anticompetitive foreclosure that they produce.

INFRINGEMENT ACTIONS

Differently from the above described IP administrative procedures, infringement actions are not inherently exclusionary. Yet, under specific conditions, monopolists can employ them in order to foreclose their actual and potential rivals or,[14] at least, in order to increase their costs.[15] For instance, when the intellectual good in question represents a competitive advantage, such as a product that consumers appreciate a lot, or a cost-reducing

---

[13] In other words, consumers benefit greatly from the availability of generic drugs, which are far cheaper than their corresponding brand name versions. Brand name drug companies lose an estimated half of their US sales during the first six months of generic production alone. See Gardiner Harris, Chris Adams, 'Drug Manufacturers Step Up Legal Attacks That Slow Generics', *Wall St. J.*, July 12, 2001, at A1; *User Fees for Prescription Drugs: Hearing Before the Sub-commission on Health and the Environment of the House Comm. on Energy and Commerce*, 102d Cong., 2d Sess. 10 (1992), where David A. Kessler (then Commissioner of FDA) stated, 'for a drug that raises $200 million a year in annual sales, assuming an 80 percent gross margin, every additional month of delay the Agency takes to review an application would cost the company about $10 million in lost opportunity'; and FTC, *Generic Drug Entry: Prior to Patent Expiration: An FTC Study*, 9 (2002) (reporting that the average generic price was half that of the brand name version, and that the availability of generic drugs saved consumers between $8 to $10 billion in 1994), available at www.ftc.gov/os/2002/07/genericdrugstudy.pdf. Because so much is at stake, it should not marvel that manufacturers of brand name drugs would do everything in their power to thwart or delay a generic drug's entry into the market. By the same token, hence, it should not marvel that the fraudulent administrative procedures that shelter the monopolized market from new entrants do harm consumer welfare.

[14] See James D. Hurwitz & Debra Simmons Neveu, 'The Noerr Doctrine: Its Significance and Current Interpretation', in *The Political Economy of Regulation: Private Interests in The Regulatory Process* 33 (FTC Law & Econ. Conf., 1984).

[15] See, e.g., James D Hurwitz, 'Abuse of Governmental Processes, the First Amendment, and the Boundaries of Noerr', 74 *Georgetown Law Journal* 65, at 70 (1985).

process, a winning infringement action that prevents dominant firms' rivals from enjoying the intellectual resource may exclude rivals from the market or, at least, may relegate them to act in a market niche. Alternatively, a dominant firm can succeed in using legal actions as credible entry deterrence tools, when time after time it establishes a reputation for forcing each of its potential competitors to face it in courts[16] – a reputation that is credible since the monopoly income that the incumbent could lose because of the entrance is larger than the income that the potential entrant could gain thanks to the entrance.[17] Else, monopolists' infringement suits can serve to raise rivals' costs, because they cast upon defendants significant and asymmetric costs: on the one hand, IPR holders may replicate the same claim against each of their rivals, thus diminishing the costs of the claim; on the other hand, the rival, if smaller, can distribute its costs only over a smaller output.[18]

After all, setting aside the fact that many charges are easier to make than to refute,[19] broadly speaking defendants not only endure monetary costs, such as lawyers' and experts' fees, trial costs, and other miscellaneous expenses, but they also bear, even before the end of a trial, indirect costs such as, for instance, an adverse effect on reputation or a decrease in credit

---

[16] In other words, an infringement action can work as a strategic entry barrier, i.e. a barrier 'purposely erected to reduce the possibility of entry'. Suppose that before the potential competitor takes her entry decision the dominant firm has already committed resources in litigation, the entry is discouraged: 'by making binding commitments and communicating them during the pre-entry period, a strategically minded established firm is able to exploit its leadership role. If the commitments imply negative profits to the entrant in the post-entry game, then entry will be successfully deterred'. And, indeed, for a potential competitor the possibility of being sued entails negative profits. The quotations are all taken from Steven C. Salop; David T. Scheffman, 'Raising Rivals' Costs', 73 *The American Economic Review* 267, 269 (1983).

[17] Julio R. Robledo, 'Strategic Patents and Asymmetric Litigation Costs as Entry Deterrence Instruments', 15 *Economics Bulletin* 1, 2 (2005). Indeed Hurwitz, *supra* note 15, at 73 and 75 (noticing that, 'fostering a reputation for predatory conduct that induces potential entrants to opt for other investment possibilities' is a way that an incumbent may use for abusing governmental processes in order to insulate its market position from future challenge. In this regard, it has been argued that the very same creation of a reputation of aggressive behavior against entrants can represent the collateral goal of a strategic litigation). Moreover, for the literature about the role of reputation in predatory practices see, e.g., Joseph F. Brodley, Patrick Bolton, Michael H. Riordan, 'Predatory Pricing: Strategic Theory and Legal Policy', 88 *Geo. L. J.* 2241, 2300–2301; Richard Posner, *Antitrust Law: An Economic Perspective* 184–7 (1976); Frederic M. Scherer, *Industrial Market Structure and Economic Performance* 559–60 (2d ed. 1980); Oliver E. Williamson, 'Dominant Firms and the Monopoly Problem: Market Failure Considerations', 85 *Harv. L. Rev.* 1512, 1521–2 (1972).

[18] Herbert Hovenkamp, 'Post-Chicago Antitrust: A Review and Critique', 2001 *Colum. Bus. L. Rev.* 257, 277 (2001).

[19] See Bork, *supra* note 8, at 348 (observing that, if the strategy's target is a firm seeking to enter the market, 'it bears the burden of going forward with evidence' and, therefore, 'litigation expenses may be much heavier for him').

rating.[20] In addition, IP-defendants are burdened with some IP-specific costs. Even before the trial's beginning, the IPR holder may both divert the defendant's clients by menacing them with a lawsuit, and use a preliminary injunction to block the defendant's production and sales of the proprietary resource.[21] In addition, during the IP-trial, the defendant may sustain the costs of revealing sensitive information, such as information about its new products and industrial processes, marketing strategies, business plan, and customer lists. Finally, if the litigation ends in favor of the plaintiff, the defendant is obliged to support further post-trial expenses that arise not only from damages, but also from the final injunction not to use, produce, and market the proprietary resource.[22] In this last circumstance, even if the final injunction does not push the defendant out of the market, it can harm it nonetheless by relegating the defendant to employ inferior or less-appreciated products and processes so increasing its costs.

In summary, although infringement actions are not exclusionary by definition, monopolists can employ them as non-price strategic tools aimed at foreclosing actual and potential competitors or, at least, at increasing their costs.

Yet, as said many times in the previous chapters, since exclusionary behaviors do not necessarily harm consumer welfare, antitrust authorities should not prosecute them without any further inquiry about their impact on such economic variable.

As to infringement actions, economic models do not state definitely when they produce a negative impact on consumer welfare. For instance, the traditional economic model of litigation explains why a rational agent decides to sue[23] – specifically, the economic model observes that the agent deems a suit 'rational' when the expected[24] value of a favorable judgment[25]

---

20 See Gary Myers, 'Litigation as a Predatory Practice', 80 *Ky. L.J.* 565, 591(1992).

21 True, in the event of the plaintiff's losing it is possible for the defendant to recoup such pre-trial costs, but probably this recoupment will not be complete and will be time-consuming, so that meanwhile the incumbent will benefit from the raising costs strategy.

22 A final injunction will order the defendant not to carry on with certain activities such as the use, the production, and the marketing of the proprietary resource. It can also be equipped with the delivery or destruction of infringing articles.

23 The first law and economics studies about litigation were those of William M. Landes, 'An Economic Analysis of the Courts', 14 *Journal of Law and Economics* 61, (1971); John P. Gould, 'The Economics of Legal Conflicts', 2 *Journal of Legal Studies* 279 (1973); and Steven Shavell, 'Suit, Settlement, and Trial: A Theoretical Analysis under Alternative Methods for the Allocation of Legal Costs', 2 *Journal of Legal Studies* 55 (1982) (endorsing the so-called 'single-person decision-making approach', here applied).

24 After all, litigation is a risky business. Both parties face uncertainty over the probability that a trial will occur and its outcome. To the extent that the plaintiff is risk averse, this uncertainty reduces his incentive to sue by increasing the overall variance of the returns from going to court.

25 The expected value of a favorable judgment amounts to the value of the injunctive

is greater than its material costs[26] [27] and concludes that whereas rational suits are welfare-increasing by definition, strategic lawsuits[28] – such as those previously described – can harm consumer welfare,[29] at least because of the dissipation of resources that they entail.[30]

---

reliefs together with the value of the expected damages awarded, both multiplied by the subjective probability of winning. In other words, it is the value of stopping third parties from exploiting the IPR, via the enforcement of the available IP-remedies, namely: preliminary injunctions, damages, and final injunctions.

[26] In particular, when it turns to IPRs these material costs are deemed to be substantial. For instance, it has been shown that a patent infringement case can cost, on average, about $2 million for each party when there is $1 million to $25 million at risk. See American Intellectual Property Law Association, 'Report of the Economic Survey' 22 (2003), available at http://www.aipla.org.

[27] In formulas, given λ the infringement action, say $\delta B(\lambda)$ the plaintiff expected value of the infringement suit, where δ is the probability of the plaintiff's victory and $B(\lambda)$ is the victory's benefit, and say $C(\lambda)$ the action material costs. The infringement action will be rational when $\delta B(\lambda) > C(\lambda)$.

[28] Broadly speaking a firm is said to bring a strategic infringement action when it knows that the litigation will produce an additional benefit – say, $AB(\lambda)$ – that does not rest with the dispute's merits. The introduction of strategic considerations into firms' decisions, indeed, does not entail abandoning the assumption of profit maximization. The difference consists in the fact that the inequality's outcome will depend on the amount of the additional benefit. See Bone, *supra* note 6, at 534 (observing that, 'occasionally plaintiffs file meritless suits . . . hoping to secure some political or business advantage . . . [or] to delay hostile takeovers, scuttle a competitor's business plans, frustrate a project or political cause, or embarrass a political opponent or personal enemy'). Such an additional benefit, the so-called 'indirect effect' or 'collateral goal' – see Klein, *supra* note 6, at 11 – may also consist of a simple rent, namely in a wealth transfer from the defendant to the plaintiff. Further, there are several ways to gain this rent. It is possible that the plaintiff forced the defendant to conclude an otherwise inconvenient cross-licensing agreement – see, in this regard, Eric von Hippel, *The Sources of Innovation* 53 (1988). Differently, as noticed by Bone, *supra* note 6, at 529, 'when litigation costs exceed the expected value of trial, a rational plaintiff will never actually try the case, unless she has a good chance of obtaining a settlement'. This same opinion about the interest in using litigation as a vehicle to reach a settlement has been expressed when speaking specifically about IP litigation by Michael J. Meurer, 'Controlling Opportunistic and Anti-Competitive Intellectual Property Litigation' (2003), available at www.ssrn.com, and Joseph Farrell, Robert P. Merges, 'Incentives To Challenge And Defend Patents: Why Litigation Won't Reliably Fix Patent Office Errors And Why Administrative Patent Review Might Help' (2004), available at www.ssrn.com. Moreover, it has been argued that the collateral benefit that a plaintiff can earn from a strategic infringement action can be equal to the difference between 'the losses awarded under U.S. case law' about patents and the losses 'that economic models of competition indicate would allow patent holders to just capture the social value of their innovations.' – see Bryan R. Krouse, Clement G. Krouse, 'Patent Infringement: Lessons from Industrial Economics', 4 *Journal of Industry, Competition and Trade* 191 (2004).

[29] A strategic litigation aimed at extracting rents is usually named 'opportunistic litigation' – see Meurer, *supra* note 28, at 4 – and does not fall into the antitrust scope until it does not affect, at least, market price and output. For instance, it is likely that small firms' strategic lawsuits are opportunistic but not anticompetitive pursuant to Section 2 and Article 102.

[30] See Myers, *supra* note 20, at 603–604; Meurer, *supra* note 28, at 10; and Hurwitz, Simmons Neveu, *supra* note 14, at 38 (arguing that manipulating governmental processes 'may lead to dead-weight loss arising from reduced output, higher prices, and the dissipation of additional resources to maintain ill-gained market power.').

Nevertheless, as Chapter 2 explained while speaking about the 'but for test', an approach that is focused upon the distinction between rational and strategic behaviors is at the same time both under- and over-inclusive. Indeed, the twofold assumption that rational behaviors are welfare-increasing by definition while strategic behaviors are welfare-decreasing just because they entail wasteful expenses is too absolute: first, there are behaviors that do not entail significant expenses but that do harm consumer welfare, and there are as well brainless behaviors that do not harm consumer welfare, even though they do entail excessive costs; second, the easier distinction between rational and strategic actions is difficult to administer, as it requires judges and officers to inquire deeply about the costs of the monopolist.[31]

Therefore, antitrust authorities confronting dominant firms' infringement actions have no conclusive yardstick for identifying those among them that harm consumer welfare. Notwithstanding that, as the following sections show, what remains is that fraudulent and strategic infringement actions deserve, at least, to be subject to the antitrust scrutiny. They, indeed, do not contribute to the well-functioning of IP regimes.

THE LEGAL PERSPECTIVE: THE US AND EU RIGHTS OF PETITIONING AND THEIR EXCEPTIONS

The right to sue and the right to bring an administrative procedure enjoy constitutional protection on both sides of the Atlantic Ocean, as they are included in the right of petitioning, which reflects two important values. First, it ensures the existence of a communication channel between the citizens, on the one hand, and the government, on the other, so that the government can decide and act in an informed way.[32] Second, it guarantees citizens the right to present grievances to the government, provided that the nature of the grievance is addressed by the governmental agency which is petitioned.

In the United States the First Amendment to the Constitution declares broadly that the Congress shall make no law abridging the right to petition

---

[31] See, e.g., See Herbert Hovenkamp, 'The Harvard and Chicago Schools and the Dominant Firm', in *How the Chicago School Overshot the Mark* 109, 115–16 (Robert Pitofsky ed. 2008) (arguing that 'supplying false information or failing to disclose important information to a government official or standard-setting organization need not cost any more than supplying truthful information, but can create monopoly under appropriate circumstances.'); and Robert O'Donoghue & Jorge A. Padilla, *The Law and Economics of Article* 82 188 (2004).

[32] For the discussion of the role of discretion in the authorities decision-making process see footnotes 77 ff. and the accompanying text.

the government for a redress of grievances and,[33] as courts and administrative agencies are parts of the government, it encompasses as well the right of access to courts and other adjudicatory processes. Then, the *Noerr-Pennington doctrine* – a judicial-made doctrine – specifically protects those who petition the government from federal antitrust liability. After the two landmark cases – *Noerr* and *Pennington* – that concern the right to influence legislative and executive actions,[34] the Supreme Court extended the immunity to adjudicative proceedings before agencies and courts with *California Motor Transport Co. v. Trucking Unlimited*.[35] Hence, nowadays the doctrine holds that, pursuant to the First Amendment, 'genuine efforts' to affect governmental processes cannot be deemed antitrust violations, even if they plainly restrain competition or result in a monopoly, unless these attempts are a 'mere sham', i.e. attempts to interfere directly with the competitor's business using what is actually nothing more than harassment.[36]

---

[33] U.S. Const. amend. I, cl. 6. This right, along with the rights of freedom of speech, association, and assembly, is part of the broad right of expression. It guarantees an open line of communication between the people and the government so that the former can 'expose governmental waste and misconduct and [. . .] express their sentiments without resorting to violence', while the latter can 'obtain the information it needs to represent the interest of the people'. See Daniel R. Fischel, 'Antitrust Liability for Attempts to Influence Government Action: The Basis and Limits of the Noerr-Pennington Doctrine', 45 *U. Chi. L. Rev.* 80, 101 (1977).

[34] Respectively, 365 U.S. 127 (1961) and 381 U.S. 657 (1965). Namely, in *Noerr* a group of truckers alleged that a group of railroads hired a public relations firm to run a publicity campaign designed to influence public opinion, in support of legislation favouring railroads at the expense of trucker. Here the Supreme Court ruled that this activity could not be challenged under the Sherman Act, regardless of any resulting restraint of trade, even if those activities were fraudulent or deceptive, at 142. Yet, it stated that 'there may be situations in which a publicity campaign ostensibly directed toward influencing governmental action, is a mere sham to cover what is actually nothing more than an, attempt to interfere with the business relationships of competitor and the application of the Sherman Act would be justified', at 144. In *Pennington* the Court extended the antitrust immunity to the attempts to persuade officers of the executive branch of government. It was alleged that a conspiracy of UMW officials and large coal producers persuaded the State Secretary of Labour to set a minimum wage for employees of contractors selling coal to TVA. The Court held that such a behavior did not violate the Sherman Act, as it involved the act of a government official 'who is not claimed to be a co-conspirator'. On the Noerr-Pennington doctrine see, e.g., Earl W. Kintner & Joseph P. Bauer, 'Antitrust Exemptions for Private Requests for Governmental Action: A Critical Analysis of the Noerr-Pennington Doctrine', 17 *U.C. Davis L. Rev.* 549 (1984); Gary Minda, 'Interest Groups, Political Freedom, and Antitrust: A Modern Reassessment of the Noerr-Pennington Doctrine', 41 *Hastings L.J.* 905 (1990).

[35] 404 U.S. 508, 510 (1972).

[36] On this topic see, e.g., Carol Rice Andrews, 'After BE & K: The 'Difficult Constitutional Question' of Defining the First Amendment Right to Petition Courts', 39 *Houston L. Rev.* 1299 (2003) and James B. Kobak, Jr., 'Professional Real Estate Investors and the Future of Patent-Antitrust Litigation: Walker Process and Handgards Meet Noerr-Pennington', 63 *Antitrust L.J.* 185 (1994) (stating that, 'the . . . *Noerr-Pennington* doctrine is the legal system's effort to ease [the] tension' that arises when ' the exercise of rights that are fundamental to our

Analogously, in the European Union it is article 47 of the *Charter of Fundamental Rights of the European Union* that establishes that everyone whose rights and freedoms guaranteed by the law of the Union are violated has the right to an effective remedy before a tribunal,[37] where the notion of tribunal encompasses administrative agencies as well as courts. Even before the *Charter* acquired its direct binding force with the Treaty of Lisbon,[38] the compulsory meaning of article 47 was undisputed. Indeed, not only is article 47 based on article 13 of the *European Convention on Human Rights* that all EU Member States signed, but every EU Member State recognizes citizens' right to petition courts and administrative bodies to redress their injuries. Thus, in EU also the right to petition represents a general principle of law that enjoys a constitutional dignity.

Further – although EU case law about the right of petitioning is not as well as established and developed as in the US[39] – in the *French-West African ship-owners' Committees* decision, the European Commission avowed a principle that evokes the holdings of *Noerr* and *Pennington*, namely that firms may try to influence the EU and national authorities to enact legislation in their favor,[40] in some cases, even acting together.[41] Further, the European Court of Justice affirmed the freedom to petition legislative bodies in two different judgments, *Cimenteries* and *Compagnie Maritime Belge*.[42] Looking at the adjudicatory sphere, in the *Hilti* and *IPS* cases the community institutions implicitly suggested that a firm's efforts[43] to influence administrative authorities are not anticompeti-

political system may undermine the competitive process that is fundamental to our economic system').

[37] OJ 2000/C 364/01, 18 December 2000.

[38] Indeed, article 6(2) of the Treaty on European Union states that, 'The Union shall respect fundamental rights, as guaranteed by the European Convention for the Protection of Human Rights and Fundamental Freedoms signed in Rome on 4 November 1950 and as they result from the constitutional traditions common to the Member States, as general principles of Community law'.

[39] See, for a discussion of the right to lobby and petition in EU, Adrian J. Vossestein, 'Corporate Efforts to Influence Public Authorities, and the EC rules on Competition', 37 *Common Market Law Review* 1383 (2000).

[40] See EC Commission Decision, OJ L 134/1, April 1 1992, [1992], § 68.

[41] Indeed, in *Cement* the Commission stated that, 'the Commission does of course recognize the right of undertakings not only to notify the competent authorities (including the Commission itself) of any infringements of national or community provisions, but also to make a joint approach for this purpose, which necessarily presupposes the ability to hold preparatory discussions amongst themselves' – Commission Decisions, 8 November 1994, OJ 1994, L 343/1, § 53.

[42] CFI, Case T-25/95, [2000] ECR II-00491; and CG, Case C-395/96, [2000] ECR I-01365.

[43] Again, for the discussion of the role of discretion in the authorities' decision-making process see footnotes 77 ff. and the accompanying text: it is ultimately the State (and not the companies) that, via its own conduct, decides whether or not to restrict competition.

tive.[44] Moreover, the Commission first, and the Court of First Instance next, established expressly that it is only in *exceptional circumstances* that by bringing legal proceedings firms can abuse their dominant positions within the meaning of Article 102 of the Treaty.[45]

As a whole, on both sides of the Atlantic Ocean, any allegations of abuse, of either a legal action or an administrative procedure, must be considered as an exception to the general power of citizens to ask for redress of grievances. Yet, this exception needs not to be strictly interpreted, because in the adjudicatory sphere the risk of chilling the right to address courts and administrative authorities is quite low. First, the adjudicatory system is already under several restrictions, with roots in tort law and civil procedure, which do not unduly deter citizens from claiming restoration of wrongs. Moreover, while the political arena needs open streams of information between the government and citizens that might be chilled by antitrust liability, courts and administrative bodies are not supposed to host debates.[46]

THE US EXPERIENCE ABOUT DOMINANT FIRMS' INFRINGEMENT ACTIONS

US courts addressing monopolists' infringement actions do not focus on the conditions that must occur in order to show that these lawsuits shelter market power and harm consumer welfare. Rather, their analyses pivot around the circumstances that must be met in order to strip away the Constitutional immunity.

As to what represents an exception to the First Amendment, *Professional Real Estate Investors* (*PREI*)[47] is the landmark case. In *PREI*, which was

---

[44] Case T-30/89, *Hilti AG v. Commission,* [1991] ECR II-1439, § 99; and EC Commission, *XXVIth Report on Competition Policy 1996*, at §§ 157–8.

[45] Case T-111/96, *ITT Promedia NV v. EC Commission*, [1998] ECR II-2937, § 60.

[46] See Marina Lao, *Reforming the Noerr-Pennington Antitrust Immunity Doctrine*, 55 Rutgers L. Rev. 965, 1009–1010 (2003); David McGowan & Mark A. Lemley, 'Antitrust Immunity: State Action and Federalism, Petitioning and the First Amendment', 17 *Harv. J.L. & Pub. Pol'y* 293, 392 (1994) and Frederic Schauer, 'Fear, Risk and the First Amendment: Unraveling the "Chilling Effect"', 58 *B.U. L. Rev.* 685, 689–94 (1978).

[47] 508 U.S. 49 (1993) where Columbia Pictures, the copyright owner of many movies, brought a copyright infringement suit against a hotel operator group, Professional Real Estate Investors (PRE), for renting copyrighted videodiscs to hotel guests for in-room viewing. PRE filed an antitrust counterclaim asserting that the copyright suit 'was a mere sham that cloaked underlying acts' and that it violated the Sherman Act. The theory of the antitrust counterclaim was that Columbia Pictures 'did not honestly believe that the infringement claim was meritorious', but had used the suit as an anticompetitive weapon against *PREI.* On this topic see Robert J. Hoerner, 'Bad Faith Enforcement of Patents – Antitrust Considerations', 55

a judgment about a copyright infringement suit, the Supreme Court imposed order on the previously chaotic case law about sham petitioning in the adjudicatory realm, establishing a two-phase test for determining whether a single lawsuit,[48] or an administrative procedure, is a sham.[49] The Court stated that an act of petitioning an adjudicatory authority is a sham when the action is 'objectively baseless', that is to say, when no reasonable litigant could have realistically expected success on the merits;[50] and when the action has been brought in order to interfere with the business relationships of a competitor. Justice Thomas's opinion thus required an antitrust plaintiff (the monopolist's rival and IP defendant) both to demonstrate that the antitrust defendant (the monopolist and IP plaintiff) did not have a probable legal cause for suing, and to show that the litigation's aim was to harass the IP defendant (its rival in the market). More exactly, the Supreme Court held that the 'objectively baseless' requirement renders irrelevant any evidence regarding the original motivation of the dominant firm that brought the infringement action. In other words, it established that any economic consideration, indeed, can play a role only when the challenged litigation is objectively meritless and the court has to examine the litigant's subjective motivation. Only under such a hypothesis can the court wonder

Antitrust L.J. 421, 422–3 (1986) and David A. Balto & Andrew M. Wolman, 'Intellectual Property and Antitrust: General Principles', 43 *IDEA* 395, 459–65 (2003).

48 It has been discussed whether the charge of sham litigation can regard even an isolated lawsuit, or must concern a pattern of baseless, repetitive claims. The issue arises from the interpretation that lower courts did of what Justice Douglas stated in *California Motor Transport*. There, Justice Douglas observed that, 'one claim, which a court or agency may think baseless, may go unnoticed; but a pattern of baseless, repetitive claims may emerge which leads the fact-finder to conclude that the administrative and judicial processes have been abused'. A careful reading of *California Motor Transport* indicates that Justice Douglas's mention of a 'pattern of baseless, repetitive claims' was only an illustration of sham litigation, as his opinion encompasses a list of several specific forms of litigation misconduct, such as perjury, patent fraud, and bribery. Then he noticed that '[t]here are many other forms of illegal and reprehensible practice' that may be unlawful, one of which involves the pattern of litigation, which is what the antitrust plaintiffs had alleged in the instant case'. One year later *Otter Tail Power* the Supreme Court, again through a Justice Douglas majority opinion, reaffirmed and seemed to broaden somewhat the sham exception for repetitive litigation by defining it as 'the use of administrative or judicial processes where the purpose to suppress competition is evidenced by repetitive lawsuits carrying the hallmark of insubstantial claims'. – See *Otter Tail Power Co. v. United States*, 410 U.S. 366, 380 (1973). Thus, the pattern of baseless repetitive claims could be interpreted as a signal, a proof of the anticompetitive intent.

49 *PREI*, 508 US 49, at 60–63.

50 Justice Thomas described objective baselessness in various ways: for instance, as an action 'that no reasonable litigant could realistically expect success on the merits', as 'malicious prosecution', and as 'a lawsuit without probable cause'. As Justice Souter pointed out in his concurring opinion, there are differences between the 'probable cause' and the 'reasonable litigant' standards: some cases may be sufficiently weak that a reasonable litigant could not realistically expect success and yet not be so devoid of merit as to lack probable cause. See on this topic Lao, *supra* note 46, at 986.

whether the baseless suit conceals an attempt to interfere directly with a competitor's business relationships via the use of a governmental process that represents a weapon for competition, even independent of its outcome.[51] In summary, *PREI* affirmed that its two-tiered test for stripping away the First Amendment Immunity requires the antitrust plaintiff to disprove the *legal* viability of the challenged lawsuit before asking the court to judge the suit's *economic* viability.

But in *PREI* the Supreme Court did something more. In surveying the various species of illegal and reprehensible practices that may corrupt the administrative or judicial processes and result in antitrust violations, the Court expressly chose not to decide whether or, if so, to what extent *Noerr* permits the imposition of antitrust liability for litigants that act fraudulently or via other misrepresentations. Therefore, thanks to these words the Court seemed to suggest the existence of a difference between those lawsuits that fall into the sham exception according to the two-part test it just established, and a second kind of lawsuit, namely, fraudulent lawsuits.

Before *PREI*, the case law about dominant firms' infringement actions pivoted around *Walker Process* and *Handgards Doctrines*, which indeed regard fraudulent infringement actions. In the *Walker Process* case,[52] the

51 More exactly, Justice Thomas depicted the subjective motivation inquiry in two ways: first, as 'whether the baseless lawsuit conceals "an attempt to interfere directly with the business relationships of a competitor" through the 'use [of] the governmental process – as opposed to the outcome of that process – as an anticompetitive weapon"'; second, as 'whether [the litigant] was indifferent to the outcome on the merits of the . . . suit, whether any damages for infringement would be too low to justify [the litigant's] investment in the suit, or whether [the litigant] had decided to sue primarily for the benefit of collateral injuries inflicted through the use of legal process'. In other words, Justice Thomas seemed to distinguish the case where the plaintiff brings the action to win – the legal case – from the two cases where it brings the action to cast costs upon rivals, and irrespective of the costs that it sustains. This approach mimics what the model of rational litigation teaches. Not by chance, indeed, years before Judge Posner in *Grip-Pak v. Illinois Tool Works*, 694 F. 2d 466, 472 (7th Circ. 1982) argued that 'the line is crossed when [the plaintiff's] purpose is not to win favorable judgments against a competitor but to harass him, and deters others, by the process itself – regardless of outcome – of litigating'. Analogously see *Clipper Express v. Rocky Mountains Motor Tariff Bureau*, Inc., 690 F. 2d 1240, 1255–66 (9th Circ. 1983).

52 It occurred less than a year after *Pennington* and before *California Motor Transport*, and although it does not cite *Noerr Motor Freight* or *Pennington* it should be included in the line-up of *Noerr* cases (see footnote 34). Moreover, see Kobak, *supra* note 36, at 186 and 193 (noticing that, '*Walker Process* did not address *Noerr* immunity, . . . [it] has often in the past been conceived of as existing in a special patent-antitrust realm of its own' and that it 'has always seemed to exist in a sort of patent-antitrust eddy of its own outside the mainstream of the *Noerr* line of cases'). For the same opinion see also Elhauge, *supra* note 10, at 1183; and Lao, *supra* note 46, at 77 (stating that, 'fraud in the petitioning process deprives the petition, not only of its patent-derived antitrust immunity, but also of Noerr immunity that would otherwise be applicable.' Therefore, the petition as such is a sham. Therefore, *a fortiori*, the enforcement of the result of a sham petition cannot be anything more than a sham).

Supreme Court held that when a dominant firm procures a patent by committing fraud on the PTO – i.e. 'by knowing and willfully misrepresenting facts to the Patent Office' – and then tries to enforce that patent against its competitor by bringing an infringement action, the lawsuit violates Section 2 if it matches its requirements. Based on subsequent lower courts' opinions, nowadays it is understood that to prove a *Walker Process* offense the antitrust plaintiff must *first* show by apparent and persuasive evidence[53] that the monopolist-patent holder was enforcing[54] a fraudulently[55] obtained patent; and *then* demonstrate that the Section 2 requirements are satisfied.[56] In other words, the *Walker Process's doctrine* is simple: since firms that have defrauded the PTO are not afforded any protection, antitrust law can scrutinize their behavior by applying the usual Section 2 analysis.[57]

Similarly, in the two *Handgards*[58] cases the Ninth Circuit held that a monopolization (or an attempt to monopolize) offense may occur when, satisfied Section 2's requirements that the conduct has strengthened market power and harmed consumer welfare, the monopolist brings an infringement action against a rival knowing either that the patent is invalid, or that the defendant is actually not infringing the patent.

---

53 *Nobelpharma AB v. Implant Innovations, Inc.*, 141 F.3d 1059, 1069–70 (Fed. Circ. 1998).

54 Indeed, pursuant to the current law there is no antitrust violation without the enforcement of an invalid patent, i.e. the mere possession of an invalid market-dominating patent does not trigger a violation of Section 2. Therefore, given an invalid patent, a plaintiff must show that the defendant took steps to enforce it. For a discussion of how even the mere possession of an invalid patent may harm competition see Christopher R. Leslie, 'The Anticompetitive Effects of Unenforced Invalid Patents', *Minnesota Law Review* 101 (2006). Now, it is certain than bringing an infringement action means enforcing the patent. Further, this 'enforcement requirement' is for instance satisfied by threatening to sue, or by sending cease and desist letters to competitors and customers. In this regard see, e.g., *Unitherm Food Systems, Inc. v. Swift-Eckrich, Inc.*, 375 F.3d 1341 (Fed. Cir. 2004) and James B. Kobak, Jr., and Robert P. Reznick, 'Federal Circuit Ruling Portends Changes to Generic Drug Patent Infringement Litigation and Walker Process Antitrust Claims', 19 *Intellectual Property & Technology Law Journal* (2007), where the authors deal with the most recent and problematic developments of the 'enforcement requirement'.

55 More exactly, for a Walker Process claim two elements are crucial: fraud and materiality. As Justice Harlan noticed in writing his concurring opinion in the *Walker Process* case, the validity of a patent is never certain. Therefore, in order not to prosecute good faith invalid patents, a finding of fraud requires a clear and convincing evidence of a misrepresentation or omission of a material fact with the intent to deceive the patent examiner, so that the patent would not have been granted absent the fraudulent conduct. See *Nobelpharma*, 141 F.3d. at 1069–1071.

56 Indeed, as S. W. O'Donnell, 'Unified Theory of Antitrust Counterclaims in Patent Litigation', 9 *Virginia Journal of Law & Technology* 1, 14 (2004) (observing that, 'it is not the fraud against the PTO that creates the monopolization offense, but the litigation of that fraudulently obtained patent').

57 See, e.g., Steinman & Fitzpatrick, *supra* note 7, at 96–7 and Fischel, *supra* note 33, at 81–2.

58 *Handgards, Inc. v. Ethicon, Inc.*, 601 F.2d 986, 994 (9th Cir. 1979) and 743 F.2d at 1282.

As a whole, hence, though the *Walker Process* and the *Handgards* stream of cases do not cite expressly the *Noerr-Pennington doctrine*, it has always been clear that the kind of fraudulent petitions that they address – i.e. fraudulent patents and fraudulent allegations – cannot enjoy the First Amendment immunity.[59] Indeed, soon after the *Walker Process* case the Court in *California Motor Transport*, justifying a broader application of the sham exception beyond the boundaries of the legislative context, observed that misrepresentations that are condoned in the political arena are not all immunized when used in the adjudicatory process.[60] While political lobbying may entail exaggerations and falsities, political debates can remedy false statements and reveal their falsity. Instead, litigants and firms that apply to administrative agencies are supposed to be truthful since courts and agencies must rely on the information they supply to decide the case. Therefore, the *Walker Process doctrine* does nothing more than consider the case of an agency – the PTO – that has delegated to firms the factual determinations that trigger its action – the granting of a patent, whose enforcement may restrain competition. Therefore, in such a case the antitrust analysis applies: it does not scrutinize the discretionary governmental decision, but the lie that has highly conditioned that decision.[61] Indeed, the case law about the role of misrepresentation is very homogeneous: whoever make misrepresentations to an adjudicatory body (either a court or an agency) is likely to fall into the sham exception, as this threatens the fair and impartial functioning of the adjudicatory system,[62] while those who make misrepresentations in the political arena would

[59] Lao, *supra* note 46, at 1010–1012, where the author writes, 'an antitrust rule providing that material misrepresentations will not be protected under Noerr, even if the litigant is genuinely seeking a favourable outcome in litigation, is no more offensive to the Constitution than the existing rules'. This thesis has been formulated in order to reject the idea that 'without a separate misrepresentation exception and under a strict reading of Professional Real Estate Investors, even litigation tainted with fraud and used as an anticompetitive tactic could be immunized under the Noerr doctrine, on the theory that the purpose of the litigation (fraud-tainted or not) was to obtain a successful judicial outcome and not merely to harass the competitor through the litigation process itself', at 1022. Lao's worries borne from the idea that who is making the fraud is bringing the suit in the name of a successful judicial outcome, and not for the collateral gains that come just from bringing the lawsuit. Nevertheless, Justice Thomas's words cannot be interpreted as to save an action aimed to establish a falsity: the point is not saving the plaintiff who hopes to win via fraud, but the plaintiff who has a legal reason to hope.

[60] At 513. See further *Clipper Express v. Ricky Mountain tariff Bureau*, 690 F. 2d 1240, 1261 (9th Circ. 1982).

[61] Elhauge, *supra* note 10, at 1249.

[62] For instance, in *Clipper Express v. Rocky Mountain Motor Tariff Bureau*, 690 F.2d 1240, 1281 (9th Cir. 1982) the Ninth Circuit explained that falsehoods and misrepresentations are unacceptable in the adjudicatory sphere primarily because government adjudicators and administrators, unlike legislators, must rely on the parties for the accuracy of the information used to make their decisions. See on this topic Hurwitz, *supra* note 15, at 85.

usually receive Noerr-Pennington immunity.[63] Besides, given the *PREI* parameters for establishing the sham exception, any distinction between sham litigation, on one side, and *Walker Process* and *Handgards* cases, on the other, makes little sense.[64] The only unique aspect of *Walker Process* and *Handgards* is that the two doctrines identify some of the different reasons why an infringement suit may be 'objectively baseless' as required by the *PREI*'s sham litigation paradigm. Moreover, given that often courts infer *PREI*'s subjective element (i.e. the monopolist's intention to harass its rival) from the structural element (i.e. the absence of legal grounding for the monopolist's infringement action), the intention to impair competitors is explicit in cases where the patent has been enforced knowing its invalidity, or in cases where the patentee knows, or has reason to know, that the rival is not an infringer.[65]

However, even considering the *Walker Process* and the *Handgards* stream of cases that are different from the *PREI*-like sham litigation cases,[66] it must be clear that in order to understand whether the First

---

[63] In *Noerr*, indeed, the Court protected from liability even the defendants' use of misleading advertising and false information, relying on the freedom of political speech and on the need for an uninhibited flow of information to lawmakers. For a deep discussion of this topic see, e.g., Fischel, *supra* note 33, 107 who asserted that under *California Motor Transport*, unethical or abusive conduct will be labeled a sham in the adjudicatory context regardless of whether it is intended to support an actual effort to influence government; by contrast, such activity in a legislative or executive setting will not be considered a sham unless the intent to influence government is absent. Further see Bork, *supra* note 8, at 359–62 who observed not only that because of the openness of political debate are antitrust restrictions unnecessary to curb or counteract the use of false information in legislative petitioning, but also that scrutiny by antitrust enforcement agencies of lobbying or other legislative activity may be politically infeasible.

[64] See O'Donnell, *supra* note 56, at 3 and 7, who from this standpoint explains that there is no reason to distinguish a fraudulent exception from a sham exception to the *Noerr-Pennington* doctrine; Herbert Hovenkamp, Mark D. Janis & Mark A. Lemley, 1 *IP and Antitrust. An Analysis of Antitrust Principles applied to Intellectual Property Law* § 11.1 (2009); Balto, Wolman, *supra* note 47, 461.

[65] O'Donnell, *supra* note 56, at 4.

[66] For instance, see *Nobelpharma AB v. Implant Innovations* 141 F.3d 1059, 1070–1072 (Fed. Cir. 1998). There the Federal Circuit stated that, Walker Process provides an alternative 'legal ground [. . .] on which a patentee may be stripped of its immunity from the antitrust laws', independently of, or in addition to the sham litigation exception. The Eleventh and the D.C. Circuits do recognize a misrepresentation exception distinct from sham as well. Indeed, the lower courts' treatment of this issue has been confusing and inconsistent. The Third Circuit, in a span of four months, decided two misrepresentation cases slightly differently. In one case, *Armstrong Surgical Center, Inc. v. Armstrong County Memorial Hospital*, it noted that Professional Real Estate Investors left the question open and then declined to carve out a separate misrepresentation exception. In the other case, *Cheminor Drugs Ltd. v. Ethyl Corp.*, a different panel of the Third Circuit refused to recognize a distinct fraud or misrepresentation exception to Noerr. It treated misrepresentation as a variant of sham and applied a somewhat modified Professional Real Estate Investors test. For the first prong of this modified test, the court asked whether the petition was objectively baseless, 'without regard to those

Amendment immunity applies, US judges consider, first, either the basis for the action, or the existence of a fraud. Then, if and only if the IP claim is baseless, they look at the motivations of the antitrust defendant, maybe by analyzing its economic interests.

THE LITTLE EU EXPERIENCE ABOUT DOMINANT FIRMS' INFRINGEMENT ACTIONS

Up to now, the EU Commission has not prosecuted any sham litigation cases involving an IPR.[67] Except for some observations about this kind of offence made in the *AstraZeneca* decision,[68] it has dealt with only *one* alleged case of sham litigation: *ITT Promedia* – a decision that the CFI affirmed.[69]

In this case the CFI held, first and foremost, that the ability to assert one's right through the courts constitutes the expression of a general

---

facts that [were alleged to be] misrepresented.' If the misrepresentations did not 'infect the core of [petitioner's] claim and the government's resulting actions', the petition would not be considered objectively baseless and, thus, would enjoy Noerr immunity. The Ninth Circuit, likewise, made intentional misrepresentations a subset of sham, but only if they are made in the adjudicatory (not legislative) realm, and only if the misrepresentation 'deprive[s] the litigation of its legitimacy'. The Fourth Circuit declined to decide whether a fraud exception to Noerr exists after Professional Real Estate Investors but said that, even if it does, it would extend 'only to the type of fraud that deprives litigation of its legitimacy'.

[67] Among the reasons for this quantity gap between the US and EU case law, it is worthwhile to remember that in US the claims contending a sham litigation, a *Walker Process*, or an *Handgards* claim are often antitrust counterclaims that alleged infringers of IPRs use in federal courts to strike back infringement actions. Although in the EU jurisdiction an alleged infringer of a national IPR held by a monopolist could bring in its national court an antitrust counterclaim for the application of Article 102, to know there is no trace of that.

[68] Those observations were, however, ancillary to the Commission's idea about the existence of a single and articulated abusive strategy of the pharmaceutical company. See AstraZeneca (COMP/A. 37.507/F3), 15 June 2005, § 736 (hereinafter '*AstraZeneca*').

[69] European Commission, Decision of 21 May 1996, Case IV/35.268, which rejected and dismissed ITT Promedia NV's claim against Belgacom S.A; CFI, case T-111/96, *ITT Promedia NV v. Commission of the European Communities*, [1998] ECR II-2937. Besides, in connection to the topic IPRs and sham litigation two other decision can also be mentioned: *BBI/Boosey and Hawkes* (87/500/EC), July 29 1987, OJ 1987 L 286/36 and *Deccca Navigator Systems* 89/113/CEE: *Decisione della Commissione del 21 dicembre 1988 relativa ad una procedura in conformità degli articoli* 81 [ex 85] e 82 [ex 86] *del* trattato CE. In the former case, according to the allegations against the dominant firm, it pursued an unjustified litigation for copyright infringement that was eventually abandoned, but that imposed a heavy financial burden on the potential rival, delaying the launching of the new range of brass instruments. Moreover, the dominant firm allegedly cut off the rival's source of components in Germany by bringing other unjustified legal actions for 'slavish copying', suits that the dominant firm lost. But, this decision came almost ten years before *ITT Promedia*. So the Commission did not actually deal with the allegedly baseless actions of copyright infringement. In the latter case, the company knew that the patent it was enforcing had expired. Then, it tried to obtain a copyright regardless of the fact that it knew it could not be obtained. Everything was objectively baseless. The purpose was clearly anticompetitive.

principle of law that underpins the constitutional traditions common to the Member States and that is laid down in Article 6 and 13 of the European Convention for the Protection of Human Rights and the Fundamental Freedoms.[70] Then, in order to support the Commission's approach, the CFI added that, in exceptional circumstances, even bringing a lawsuit could be abusive. Indeed, as to these circumstances the Commission established that bringing a lawsuit – but not enforcing a defensive strategy[71] – violates EU competition law when the legal action cannot reasonably be considered as an attempt to establish the rights of the firm and can, hence, only serve to harass the opposite party; and when the legal action is conceived in the framework of a plan whose goal is to eliminate competition.

The first prong of the EU standard recalls the first requirement of the test used in *PREI*: the Commission has to ascertain whether the monopolist brings a legal action asserting a right that, at that moment, it cannot reasonably consider being its own. On the contrary, the second prong of the EU standard does not concern the subjective element that the US Supreme Court applied in *PREI*, perhaps because the EU notion of abuse is traditionally an objective one. However, the second EU prong – i.e. the requirement that the unreasonable action is part of a plan to eliminate competition – resembles another US idea, namely the idea that the anticompetitive intent of a plaintiff can be derived from the existence of a pattern of baseless, repetitive lawsuits.[72]

As a whole, thus, the EU approach does not differ a lot from the US one; it focuses on the conditions – i.e. the lack of basis for the action and the existence of an overall anticompetitive strategy – that must be met in order to strip away the constitutional immunity – conditions that, according to the CFI, have to be interpreted strictly.[73]

THE US EXPERIENCE ABOUT DOMINANT FIRMS' IP ADMINISTRATIVE PROCEDURES

In the US, administrative procedures do not enjoy the First Amendment immunity when either they are fraudulent or the above-described two-phase *PREI* test applies.

---

70 See CFI, case T-111/96, *ITT Promedia NV v. Commission of the European Communities*, [1998] ECR II-2937, § 60.

71 *AstraZeneca*, § 737, where the Commission wrote, 'the conduct of defense cannot be equated, as a matter of course, to the institution of legal proceedings'.

72 See footnote 52 for the description of *California Motor Transport*.

73 See CFI, case T-111/96, *ITT Promedia NV v. Commission of the European Communities*, [1998] ECR II-2937.

Gaming is not persuading or influencing.[74] Therefore, any attempt to cheat administrative bodies cannot deserve any kind of immunity. For instance, the willful registration in the Orange Book of a clearly invalid patent as well as the registration of a patent that obviously does not cover the drug claimed is vulnerable to antitrust scrutiny.[75]

Instead, in order to strip away the immunity that covers non-fraudulent administrative procedures, in accordance with *PREI*, the antitrust plaintiff has to prove, first, that the monopolist's administrative procedure – think, for instance, to an FDA's procedure[76] – lacks grounding and, second, that it has been enforced in order to harass the monopolist's competitors. By and large, the legal standards and principles underpinning the application of

---

[74] See Hurwitz, *supra* note 15, 83.

[75] See Daniel J. Davis, 'The Fraud Exception to the Noerr-Pennington Doctrine in Judicial and Administrative Proceedings', *U. Chi. L. Rev.* 325, 343 (2002). Moreover, see *In re Biovail Corp*, 2002 WL 727033 (FTC No. 011 0094, April 23, 2002). In 1995 Biovail, a manufacturer of branded and generic drugs, received FDA approval to market Tiazac, a branded prescription pharmaceutical. Andrx, a company that develops generic versions of branded pharmaceuticals, was the first company to submit an ANDA to the FDA to manufacture and sell a generic version of Tiazac, stating that its generic product would not infringe the listed patent Tiazac. Within 45 days of this filing, Biovail filed a patent infringement action against Andrx. The district court ruled on that Andrx's generic version of Tiazac did not infringe Biovail's patent, and Biovail appealed. While the appeal was still pending, the FDA tentatively approved Andrx's ANDA, but before Andrx could enter the market with its generic Tiazac equivalent, Biovail listed a second patent in the Orange Book as claiming Tiazac. More exactly, Biovail acquired an exclusive license to this patent from another company, DOV. As a consequence of this new listing, Andrx filed another certification stating that its generic did not infringe the Biovail's patent, but within the 45-day period, Biovail filed another patent infringement suit against Andrx. After learning that DOV could not give Andrx a license due to its exclusive agreement with Biovail, Andrx petitioned the FDA to require Biovail to delist the patent from the Orange Book. The FDA sought confirmation from Biovail that the patent was properly listed for Tiazac. Biovail submitted a declaration to the FDA stating that the patent was eligible for Orange Book listing in connection with Tiazac. As a result of Biovail's declaration, the FDA decided not to de-list the patent. The consent order requires Biovail to: (1) transfer certain rights in the acquired patent back to their original owner; (2) terminate its infringement suit against the generic competitor, thereby ending the 30-month stay; (3) refrain from any action that would trigger another 30-month stay; (4) refrain from future improper Orange Book listing practices; and (5) provide the FTC with prior notice of future acquisitions of any patents it intends to list in the Orange Book.

[76] As Steinhauer, *supra* note 7, at 680 explained, immunity allows avoiding millionaire settlements, because 'when antitrust claims are not dismissed in their entirety, class actions arising from Hatch-Waxman litigation are typically settled following extensive discovery. See e.g., *In re Remeron End-Payor Antitrust Litig.*, 2005 US Dist LEXIS 27011, at *14 (D. N.J. Sept. 13, 2005) (approximately $39 million settlement); *In re Remeron Direct Purchaser Antitrust Litig.*, 2005 US Dist. LEXIS 27013, *2; *8 (D. N.J. Nov. 9, 2005) ($75 million settlement); *Stop & Shop Supermarket Co. v. SmithKline Beecham Corp.*, 2005 U.S. Dist. LEXIS 9705, at *2; 20 (E.D. Pa. May 20, 2005) ($100 million settlement); *Nichols v. SmithKline Beecham Corp.*, 2005 US Dist. LEXIS 7061, at *24 (E.D. Pa. Apr. 22, 2005) ($65 million settlement); *In re Relafen Antitrust Litig.*, 231 F.R.D. 52, 63 (D. Mass. 2005) ($75 million settlement); *In re Cardizem CD Antitrust Litig.*, [cited in *In re Visa Check/Mastermoney Antitrust Litig.*, 297 F. Supp. 2d 503, 525 n.33 (E.D.N.Y 2003)] ($110 million settlement)'.

PREI to infringement actions hold also in connection with administrative procedures. What that changes – which represents the core of this section – is evaluating whether monopolists' administrative procedures may be objectively baseless and, even, whether they can amount to 'acts of petitioning'.

In contrast to court proceedings, indeed, it may be difficult to show the objective absence of grounding in the administrative context, because agencies enjoy greater policymaking discretion than the courts do. In other words, distinguishing legitimate political petitioning from arguably improper use of administrative processes could be complex,[77] because the standards for approval of administrative applications make reference to policy determinations and to undefined considerations of public interest.[78] Nevertheless, when the procedures under review involve significant factual inquiries and when applicants must submit significant and specific information, administrative proceedings tend to rely on the information that the parties provide: they lose their 'political, discretionary soul', that is, they result more from firms' acts than from agencies' choices.[79] For instance in two recent judgments – *In re Buspirone Patent Litigation*[80] and *Organon Inc. v. Mylan Pharms., Inc.*[81] – US courts have affirmed, following the FTC suggestion,[82] that the act of listing drugs in the Orange Book is a kind of

---

77 See Noah, *supra* note 4, at 6.

78 Indeed, the Federal Circuit held that the First Amendment rationale for *Noerr* immunity applied only when the government acts after an independent review of the merits of a petition, and not when the government acts merely in a ministerial or nondiscretionary capacity in direct reliance on the representations made by private parties. See *In re Buspirone Patent & Antitrust Litig*., 185 F. Supp. 2d 363, 369–70 (S.D.N.Y 2002).

79 See, e.g., Noah, *supra* note 4, at 2; Bork , *supra* note 8, at 348–9; Elhauge, *supra* note 10, at 1250; Hurwitz, *supra* note 15, at 119–26; Minda, *supra* note 34, at 999–1001; and David L. Meyer, Note, *A Standard for Tailoring Noerr-Pennington Immunity More Closely to the First Amendment Mandate*, 95 Yale L.J . 832, 846 (1986). Indeed, the APA separates administrative proceedings into two worlds depending on whether they result in 'rules' or 'orders'. Rulemaking proceedings lead to rules, and adjudicatory proceedings lead to orders.

80 *In re Buspirone* involves allegations that Bristol-Myers Squibb Co. (BMS) violated the antitrust laws by fraudulently listing a patent on its branded drug, BuSpar, in the FDA's Orange Book, thereby foreclosing generic competition. Bristol-Myers Squibb ('BMS') is a company that develops, manufactures, and distributes prescription pharmaceutical products (including the anti-anxiety drug, BuSpar, and two anti-cancer drugs, Taxol and Platinol) and other consumer health care products. In a complaint dated March 7, 2003, the FTC alleged that BMS had engaged in a decade-long pattern of anticompetitive conduct in order to delay generic competition to BuSpar, Taxol and Platinol. The FTC complaint charged that BMS willfully maintained its monopoly over each of the three products by abusing government regulatory processes by, amongst other things, 'strategically gaming the Hatch-Waxman 30-month provision' through the listing in the Orange Book of patents which did not meet the listing criteria.

81 293 F. Supp. 2d 453, 455 (D. N.J. 2003).

82 Indeed, in its *amicus* brief, the FTC opposed the application of the Noerr-Pennington Immunity arguing that submitting patent information for listing in the Orange Book did not constitute 'petitioning' the FDA.

mechanical ministerial function acted upon by government functionaries, where there is no attempt to persuade any government decision-maker, and no government decision-maker makes an evaluative decision. Therefore, courts can easily ascertain whether such an act is objectively baseless. Better, in connection to the listing of drugs in the Orange book, courts can even avoid applying the *PREI* test, because such an act is not even an act of petitioning.[83] It is, hence, clearly subject to the antitrust scrutiny.[84]

THE EU EXPERIENCE ABOUT DOMINANT FIRMS' ADMINISTRATIVE PROCEDURES

The EU Commission has prosecuted only one case addressing abusive use of an IP-specific administrative procedure.[85] In the *AstraZeneca*[86] decision, the European Commission observed that a patentee with monopoly power might use administrative procedures in a harmful way,[87] that is to say, in

---

[83] A 'petition' is an attempt to persuade the government to take some action and, therefore, communications to the government that do not have this persuasion component should fall outside the scope of Noerr. The term 'petition' in this context broadly refers to any formal or informal request directed to a government official or entity, ranging from lobbying legislators to filing claims before a court.

[84] Id. at 369–73. The court added the gloss that even if Bristol-Myers' listing activities were protected under the *Noerr-Pennington* doctrine, antitrust plaintiffs had sufficiently pleaded that Bristol-Myers had misrepresented the scope of the patent in its submissions to the FDA to allow a *Walker Process* claim to proceed. Id. at 373–5. Moreover, see Bork, *supra* note 8, at 362 (elaborating further this hypothetical case and suggesting that such conduct should constitute a violation of the antitrust laws); Hurwitz, *supra* note 15, at 69 (arguing that, 'Aggressively self-serving petitions, objections, and arguments are the norm, and the visible bounds of "proper" conduct are faint at best.'); and Easterbrook, *supra* note 10, at 97–8 (observing, that 'A statute requiring "certificates of public interest, convenience, and necessity" or other licenses as conditions of entry is more likely to be the handiwork of trade groups seeking to slow down or interdict competition from new entrants than it is to be a method of "protecting the public"'). Similarly, the 'zone of interest' requirement of standing doctrine has not prevented competitors from pressing the interests of consumers in reviewing courts.

[85] Yet, see the following opening of proceeding, COMP/39.612 – *Perindopril (Servier)*, available at http://ec.europa.eu/competition/antitrust/cases/decisions/39612/opening_proceedings.pdf; and COMP/39.246 – *Boehringer*, available at http://ec.europa.eu/competition/antitrust/cases/decisions/39246/initiations.pdf.

[86] See Jacques-Philippe Gunther, Charlotte Breuvart, 'Misuse of Patent and Drug Regulatory Approval Systems in the Pharmaceutical Industry: An Analysis of US And EU Converging Approaches', 26 *E.C.L.R.* 669 (2005), and Emmanuel Dieny, 'The Pharmaceutical Industry and Competition Law between the Present and the Future', 28 *E.C.L.R.* 223 (2007).

[87] Indeed, the Commission clearly stated in connection to each of the two considered abuses that, 'the use of public procedures and regulation, including administrative and judicial processes, may . . ., in specific circumstances, constitute an abuse' and that, 'the abuse concerns AstraZeneca's misuse of government procedures. It does not concern AstraZeneca's use of its intellectual property rights'. See *AstraZeneca* §§ 328 and 817.

order to keep generics' producers away from the market and, hence, harm consumer welfare. Consistent with the US approach, the Commission clarified that, as long as the enforcement of public procedures does not require administrative authorities to enforce discretionary powers, that is to say, to judge the merit of the dominant firm's applications, the monopolist is liable for the anticompetitive effects that follow from the enforcement of those public procedures. Afterwards, the CFI concurred with the Commission by holding that dominant firms abuse their monopoly power when they submit objectively misleading representations 'which are of such nature as to lead' the administrative authority to make a mistake[88]. In other words, EU institutions share with US courts the seminal idea that a firm may be held responsible for harm to competition, as long as it has actually been free to affect competition – a scenario that cannot occur when agencies make substantive decisions, but that does happen when the agencies just rubber stamp.

Then, in the *AstraZeneca* decision the Commission found two different abuses: the fraudulent obtaining of some SPCs and the unusual withdrawal of the authorization to market a particular formulation of the branded drug.

With respect to grant of SPCs, usually national patent offices grant SPCs relying on information supplied by companies in their applications,[89] and are not obliged (in contrast to normal patent assessments) to consider whether the products were innovative. Given hence that according to the US perspective requesting SPCs is not even an act of petitioning, in the *AstraZeneca* decision the Commission found it illegal,[90] and the CFI affirmed its decision because AstraZeneca *knowingly* gave a *misleading representation* about the date of the first authorization to market the patented product – a misrepresentation *without which* the SPC would not been obtained or, at least, would not have had the same duration.[91] In other words, the Commission seemed to judge the *AstraZeneca* behavior according to the same criteria that a US court would have used in analyzing the fraudulent procurement of a patent in a *Walker Process Case*. It noticed not only the clear anticompetitive effect of the monopolist's practice and the (again, clear) materiality of the misrepresented information. It also

---

88 See CFI, Astrazeneca, 1 July 2010, case T-321/05, § 361, available at http://curia.europa.eu/.

89 As said in a previous chapter, obtaining an SPC means enforcing a patent. For the opposite idea – namely that 'AstraZeneca does not only concern the abusive exercise of intellectual but also the abusive obtaining, protection and extension of intellectual property rights themselves' see Gunther and Breuvart, *supra* note 86, at 679.

90 See *AstraZeneca*, §§ 328 and 820.

91 *Id.*, §§ 145, 626 and 630.

observed from several AstraZeneca internal documents that AstraZeneca's conduct was intentionally fraudulent and not the result either of a mistake or an innocent misinterpretation of the law.

Instead, the Commission applied different criteria when it dealt with AstraZeneca's choice to replace the marketing authorizations for capsules, with the marketing authorization for the corresponding tablet formulation – a choice that blocked the entrance of generics and parallel importers, because at that time of the facts those last could obtain a marketing authorization for specific product only if there was an existing reference marketing authorization for the original corresponding medicinal product. Therefore, the withdrawal of the authorization for capsules prevented them from entering that market.

In analyzing this second abuse the Commission first stated that, 'single acts involving the launch, withdrawal or requests for deregistration of a pharmaceutical product would not normally be regarded as an abuse'.[92] Then, it used several objective elements to rebut this presumption in the case before it, such as the selective nature of the switch between 'capsules/tablets'; the ability of the withdrawal to eliminate generics and parallel import; and the absence of a rational business justification, providing further that the practice was really unusual for the industry.[93] In other words, in this second abuse scenario there was no fraudulent statement to suggest the harmful nature of the procedure. This was deemed to be a strategic tool that does not boast any raison d'etre but the exclusion of potential rivals.

Therefore, the Commission's evaluation can be interpreted according to two different views. It is possible that the Commission held the switch from capsules to tablets together with the withdrawal of the market authorization harmful without establishing any particular standard, but only applying the 'old fashion' idea that a dominant firm carries the special responsibility.[94] Alternatively, it is possible that the Commission made its finding based on the fact that the practice was unconventional for the whole industry and, hence, strategically capable of producing anticompetitive foreclosure in the absence of a business justification for it. It this was true, then one could argue that the Commission made an economic analysis of AstraZeneca's conduct, assuming that its unconventional nature was evidence of its irrational nature. The CFI seems to concur with this second interpretation.[95]

---

[92] Id., § 792.

[93] For a detailed discussion of these elements, see AstraZeneca (COMP/A. 37.507/F3), 15 June 2005, §§ 794–810.

[94] See, for instance, Dieny, *supra* note 86, at 224–5.

[95] See CFI, Astrazeneca, 1 July 2010, case T-321/05, § 694, available at http://curia.europa.eu/.

THE CONVERGENT US AND EU APPROACHES

The previous analysis of the US and EU case law about dominant firms' judicial and administrative IP processes shows that the antitrust authorities of the two jurisdictions converge in arguing that these behaviors can be prosecuted only when two conditions occur at the same time: (a) the constitutional immunity, protecting the right of citizen to petition the government, does not apply; *and* (b) the conduct under review satisfies Section 2 and Article 102's requirements.

The condition *subsection* (b) shows that, in both jurisdictions, antitrust authorities avoided using competition law as an extra-remedy for fraudulent judicial and administrative IP processes that did not infringe competition law. Thus – one should conclude that – harm to dynamic efficiency, which arguably happens when IPR holders misuse their rights by bringing fraudulent actions, cannot work as a stand-alone source of antitrust liability: in order to trigger the enforcement of Section 2 and Article 102, a likely harm to innovation is not enough.

As to the condition *subsection* (a), US and EU antitrust authorities converged in establishing somehow analogous criteria for stripping away constitutional immunity. They focused on objective elements, such as the grounds of the regarded legal/administrative actions; the existence of a fraud; the existence of an overall anticompetitive plan; or the praxis of the industry. Then, they considered the intent of firms. Yet, US courts relied on such elements only subordinately and using the economic cost-benefit analysis in order to decipher it; further, the EU consideration of this subjective element remains quite heterodox.

Arguably, antitrust authorities that drive under antitrust scrutiny fraudulent actions 'played it safe'. In other words, they choose to explore those behaviors that certainly cannot produce any countervailing value against the anticompetitive effects that they may entail.

Instead, when they choose to scrutinise non-fraudulent legal and administrative actions they affirm the idea that even IP legal tools that are fully consistent with IP regimes can, however, violate antitrust law. In other words, by inquiring whether valid infringement actions or IP administrative procedures can fall under Section 2 and Article102, antitrust authorities conceive the idea that, in some specific circumstances, even what is proper for IP regimes becomes a tool for sheltering market power and harming consumer welfare. In particular, as to these specific circumstances, antitrust authorities evoke what economic thinking says about rational and strategic actions. Indeed, the absence of legal grounds could work as a proxy – actually, not a perfect one, because it is not focused on costs, but on legal motives[96] – for irrationality.[97] The US choice to read IP plaintiffs' intent in the light of their expectations about the benefits and costs of their actions, as well as the EU decisions to search for a pattern of legal action, could signal the existence of a general exclusionary strategy meant to raise rivals' costs.

---

[96] See also Kobak, *supra* note 3, 203.
[97] Myers, *supra* note 20, at 19.

7. Conclusion

Nowadays, the EU jurisdiction finally concurs with the US jurisdiction in making antitrust law pivot around economics (Chapters 1 and 2). In dealing with the enforcement of antitrust provisions this means that, once chosen what economic model better explains the facts in question, antitrust authorities appreciate firms' practices by verifying whether the scenario where the practices took place fits the theoretical hypothesis underpinning the selected economic model (Chapter 2). But, when the economic theory reaches its unsettled edges and cannot explain the facts in question in a conclusive way, the choice to make antitrust law pivot around economics not only morphs the decision to select a specific economic model into a policy choice, but also leaves antitrust authorities with no definitive benchmark for their assessments (Chapter 1).

This is what happens when economics is required to explain how market monopolies and IPRs affect competition and innovation. On the one side, IP provisions and the antitrust rules about the scope of market monopolies govern altogether what intellectual resources monopolists may use, via what behaviors they can exploit them, and what benefits coming from market monopolies and IPRs monopolists can appropriate. Yet, on the other side, economics cannot fix from an *ex ante* and universal perspective the optimal level of intellectual resources that should be made available to monopolists, the catalog of monopolists' harmful behaviors, and how many benefits are enough for monopolists to compete and innovate, across times, at a level which is optimal for the whole society. In summary, from an economic standpoint, antitrust rules about monopolists – that is to say, Section 2 of the Sherman Act and Article 102 of the TFEU – as well as patent and copyright provisions are thought to govern mechanisms of appropriation (Chapter 2), but economic theory does not know how many opportunities and incentives firms need to enjoy over time in order to promote competition and innovation (Chapter 1).

Now, for antitrust authorities judging dominant firms' behaviors involving IPRs, the absence of such an ideal yardstick to measure how broad and lasting dominant firms' IPRs should be has represented an issue, especially because antitrust authorities should point their enforcing action to further competition and innovation (Chapter 2). Indeed, since innovation can drive economic growth far more than the elimination of static inefficiencies, *nowadays* US and EU antitrust authorities expressly acknowledge that they want to look not only at firms' behaviors that may worsen market performances in terms of price and output – that is to say, at firms' conduct that may harm short run-consumer welfare – but also at firms' practices that may make market outcomes worse in terms of quality, variety, and rate of innovation – that is to say, at business behaviors that may harm long-run consumer welfare (Chapter 2).

Actually, over the years US and EU antitrust authorities dealing with dominant firms' behaviors involving IPRs have already taken somehow different paths in order to protect innovation (Chapters 3 to 6).

Various interrelated policy choices, some of which are connected to the jurisdictional and cultural backgrounds of US and EU judges and officers – and, hence, independent from the policy aims and enforcing features of Section 2 and article 102 – explain the sometimes divergent, sometimes convergent, US and EU choices.

First, recall that several economic models can establish, under highly detailed hypothesis, whether specific monopolists' behaviors fall under Section 2 and Article 102 (Chapters 3 to 6). These models are quite sophisticated and thorough. Therefore, antitrust authorities have always had to decide – and this is the *first* of the here-listed policy choices that affect the US and EU approaches towards dominant firms' practices involving IPRs – the *level of complexity that they want to introduce in their enforcing activity*. The more self-confidence antitrust authorities have, the more they distrust market forces and innovations' displacing powers, the lower they deem the risk of false positives, and the more they accept to base their analysis on sophisticated economic models that somehow venture to give a new shape to dominant firms' IPRs from an *ex post* case-by-case perspective. In particular, sometimes the two jurisdictions converged in preferring not to pay attention to these complicated economic models. For instance, in order not to seriously affect firms' incentives to innovate and compete via innovation, US courts and EU institutions have never prosecuted internally developed patents. If they acted against the mere ownership of these IPRs, they acted against *acquired* and *licensed* patents (Chapter 3). Other times, both US and EU antitrust authorities accepted to use the same sophisticated post-Chicago economic theory. It happened in the Microsoft cases regarding Microsoft's System Innovations and Microsoft's refusals to deal, where EU antitrust authorities shared with US courts the idea that Microsoft was sheltering its dominance in the middleware by leveraging its monopoly over secondary markets (Chapters 4 and 5). Analogously, US courts and EU antitrust institutions did not 'play it safe' when they chose to detect when dominant firms used valid infringement actions and IP administrative procedures in a strategic way. They could have flattered on the idea that sole fraudulent (not IP-consistent) judicial and administrative actions were harmful: instead they decided to follow complicated analyses in order to also bring IP consistent infringement and administrative actions under the antitrust scrutiny (Chapter 6). However, from the here-developed analysis of the arguments that US and EU antitrust authorities elaborated in their case law it arises that the attitude of the latter seems more unprejudiced than that of the former. Nowadays, EU antitrust authorities want to prohibit dominant firms' behaviors even when harm to consumer welfare is only likely (Chapter 2). Further, also on the base of heterodox economic theories, they are willing to elaborate long-run analyses, where they try to forecast how market structure will develop, how innovation will evolve, and who is in the best position to innovate and compete. It happened clearly in the Microsoft cases about System Innovations, when EU antitrust authorities predicted the standardization effect in the market of music players and the block to future innovation in the markets of music players and browsers (Chapter 4). It happened also when EU antitrust authorities dealt with refusals to deal cases: whereas the US courts of the Reagan and Bush administrations have never imposed a duty to deal questioning that monopolist's rivals can use the monopolist's properties – in case for pursuing innovation – better than their legitimate owners, EU did embrace such a social-planning perspective, arguing that, because of their blocking effects on rivals' innovations and new products, monopolists' IPRs were not only failing in boosting innovation, but also morphing industries' innovative paths in favor of monopolists (Chapter 5).

Indeed – and this is the *second* policy issue that arises from what has just been noticed – US courts have often been very liberal as to *monopolists' right to keep on searching for competitive advantages* that, like patented and copyrighted innovations, strengthen market power at their rivals' expenses. They allow any kind of monopolists' proprietary innovations: with the sole exception of sham innovations, they permit even those System Innovations that traditionally create 'social alarm' by impairing the existing *status quo*, i.e. rivals' existing market positions on secondary markets. US judges, indeed, generally rejected any intrusion of considerations of promoting welfare into business relationships leaving monopolists free to strengthen their dominance, in case via IPRs that further protect their competitive advantages, as long as monopolists' behaviors are able to increase consumer welfare via innovations (Chapters 4 and 5). EU antitrust institutions, instead, have never prosecuted the innovations of mono-product monopolists, but have looked with suspicion both at monopolists' System Innovations and at those monopolists' intellectual goods that were deemed indispensable for rivals' new products and processes (Chapters

4 and 5). In those circumstances, by obliging monopolists to share their revolutionary System Innovations and necessary intellectual goods, EU antitrust authorities sketched *two interrelated policy guidelines*, with which US courts clearly did not concur. *In general*, EU dominant firms may be forced to act as their rivals' trustee: they could be called upon to support their rivals' ability to make their own current products and, if possible, to generate follow-on new products and processes, without being the only one to enjoy their competitive advantages. *In particular*, if IPRs protect these competitive advantages, antitrust law is legitimized to neutralize them in order not only to protect competition, but also to boost innovation.

From this perspective, hence, two further policy attitudes arise, i.e. the *third* and *fourth* of the policy variables here-listed: in the first place, whereas US courts seemed to believe that existing monopolists deserve to enjoy their dominant positions and seem to trust their ability to enhance competition, EU antitrust authorities have a more skeptical *approach towards monopolists' past and present merits*. Arguably, this approach roots in a skein of factors: from the fact that, in the past, European governments sustained – at least, partially – monopolists' investments in innovations and other competitive advantages, to the spell that some new economic theories, such as the path dependence doctrine, have had on the more 'unprejudiced' EU institutions, that use them to argue that in some industries firms that happened to be monopolists do not really deserve that position (Chapter 2 and 5).

In the second place, as to *the role that antitrust authorities grant to IPRs and IP cultures in shaping their decisions*, US courts have been more willing to preserve the *ex ante* and not market-specific pattern of incentives created by federal IP legislators, even when the IPR holder was a monopolist and the market in question was favorable to monopolies. Beyond the adversity to the risk of false positives – they argued – courts have no right to second guess what legislators have decided because, especially in the most recent reforms, they have already struck a balance among the rights of IP owners, the rights of consumers, and the concerns for a competitive and innovative marketplace, trying to please as many conflicting interests as possible. In contrast, EU antitrust authorities made an *ex post* and case-by-case analysis of that pattern of incentives: they have been willing to give another shape to dominant firms' IPRs not only when it was argued that their rapid intervention redresses the unfair IPRs that lobbies contributed to design – an argument that, incidentally, works in support of any kind of intervention, because it reduces the separation of power argument to a 'formal argument' – but also when the specific IPRs in question failed in spurring future innovation (Chapters 2 and 5).

These are the reasons why EU institutions took such an approach

(Chapter 5): primary, whereas in the United States judges enforcing antitrust law consider the principles underpinning the IP systems in their decision making processes, *the EU experience lacks an IP communitarian culture* that could influence the communitarian antitrust approach. Next, because of their *primacy over national IP legislators*, EU antitrust authorities enjoy a vertical institutional order that helps to nullify the Montesquieu separation of power argument so dear to US courts. Third – and, perhaps, more importantly – EU institutions hold the principle that *antitrust law protects the public interest*, whereas patents and copyrights are private rights. The EU idea seems to be that freedom of contract and property rights – i.e. the levers of private ordering – are not enough to guarantee the protection of competition and the boost of innovation. A public intervention is needed, at least in order to prohibit the practices that, although legitimated by freedom of contract and property rights, harm competition and innovation. After all, the idea that competition law is thought to preserve a general order that is superior to the order that private parties create via property rights and contracts could be supported by the already mentioned EU belief that public powers act better than private parties in taking care of competitive and innovative markets – a belief that has roots in the EU historical experience as well as in its conception of the relationship between markets and public powers (Chapter 5).

As to *the final* of the policy choices here listed to explain the US and EU approaches towards the antitrust-IP interface, in opposition to the attitude to intervene against valid IPRs and against IP-consistent conduct, it arises that in neither jurisdictions do antitrust authorities try to use competition law as an extra-remedy against behaviors that violate IP laws. In other words, nowadays neither US courts nor EU antitrust institution choose to look for *an over-reaching use of competition law*.

In summary, when the economic theory that underpins the antitrust analysis reaches its epistemological limits as it happens when dominant firms' IP-consistent behaviors strengthen their market power and affect consumer welfare over the short and long run, even two jurisdictions that want their aims to converge may adopt different decisions, which are however influenced by other cultural and jurisdictional variables.

Bibliography

Abramovitz, Moses (1956) 'Resource and Output Trends in the US since 1870', **46** *Am. Econ. Rev.*, 5.

Abramowicz, Michael (2003) 'Perfecting Patent Prizes', **56** *Vand. L. Rev.*, 115.

Ackerman, Bruce A. (1975) *Economic Foundations of Property Law*, Boston, Little, Brown & Co.

Adams, William J. & Janet L. Yellen (1976) 'Commodity Bundling and the Burden of Monopoly', **90** *Quarterly J. Econ.*, 475.

Aghion, Philippe et al., (2005) 'Competition and Innovation: An Inverted-U Relationship', **120** *Quarterly J. Econ.*, 701.

Ahlborn, Christian, David S. Evans & Jorge A. Padilla, (2004) 'The Antitrust Economics of Tying – A Farewell to Per Se Illegality', **49** *Antitrust Bull.*, 287.

Akman, Pinar (2007), *Searching for The Long-Lost Soul of Article 82 EC*, available at http://ssrn.com.

Alchian, Armen & William R. Allen (1983), *Exchange and Production: Competition, Coordination, and Control*, Belmont, Ca, Wadsworth Publishing Company.

Alese, Femi (2008), *Federal Antitrust and EC Competition Law Analysis*, Aldershot, Ashgate Publishing Limited.

Almeida, Alexandre & Aurora A.C. Teixeira (2007), *Does Patenting Negatively Impact on R&D Investments? An International Panel Data Assessment*, available at www.ftc.gov/os/2003/10/innovationrptsummary.pdf.

Amato, Giuliano, (1997) *Antitrust and the Bounds of Power: The Dilemma of Liberal Democracy in the History of the Market*, Oxford, Hart Publishing.

Anderman, Steven D. (ed.) (2007), *The Interface between Intellectual Property Rights and Competition Policy*, Cambridge, Cambridge University Press.

Andrews, Carol Rice (2003), 'After BE & K: The "Difficult Constitutional Question" of Defining the First Amendment Right to Petition Courts', **39** *Houston L. Rev.*, 1299.

Angland, Joseph (2008), 'The Justice Department's Section 2 Report: In Search of a General Theory of Exclusionary Conduct', *The Online Magazine for Global Competition*, 6.

Apostolopoulos, Haris (2007), 'Refusal to deal Cases of IP Rights at the Aftermarket in the US and EU Law: Converging of both Law Systems through Speaking the Same Language of Law and Economics', **7** *Chi.-Kent J. Int'l Comp. L.*, 144.

Areeda, Phillip E. & Herbert Hovenkamp, *Antitrust Law: An Analysis of Antitrust Principles and Their Application,* New York, Aspen Publishers.

Areeda, Phillip E. (1990), 'The Essential Facilities Doctrine: An Epithet in Need of Limiting Principles', **58** *Antitrust L.J.,* 841.

Areeda, Philip & Donald F. Turner (1975), 'Predatory Pricing and Related Practices under Section 2 of the Sherman Act', **88** *Harv. L. Rev.*, 697.

Armstrong, Mark & Robert Porter (eds.) (2003), *Handbook of Industrial Organization*, Amsterdam, North-Holland Publishing Company.

Armstrong, Mark (2002), 'The Theory of Access Pricing and Interconnection', in Martin E. Cave, Sumit K. Majumdar, & Ingo Vogelsang (eds), *Handbook of Telecommunication Economics,* 1, Amsterdam, Elsevier B.V.

Arpon Almudena de Mendivil y de Aldama (2008), 'Exclusionary Conduct and Consumer Welfare: Effects in Competition, Justifications and Efficiencies. What is the Right Balance?', in Barry E. Hawk (ed.) (2009) *International Antitrust & Policy: Annual Proceedings of the Fordham Corporate Law Institute,* New York, Juris Publishing,1.

Arthur, Thomas C. (1986), 'Farewell to the Sea of Doubt: Jettisoning the Constitutional Sherman Act', **74** *Cal. L. Rev.*, 263.

Arthur, W. Brian (2004), *Increasing Returns and Path Dependence in the Economy*, Ann Arbor, Mi, University of Michigan Press.

Arthur, W. Brian (1990), 'Positive Feedback in the Economy', **262** *Scientific Am.,* 92.

Audretsch, David, William Baumol & Andrew Burke (2001), 'Competition Policy in Dynamic Markets', **19** *International Journal of Industrial Organization*, 613.

Ayres, Ian & Paul Klemperer (1999), '"Limiting Patentees" Market Power Without Reducing Innovation Incentives: The Perverse Benefits of Uncertainty and Non-Injunctive Remedies', **97** *Mich. L. Rev.*, 985.

Bain, Joe S. (1959), *Industrial organization*, New York, John Wiley & Sons.

Bain, Joe S. (1956), *Barriers to New Competition*, Cambridge, Ma, Harvard University Press.

Bainbridge, David I. (2007), *Intellectual Property,* Harlow, Pearson Education Limited.

Baker, Donald I. & William Blumenthal (1986), 'Ideological Cycles and Unstable Antitrust Rules', **31** *Antitrust Bull.*, 323.

Baker, Jonathan B. (2008), 'Beyond Schumpeter vs. Arrow: How Antitrust Fosters Innovation', **74** *Antitrust L. J.*, 575.

Baker, Jonathan B. (2003), 'The Case for Antitrust Enforcement', **17** *J. Econ. Perspectives*, 27.

Baker, Jonathan B. (1999), 'Promoting Innovation Competition through the Aspen/Kodak Rule', **7** *Geo. Mason L. Rev.*, 495.

Baker, Jonathan B. (1989), 'Recent Developments in Economics That Challenge Chicago School Views', **58** *Antitrust L. J.*, 645.

Bakos, Yannis & Eric Brynjolfsson (1999), 'Bundling Information Goods: Prices, Profits, and Efficiency', **45** *Mgmt. Sci.*, 1613.

Baldwin, William L. & John T. Scott (1987), *Market Structure and Technological Change*, New York, Harwood Academic Publishers.

Baldwin, William L. & G. L. Childs (1969), 'The Fast Second and Rivalry in Research and Development', *S. Econ. J.*, 18.

Balmer, Thomas A. (1980), 'Sham Litigation and the Antitrust Laws', **29** *Buff. L. Rev.*, 39.

Balto, David A. & Andrew M. Wolman (2003), 'Intellectual Property and Antitrust: General Principles', **43** *IDEA*, 395.

Balto, J. David & Robert Pitofsky (2001), 'Challenges of the New Economy: Issues at the Intersection of Antitrust and the New Economy', **68** *Antitrust L.J.*, 913.

Barnett, Jonathan M. (2004), 'Private Protection of Patentable Goods', **25** *Cardozo L. Rev.*, 1251.

Barnett, Thomas (2007), 'Maximizing Welfare through Technological Innovation', available at http://www.usdoj.gov/atr/public/speeches/227291.pdf.

Bauer, Joseph P. (2006), 'Refusal to Deal with Competitors by Owners of Patents and Copyrights: Reflections on the Image Technical and Xerox Decisions', **55** *DePaul l. rev.*, 1211.

Baumol, William J. (2002), *The Free-Market Innovation Machine: Analyzing The Growth Miracle Of Capitalism*, Woodstock, Princeton University Press.

Baumol, William J., John C. Panzar & Robert D. Willig (1982), *Contestable Markets and the Theory of Industry Structure*, San Diego, Harcourt Brace Jovanovich.

Bayus, Barry L. & William P. Putsis (1999), 'Product Proliferation: An Empirical Analysis of Product Line Determinants and Market Outcomes', **18** *Marketing Science*, 137.

Beck, Roger L. (1981), 'Competition for Patent Monopolies', **3** *Res. L. & Econ.*, 91.

Becker, Gary (1976), *The Economic Approach to Human Behavior*, Chicago, University of Chicago Press.

Becker, Lawrence C. (1993), 'Deserving to Own Intellectual Property', **68** *Chicago-Kent Law Review*, 609.

Bentley, Lionel & Brad Sherman (2009), *Intellectual Property Law*, Oxford, Oxford University Press.
Bernheim, B. Douglas & Michael Whinston (1998), 'Exclusive Dealing', **106** *J. Pol. Econ.*, 64.
Besen, Stanley M., *Intellectual Property* (1998), in *The New Palgrave Dictionary of Economics and the Law,* London, Macmillan Press.
Besen, Stanley M. & Joseph Farrell (1994), 'Choosing How to Compete: Strategies and Tactics in Standardization', *J. Econ. Persp.*, 117.
Besen, Stanley M. & Leo J. Raskind (1991), 'An Introduction to the Law and Economics of Intellectual Property', **5** *J. Econ. Persp.*, 3.
Bloch, Robert E. et al. (2006), 'A Comparative Analysis of Article 82 and Section 2 of the Sherman Act', **7** *Business Law International*, 148.
Bessen, James & Michael J. Meurer (2008), *Patent Failure: How Judges, Bureaucrats, and Lawyers Put Innovators at Risk,* Princeton, NJ, Princeton University Press.
Bessen, James (2003), 'Patent Thickets: Strategic Patenting of Complex Technologies', available at www.ssrn.com.
Bessen, James & Eric Maskin, 'Sequential Innovation, Patents, and Imitation' (2000), available at www.ssrn.com.
Bloom, Margaret (2005), 'The US and EU Move Towards Substantial Antitrust Convergence on Consumer Welfare Based Enforcement', **19** *SUM Antitrust*, 18.
Blumenthal, William, *Clear Agency Guidelines: Lessons from 1982* (2000), **68** *Antitrust L. J.*, 5.
Bohannan, Christina (2006), 'Reclaiming Copyright', **23** *Cardozo Arts & Ent. L. J.*, 567.
Bone, Robert G., 'Modeling Frivolous Suits', **145** *U. Pa. L. Rev.*, 519.
Bork, Robert H. (1978), *The Antitrust Paradox,* New York, Free Press.
Bork, Robert H. (1966), 'Legislative Intent and the Policy of the Sherman Act', **9** *J. L. & Econ.*, 7, 714.
Boscheck, Ralf (2007), 'Competitive Advantage and the Regulation of Dominant Firms', **30** *World Competition*, 463.
Bourgeois, Hendrik (2009), 'The Chilling Effects of Article 82 Enforcement', in Barry E. Hawk (ed) *International Antitrust & Policy: Annual Proceedings of the Fordham Corporate Law Institute 2008*, New York, Juris Publishing.
Boudin, Michael (1986), 'Antitrust Doctrine and the Sway of Metaphor', **75** *Geo. L.J.*, 395.
Bowman, Ward Jr. (1973), *Patent and Antitrust Law: A Legal and Economic Appraisal,* Chicago, University of Chicago Press.
Boyle, Peter M. et al. (2002), 'Antitrust Law at the Federal Circuit: Red Light or Green Light at the IP-Antitrust Intersection?', **69** *Antitrust L.J.*, 739.

Brennan, Timothy J., 'Should Innovation Rationalize Supra-Competitive Prices? A Skeptical Speculation 15–17', prepared for the Pros and Cons of High Prices Seminar, Swedish Competition Authority/ Konkurrensverket Stockholm, Sweden, November 9, 2007.

Breyer, Stephen (1970), 'The Uneasy Case for Copyright: A Study of Copyright in Books, Photocopies, and Computer Programs', **84** *Harv. L. Rev.,* 281.

Brodley, Joseph F., Patrick Bolton, Michael H. Riordan (2000), 'Predatory Pricing: Strategic Theory and Legal Policy', **88** *Geo. L. J.,* 2241.

Brodley, Joseph F. (1987), 'The Economic Goals of Antitrust: Efficiency, Consumer Welfare, and Technological Progress', **62** *N.Y.U. L. Rev.*, 1020.

Brunell, Richard M. (2001), 'Appropriability in Antitrust: How Much is Enough?', **69** *Antitrust L. J.*, 1.

Bruzzone, Ginevra, Marco Boccaccio (2009), 'Impact-Based Assesment and Use of Legal Presumptions in EC Competition Law: The Search for the Proper Mix', **32** *World Competition,* 465.

Bruzzone, Ginevra & Marco Boccaccio, 'Identyfying infringemente of comptetition rules: the role of economic and legal thinking', paper presented to the VIII Conference 'Antitrust Between EC Law and National Law' 10, Treviso, 22–23 May 2008, available at http://www.emagazine.assonime.it/upload/Identifying%20infringements%20def.pdf.

Bryan, R. & Clement G. Krouse (2004), 'Patent Infringement: Lessons from Industrial Economics', **4** *Journal of Industry, Competition and Trade,* 191.

Buccirossi, Paolo (ed.) (2008), *Handbook of Antitrust Economics,* Cambridge, Ma, The MIT Press.

Buckley, Meg (2004), 'Licensing Intellectual Property: Competition and Definitions of Abuse of a Dominant Position in the United States and the European Union', **29** *Brook. J. Int'l L.,* 797.

Budzinsky, Oliver (2009), 'Modern Industrial Economics and Competition Policy: Open Problems and Possible Limits', available at www.ssrn.com.

Burtis, Michelle M. (2003), 'Modern Industrial Organization: A Comment', **12** *Geo. Mason L. Rev.*, 39.

Burtis, Michelle M. & Bruce H. Kobayashi (2001), 'Why an Original Can Be Better Than a Copy: Intellectual Property, The Antitrust Refusal to Deal, and ISO Antitrust Litigation', **9** *Sup. Ct. Econ. Rev.*, 143.

Buttigieg, Eugene (2009), *Competition Law: Safeguarding the Consumer Interest. A Comparative Analysis of US Antitrust Law and EC Competition Law,* The Netherlands, Kluwer Law International.

Buttigieg, Eugene (2005), 'Consumer Interests and the Antitrust Approach to Abusive Practices by Dominant Firms', *EBLR*, 1191.

Calvani, Terry & Craig Sibarium (1990), 'Antitrust Today: Maturity or Decline', **35** *Antitrust Bull.,* 123.

Calvani, Terry (1985), 'Non-Price Predation: A New Antitrust Horizon', **54** *Antitrust L. J.*, 409.

Candrillo, Steve P. (1998), 'An Economic Analysis of Intellectual Property Rights: Justifications and Problems of Exclusive Rights, Incentives to Generate Information, and the Alternative of a Government-run Reward System', **9** *Fordham Intell. Prop. Media & Ent. L.J.*, 301.

Cantner, Uwe, Franco Malerba (eds.) (2007), *Innovation, Industrial Dynamics and Structural Transformation: Schumpeterian Legacies,* Leipzig, Springer.

Carlson, Steven C. (1999), 'Patent Pools and Antitrust Dilemma', **16** *Yale Journal on Regulation,* 359.

Carlton, Dennis W. & Ken Heyer (2008), 'Appropriate Antitrust Policy Towards Single-Firm Conduct', available at http://ssrn.com/abstract=1111665.

Carlton, Dennis W. (2007), 'Does Antitrust Need to be Modernized?', available at http://ssrn.com.

Carlton, Dennis W. (2004), 'Using Economics to Improve Antitrust Policy', **2004** *Columbia Business Law Review,* 283.

Carlton, Dennis W. (2003), 'The Relevance for Antitrust Policy of Theoretical and Empirical Advances in Industrial Organization', **12** *Geo. Mason L. Rev.,* 47.

Carlton, Dennis W. (2001), 'A General Analysis of Exclusionary Conduct and Refusal to Deal-Why Aspen and Kodak Are Misguided', **68** *Antitrust L.J.*, 659.

Carlton, Dennis W. & Jeffrey M. Perloff (2005), *Modern Industrial Organization,* Boston, Addison-Wesley.

Carlton, Dennis W. & Michael Waldman (2002), 'The Strategic Use of Tying to Preserve and Create Market Power in Evolving Industries', **33** *Rand Journal of Economics,* 194.

Carrier, Michael A. (2006), 'Refusals to License Intellectual Property after Trinko', **55** *DePaul L. Rev.*, 1191.

Carrier, Michael A. (2005), 'Of Trinko, Tea Leaves, and Intellectual Property', *Journal of Corporation Law,* 101, 108.

Carrier, Michael A. (2004), 'Cabining Intellectual Property through a Property Paradigm', **54** *Duke L. J.*, 1.

Carroll, Glenn R. & David J. Teece (eds.) (1999), *Markets and Hierarchies. The Transaction Cost Economics Perspective,* Oxford, Oxford University Press.

Cass, Ronald A. & Keith N. Hylton (2001), 'Antitrust Intent', **74** *S. Cal. L. Rev.*, 657.

Cass, Ronald A. & Keith N. Hylton (1999), 'Preserving Competition: Economic Analysis, Legal Standards and Microsoft', **8** *Geo. Mason L. Rev.*, 1.

Cavanagh, Edward D. (2006), 'Trinko: A Kinder, Gentler Approach To Dominant Firms Under the Antitrust Laws?', available at www.ssrn.com.

Ceccagnoli, Marco (2007), 'Appropriability, Preemption, and Firm Performance', available at www.ssrn.com.

Chalmers, Damian et al. (2006), *European Union Law, Text and Materials*, Cambridge, Cambridge University Press.

Chan, Ka Man & Yue Kuen Kwok (2007), 'Asymmetric Preemptive Patenting Races and Sleeping Patents', available at www.ssrn.com.

Cherensky, Steven (1993), 'Agreements, Property, and Personhood', **81** *Cal. L. Rev.* 595.

Chin, Yee Wah (1998), 'Unilateral Technology Suppression: Appropriate Antitrust and Patent Law Remedies', **66** *Antitrust L. J.*, 441.

Choi, Jay P., Gwanghoon Lee & Christodoulos Stefanadis (2003), 'The Effects of Integration on R&D Incentives in Systems Markets', **5** *Netnomics*, 21.

Choi, Jay P. & Christodoulos Stefanadis (2001), 'Tying, Investment, and the Dynamic Leverage Theory', **32** *Rand Journal of Economics,* 52.

Choi, Jay P. (1998), 'Tying and Innovation: A Dynamic Analysis of Tying Arrangements', available at http://ssrn.com.

Choi, Jay P. (1996), 'Informational Leverage and the Endogenous Timing of Product Introductions', available at http://ideas.repec.org/p/clu/wpaper/1996_03.html.

Christensen, Clayton M. (1997), *The Innovator's Dilemma,* Boston, Ma, Harvard University Press.

Church, J. & N. Gandal (1992), 'Networks Effects, Software Provision and Standardization', **40** *Journal of Industrial Economics,* 85.

Clarke-Smith, Jennifer M. (2002), 'The Development of the Monopolistic Leveraging Theory and Its Appropriate Role in Antitrust Law', **52** *Cath. U. L. Rev.,* 279.

Clark, John Maurice (1940), 'Toward a Concept of Workable Competition', **20** *American Economic Review,* 241.

Coco, Rita (2008), 'Antitrust Liability for Refusal to License Intellectual Property: A Comparative Analysis and the International Setting', **12** *Marq. Intell. Prop. L. Rev.,* 1.

Cohen, Felix (1935), 'Transcendental Nonsense and the Functional Approach', **35** *Colum. L. Rev.,* 809.

Cohen, Joel M. & Arthur J. Burke (1998), 'An Overview of the Antitrust Analysis of Suppression of Technology', **66** *Antitrust L. J.* 420.

Cohen, Wesley M., Richard R. Nelson, & John Walsh (2000), 'Protecting their Intellectual Assets: Appropriability Conditions and Why U.S. Manufacturing Firms Patent (or Not)', NBER Working Paper Series, no. 7552.
Comanor, William S. & Thomas A. Wilson (1979), 'The Effect of Advertising on Competition: A Survey', **17** *J. Econ. Lit.,* 453.
Cooper Feldman, Robin (1999), 'Defensive Leveraging in Antitrust', **87** *Geo. L. J.,* 2079, 2087.
Cornish, William R. & David Llewelyn (1999), *Intellectual Property: Patents, Copyright, Trade marks and Allied Rights,* London, Sweet & Maxwell.
Correia, Edward O.(1995), 'Antitrust and Liberalism', **40** *Antitrust Bull.,* 99.
Cotter, Thomas F. (2007), 'Misuse', **44** *Hous. L. Rev.,* 901.
Cotter, Thomas F. (2006), 'The Procompetitive Interest in Intellectual Property Law', **48** *Wm. & Mary L. Rev.*, 483.
Cotter, Thomas(1999), 'Intellectual Property and the Essential Facilities Doctrine', **44** *Antitrust Bulletin,* 211, 214 and 250.
Cowling, Keith & Dennis C. Mueller (1978), 'The Social Costs of Monopoly', **88** *Econ. J.,* 727.
Crandall, Robert W. & Clifford Winston (2003), 'Does Antitrust Policy Improve Consumer Welfare? Assessing the Evidence', **17** *J. Econ. Perspectives,* 3.
Crane, Daniel A. (2002), 'Exit Payments in Settlement of Patent Infringement Lawsuits: Antitrust Rules and Economic Implications', **54** *Fla. L. Rev.*, 747.
Crew, Eugene (1998), 'Foreword: Symposium on Antitrust and the Suppression of Technology in the United States and Europe: Is There a Remedy?', **66** *Antitrust L. J.*, 415.
Curtis Eaton, B. and Richard G. Harris (eds.) (1997), *Trade, Technology and Economics*, Cheltenham, Edward Elgar Publishing.
Curtis Eaton, B. & Richard G. Lipsey (1979), 'The Theory of Market Preemption: The Persistence of Excess Capacity and Monopoly in Growing Spatial Markets', **46** *Economica,* 149.
Cseres, Katalin J. (2005), *Competition Law and Consumer Protection,* The Hague, Kluwer Law International.
Cucinotta, Antonio, Roberto Pardolesi & Roger Van den Bergh (eds.) (2002), *Post-Chicago Developments in Antitrust Law*, Cheltenham, Edward Elgar Publishing.
Czapracka, Katarzyna A. (2007), 'Where Antitrust Ends and IP Begins – On The Roots Of The Transatlantic Clashes', **9** *Yale J. L. & Tech.*, 44.
Damich, Edward J. (1988), 'The Right of Personality: A Common Law Basis for the Protection of Moral Rights', **23** *Ga. L. Rev.,* 1.

David, J. (1988) 'Rethinking the Monopolist's Duty to Deal: a Legal and Economic Critique of the Doctrine of Essential Facilities', **74** *Van. L. Rev.,* 1069, 1089 and 1093.

David, Paul (2002), 'Does the Economy Need All the Old IPR Institutions? Digital Information Goods and Access to Knowledge for Economic Development', Address at the Wider Conference on The New Economy in Development (May 11, 2002).

David, Paul (1993), 'Intellectual Property Institutions and the Panda's Thumb: Patents, Copyrights, and Trade Secrets in Economic Theory and History', in Mitchell B. Wallerstein, Mary E. Mogee and Roberta A. Schoen (eds), *Global Dimensions of Intellectual Property Rights in Science & Technology* 19, 54–57.

David, Paul A. (1985), 'Clio and the Economics of QWERT*Y*', **75** *Am. Econ. Rev.,* 332.

Davis, Daniel J. (2002), 'The Fraud Exception to the Noerr-Pennington Doctrine in Judicial and Administrative Proceedings', *U. Chi. L. Rev.,* 325.

Davis, Ronald W. (2008), 'The Antitrust Division's Report on Section 2: Firm Foundations for Enforcement or a Bridge to Nowhere?', **23** *Antitrust,* 42.

Driscoll, Ronald W. & Jennifer M. 'The Urge to Convergence – The New EU Discussion Paper on Abuse of a Dominant Position', **20** *SPG Antitrust*, 82.

Decker, Christopher (2009), *Economics and the Enforcement of European Competition Law,* Cheltenham, Edward Elgar Publishing.

Delrahim, Makan(2004), 'Forcing Firms to Share the Sandbox: Compulsory Licensing of Intellectual Property Rights and Antitrust', available at http://www.justice.gov/atr/public/speeches/203627.htmDemsetz, Harold (1982), 'Barriers to Entry', **72** *Am. Econ. Rev.*, 47.

Demsetz, Harold (1967), 'Toward a Theory of Property Rights', **57** *Am. Econ. Rev,* 347.

Denicolò, Vincenzo (2000), 'Compatibility and Bundling with Generalist and Specialist Firms', **2** *Journal of Industrial Economics,* 177.

Denicolò, Vincenzo (1996), 'Patent Races and Optimal Patent Breadth and Length', **44** *Journal of Industrial Economics,* 249.

Derzko, Natalie M. (2005), 'The Impact of Recent Reforms of the Hatch-Waxman Scheme on Orange Book Strategic Behavior and Pharmaceutical Innovation', **45** *IDEA,* 165.

De Smet, Dieter (2008), 'The Diametrically Opposed Principles of US and EU Antitrust Policy', **29** *E.C.L.R.*, 356.

Devlin, Alan & Michael Jacobs (2009), 'Antitrust Divergence and the Limits of Economics', available at www.ssrn.com.

Devlin, Alan (2009), 'The Stochastic Relationship between Patents and Antitrust', **5** *Journal of Competition Law and Economics*, 75.

Devlin, Alan (2007), 'A Neo-Chicago Perspective on the Law of Product Tying', **44** *Am. Bus. L.J.*, 521.

Dieny, Emmanuel (2007), 'The Pharmaceutical Industry and Competition Law between the Present and the Future', **28** *E.C.L.R.*, 223.

Dixit, Avinash (1980), 'The Role of Investment in Entry-Deterrence', **90** *Economic Journal*, 95.

Dolmans, Maurits & Thomas Graf (2004), 'Analysis of Tying under Article 82 EC: The European Commission's Microsoft Decision in Perspective', 27 *World Competition Law & Economics Review,* 225.

Dorfman, Nancy S. (1987), *Innovation and Market Structure: Lessons from the Computer and Semiconductor Industries,* Cambridge, Ballinger Publishing Company.

Dosi, Giovanni, Luigi Marengo, Corrado Pasquali and Marco Valente (2009), 'Appropriability, Patents, and Rates of Innovation in Complex Products Industries', LEM Papers Series 2009/05, Laboratory of Economics and Management (LEM), Sant'Anna School of Advanced Studies, Pisa, Italy.

Dosi, Giovanni et al. (1988), *Technical Change and Economic Theory,* London, Pinter Publishers.

Dosi, Giovanni, Luigi Marengo, & Corrado Pasquali (2007), 'Knowledge, Competition and Innovation: Is Strong IPR Protection Really Needed for More and Better Innovations?', **13** *Mich. Telecomm. Tech. L. Rev.,* 471.

Dosi, Giovanni, Luigi Marengo and Corrado Pasquali (2006), 'How Much Should Society Fuel the Greed of Innovators? On the Relations Between Appropriability, Opportunities and Rates of Innovation', available at ideas.repec.org/p/ssa/lemwps/2006-17.html.

Dosi, Giovanni (1982), 'Technological Paradigms and Technological Trajectories: A Suggested Interpretation of the Determinant and Direction of Technological Change', **11** *Res. Pol'y,* 147.

Drexl, Josef, Laurence Idot, Joel Moneger (eds.) (2009), *Economic Theory and Competition Law,* Cheltenham, Edward Elgar Publishing.

Drexl, Joseph (2009), 'Real Knowledge is To Know the Extent of One's Own Ignorance: on the Consumer Harm Approach in Innovation-Related Competition Cases', available at www.ssrn.com.

Drexl, Josef (ed.) (2008), *Research Handbook on Intellectual Property and Competition Law,* Cheltenham, Edward Elgar Publishing.

Dunford, Richard (1987), 'The Suppression of Technology as a Strategy for Controlling Resource Dependence', **32** *Admin. Sci. Q.,* 512, 513.

Dusollier, Severine (2005), 'Technology as an Imperative for Regulating

Copyright: From the Public Exploitation to the Private Use of the Work', **27** *European Intellectual Property Review,* 201.

Dusollier, Severine (2003), 'Exceptions and Technological Measures in the European Copyright Directive of 2001 – An Empty Promise', **34** *IIC,* 62.

EAGCP, 'An Economic Approach to Article 82', available at http://ec.europa.eu/comm/competition/antitrust/art82/index.html.

Easterbrook, Frank H. (1990), ' Intellectual Property is Still Property', **13** *Harv. J. L. Pub. Pol.,* 1.

Easterbrook, Frank H. (1986), 'Workable Antitrust Policy ', **84** *Mich. L. Rev.,* 1696.

Easterbrook, Frank H. (1984a), ' Foreword: The Court and the Economic System in The Supreme Court 1983 Term', **98** *Harv. L. Rev.*, 4.

Easterbrook, Frank H. (1984b), 'The Limits of Antitrust ', **63** *Texas L. Rev.*, 1, 2.

Easterbrook, Frank H. (1981), 'Predatory Strategies and Counterstrategies', **48** *U. Chi. L. Rev.,* 263.

Easterbrook, Frank H. (1980), 'An Economical and Legal Analysis of Physical Tie-Ins', 89 *Yale L. J.*, 769.

Economides, Nicolas (2007), 'Hit and Miss: Leverage, Sacrifice, and Refusal to Deal in the Supreme Court Decision in Trinko', **10** *Vand. J. Ent. & Tech. L.*, 121.

Economides, Nicholas (2006) , 'Public Policy in Network Industries', available at www.ssrn.com.

Economides, Nicholas & Lawrence J. White (1994), 'Networks and Compatibility: Implications for Antitrust', **38** *European Economic Review,* 651.

Economides, Nicholas & Steven C. Salop (1992), 'Competition and Integration Among Complements, and Network Market Structure', **40** *Journal of Industrial Economics*, 105.

Economides, Nicholas (1989), 'Desirability of Compatibility in the Absence of Network Externalities', 79 *American Economic Review*, 1165.

Edquist, Charles, Leif Hommen & Maureen McKelvey (2001), *Innovation and Employment, Process versus Product Innovation,* Cheltenham, Edward Elgar Publishing.

Ehlermann, Claus-Dieter & Isabela Atanasiu (eds.) (2006), *European Competition Law Annual 2005: The Interaction between Competition Law and Intellectual Property Law,* Oxford, Hart Publishing.

Ehlermann, Claus-Dieter & Isabela Atanasiu (eds.) (2003), *European Competition Law Annual 2003: What is an Abuse of Dominant Position?,* Oxford, Hart Publishing.

Ehlermann ,Claus-Dieter & Laraine L. Laudati, (eds.) (1998), *European Competition Law Annual 1997: Objectives of Competition Policy*, Oxford, Hart Publishing.

Eilmansberger, Thomas (2005), 'How to Distinguish Good from Bad Competition under Article 82 EC: In Search of Clearer and More Coherent Standards for Anti-Competitive Abuses', **42** *Common Market Law Review,* 129.

Eisenach, Jeffrey A. & Thomas M. Lenard (eds.) (1999), *Competition, Innovation and the Microsoft Monopoly: Antitrust in the Digital Marketplace,* Norwell, Ma, Kluwer Academic Publishers.

Elhauge, Einer R. (2003), 'Defining Better Monopolization Standards', **56** *Stan. L. Rev.,* 253.

Elhauge, Einer R. (2003), 'Why Above-cost Price Cuts to Drive Out Entrants are Not Predatory', **112** *Yale L. J.,* 681.

Elhauge, Einer (1992), 'Making Sense of Antitrust Petitioning Immunity', **80** *Cal. L. Rev.,* 1177.

Ellig, Jerry (ed.) (2001), *Dynamic Competition and Public Policy: Technology, Innovation, and Antitrust Issues,* Cheltenham, Edward Elgar Publishing.

Elzinga, Kenneth G. & David E. Mills (1999), 'PC Software', **44** *Antitrust Bull.,*739.

Epstein, Richard (1998), *Principles for a Free Society: Reconciling Individual Liberty with the Common Good,* New York, Basic Books.

Epstein, Richard A. (1985), *Takings, Private Property and the Power of Eminent Domain,* Boston, Ma, Harvard University Press, 65.

Erramouspe, Matthew (1996), 'Comment, Staking Patent Claims on the Human Blueprint: Rewards and Rent-dissipating Races', **43** *UCLA L. Rev.,* 961.

Etzkowitz, Henry (1984), 'Solar Versus Nuclear Energy: Autonomous or Dependent Technology?', **31** *Soc. Probs.,* 417.

Evans, David (2005), ' How Economists Can Help Courts Design Competition Rules: An EU and US Perspective ', **28** *World Competition,* 93.

Evans, David S. & Michael Salinger (2005), 'Why Do Firms Bundle and Tie? Evidence from Competitive Markets and Implications for Tying Law', **22** *Yale J. Reg.,* 37.

Evans, David S. & A. Jorge A. Padilla (2005), 'Designing Antitrust Rules for Assessing Unilateral Practice: A Neo Chicago Approach', **72** *U. Chi. L. Rev.,* 27.

Evans, David S. & A. Jorge Padilla (2004), 'Tying under Article 82 EC and the Microsoft Decision: A Comment on Dolmans and Graf ', **27** *World Competition Law & Economics Review,* 503.

Evans, David S., Jorge A. Padilla & Michele Polo (2002), 'Tying in Platform Software: Reasons for a Rule-of-Reason Standard in European Competition Law', 25 *World Competition Law & Economics Review,* 509.

Evans, David S. & Richard Schmalensee (1995), 'Economic Aspects of

Payment Card Systems and Antitrust Policy Toward Joint Ventures', **63** *Antitrust L.J.,* 861.
Ezrachi, Ariel (ed.) (2009), *Article 82 EC: Reflections on its Recent Evolution,* Oxford, Hart Publishing.
Fagerberg, Jan, David C. Mowery & Richard R. Nelson (2005), *The Oxford Handbook of Innovation,* Oxford, Oxford University Press.
Farrell, Joseph & Robert P. Merges (2004), 'Incentives To Challenge And Defend Patents: Why Litigation Won't Reliably Fix Patent Office Errors And Why Administrative Patent Review Might Help', available at www.ssrn.com.
Farrell, Joseph, Hunter K. Monroe & Garth Saloner (1998), 'The Vertical Organization of Industry: Incompatibility versus Compatibility', **7** *Journal of Economics and Management Strategy,* 143.
Farrell, Joseph & Garth Saloner (1986), 'Installed Base Compatibility: Innovation, Product Preannouncement, and Predation', **76** *The American Economic Review,* 940.
Farrell, Joseph (1986), 'How Effective is Potential Competition', **9** *Econ. Letters,* 67.
Farrell, Joseph & Garth Saloner (1985), 'Standardization, Compatibility, and Innovation', **16** *Rand J. Econ.*, 70.
Fellmeth, Robert C. (1981), 'Suppression and Other Antitrust Concerns', in John H. Minon & William H. Lawrence (eds), *Legal Aspects of Solar Technology,* Lexington Ma, Lexington Books, 197.
First, Harry & Andrew I. Gavil (2006), 'Re-framing Windows: The Durable Meaning of the Microsoft Antitrust Litigation', *2006 Utah L. Rev.,* 641.
First, Harry (2006), 'Microsoft and the Evolution of the Intellectual Property Concept', *Wis. L. Rev.,* 1369.
Fischel, Daniel R. (1977), 'Antitrust Liability for Attempts to Influence Government Action: The Basis and Limits of the Noerr-Pennington Doctrine', **45** *U. Chi. L. Rev.,* 80.
Fisher, Franklin M., Daniel L. Rubinfeld, Richard L. Schmalensee & David S. Evans (2000), *Did Microsoft Harm Consumers? Two Opposing Views,* Washington, DC, AEI Press.
Fisher, Franklin M. (2000), 'The IBM and Microsoft Cases: What's the Difference', **90** *Am. Econ. Rev.*, 180.
Fisher, Franklin M., John J. McGowan & Joen E. Greenwood (1983), *Folded, Spindled, and Mutilated: Economic Analysis and U.S. v. IBM,* Boston, The MIT Press, 165.
Flynn, John J. (1998), 'Antitrust Policy, Innovation Efficiencies, and the Suppression of Technology', **66** *Antitrust L. J.,* 487.
Flynn, John J. (1988), 'The Reagan Administration's Antitrust Policy,

"Original Intent" and the Legislative History of the Sherman Act', 33 *Antitrust Bull.*, 259.

Flynn, John J. (1977), 'Introduction, Antitrust Jurisprudence: A Symposium on the Economic, Political and Social Goals of Antitrust Policy', **125** *U. Pa. L. Rev.*, 1182.

Forrester, Ian C. (2005), 'Regulating Intellectual Property Via Competition? Or Regulating Competition Via Intellectual Property? Competition and Intellectual Property: Ten Years on, the Debate Still Flourishes', available at http://www.eui.eu/RSCAS/Research/Competition/2005/200510-CompForrester.pdf.

Forrester, Ian S. (2005), 'Article 82: Remedies in Search of Theories? ', *Fordham Int'l L. J.*, 919, 920.

Foss, Nicolai J. (2000), *The Theory of the Firm*, London, Routledge.

Foss, Nicolai J. (1994), 'The Biological Analogy and the Theory of the Firm: Marshall and Monopolistic Competition', **28** *Journal of Economic Issues,* 1115.

Foss, Nicolai J. (1993), 'Theories of the Firm: Contractual and Competence Perspectives', **9** *Journal of Evolutionary Economics,* 127.

Fox, Eleanor M. (2005), 'Is There Life After Trinko? The Silent Revolution of Section 2 of the Sherman Act', **73** *Antitrust L.J.,* 153.

Fox, Eleanor M. (2003), 'We Protect Competition, You Protect Competitors', **26** *World Competition,* 149.

Fox, Eleanor M., Lawrence A. Sullivan (1987), 'Antitrust – Retrospective and Prospective: Where Are We Coming From? Where Are We Going?', **62** *N. Y. U. L. Rev.*, 936.

Fox, Eleanor M. (1986), 'The Politics of Law and Economics in Judicial Decision Making: Antitrust as a Window', **61** *N. Y. U. L. Rev.,* 554.

Friedman, Aryeh S. (1986), 'Law and the Innovative Process: Preliminary Reflections, 1986', *Colum. Bus. L. Rev.,* 1.

Frischmann, Brett & Spencer Weber Waller (2008), 'Revitalizing Essential Facilities', **75** *Antitrust L.J.,* 1.

Frost, George E. (1946), 'Legal Incidents of Non-Use of Patented Inventions Reconsidered', **14** *Geo. Wash. L. Rev.,* 273.

Fudenberg, Drew et al. (1983), 'Preemption, Leapfrogging and Competition in Patent Races', **22** *The European Economic Review,* 3.

Furse, Mark (2004), *Competition Law of the EC and UK*, Oxford, Oxford University Press.

Gal, Michal S. (2004), 'Monopoly Pricing as an Antitrust Offense in the U.S. and the EC: Two Systems of Belief About Monopoly?', **49** *Antitrust Bull.,* 343.

Gallini, Nancy (2002), 'The Economics of Patents: Lessons from Recent U.S. Patent Reform', **16** *Journal of Economic Perspectives,* 131.

Gambrell, James B. (2000), 'The Evolving Interplay of Patent Rights and Antitrust Restraints in the Federal Circuit', **9** *Tex. Intell. Prop. L.J.,* 137.

Gandal, Neil, Michael Kende & Rafael Rob (2000), 'The Dynamics of Technological Adoption in Hardware/Software Systems: The Case of Compact Disc Players', **31** *Rand J. Econ.,* 43.

Gandal, Neil (1995), 'Competing Compatibility Standards and Network Externalities in the PC Software Market', **77** *Rev. Econ. & Stat.,* 599.

Garza, Deborah A. (2001), 'A Comparative Analysis of the Clinton Antitrust program and Suggestion of Changes to Come', **15** *Antitrust,* 64.

Gavil, Andrew I. , William E. Kovacic, & Jonathan B. Baker (2008), *Antitrust Law in Perspective: Cases, Concepts and Problems in Competition Policy,* St. Paul, Mn, Thomson-West.

Gavil, Andrew I. (2004), 'Exclusionary Distribution Strategies by Dominant Firms: Striking a Better Balance', **72** *Antitrust L. J.*, 3.

Gaynor, Daniel E. (2006), 'Technological Tying', available at *www.ftc.gov/be/workpapers/wp284.pdf.*

Genevaz, Simon(2004), 'Against Immunity for Unilateral Refusals to Deal in Intellectual Property: Why Antitrust Law Should Not Distinguish Between IP and Other Property Rights', **19** *Berkeley Technology L. J.*, 741.

Gerardin, Damien (2004), 'Limiting the Scope of Article 82 EC: What Can the EU Learn from the US Supreme Court's Judgment in Trinko, in the Wake of Microsoft, IMS and Deutsche Telekom?', **41** *C.M. L. Rev.,* 1519.

Gerber, David J. (2007), 'The Future of Article 82: Dissecting the Conflict 12–13', paper presented at the 12th Annual Competition Law and Policy Workshop, Robert Schuman Centre EUI, Florence, available at http://www.eui.eu/RSCAS/Research/Competition/2007(papers).shtml.

Gerber, David J. (2005), 'Competition Law' chapter in the *Oxford Handbook of Comparative Law* 1, available on http://ssrn.com.

Gerber, David J. (1998), 'Law and the Abuse of Economic Power in Europe', **62** *Tulane L. Rev.,* 85.

Gerber, David J. (1988), *Law and Competition in Twentieth-Century Europe Gerber*, Oxford, Oxford University Press.

Geroski, Paul A. (1990), 'Innovation, Technological Opportunity, and Market Structure', **42** *Oxford Econ. Papers,* 586.

Ghidini, Gustavo (2006), *Intellectual Property and Competition Law,* Cheltenham, Edward Elgar Publishing.

Ghosal, Vivek & John Stennek (eds.) (2007), *The Political Economy of Antitrust*, Amsterdam, Elsevier.

Glader, Marcus (2006), *Innovation Markets and Competition Analysis,* Cheltenham, Edward Elgar Publishing.

Gifford, Daniel J. (2002), 'The Antitrust/Intellectual Property Interface: An Emerging Solution to an Intractable Problem', **31** *Hofstra L. Rev.,* 363, 409.

Gilbert, Richard J. (2007), 'Holding Innovation to an Antitrust Standard', **3** *Competition Policy International,* 47.

Gilbert, Richard J. & Michael H. Riordan (2007), 'Product Improvement and Technological Tying in a Winner-Take-All Market', **15** *The Journal of Industrial Economics,* 113.

Gilbert, Richard J. & Willard K. Tom (2001), 'Is Innovation King at the Antitrust Agencies? The Intellectual Property Guidelines Five Years Later', **69** *Antitrust L. J.,* 43.

Gilbert, Richard J. & Carl Shapiro (1996), 'An Economic Analysis of Unilateral Refusals to License Intellectual Property', **93** *Proc. Nat'l Acad. Sci.,* 12749, 12754, available at http://pnas.org/cgi/reprint/93/23/12749.pdf.

Gilbert, Richard J. & Steven C. Sunshine (1995), 'Incorporating Dynamic Efficiency Concerns in Merger Analysis: The Use of Innovation Markets', **63** *Antitrust L. J.,* 569.

Gilbert, Richard J. (1992), 'Symposium of Compatibility: Incentives and Market Structure', **40** *The Journal of Industrial Economics,* 1.

Gilbert, Richard & Carl Shapiro (1990), 'Optimal Patent Length and Breadth', **21** *Rand Journal of Economics,* 106.

Gilbert, Richard & Oliver Williamson (1988), 'Antitrust Policy ', in Peter Newman (ed) *The New Palgrave Dictionary of Economics and the Law,* New York, Macmillan, 82.

Gilbert, Richard J. & David M.G. Newbery (1982), 'Preemptive Patenting and the Persistence of Monopoly', **72** *Am. Econ. Rev.,* 514.

Ginsburg, Douglas H. (2006), 'An Introduction to Bork *(1966)*', **2** *Competition Pol'y Int'l,* 225.

Ginsburg, Jane C. (2005), 'Legal Protection of Technological Measures Protecting Works of Authorship: International Obligations and the US Experience', available at http://lsr.nellco.org/columbia/pllt/papers/0593.

Ginsburg, Jane C. (1990), 'Creation and Commercial Value: Copyright Protection of Works of Information', **90** *Colum. L. Rev.,* 1865.

Ginsburg, Jane C. (1990), 'A Tale of Two Copyrights: Literary Property in Revolutionary France and America', **64** *Tul. L. Rev.,* 991.

Goldstein, Paul (1971), 'The Competitive Mandate: From Sears Tolear', **59** *Cal. L. Rev.,* 971.

Gordon, Wendy J. (2002), 'Authors, Publishers, and Public Goods: Trading Gold for Dross', **36** *Loyola L. Rev.,* 159.

Gordon, Wendy J. (1999), 'Introduction', **108** *Yale L. J.,* 1611.

Gordon, Wendy J. (1993), 'A Property Right in Self-Expression: Equality and Individualism in the Natural Law of Intellectual Property', **102** *Yale L. J.,* 1533.

Gormsen, Liza Lovdahl (2010), *A Principled Approach to Abuse of Dominance in European Competition Law,* Cambridge, Cambridge University Press.

Gormsen, Liza Lovdahl (2006), 'Article 82: Where are We Coming from and Where are We Going To?', **2** *Comp. L. Rev.*, 5.

Gould, John P. (1973), 'The Economics of Legal Conflicts', **2** *Journal of Legal Studies,* 279.

Grady, Mark F. & Jay I. Alexander (1992), 'Patent Law and Rent Dissipation', **78** *Vand. L. Rev.,* 305.

Green, Jerry R. & Suzanne Scotchmer (1995), 'On the Division of Profit in Sequential Innovation', **26** *Rand J. Econ.,* 20.

Griliches, Zvi (1992), 'The Search for R&D Spillovers', **94** *Scandinavian Journal of Economics,* 29.

Gruca, Thomas S. & D. Sudharshan (1995), 'A Framework for Entry Deterrence Strategy: The Competitive Environments, Choices, and Consequences', **59** *Journal of Marketing,* 44.

Gual, Jorde (2007), 'Time to Rethink Merger Policy', **3** *Competition Policy International,* available at http://ssrn.com/abstract=987093.

Gunther, Jacques-Philippe, Charlotte Breuvart (2005), 'Misuse of Patent and Drug Regulatory Approval Systems in the Pharmaceutical Industry: An Analysis of US and EU Converging Approaches', **26** *E.C.L.R.,* 669.

Hall, Bronwyn & Rose Marie Ham (1989), 'The Patent Paradox Revisited: Determinants of Patenting in the US Semiconductor Industry, 1980–94', NBER Working Paper Series, no. 7062.

Ham, Rosemarie Ziedonis & Bronwyn H. Hall (2001), 'The Effects of Strengthening Patent Rights on Firms Engaged in Cumulative Innovation: Insights from the Semiconductor Industry', **32** *Rand Journal of Economics,* 101.

Hamilton, Walton H. (1941), *Patents and Free Enterprise. Investigation of Concentration of Economic Power*, Washington, U.S. Govt. Print. Off.

Handler, Milton & Richard A. De Sevo (1984), 'The Noerr Doctrine and Its Sham Exception', **6** *Cardozo L. Rev.,* 1.

Hardin, Garrett (1968), 'The Tragedy of the Commons', **162** *Science,* 1243.

Harris, Gardiner, Chris Adams (2001), 'Drug Manufacturers Step Up Legal Attacks That Slow Generics', *WALL ST. J.,* July 12 2001, at A1.

Hart, David M. (2001), 'Antitrust and Technological Innovation in US: Ideas, Institutions, Decisions, and Impacts, 1890–2000', **30** *Research Policy,* 923.

Hart, Robert J. (2006), 'Interoperability Information and the Microsoft Decision', **28** *E.I.P.R.,* 361.

Hatch, Orrin G. & Thomas R. Lee (2002), '"To Promote the Progress of Science": The Copyright Clause and Congress's Power to Extend Copyrights', **16** *Harv. J. L. & Tech.*, 1.

Hatch, Orrin G. (1998), 'Toward a Principled Approach to Copyright Legislation at the Turn of the Millennium', **59** *U. Pitt. L. Rev.*, 719.

Hay, Donald A. (1976), 'Sequential Entry and Entry-Deterring Strategies in Spatial Competition', **28** *Oxford Economic Papers,* 240.

Hayek, Friederich A. (1937), 'Economics and Knowledge', **4** *Economics* 33.

Heiner, David A. (2005), 'Assessing Tying Claims in the Context of Software Integration: A Suggested Framework for Applying the Rule Of Reason Analysis', **72** *U. Chi. L. Rev.*, 123.

Heller, Michael & Rebecca Eisenberg (1998), 'Can Patents Deter Innovation? The Anticommons in Biomedical Research', **280** *Science,* 698.

Hettinger, Edwin C. (1989), 'Justifying Intellectual Property', **18** *Philosophy and Public Affairs,* 31, 37.

Heyer, Ken (2005), 'A World of Uncertainty: Economics and the Globalization of Antitrust', **72** *Antitrust L.J.*, 375.

Hodgson, Geoffrey M. (1993), *Economics and Evolution*, Ann Arbor, Mi, University of Michigan Press.

Hoerner, Robert J. (1986), 'Bad Faith Enforcement of Patents – Antitrust Considerations', **55** *Antitrust L.J.*, 421.

Hotelling, Harold (1929), 'Stability in Competition', **39** *Economic Journal*, 41.

Hovenkamp, Herbert, Mark D. Janis & Mark A. Lemley (2009), *IP and Antitrust. An Analysis of Antitrust Principles Applied to Intellectual Property Law,* New York, Aspen.

Hovenkamp, Herbert (2007), 'The Legal Periphery of Dominant Firm Conduct', available at https://ssrn.com.

Hovenkamp, Herbert J. (2008), 'Innovation and the Domain of Competition Policy', available at https://ssrn.com.

Hovenkamp, Herbert (2005), 'Exclusion and the Sherman Act', **72** *U. Chi. L. Rev.*, 147.

Hovenkamp, Herbert (2005), *The Antitrust Enterprise: Principle and Execution,* Cambridge, Ma, Harvard University Press.

Hovenkamp, Herbert (2005), 'IP and Antitrust Policy: A Brief Historical Overview', 5, available at https://ssrn.com.

Hovenkamp, Herbert (2001), 'Post-Chicago Antitrust: A Review and Critique', 2001 *Colum. Bus. L. Rev.*, 257.

Hovenkamp, Herbert (1993), 'The Marginalist Revolution in Legal Thought', **46** *Vand. L. Rev.*, 305.

Hovenkamp, Herbert (1989), 'The Antitrust Movement and the Rise of Industrial Organization', **68** *Tex. L. Rev.*, 105.

Hovenkamp, Herbert (1989), 'The Sherman Act and the Classical Theory of Competition', **74** *Iowa L. Rev.,* 1019.

Hovenkamp, Herbert (1985), 'Antitrust Policy after Chicago', **84** *Mich. L. R.,* 213.

Hovenkamp, Herbert (1982), 'Distributive Justice and the Antitrust Laws', **51** *Geo. Wash. L. Rev.,* 1.

Howarth, David & Kathryn McMahon (2008), '"Windows Has Performed an Illegal Operation": The Court of First Instance's Judgment in Microsoft v. Commission', 29 E. *C. L. R.,* 117.

Hughes, Justin (1988), 'The Philosophy of Intellectual Property', **77** *Geo. L. J.,* 287.

Hunt, Robert M.. (2006), 'When Do More Patents Reduce R&D?', available at http://ideas.repec.org/e/phu40.html.

Hunt, Robert M. (1999), 'Patent Reform: A Mixed Blessing for the U.S. Economy?', available at http://ideas.repec.org/a/fip/fedpbr/y1999inovp15-29.html.

Hurt, Robert M. & R. Schuchman (1966), 'The Economic Rationale for Copyright', **56** *Am. Econ. Rev.,* 421.

Hurwitz, James D (1985), 'Abuse of Governmental Processes, the First Amendment, and the Boundaries of Noerr', **74** *Georgetown Law Journal,* 65.

Hurwitz, James D. & William E. Kovacic (1982), 'Judicial Analysis of Predation: The Emerging Trends', 35 *Vand. L. Rev.,* 63.

Hylton, Keith N. (1991), 'Economic Rents and Essential Facilities', in 1991 *B.Y.U. L. Rev.,* 1243.

Immordino, Giovanni & Michele Polo (2008), 'Judicial Errors and Innovative Activity', CSEF Discussion Paper no. 196.

Jacobs, Jonathan M. (2001), 'Do We Need a "New Economy" Exception for Antitrust?', **16** *Antitrust,* 89.

Jacobs, Michael S. (1996), 'An Essay on the Normative Foundations of Antitrust Economics', **74** *North Carolina L. Rev.,* 219.

Jaffe, Adam B., Josh Lerner & Scott Stern (eds.) (2006), *Innovation Policy and the Economy,* Boston, Ma, The MIT Press.

Jaffe, Adam B. (2000), 'The U.S. Patent System in Transition: Policy Innovation and the Innovation Process', **29** *Research Policy,* 531.

Jebsen, Per & Robert Stevens (1996), 'Assumptions, Goals and Dominant Undertakings: The Regulation of Competition under Article 86 of the European Union', **64** *Antitrust L. J.,* 443.

Johnson, William R. (1985), 'The Economics of Copying', **93** *J. Pol. Econ.,* 158, 172.

Joliet, René (1970), *Monopolization and Abuse of Dominant Position,* The Hague, Martinus Nijhoff.

Jones, Alison & Brenda Sufrin (2008), *EC Competition Law,* Oxford, Oxford University Press.
Jones, Charles I. & John C. Williams (1998), 'Measuring the Social Return to R&D', **113** *Quarterly J. Econ.*, 1119.
Jorde, Thomas M. & David J. Teece (1993), 'Rule of Reason Analysis of Horizontal Arrangements: Agreements Designed to Advance Innovation and Commercialized Technology', **61** *Antitrust L. J.,* 579.
Jorde, Thomas M. & David J. Teece (eds.) (1992), *Antitrust, Innovation, and Competitiveness,* Oxford, The Oxford University Press.
Joskow, Paul L. (1991), 'The Role of Transaction Cost Economics in Antitrust and Public Utility Regulatory Policies', **7** *J. L. Econ. & Organ.,* 53.
Jovanovic, Boyan (1982), 'Selection and the Evolution of Industry', **50** *Econometrica,* 649.
Kallay, Dina (2004), *The Law and Economics of Antitrust and Intellectual Property. An Austrian Approach,* Cheltenham, Edward Elgar Publishing.
Kanter, Daniel (2006), 'IP and Compulsory Licensing on Both Sides of the Atlantic – An Appropriate Antitrust Remedy or Cutback to Innovation', 27(7) *E.C.L.R.,* 351, 355.
Kaplow, Louis (1985), 'Extension of Monopoly Power Through Leverage', **85** *Colum. L. Rev.,* 515.
Karp, Larry S. & Jeffrey Perloff (1996), 'The Optimal Suppression of a Low-Cost Technology by a Durable-Good Monopoly', **27** *Rand Journal of Economics,* 346.
Katz, Ariel (2002), 'Intellectual Property Rights and Antitrust Policy: Four Principles for a Complex World', **1** *Journal of Telecommunications & High Technology Law,* 325, 351.
Katz, Michael L. & Joseph Farrell (2000), 'Innovation, Rent Extraction, and Integration in System Markets', **48** *Journal of Industrial Economics,* 413.
Katz, Michael L. & Carl Shapiro (1994), 'Systems Competition and Network Effects', **5** *Journal of Economic Perspectives,* 93.
Katz, Michael L. & Carl Shapiro (1986), 'Product Compatibility Choice in a Market with Technological Choices', **38** *Oxford Economic Series,* 146.
Katz, Michael L. & Carl Shapiro (1986), 'Network Externalities, Competition, and Compatibility', **75** *Am. Econ. Rev.*, 93.
Katz, Michael L. & Carl Shapiro (1986), 'Technology Adoption in the Presence of Network Externalities', **94** *J. Pol. Econ.,* 822.
Katz, Michael L. & Howard A. Shelanski (2005), '"Schumpeterian" Competition and Antitrust Policy in High-Tech Markets', available at http://ssrn.com.

Katz, Michael (1951), 'The Doctrine of Moral Rights and American Copyright Law – A Proposal', **24** *S. Cal. L. Rev.*, 375, 391–409.

Kaufman, Bruce W. et al. (1970), 'Suppressing Technology: The Automobile Air Pollution Case', **3** *Antitrust Law and Economics Review*, 111.

Kaufmann, Jack (1998), 'Afterword: Symposium on Antitrust and the Suppression of Technology in the United States and Europe: Is There a Remedy?', **66** *Antitrust L. J.*, 527.

Kaysen, Carl, Donald F. Turner (1959), *Antitrust Policy; An Economic and Legal Analysis,* Cambridge, Ma, Harvard University Press.

Kieff, F. Scott (2001), 'Facilitating Scientific Research: Intellectual Property Rights and the Norms of Science – A Response to Rai and Eisenberg', **95** *Nw. U. L. Rev.*, 691.

Kintner, Earl W. & Joseph P. Bauer (1984), 'Antitrust Exemptions for Private Requests for Governmental Action: A Critical Analysis of the Noerr-Pennington Doctrine', **17** *U.C. Davis L. Rev.*, 549.

Kirzner, Israel (ed.)(1982), *Methods, Process and Austrian Economics,* Lexington, Ma, Lexington Books.

Kirzner, Israel (1973), *Competition and Entrepreneurship,* Chicago, University of Chicago Press.

Kitch, Edmund W. (2000), 'Elementary and Persistent Errors in the Economic Analysis of Intellectual Property', **53** *Vand. L. Rev.*, 1727, 1740.

Kitch, Edmund W. (1977), 'The Nature and Function of the Patent System', **20** *J. L. & Econ.*, 265.

Klein, Christopher C. (1989), 'The Economics of Sham Litigation: Theory, Cases, and Policy', Bureau of Economics Staff – Report to the Federal Trade Commission 20, available at www.ftc.gov.

Klein, Christopher C. (1986), 'Strategic Sham Litigation: Economic Incentives in the Context of the Case Law', **6** *International Review of Law and Economics,* 241.

Klein, Joel & Preeta Bansal (1996), 'International Antitrust Enforcement in the Computer Industry', **41** *Vill. L. Rev.*, 173.

Klein, Peter (2000), 'New Institutional Economics', in Boudewijn Bouckaert & Gerrit De Geest (eds.) *Encyclopedia of Law and Economics*, Cheltenham, *Edward Elgar Publishing,* 456.

Klemperer, Paul (1990), 'How Broad Should the Scope of Patent Protection Be?', **21** *Rand Journal of Economics,* 113.

Kobak, James B., Jr., and Robert P. Reznick (2007), 'Federal Circuit Ruling Portends Changes to Generic Drug Patent Infringement Litigation and Walker Process Antitrust Claims', **19** *Intellectual Property & Technology Law Journal*, 1.

Kobak, James B. Jr. (2001), 'The Federal Circuit as a Competition

Law Court', available at www.hugheshubbard.com/files/tbl_s20NewsPring%5CPDFUpload103%5C701%5CJournal_Patent_Trademark_August_2001.pdf.

Kobak, James B., Jr. (1994), 'Professional Real Estate Investors and the Future of Patent-Antitrust Litigation: Walker Process and Handgards Meet Noerr-Pennington', **63** *Antitrust L.J.*, 185.

Kobak, James B., Jr. (1996), 'Running the Gauntlet: Antitrust and Intellectual Property Pitfalls on the Two Sides of the Atlantic', **64** *Antitrust L. J.*, 341.

Kobayashi, Bruce H. (2005), 'Does Economics Provide a Reliable Guide to Regulating Commodity Bundling by Firms? A Survey of the Economic Literature', **1** *Journal of Competition Law & Economics*, 707.

Kobayashi, Bruce H. (1997), 'Game Theory and Antitrust: A Post-Mortem', **5** *Geo. Mason L. Rev.*, 411.

Kolay, Sreya & Greg Shaffer (2003), 'Bundling and Menus of Two-Part Tariffs', **51** *J. Ind. Econ.*, 383.

Kolasky, William J. (2004), 'What Is Competition? A Comparison of the U.S. and European Perspectives', **49** *Antitrust Bull.*, 29.

Korah, Valentine (2002), 'The Interface between Intellectual Property and Antitrust: The European Experience', **69** *Antitrust L. J.*, 801.

Kovacic, William (2007), 'The Intellectual DNA of Modern U.S. Competition Law for Dominant Firm Conduct: The Chicago/Harvard Double Helix', **2007** *Colum. Bus. L. Rev.*, 1.

Kovacic, William E. (2003), 'The Modern Evolution of U.S. Competition Policy Enforcement Norms', **71** *Antitrust L.J.*, 377, 448–60.

Kovacic, William E. & Carl Shapiro (2000), 'Antitrust Policy: A Century of Economic and Legal Thinking', **14** *J. Econ. Persp.*, 43.

Kovacic, William E. (1992), 'The Influence of Economics on Antitrust Law', **30** *Econ. Inquir.*, 294.

Krafft, Jackie (ed.) (2000), *The Process of Competition*, Cheltenham, *Edward Elgar*.

Krueger, Anne O. (1974), 'The Political Economy of the Rent-Seeking Society', **64** *Am. Econ. Rev.*, 291.

Kukkonen, Carl A. (1998), 'The Use of Patent Licensing Center as an Intermediary for Facilitating the Licensing of Commercially Viable, Unused Patents', **3** *Va. J. L. & Tech.*, 10.

Kwall, Roberta R. (1985), 'Copyright and the Moral Right: Is an American Marriage Possible?', **38** *Vand. L. Rev.*, 1.

Kwoka, John E. & Lawrence J. White (eds.) (2003), *The Antitrust Revolution*, Oxford, Oxford University Press.

Lachmann, L. M. (1986), *The Market as an Economic Process*, New York, Basil Blackwell.

Laffont, Jean-Jacques & Jean Tirole (2000), *Competition in Telecommunications,* Cambridge, Ma, The MIT Press.
Lancaster, Kelvin (1990), 'The Economics of Product Variety: A Survey', **9** *Marketing Science,* 189.
Lande, Robert H. (1988), 'The Rise and (Coming) Fall of Efficiency as the Ruler of Antitrust', **33** *Antitrust Bulletin,* 429.
Lande, Robert H. (1982), 'Wealth Transfers as the Original and Primary Concern of Antitrust: The Efficiency Interpretation Challenged', **34** *Hastings L. J.,* 65.
Landers, Amy L. (2006), 'Liquid Patents', **84** *Denver University L. Rev.,*199.
Landes, William M. (2004), 'Empirical Analysis of Intellectual Property Litigation: Some Preliminary Results', **41** *Hous. L. Rev.,* 749.
Landes, William M. & Richard A. Posner (2003), *The Economic Structure of Intellectual Property Law,* Cambridge, Ma, Harvard University Press.
Landes, William M. & Richard A. Posner (2003), 'Indefinitely Renewable Copyright', **70** *U. Chi. L. Rev.,* 471.
Landes, William M. & Richard A. Posner (1989), 'An Economic Analysis of Copyright Law', **18** *J. Legal Studies,* 325.
Landes, William M. & Richard A. Posner (1981), 'Market Power in Antitrust Cases', **94** *Harv. L. Rev.,* 937.
Landes, William M. (1971), 'An Economic Analysis of the Courts', **14** *Journal of Law and Economics,* 61.
Langer, Jurian (2007), *Tying and Bundling as a Leveraging Concern under EC Competition Law,* The Netherlands, Kluwer Law International, 49.
Langlois, Richard N. (1986), *Economics as a Process: Essays in the New Institutional Economics,* New York, Cambridge University Press.
Lao, Marina (2009), 'Networks, Access, and "Essential Facilities": From Terminal Road to Microsoft', **62** *SMU L. Rev.,* 557.
Lao, Marina (2005), 'Aspen Skiing and Trinko: Antitrust Intent and Sacrifice', **73** *Antitrust L. J.,* 171.
Lao, Marina (2003), 'Reforming the Noerr-Pennington Antitrust Immunity Doctrine', **55** *Rutgers L. Rev.,* 965.
Lee, Kirby W. (2003), 'Permitted Use of Patented Inventions in the United States: Why Prescription Drugs Do Not Merit Compulsory Licensing', **36** *Ind. L. Rev.,* 175.
Lehmann, Michael (1985), 'The Theory of Property Rights and the Protection of Intellectual and Industrial Property', **16** *International Review of Industrial Property and Copyright Law,* 525.
Leibenstein, Harvey (1966), 'Allocative Efficiency vs. "X-Efficiency"', **56** *Am. Econ. Rev.,* 392.
Lemley, Mark A. (2005), 'Property, Intellectual Property, and Free Riding', **83** *Tex. L. Rev.,* 1031.

Lemley, Mark A. & Carl Shapiro (2005), 'Probabilistic Patents', **19** *Journal of Economic Perspectives,* 75.
Lemley, Mark A. (2004), 'Ex ante versus ex post Justifications for Intellectual Property', **71** *U. Chi. L. Rev.,* 129.
Lemley, Mark A. & David McGowan (1998), 'Legal Implications of Network Economic Effects', **86** *Cal. L. Rev.,* 479.
Lemley, Mark A. (1997), 'The Economics of Improvement in Intellectual Property Law', **75** *Tex. L. Rev.,* 989.
Leslie, Christopher R. (2006), 'The Anticompetitive Effects of Unenforced Invalid Patents', **91** *Minn. L. Rev.,* 101.
Levey, Robert A. (2005), 'Microsoft and the Browser Wars', **31** *Conn. L. Rev.,* 1321.
Lévêque, François & Howard Shelanski (eds.) (2005), *Antitrust and IPRs. EU and US Perspectives,* Cheltenham, Edward Elgar Publishing.
Lévêque, François(2005), 'Innovation, Leveraging and Essential Facilities: Interoperability Licensing in the EU Microsoft Case', in *Antitrust, Patents, and Copyright* 103, 107–08, available at www.ssrn.com.
Lévêque, François and Yann Ménière (2004), *The Economics of Patents and Copyright,* Berkeley Electronic Press.
Levin, Richard C. et al. (1987), 'Appropriating the Returns from Industrial Research and Development', **3** *Brookings Papers on Economic Activity,* 783.
Levin, Richard C. et al. (1985), 'R&D Appropriability, Opportunity and Market Structure: New Evidence on Some Schumpeterian Hypotheses', **75** *Am. Econ. Rev.,* 20.
Lewin, Peter (2007), 'Creativity or Coercion: Alternative Perspectives on Rights to Intellectual Property', **71** *Journal of Business Ethics,* 441.
Liebowitz, Stan J. and Stephen E. Margolis (1995), 'Path Dependence, Lock-In and History', **11** *J. L. Econ.. & Org.*, 205.
Liebowitz, Stan J. and Stephen E. Margolis (1994), 'Network Externality: An Uncommon Tragedy', **8** *J. Econ. Persp.*
Liebowitz, Stan J. and Stephen E. Margolis (1990), 'The Fable of the Keys', **33** *J. L. & Econ.,* 1.
Lipsky, Abbott B. & J. Gregory Sidak (1999), 'Essential Facilities', **51** *Stan. L. Rev.,* 1187, 1248.
Liu, Joseph P. (2002), 'Copyright and Time: A Proposal', **101** *Mich. L. Rev.,* 409.
Loewenthal, Paul-John (2005), 'The Defence of "Objective Justification" in the Application of Article 82 EC', **28** *World Competition,* 455.
Lofaro, Andrea & Derek Ridyard (2002), 'Beyond Bork: New Economic Theories of Exclusion in Merger Cases', **23** *European Competition Law Review,* 153.

Lopatka, John E. (2000), 'United States v. IBM: A Monument to Arrogance', **68** *Antitrust L.J.,* 145.

Lopatka, John E. & William H. Page (1999), 'Antitrust on Internet Time: Microsoft and the Law of Economics and Exclusion', **7** *Sup. Ct. Econ. Rev.,* 157.

Lopatka, John E. & William H. Page (1995), 'Microsoft, Monopolization, and Network Externalities: Some Abuses of Economic Theory in Antitrust Decision Making', **40** *Antitrust Bull.,* 317.

Lundvall, Bengt-Åke (1992), *National Systems of Innovation: Towards a Theory of Innovation and Interactive Learning*, London: Pinter Publisher.

Lowe, Philip & Lucas Peeperkorn (2005), 'Intellectual Property: How Special is it For the Purposes of Competition Law Enforcement?', available at http://www.eui.eu/RSCAS/Research/Competition/2005(papers).shtml.

Lowe, Philip (2004), *DG Competition's Review of the Policy on Abuse of Dominance*, in Barry E. Hawk (ed) *International Antitrust & Policy: Annual Proceedings of the Fordham Corporate Law Institute 2003,* New York, Juris Publishing, 170.

Lugard, Paul & Leigh Hancher (eds.) (2005) *On The Merits: Current Issues In Competition Law and Policy,* Mortsel, Intersentia .

Machovec, Frank M. (1995), *Perfect Competition and the Transformation of Economics*, London, Routledge.

Mackie-Mason, Jeffrey K. (2006), 'What to do about Unilateral Refusals to License?', available at www.ssrn.com.

Malerba, Franco & Stefano Brusoni (eds.) (2007), *Perspectives on Innovation*, Cambridge, Cambridge University Press.

Marenco, Giuliano (2002), 'The Birth of Modern Competition Law in Europe', in Armin von Bogdandy, Petros C. Mavroidis, Yves Mény (eds), *European Integration and International Coordination: Studies in Transnational Economic Law in Honour of Claus Dieter Ehlermann,* The Hague, Kluwer International Law.

Marengo, Luigi & Simonetta Vezzoso (2006), 'Dynamic Inefficiencies of Intellectual Property Rights from an Evolutionary/Problem-Solving Perspective: Some Insights on Computer Software and Reverse Engineering 2', available at www.ssrn.com.

Marshall, Alfred (1920), *Principles of Economics*, London, Macmillan

Mason, Edward S. (1949), 'The Current State of the Monopoly Problem in the United States', **62** *Harv. L. Rev.,* 1265.

Martin, Stephen (2007), 'The Goals of Antitrust and Competition Policy', available at http://ssrn.com.

Matutes, Carmen & Pierre Regibeau (1996), 'A Selective Review of the Economics of Standardization. Entry Deterrence, Technological

Progress and International Competition', **12** *European Journal of Political Economy,* 183.

Matutes, Carmen & Pierre Regibeau (1988), 'Mix and Match Product Compatibility without Network Externalities', **19** *Rand Journal of Economics,* 221.

May, James (1989), 'Antitrust in the Formative Era: Political and Economic Theory in Constitutional and Antitrust Analysis, 1880–1918', **50** *Ohio St. L. J.*, 257.

Mazzoleni, Roberto & Richard R. Nelson (1998), 'The Benefits and Costs of Strong Patent Protection: A Contribution to the Current Debate', **27** *Research Policy,* 273.

McAfee, Preston R, John McMillan, & Michael D. Whinston (1989), 'Multiproduct Monopoly, Commodity Bundling, and Correlation of Values', **104** *Quarterly Journal of Economics,* 371.

McAfee, Preston R., Hugo M. Mialon, Sue H. Mialon (2005), 'Private Antitrust Litigation: Procompetitive or Anticompetitive?', available at http://userwww.service.emory.edu/~hmialon/PrivateAntitrustEnforcementProOrAntiCompetitivMcDonald, J. Bruce (2005), 'Section 2 and Article 82: Cowboys and Gentlemen', available at www.usdoj.gov/atr/public/speeches/210873.htm.

McDonough III, James F. (2006), 'The Myth of the Patent Troll: An Alternative View of the Function of Patent Dealers in an Idea Economy', **56** *Emory L. J.,* 189.

McFetridge, Donald G. & Douglas A. Smith (1980), 'Patents, Prospects, and Economic Surplus: A Comment', **23** *J. L. & Econ.,* 197.

McGowan, David (1996), 'Regulating Competition in the Information Age: Computer Software as an Essential Facility Under the Sherman Act', **18** *Hastings Comm. & Ent. L.J.*, 771.

McGowan, David & Mark A. Lemley (1994), 'Antitrust Immunity: State Action and Federalism, Petitioning and the First Amendment', **17** *Harv. J.L. & Pub. Pol'y,* 293.

McNulty, Paul J. (1968), 'Economic Theory and the Meaning of Competition', **82** *Quarterly Journal of Economics,* 639.

McNulty, Paul J. (1967), 'A Note on the History of Perfect Competition', **75** *J. Pol. Econ.,* 395.

McNutt, Patrick A.. (2005), *Law, Economics and Antitrust towards a New Perspective,* Cheltenham, *Edward Elgar Publishing.*

Meinberg, Henrik (2006), 'From Magill to IMS Health: The New Product Requirement and the Diversity of Intellectual Property Rights', 28(7) *E.I.P.R.,* 398.

Meinhardt, Peter (1946), *Inventions, Patents and Monopoly,* London, Stevens & Sons.

Melamed, Douglas (2005), 'Exclusionary Conduct under the Antitrust Laws: Balancing, Sacrifice and Refusals to Deal', **20** *Berkeley Tech. L. J.*, 1247.

Melamed, A. Douglas & Ali M. Stoeppelwerth (2002), 'The CSU Case: Facts, Formalism and the Intersection of Antitrust and Intellectual Property', **10** *George Mason L. Rev.*, 407.

Melissa, K., 'Monopolistic Tendencies of Brand-Name Drug Companies in Pharmaceutical Industry', **15** *J.L.& COM.*, 357.

Merges, Robert P. (2000), 'One Hundred Years of Solicitude: Intellectual Property Law', 1900–2000, **88** *Cal. L. Rev.*, 2187.

Merges, Robert P. (2000), 'Intellectual Property Rights and the New Institutional Economics',**53** *Vand. L. Rev.*, 1857.

Merges, Robert P. & Glenn H. Reynolds (2000), 'The Proper Scope of the Copyright and Patent Power', **37** *Harv. J. on Legis.*, 45.

Merges, Robert P. (1994) 'Of Property Rules, Coase, and Intellectual Property', **94** *Colum. L. Rev.*, 2655.

Merges, Robert P. and Richard R. Nelson (1994), 'On Limiting or Encouraging Rivalry in Technical Progress: the Effects of Patent Scope Decisions', **25** *Journal of Economic Behavior and Organization,* 1, 2.

Merges, Robert P. (1992), 'Rent Control in the Patent District: Observations on the Grady-Alexander Thesis', **78** *Vand. L. Rev.*, 359.

Merges, Robert P. & Richard R. Nelson (1990), 'On the Complex Economics of Patent Scope', **90** *Colum. L. Rev.*, 839.

Merrill, Thomas W. (1998), 'Property and the Right to Exclude', **77** *Neb. L. Rev.*, 730.

Mertikopoulou, Victoria (2007), 'DG's Competition Discussion Paper on the Application of Article 82 of the EC Treaty to Exclusionary Abuses: the Proposed Economic Reform from a Legal Point of View', **28** *ECLR,* 241.

Meurer, Michael J. (2003), 'Controlling Opportunistic and Anti-Competitive Intellectual Property Litigation', available at www.ssrn.com.

Meyer, David L. (1986), Note, 'A Standard for Tailoring Noerr-Pennington Immunity More Closely to the First Amendment Mandate', **95** *Yale L.J* . 832.

Michelman, Frank I. (1967), 'Property, Utility, and Fairness: Comments on the Ethical Foundations of "Just Compensation" Law', **80** *Harv. L. Rev.*, 1165.

Miller III, James C. & Paul Pautler (1985), 'Predation: The Changing View in Economics and the Law', **28** *Journal of Law and Economics,* 495.

Millon, David S. (1988), 'The Sherman Act and the Balance of Power', **61** *S. Cal. L. Rev.*, 1219, 1255.

Minda, Gary (1995), 'Antitrust at Century's End', **48** *S.M.U. L. Rev.*, 1749.

Minda, Gary (1990), 'Interest Groups, Political Freedom, and Antitrust: A Modern Reassessment of the Noerr-Pennington Doctrine', **41** *Hastings L.J.,* 905.

Montagnani, Maria Lillà (2006), 'Predatory and Exclusionary Innovation: Which Legal Standard for Software Integration in the Context of the Competition v. Intellectual Property Rights Clash?', **37** *IIC,* 304.

Monti, Girogio (2007), *EC Competition Law,* Cambridge, Cambridge University Press.

Moore, Adam D. (2001), *Intellectual Property & Information Control. Philosophic Foundations and Contemporary Issues, Piscataway*, NJ, Transaction Publishing Rutgers.

Möschel, Wernhard (1989), 'Competition Policy from an Ordo Point of View', in Alan Peacock and Hans Willgerodt, (eds), *German Neo-liberals and the Social Market Economy,* London, MacMillan, 146.

Moss, Scott (1984), 'The History of the Theory of the Firm from Marshall to Robinson and Chamberlin: The Source of Positivism in Economics', **51** *Economica,* 307.

Motta, Massimo (2004), *Competition Policy,* Cambridge, Cambridge University Press.

Munzer, Stephen R. (ed.) (2001), *New Essays in the Legal and Political Theory of Property,* Cambridge, Cambridge University Press.

Muris, Timothy J. (2002), 'Generic Pharmaceuticals: Marketplace Access and Consumer Issues: Hearing Before the S. Comm. on Commerce, Science & Transportation, 107th Cong. 23–24 (2002)', available at http://www.ftc.gov/os/2002/04/pharmatestimony.htm.

Muris, Timothy J. (1997), 'Economics and Antitrust', **5** *Geo. Mason L. Rev.,* 303.

Myers, Gary (1992), 'Litigation as a Predatory Practice', **80** *Ky. L.J.,* 565.

Nalebuff, Barry (2004), 'Bundling as an Entry Barrier', **119** *Quart. J. Bus. Econ.,* 159.

Nalebuff, Barry (2003), 'Bundling, Tying and Portfolio Effects', available at www.berr.gov.uk/files/file14774.pdf.

Nelson, Richard R. (1996), *The Sources of Economic Growth,* Cambridge, Ma, Harvard University Press, 87.

Nelson, Richard R. & Sidney G. Winter (1982), *An Evolutionary Theory of Economic Change*, Cambridge, Ma, Belknap Press of Harvard University Press.

Nelson, Richard R. (1959), 'The Simple Economics of Basic Scientific Research', **67** *J. Pol. Econ.,* 297.

Netanel, Neil Weinstock (1996), 'Copyright and a Democratic Civil Society', **106** *Yale L. J.,* 283.

Newcomb Hohfeld, Wesley (1917), 'Fundamental Legal Conceptions as Applied in Judicial Reasoning', **26** *Yale L.J.,* 710.

Newcomb Hohfeld, Wesley (1913), 'Some Fundamental Legal Conceptions as Applied in Judicial Reasoning', **23** *Yale L.J.,* 16.

Niels, Gunnar & Adriaan Kate (2004), 'Introduction: Antitrust in the U.S. and the EU – Converging or Diverging Paths?', **49** *Antitrust Bull.,* 1.

Nordhaus, William D. (1969), *Invention, Growth, and Economic Welfare*, Boston, Ma, The MIT Press.

O'Donnell, S. W.(2004), 'Unified Theory of Antitrust Counterclaims in Patent Litigation', **9** *Virginia Journal Of Law & Technology*, 1.

O'Donoghue, Robert & Jorge A. Padilla (2004), *The Law and Economics of Article 82,* Oxford, Hart Publishing.

OECD (2007), 'Guidance to Business on Monopolization and Abuse of Dominance', available at http://www.oecd.org/dataoecd/50/33/40880976.pdf.

OECD (2005), 'Competition on the Merits', available at http://www.oecd.org/dataoecd/7/13/35911017.pdf.

Oettinger, Nicholas (2001), 'In re Independent Service Organizations Antitrust Litigation', **16** *Berkeley Tech. L.J.,* 323.

Ordover, Janusz A., Garth Saloner & Steven Salop (1990), 'Equilibrium Vertical Foreclosure', **80** *Am. Econ. Rev.,* 127.

Ordover, Janusz A. (1985), 'Economic Foundations and Considerations in Protecting Industrial and Intellectual Property', **53** *Antitrust L. J.*, 503.

Ordover, Janusz A., Alan O. Sykes, & Robert D. Willig (1983), 'Predatory Systems Rivalry: A Reply', **83** *Colum. L. Rev.,* 1150.

Ordover, Janusz & Robert Willig (1981), 'An Economic Definition of Predation Pricing and Product Innovation', **91** *Yale L. J.*, 8.

Owen, Bruce M. & Ronald Braeutigam (1978), *The Regulation Game: Strategic Use of the Administrative Process,* Cambridge, Ma: Ballinger Pub. Co.

Page, William H. (1996), 'Areeda, Chicago, and Antitrust Injury: Economic Efficiency and Legal Process', **41** *Antitrust Bull.,* 909.

Page, William H. (1991), 'Ideological Conflict and the Origins of Antitrust Policy', 66 *Tul. L. Rev.* 1.

Palmer, Tom G. (1990), 'Are Patents and Copyrights Morally Justified?', **13** *Harvard Journal of Law and Public Policy,* 817.

Palomeras, Neus (2003), 'Sleeping Patents: Any Reason to Wake Up?', Working Paper no. 506, available at www.ebcenter.org.

Pate, R. Hewitt (2005), 'Exclusionary Conduct: Refusals to Deal and Bundling and Loyalty Discounts', Testimony before the Antitrust Modernization Commission (September 29, 2005).

Pate, R. Hewitt (2005), 'Competition and Intellectual Property in the US:

Licensing Freedom and the Limits of Antitrust', available at http://www.eui.eu/RSCAS/Research/Competition/2005(papers).shtml.

Pate, R. Hewitt 2004, 'The Common Law Approach and Improving Standards for Analyzing Single Firm Conduct', in Barry E. Hawk (ed), *International Law Policy: Fordham Corporate Law 2003,* New York, Juris Publishing, 195.

Pate, R. Hewitt (2002), 'Refusals to Deal and Intellectual Property Rights', **10** *Geo. Mason L. Rev.,* 429.

Patry, William F. (1996), 'Copyright and the Legislative Process: A Personal Perspective', **14** *Cardozo Arts & Ent. L. J.,* 139.

Patterson, Mark R. (2003), 'The Sacrifice of Profits in Non-Price Predation', **18** *Antitrust,* 37.

Peltzman, Sam (1996), 'The Handbook of Industrial Organization: A Review Article', **99** *J. Pol. Econ.,* 201.

Peritz, Rudoph (2001), 'Re-Thinking US v Microsoft in Light of the EC Case', available at http://ssrn.com/abstract=571803.

Peritz, Rudolph J. R. (1996), *Competition Policy in America 1888–1992: History, Rhetoric, Law*, New York, Oxford University Press.

Perrine, James (1995), 'Defining the Sham Litigation to the Noerr-Pennington Antitrust Immunity Doctrine: An Analysis of the Professional Real Estate Investors v. Columbia Pictures Industries Decision', **46** *Ala. L. Rev.,* 815.

Peterson, Shorey(1957), 'Antitrust and the Classic Model', **47** *Am. Econ. Rev.,* 60.

Piraino, Thomas A. (1998), 'An Antitrust Remedy for Monopoly Leveraging by Electronic Networks', **93** *Nw. U. L. Rev.,* 1.

Pitofsky, Robert (ed.) (2008), *How the Chicago School Overshot the Mark*, New York, Oxford University Press.

Pitofsky, Robert (2005), 'Past, Present and Future Antitrust Enforcement at the Federal Trade of Commission', **72** *U. Chi. L. Rev.,* 209.

Pitofsky, Robert, Donna Patterson & Jonathan Hooks (2002), 'The Essential Facilities Doctrine Under U.S. Antitrust Law', **70** *Antitrust L.J.,* 443.

Pitofsky, Robert (2001), 'Challenges of the New Economy: Issues at the Intersection of Antitrust and Intellectual Property', **68** *Antitrust L.J.,* 913, 919–23.

Pitofsky, Robert (2001), 'Antitrust and Intellectual Property: Unresolved Issues at the Heart of the New Economy', **16** *Berkeley Tech. L. J.,* 535.

Pitofsky, Robert (1979), *The Political Content of Antitrust*, **127** *U. Pa. L. Rev.,* 1051.

Plant, Arnold (1934), 'The Economic Theory Concerning Patents for Inventions', **1** *Economica,* 67.

Polanyi, Michael (1958), *Personal Knowledge. Towards a Post Critical Philosophy*, London, Routledge.

Ponsoldt, James F. & Christopher D. David (2007), 'A Comparison between U.S. and E.U. Antitrust Treatment of Tying Claims against Microsoft: When should the Bundling of Computer Software be Permitted', **27** *Nw. J. Int'l L. & Bus.,* 421.

Posner, Richard A. (2000), 'Antitrust in the New Economy 3', available at www.ssrn.com.

Posner, Richard A. (2005), 'Intellectual Property: The Law and Economics Approach', **19** *Journal of Economic Perspectives* 57.

Posner, Richard A. (2003), *Economic Analysis of Law*, New York, Aspen Law & Business.

Posner, Richard A. (1979), 'The Chicago School of Antitrust Analysis', **127** *U. Pa. L. Rev.,* 925.

Posner, Richard A. (1976), *Antitrust Law,* Chicago, University of Chicago Press.

Posner, Richard (1975), 'The Social Costs of Monopoly and Regulation', **83** *J. Pol. Econ.,* 807.

Posner, Richard A. (1973), 'An Economic Approach to Legal Procedure and Judicial Administration', **2** *Journal of Legal Studies,* 399.

Priest, George L. (1986), 'What Economists Can Tell Lawyers About Intellectual Property: Comment on Cheung', **8** *Res. L. & Econ.,* 19.

Radin, Margaret Jane (1982), 'Property and Personhood', **34** *Stan. L. Rev.*, 957.

Rahnasto, Ilkka (2002), *Intellectual Property Rights, External Effects and Antitrust Law*, Oxford, Oxford University Press, 49.

Rasmussen, Eric (1991), 'Naked Exclusion', **81** *Am. Econ. Rev.*,1137.

Reinganum, Jennifer F. (1983), 'Uncertain Innovation and the Persistence of Monopoly', **73** *Am. Econ. Rev*., 741.

Reitzig, Marcus et al. (2006), 'On Sharks, Trolls, and Other Patent Animals – "Being Infringed" as a Normatively Induced Innovation Exploitation Strategy', available at http://ssrn.com/abstract=885914.

Rey, Patrick & Jean Tirole (2006), 'A Primer on Foreclosure 1', available at http://idei.fr/doc/by/tirole/primer.pdf.

Rey, Patrick, Paul Seabright, & Jean Tirole (2001), 'The Activities of a Monopoly Firm in Adjacent Competitive Markets: Economic Consequences and Implications for Competition Policy', available at http://ideas.repec.org/p/ide/wpaper/660.html.

Ridyard, Derek (2004), 'Compulsory Access Under EC Competition Law – A New Doctrine of "Convenient Facilities" and the Case for Price Regulation', **25**(11) *European Competition L. Rev.,* 670.

Ritter, Cyril (2005), 'Refusal to Deal and "Essential Facilities": Does

Intellectual Property Require Special Deference Compared to Tangible Property?', 28(3) *World Competition,* 281.
Robledo, Julio R. (2005), 'Strategic Patents and Asymmetric Litigation Costs as Entry Deterrence Instruments', **15** *Economics Bulletin,* 1, 2.
Roeder, Martin A. (1940), 'The Doctrine of Moral Rights: A Study in the Law of Artists, Authors and Creators', **53** *Harv. L. Rev.,* 554.
Röller, LarsHendrik & Oliver Stehmann (2005), 'The Year 2005 at DG Competition: The Trend towards a more Effects-based Approach', **29** *Review of Industrial Organization,* 281.
Rommer, Paul (1992), 'When Should We Use Intellectual Property Rights', **92** *Am. Econ. Rev.,* 213.
Rose, Mark (1993), *Authors and Owners: The Invention of Copyright,* Cambridge, Ma, Harvard University Press.
Rousseva, Ekaterina (2010), *Rethinking Exclusionary Abuses in EU Competition Law*, New York, Hart Publishing.
Rousseva, Ekaterina (2006), 'The Concept of "Objective Justification" of an Abuse of a Dominant Position: Can It Help to Modernize the Analysis under Article 82 EC?', **2** *Comp. L. Rev.,* 27.
Rubinfeld, Daniel L. (2001), 'Antitrust Policy', in Neil J. Smelser and Paul B. Baltes (ed.), *1 International Encyclopedia of the Social and Behavioral Sciences* 553.
Rubinfeld, Daniel L. (1998), 'Antitrust Enforcement in Dynamic Network Industries', **43** *Antitrust Bull.,* 859.
Sakakibara, Mariko & Lee Branstetter (2001), 'Do Stronger Patents Induce More Innovation? Evidence from the 1988 Japanese Patent Law Reforms', **32** *Rand Journal of Economics,* 77.
Salant, Stephen (1984), 'Preemptive Patenting and the Persistence of Monopoly: Comment', **74** *Am. Econ. Rev.,* 247.
Salinger, Michael A. (1995), 'A Graphical Analysis of Bundling', **68** *J. Bus.*,85.
Salop, Steven C. (2010), 'An Administrable and Efficient Standard for Refusals to Deal and Price Squeezers by an Unregulated, Vertically Integrated Monopolist', available at www.ssrn.com.
Salop, Steven C. (2006), 'Exclusionary Conduct, Effect on Consumers, and the Flawed Profit-Sacrificed Standard', **73** *Antitrust L. J.,* 311.
Salop, Steven C. & R. Craig Romaine (1999), 'Preserving Monopoly: Economic Analysis, Legal Standards, and Microsoft', **7** *Geo. Mason L. Rev.,* 617.
Salop, Steven C. (1986), 'Measuring Ease of Entry', **31** *Antitrust Bull.,* 551.
Salop, Steven C. and Lawrence J. White (1986), 'Economic Analysis of Private Antitrust Litigation', **74** *Geo. L.J.,* 1001.

Salop, Steven C. & David Scheffman (1983), 'Raising Rivals' Costs', **73** *Am. Econ. Rev.*, 267.

Salop, Steven C. (ed.) (1981), *Strategy, Predation, and Antitrust Analysis*, Washington, Federal Trade Commission, Bureau of Economics.

Sampsung X. Shi (2008), 'Knowledge and Its Inventors/Carriers in Evolutionary Economics: Towards A Relational Theory of Authorship and Copyright 2', available at www.ssrn.com.

Samuelson, Pam (2003), 'Copyright and Freedom of Expression in Historical Perspective', **10** *J. Intell. Prop. L.*, 319.

Samuelson, Pamela et al. (1994), 'A Manifesto Concerning the Legal Protection of Computer Programs', **94** *Colum. L. Rev.*, 2308.

Sanders, Barkey S. (1964), 'Patterns of Commercial Exploitation of Patented Inventions by Large and Small Corporations', **8** *Pat., Trademark, & Copyright J. Res. & Educ.*, 51.

Sanfilippo, Luca (1995), 'Abuse of Freedom of Conduct: Neighbouring Markets and Application of Article 86', *EBLR*, 6.

Sankaran, Sri Krishna (2000), 'Patent Flooding in the United States and Japan', **40** *IDEA, The Journal of Law and Technology*, 393.

Saunders, Kurt M. & Linda Levine (2002), 'Better, Faster, Cheaper – Later: What Happens When Technologies Are Suppressed', **11** *Mich. Telecomm. & Tech. L. Rev.*, 1.

Saunders, Kurt M. (2002), 'Patent Nonuse and the Role of Public Interest as a Deterrent to Technology Suppression', **15** *Harv. J.L. & Tech.*, 389.

Schanzenbach, Max (2002), 'Network Effects and Antitrust Law: Predation, Affirmative Defenses, and the Case of U.S. v. Microsoft', *2002 Stan. Tech. L. Rev.*, 4.

Schauer, Frederick (1978), 'Fear, Risk and the First Amendment: Unraveling the "Chilling Effect"', **58** *B.U. L. Rev.*, 685.

Scheffman, David T. & Richard S. Higgins (2003), 'Twenty Years of Raising Rivals' Costs: History, Assessment, and Future', **12** *Geo. Mason L. Rev.*, 371.

Schelling, Thomas C. (1960), *The Strategy of Conflict*, Cambridge Ma, Harvard University Press.

Scherer, Frederic M. (2005), *Patents. Economics, Policy and Measurement*, Cheltenham, Edward Elgar Publishing.

Scherer, Frederic M. (2005), 'Technological Innovation and Monopolization', available at: http://ssrn.com/abstract=1103594.

Scherer, Frederic M. & Dietmar Harhoff (2000), 'Technology Policy for a World of Skew-distributed Outcomes', **29** *Res. Policy*, 559.

Scherer, Frederic M. (1992), 'Schumpeter and Plausible Capitalism', **30** *Journal of Economic Literature*, 1416.

Scherer, Frederic M. & David Ross (1990), *Industrial Market Structure and Economic Performance*, Boston, Houghton-Mifflin Company.
Scherer, Frederic M. (1987), 'Antitrust, Efficiency, and Progress', **62** *N. Y. U. L. Rev.*, 998.
Scherer, Frederic M. (1979), 'The Welfare Economics of Product Variety: An Application to the Ready-to-Eat Cereals Industry', **28** *The Journal of Industrial Economics,* 113.
Scherer, Frederic M. (1972), 'Nordhaus's Theory of Optimal Patent Life: A Geometric Reinterpretation', **62** *Am. Econ. Rev.*, 422.
Scherer, Frederic M. (1967), 'Market Structure and the Employment of Scientists and Engineers', **57** *Am. Econ. Rev.*, 524.
Schlesinger Jr., Arthur (1986), *The Cycles of American History*, Boston, Houghton Mifflin.
Schmalensee, Richard A. (2000), 'Antitrust Issues in Schumpeterian Industries', **90** *Am. Econ. Rev.*, 192.
Schmalensee, Richard & Robert D. Willig (eds.) (1989), *Handbook of Industrial Organization*, North-Holland, Amsterdam.
Schmalensee, Richard (1984), 'Gaussian Demand and Commodity Bundling', **57** *Journal of Business,* 211.
Schmalensee, Richard (1982), 'Commodity Bundling by Single Product Monopolies', **25** *J. L. & Econ.*, 67.
Schmalensee, Richard (1978), 'Entry Deterrence in the Ready-to-Eat Breakfast Cereal Industry', **9** *The Bell Journal of Economics,* 305.
Schmookler, Jacob (1966), *Invention and Economic Growth*, Cambridge, Ma, Harvard University Press, 166.
Schumpeter, Joseph (1942), *Capitalism, Socialism, and Democracy*, London, Routledge.
Screpanti, Ernesto & Stefano Zamagni (2005), *An Outline of the History of Economic Thought*, Oxford, Oxford University Press.
Scotchmer, Suzanne (1991), 'Standing on the Shoulders of Giants: Cumulative Research and the Patent Law', **5** *J. Econ. Persp.*, 29.
Scotchmer, Suzanne & Jerry Green (1990), 'Novelty and Disclosure in Patent Law', **21** *Rand J. Econ.*, 131.
Schwartz, Louis B. (1979), '"Justice" and other Non-Economic Goals of Antitrust', **127** *U. Pa. L. Rev.*, 1076.
Shavell, Steven & Tanguy van Ypersele (2001), 'Rewards versus Intellectual Property Rights', **44** *J. L. & Econ.*, 525. Sidak, Joseph G. (2001), 'An Antitrust Rule for Software Integration', **18** *Yale Journal on Regulation,* 1, 15–20.
Shavell, Steven (1982), 'Suit, Settlement, and Trial: A Theoretical Analysis under Alternative Methods for the Allocation of Legal Costs', **2** *Journal of Legal Studies,* 55.

Shughart II, William F. (2000), 'The Fleeting Reagan Antitrust Revolution', **45** *Antitrust Bulletin,* 271.

Shughart II, William F. (1990), 'Private Antitrust Enforcement: Compensation, Deterrence, or Extortion?', **13** *Regulation,* 53.

Sidak, Joseph G. (1983), 'Debunking Predatory Innovation', **83** *Colum. L. Rev.*, 1121.

Silbey, Jessica (2008), 'The Mythical Beginnings of Intellectual Property', **15** *Geo. Mason L. Rev.,* 319.

Simmons, Ian, Patrick Lynch, & Theodore H. Frank (2002), '"I Know It When I See It": Defining And Demonstrating "Blocking patents"', **16** *Antitrust,* 48.

Sinclair, Duncan (2004), 'Abuse of Dominance at a Crossroads – Potential Effect, Object and Appreciability under Article 82 EC', **8** *E.C.L.R.,* 491.

Smith, Neil A. (1971), 'Fraud upon the Patent Office as a Violation of the Sherman Antitrust Law', **53** *J. Pat. and Trademark Off. Soc'y,* 423.

Sobel, Gerald (1984), 'The Antitrust Interface with Patents and Innovation: Acquisition of Patents, Improvement Patents and Grant-Backs, Non-Use, Fraud on the Patent Office, Development of New Products and Joint Research', **53** *Antitrust L. J.,* 681.

Solow, Robert M. (1957), 'Technical Change and the Aggregate Production Function', **39** *Rev. of Economics and Statistics,* 312.

Solow, Robert M. (1956), 'A Contribution to the Theory of Economic Growth', **70** *Quarterly J. Econ.,* 65.

Soma, John T. & Kevin B. Davis (2000), 'Network Effects in Technology Markets: Applying the Lessons of Intel and Microsoft to Future Clashes between Antitrust and Intellectual Property', **8** *J. Intell. Prop. L.,* 1.

Sosnick, Stephen (2006), 'A Critique of the Concept of Workable Competition', **72** *Quarterly Journal of Economics,* 380.

Steinhauer, Esther H. (2006), 'Is Noerr-Pennington Immunity Still a Viable Defense Against Antitrust Claims Arising From Hatch-Waxman Litigation?', **61** *Food and Drug Law Journal,* 679.

Steinman, David R. & Danielle S. Fitzpatrick (2001), 'Antitrust Counterclaims in Patent Infringement Cases: A Guide to Walker Process and Sham-Litigation Claims', **10** *Tex. Intell. Prop. L.J.,* 95.

Stemple, Dayton R. (1952), 'Nonuser of Paper Patents', **34** *J. Pat. Off. Soc'y,* 23.

Sterk, Stewart E. (1996), 'Rhetoric and Reality in Copyright Law', **94** *Mich. L. Rev.*, 1197.

Stigler, George 1987, 'Competition', in John Eatwell, Murray Milgate & Peter Newman (eds), *The New Palgrave. A Dictionary of Economics*, London, Macmillan Press, 51.

Stigler, George J. (1968), *The Organization of Industry*, Chicago, The University of Chicago Press, 67.

Stigler, George J. (1964), 'US v. Loew's Inc.: A Note on Block Booking', **1963** *Supreme Court Review,* 152.

Stigler, George J. (1957), 'Perfect Competition. Historically Contemplated', **65** *Journal of Political Economy,* 1.

Stigler, George J. (1946), *The Theory of Price,* New York, Macmillan.

Stiglitz, Joseph (1987), 'Technological Change, Sunk Costs, and Competition', *Brookings Papers on Econ. Activity,* 883.

Stratakis, Alexandros (2006), 'Comparative Analysis of the US And EU Approach and Enforcement of the Essential Facilities Doctrine', 27(8) *E.C.L.R.,* 434, 436.

Stremersch, Stefan & Gerard J. Tellis (2002), 'Strategic Bundling of Products and Prices: A New Synthesis for Marketing', **66** *J. Mkt'g,* 55.

Sullivan, E. Thomas (1990), *The Political Economy of the Sherman Act: The First One Hundred Years,* Oxford, Oxford University Press.

Sullivan, Lawrence A. (1980), 'Antitrust, Microeconomics, and Politics: Reflection on Some Recent Relationships', **68** *Cal. L. Rev.,* 1, 2.

Sunder, Madhavi (2006), 'IP^3', **59** *Stanford L. R.,* 257.

Symeonides, George (1996), 'Innovation, Firm Size and Market Structure: Schumpeterian Hypotheses and Some New Themes § 44', Economics Department Working Papers No. 161, London School of Economics.

Szulanski, Gabriel (2000), 'Appropriability and the Challenge of Scope: Banc One Routinizes Replication', in Giovanni Dosi, Richard R. Nelson, and Sidney G. Winter, (eds), *The Nature and Dynamics of Organizational Capabilities,* Oxford, Oxford University Press, 69.

Teece, David J. & Mary Coleman (1998), 'The Meaning of Monopoly: Antitrust Analysis in High-Technology Industries', **18** *Antitrust Bull.,* 801.

Teece, David J. (1986), 'Profiting from Technological Innovation: Implications for Integration, Collaboration, Licensing and Public Policy', in **15** *Research Policy,* 285.

Temple Lang, John (2004), 'Anticompetitive Non-Pricing Abuses Under European and National Antitrust Law', in Barry E. Hawk (ed.), *2003 Fordham Corporate Law Institute 235–240,* New York, Juris Publishing.

Temple Lang, John (2003), 'Anticompetitive Abuses Involving Intellectual Property Rights', available at, http://www.eui.eu/RSCAS/Research/Competition/2003/200306COMP-TempleLang-sIII.pdf.

Temple Lang, John & Robert O'Donoghue (2002), 'Defining Legitimate Competition: How to Clarify Pricing Abuses Under Article 82 EC', **26** *Fordham International Law Journal,* 83.

Thorelli, Hans B. (1955), *The Federal Antitrust Policy: Origination of an American Tradition*, Baltimore, Md.: The Johns Hopkins Press.

Tirole, Jean (2004), 'The Analysis of Tying Cases: A Primer 15', available at http://www.ssrn.com/.

Tirole, Jean (1988), *The Theory of Industrial Organization*, Boston, The MIT Press.

Torremans, Paul (2008), *Intellectual Property Law*, Oxford, Oxford University Press.

Touffut, Jean-Phillipe (ed.) (2003), *Institutions, Innovation and Growth: Selected Economic Papers*, Cheltenham, *Edward Elgar Publishing.*

Tullock, Gordon (1967), 'The Welfare Costs of Tariffs, Monopolies and Theft', **5** *W. Econ. J.*, 224.

Ullrich, Hanns (1989), 'The Importance of Industrial Property Law and Other Legal Measures in the Promotion of Technological Innovation', **28** *Industrial Property* 102–103.

Van Bael, Ivo, & Jean-Francois Bellis (2004), *Competition Law of the European Community*, The Hague, Kluwer Law International.

Van Cayseele, Patrick, & Roger Van den Bergh (1999), 'Antitrust Law', in Boudewijn Bouckaert & Gerrit De Geest (eds.), *Encyclopedia of Law and Economics*, Cheltenham, *Edward Elgar,* 467.

Van Cayseele, Patrick (1998), 'Market Structure and Innovation: A Survey', **146** *De Economist,* 391.

Van den Bergh, Roger J. & Peter D. (2006), *Camesasca, European Competition Law and Economics: A Comparative Perspective*, London, Sweet and Maxwell.

Van den Bergh, Roger (1996), 'Modern Industrial Organization versus Old-Fashioned European Competition Law', **17** *European Competition Law Review,* 75.

Venit, James S. (2005), 'Article 82: The Last Frontier – Fighting Fire with Fire?', **28** *Fordham Int'l L. J,* 1157.

Vezzoso, Simonetta (2006), 'The Incentives Balance Test in the EU Microsoft Case: a Pro-Innovation "Economic-Based" Approach', **27** *E.C.L.R.*, 382.

Vickers, John (1995), 'The Concepts of Competition', **47** *Oxford Economic Papers,* 1.

Vickers, John (1985), 'Pre-Emptive Patenting, Joint Ventures, and the Persistence of Oligopoly', **3** *International Journal of Industrial Organization,* 261.

Viscusi, W. Kip, John M. Vernon & Joseph E. Harrington, Jr (2005), *Economics of Regulation and Antitrust*, Boston, The MIT Press.

Völcker, Sven (2004), 'Developments in EC Competition Law in 2003: An Overview', **41** *Common Market Law Review,* 1027.

von Hippel, Eric (1998), *The Sources of Innovation,* Oxford, Oxford University Press, 53.

von Mises, Ludwig (1949), *Human Action: A Treatise on Economics,* New Haven: Yale University Press,

von Neumann, John & Oskar Morgenstern (1944), *Theory of Games and Economic Behavior*, *Princeton*, NJ, Princeton University Press.

von Weizsacker, Carl C. (1980), *Barriers to Entry. A Theoretical Treatment*, Berlin, Springer-Verlag.

Vossestein, Adrian J. (2000), 'Corporate Efforts to Influence Public Authorithies, and the EC rules on Competition', **37** *Common Market Law Review,* 1383.

Walker, Mike & Simon Bishop (2002), *The Economics EC Competition Law: Concepts, Application and Measurement,* London, Sweet and Maxwell.

Wallerstein, Mitchel B., Mary Ellen Mogee, & Roberta Schoen (eds.) (1993), *Global Dimensions of Intellectual Property Rights in Science & Technology,* Washington, National Academies Press.

Watt, Richard (2000), Copyright and Economic Theory: Friends or Foes?, Cheltenham, Elgar Edward Publishing.

Weber Waller, Spencer (2008), 'Areeda, Epithets, and Essential Facilities', **2008** *Wis. L. Rev.*, 359.

Weeds, Helen (1999), 'Sleeping Patents and Compulsory Licensing: An Options Analysis', available at http://privatewww.essex.ac.uk/~hfweeds/sleeping%20patents.pdf.

Weinreb, Lloyd (1998), 'Copyright for Functional Expression', **111** *Harv. L. Rev.*, 1149.

Werden, Gregory J. (2006), 'Identifying Single-Firm Exclusionary Conduct: From Vague Concepts to Administrable Rules', 33rd Annual Conference on International Antitrust Law & Policy, Fordham Corporate Law Institute, New York, September 14–15.

Werden, Gregory J. (2001), 'Network Effects and Conditions of Entry, Lessons from the Microsoft Case', **69** *Antitrust L. J.*, 87.

Werden, Gregory J. (1987), 'The Law and Economics of the Essential Facility Doctrine', **32** *St. Louis U. L.J.*, 433.

Whinston, Michael D. (1990), 'Tying, Foreclosure, and Exclusion', **80** *Am. Econ. Rev.*, 837, 845.

Whish, Richard (2008), *Competition Law*, Oxford, Oxford University Press.

Willard K. Tom & Joshua A. Newberg (1997), 'Antitrust and Intellectual Property: From Separate Spheres to Unified Field', **66** *Antitrust L.J.*, 167.

Williamson, Oliver (1987), 'Delimiting Antitrust', **76** *Geo. L. J.*, 271.

Williamson, Oliver E. (1972), 'Dominant Firms and the Monopoly Problem: Market Failure Considerations', **85** *Harv. L. Rev.*, 1512.

Winter, Ralph (1984), 'The Use of Adjudicative Processes to Injure

Competitors', in *The Political Economy of Regulation: Private Interests in the Regulatory Process* 278 (FTC Law & Econ. Conf.,)

Winter, Sydney G. (2006), 'The Logic of Appropriability: From Schumpeter to Arrow to Teece', **35** *Research Policy,* 1110.

Wood, Diane P. (2004), 'The U.S. Antitrust Laws in a Global Context', **2004** *Colum. Bus. L. Rev.,* 265.

Yen, Alfred C. (1990), 'Restoring the Natural Law: Copyright as Labor and Possession', **91** *Ohio St. L. J.,* 517.

Zerbe, Jr, Richard O. & William Kovacic (eds.) (1995), *Research in Law and Economics,* Amsterdam, Elsevier.

Index